PENGUIN BOOKS

JAMES BALDWIN: A BIOGRAPHY

David Leeming is Professor of English and Comparative Literature at the University of Connecticut. He has also written *The World of Myth* (OUP, 1990).

James Baldwin: A Biography

DAVID LEEMING

PENGUIN BOOKS

PENGUIN BOOKS

Published by the Penguin Group
Penguin Books Ltd, 27 Wrights Lane, London W8 5TZ, England
Penguin Books USA Inc., 375 Hudson Street, New York, New York 10014, USA
Penguin Books Australia Ltd, Ringwood, Victoria, Australia
Penguin Books Canada Ltd, 10 Alcorn Avenue, Toronto, Ontario, Canada M4V 3B2
Penguin Books (NZ) Ltd, 182–190 Wairau Road, Auckland 10, New Zealand

Penguin Books Ltd, Registered Offices: Harmondsworth, Middlesex, England

First published by Michael Joseph 1994
Published in Penguin Books 1995
1 3 5 7 9 10 8 6 4 2

Owing to limitations of space, all permissions to reprint previously published and unpublished material can be found immediately following the index

Printed in England by Clays Ltd, St Ives plc

For

David

In Memory of

Jimmy,

Beauford, Bernard, Ellis, Mary, Orilla, Sam,

and all

the "many thousands gone"

And they, whether they will hear, or whether they will forbear, . . . yet shall they know that there hath been a prophet among them.

—Ezekiel 2:5

I ain't good looking, but I'm somebody's angel child.

—Bessie Smith
"Reckless Blues"

Photographic Credits

First insert

Esther Jackson: with Martin Luther King, Jr.

Irmeli Jung: in Paris in the sixties

Theodore Pelatowski: The Melodeers; an "Elisha"

Leslie Schenck: Baldwin in his twenties

Steve Schapiro/Black Star: in the pulpit, 1963; in the South, 1963; in Louisiana, 1963; with Lena Horne

Stan Weir: Connie Williams

Second insert

ATV London: with David Baldwin in London

Courtesy of Bowling Green State University, Office of Public Relations: teaching at Bowling Green

Sam Floyd: with Bill Belli

Carlos Freire: with Bernard Hassell

David Leeming: Mary Painter; the final bed, Saint-Paul-de-Vence; the welcome table

Sedat Pakay: with Bertice Redding; on the Bosphorus in the sixties

Max Petrus: with Beauford Delaney

Contents

Preface and Acknowledgements

The primary source for the information contained in this book is James Baldwin himself. I met Baldwin in 1961 during his first visit to Istanbul, where I was working as a teacher. We saw each other again when he came back to Istanbul during 1962 and 1963. When I began graduate work at New York University in 1963, Baldwin hired me as a part-time secretary in charge of sorting his manuscripts and papers. Eventually I did some correspondence and research for him and accompanied him on lecture trips. Later, early in 1966, he invited me to go with him back to Istanbul as a companion-translator-secretary, and there he, his brother David, and I shared a house while Jimmy completed *Tell Me How Long the Train's Been Gone*.

During the 1970s when I saw Jimmy from time to time in New York, we talked about the possibility of my writing a biography. Years earlier we had considered the project more in fun than in earnest. He sometimes introduced me as "my Boswell." Like most writers, Baldwin preferred to be, through his works, his own biographer. But over the years he came to realize that biographies would be written, and in 1977 he gave me an authorization letter, promising access to his papers—a promise he fulfilled—and, insofar as he could help, access to his friends and relatives. It should be noted that this biography is in no way authorized by his estate.

During the 1980s Baldwin and I had formal interviews in New York, in Amherst, where he was teaching, in Connecticut, where he visited my wife and me several times, and in Saint-Paul-de-Vence, where we visited him.

After Jimmy's funeral in New York, I returned to France at David Baldwin's request, to collect the Baldwin papers. Later I sorted them in Jimmy's New York apartment and was able to add the information they contained to what I had already learned from the papers I had sorted in the early sixties. Other information came from the interviews and meetings with Baldwin in the 1970s and 1980s, and from extensive conversations in New York and in our Istanbul house in the 1960s.

Our conversations over the years covered every imaginable subject. Baldwin talked about his loves, his disappointments in love, about what he considered his role as a witness, about literature, about his works, about America and about history. He told me about his school experiences, about his first favorite teacher, a young white woman from the Middle West called "Bill" Miller, about Connie Williams, the owner of the Calypso Cafe in Greenwich Village, where he worked in the 1940s. He spoke of his trips South, of his "spiritual father," the painter Beauford Delaney, and mentors like Sterling Brown and Kenneth Clark. He also talked about race, about homosexuality, about his loneliness, about his family. Our last "interview" occurred two days before he died as I sat up with him during the night in Saint-Paul-de-Vence. Characteristically, the conversation, although necessarily disjointed and sometimes incoherent, ranged from the denied pleasures of a scotch and a cigarette to the "devastating" economy of Jane Austen, to the impossibility of holding food down, to religion.

Almost from the moment I met Baldwin, I recognized that I was in the presence of a highly complex, troubled, and driven individual who was more intensely serious than anyone I had ever met. This is not to say he did not enjoy life or that he had no sense of humor. He was a man who laughed a lot and who knew how to make others laugh. And while clearly obsessed by what he saw as a witnessing role, he was just as committed to the life of the senses; when he ate a meal, smoked a cigarette, sipped on a scotch, or touched another human being, he did so with deep pleasure that was evident and with an incomparable elegance and care. And he spent his whole life longing to be picked up and sheltered by what he thought of as the power of love in arms stronger than his own.

Baldwin was a lonely and extremely vulnerable man. His vulnerability made him sometimes overly defensive—even, some would say, "paranoid." In pursuit of love and approval he squandered money and time and sometimes hurt people. He was a man, like most people, with evident neuroses. He was not a saint, he was not always psychologically or emotionally stable. But he *was* a prophet.

It was the calling to bear witness to the truth that dominated Baldwin's being, and in this role he could be harsh, uncompromising, and even brutally cruel. He knew that the combination of his heritage as an African-American, his early "God-given" talent with words, and even his mysterious parentage and his sexual "ambivalence" made it inevitable that he be an outsider, a stranger condemned like Jonah to preach and convert, even as he longed simply to live. Like it or not, he was called, and to the extent that he attempted to refuse the call in his life he found himself psychologically trapped in the belly of the whale.

Baldwin was a prophet not so much in the tradition of foreseeing events—although *The Fire Next Time* bears witness to the fact that he sometimes did precisely that—as in the tradition of the Old Testament. Like Ezekiel, Isaiah, Jeremiah, and Samuel, whose words and agonies he knew from his days as a child preacher in Harlem, he understood that as a witness he must often stand alone in anger against a nation that seemed intent on not "keeping the faith." He knew that his childhood "salvation" on the threshing floor of his church was but the preface to a life of searching on the universal threshing floor of personal and societal pain.

Baldwin's prophecy took many forms. His essays stand out as among the most articulate expressions we have of the human condition in his time. The collections *Notes of a Native Son* and *Nobody Knows My Name*, and the long essay *The Fire Next Time*, have already become classics. In three plays, many short stories, and six novels, including, most notably, *Go Tell It on the Mountain*, *Giovanni's Room*, "Sonny's Blues," and *Another Country*, Baldwin creates parables to illustrate, in the private and personal realm of human relationships, the words of his essays.

Baldwin was a writer who could combine the cadences of the King James Bible and Henry James with what he liked to call the "beat" of African-American culture. His audience was the whole "nation," and he incorporated the whole nation into his voice. His was the "voice in the wilderness" that preached the necessity of touching. In his personal life and his work, he took the side of those who were made into exiles and outcasts by barriers of race, sex, and class or who turned away from safety and chose the honorable path of tearing down such barriers. But he mourned for those who had created the barriers and had unwittingly allowed themselves to be destroyed by them.

IN THIS BIOGRAPHY of James Baldwin I have been helped not only by the subject himself but by a large number of witnesses to his life and work, the most important of whom has been his brother David. David Baldwin has generously granted me several interviews, answered countless questions, and given me full access to his extensive correspondence with his brother. Most important, he has provided encouragement and support throughout this long process.

Another significant source of information has been the material collected by Karen Thorsen, Bill Miles, Douglas Dempsey, and their staff for the PBS documentary *James Baldwin: The Price of the Ticket*, for which both David Baldwin and I were consultants. This material includes detailed interviews with Ishmael Reed, Maya Angelou, Amiri Baraka, William Styron, Bobby Short, Engin Cezzar, Lucien Happersberger, Emile Capouya, and Yasar Kemal, to mention only a few, and boxes of supporting material.

Baldwin's friend and mine, Sedat Pakay, provided some of the photographs contained in the book and advised me on others to use. Dick Fontaine was also an important source for photographs.

Other interviews, letters, and photographs have been provided by too many people to mention them all here. I am especially grateful to Orilla Miller Winfield, who knew Baldwin as a child and who has only recently died, to Connie Williams, Claire Burch, and Stan Weir, who knew him in his Village days, to Mary Keen Blumenau, Otto and Priscilla Friedrich, Herbert Gold, Richard Olney, Tom Maltais, Themistocles Hoetis, and Bosley Bratman Wilder, all of whom knew him first during the early Paris period.

Other close Baldwin friends and associates who were particularly helpful were Valerie Sordello, the Roux family at the Colombe d'Or in Saint-Paul-de-Vence, Donna Schrader, Pat Mikell, Ernest Champion, Cynthia Packard, Brock Peters, Dick Fontaine, Ruth Dean, Richard Long, Calua Dundy, Katherine Shipley, James Silberman, Lloyd Richards, Lonie Levister, Raleigh Trevelyan, Horace Ove, Catherine McLaughlin, Anton Phillips, and especially Bill Belli, Engin Cezzar, Marc Crawford, Cecil Brown, Kay Boyle, David Moses, and Lucien Happersberger.

Four of my most important informants, who became my close friends during the time I knew Baldwin, were Beauford Delaney, Bernard Hassell, Sam Floyd, and Mary Painter. Beauford died in 1979, Sam in 1986, and the others only recently. Other than his family and, perhaps, Lucien Happersberger, no one knew Baldwin better than Beauford, Mary, Sam, and Bernard.

Earlier biographies—by Fern Eckman, W. J. Weatherby, and James Campbell—have been useful, as have conversations over the years with many members of the Baldwin family. Critical works and collections by many scholars, including Horace Porter, Fred Standley, Louis Pratt, and Quincy Troupe have been helpful as well.

Significant financial support for the project has been provided by research grants from the University of Connecticut, the National Endowment for the Humanities, the Fondation Camargo, and the Schomburg Center for Research in Black Culture at 135th Street and Malcolm X Boulevard, where I was a scholar-in-residence for a semester and where Baldwin did much of his early reading.

Valuable research assistance was provided by Karin Swann in California and Lisa Gitelman in New York, and important ideas were suggested by my graduate students at the University of Connecticut.

Finally, there are people who in some cases have provided information and who in all cases have provided significant moral support. The late Ellis Haizlipp, Michel Fabre, Howard Dodson, and many people at the Schomburg Center, Jim Hatch and the Hatch-Billops Archives, Richard Newman, Gerald O'Grady, and Sedat Pakay, Joe Wood, Henry Louis Gates, Jr., Arnold Rampersad, Florence Ladd, Don Belton, the late Melvin Dixon, Houston Baker, Jr., David and Lee Porter, Peter and Rosemary Shiras, Stephen Spender, the late Richard Ellmann, Ernest Champion, Leon Edel, Geoffrey Wolff, Faith Childs, Krysia Jopek, Jake and Susanne Page, James and Pamela Morton, Amanda Huston-Hamilton, Veronica Skurat, Charles Hargreaves and Natasha Milne, Dalia Kandiyoti, John Lankenau, Petter Juel-Larsen, Douglas Dempsey and Karen Thorsen, and my editor, Ashbel Green, come immediately to mind, as do all of my friends in Stonington and at the University of Connecticut. And most of all, I have been supported by my family—Pam, both Margarets, Juliet, and Paul.

In a few cases it has seemed necessary, in the interest of preserving privacy, to change names. When the Baldwin papers become available to scholars at large there will certainly be other Baldwin books to be written, perhaps even Baldwin biographies from different perspectives than mine. His letters are moving and telling documents that should be collected and published. A James Baldwin autobiography needs to be extracted from his writings. And there are any number of scholarly works called for by Baldwin's manuscript revisions alone. My hope is that this biography will serve as a useful source for those who continue the search for James Baldwin.

Stonington, Connecticut
1993

publications by many scholars, including [illegible] Hagstrum, Morton Paley, [illegible] [illegible], and [illegible] [illegible] have been helpful as well.

[illegible] financial support for the project has been provided by research grants from the University of Connecticut, the National Endowment for the Humanities, the Huntington Library, and the [illegible] Center for [illegible] [illegible] [illegible] [illegible] and [illegible] [illegible] [illegible] [illegible] [illegible] [illegible].

[illegible] research assistance was provided [illegible] [illegible] [illegible] [illegible] [illegible] [illegible] by [illegible] graduate students at the University of Connecticut.

I thank [illegible] [illegible] [illegible] [illegible] [illegible] [illegible] [illegible] [illegible] [illegible] [illegible] [illegible] [illegible]

[illegible] [illegible] [illegible] [illegible] [illegible] [illegible] [illegible] [illegible]

[illegible]

JAMES BALDWIN

JAMES BALDWIN: A BIOGRAPHY

CHAPTER 1

The Harlem Life

Go tell it on the mountain,
over the hills and everywhere.
Go tell it on the mountain
that Jesus Christ is born.
—old song

Illegitimacy and an almost obsessive preoccupation with his stepfather were constant themes in the life and works of James Baldwin. The circumstance of his birth, to Berdis Jones on August 2, 1924, in New York City's Harlem Hospital, was later to symbolize for him the illegitimacy attached to an entire race within the American nation. If Baldwin ever knew who his real father was, he kept the knowledge to himself. He preferred to use the fact of his illegitimacy, as he did his minority status and his homosexuality, as supporting material for a mythical or representative persona indicated in such titles as *Nobody Knows My Name*, *No Name in the Street*, or "Stranger in the Village."

It is true that much of Baldwin's early life was concerned with a search for a father, but not for a biological father—he nearly always referred to his stepfather as his "father" and seemed satisfied to think of him as such. His search was, rather, for what an ideal father might have been for him—a source of self-esteem who would have supported and guided him in his quest to become a writer and a "preacher." And by extension, his search was a symbolic one for the birthright denied him and all "colored," "negro," or "black" people, so defined by others who insist on thinking of themselves as "white."

That Baldwin would approach his life's story metaphorically and symbolically was evident even before he was to speak of his illegitimacy. The first important nonfictional autobiographical statement is the 1955 essay "Notes of a Native Son," in which, as Horace

Porter has recognized, Baldwin strikes a "universal note, connecting his life and family to all mankind." In the autobiographical notes to the collection of which "Notes of a Native Son" was the title essay, Baldwin spoke of the importance of being forced early in his life to recognize that he was "a kind of bastard of the West." Baldwin was not a conceited man, but he was to look back upon his birth and his childhood as part of a prophetic mission. He saw himself as, like it or not, born to "save" others through the word.

As a child he had a favorite hill in Central Park, where he would escape whenever possible, look out over the great city, and, like his fictional character, John, in *Go Tell It on the Mountain*, dream of a messianic future:

> He felt like a long-awaited conqueror at whose feet flowers would be strewn, and before whom multitudes cried, Hosanna! He would be, of all, the mightiest, the most beloved, the Lord's anointed; and he would live in this shining city which his ancestors had seen with longing from far away.

The writer/spokesman-to-be was born, like so many mythic heroes, in an overlooked place where pain and deprivation were common, a place that remains today an appropriate metaphor for the spiritual meanness of the larger surrounding community, which both fears and ignores it. Rising out of Harlem, James Baldwin used the mystery of his parentage and his humble birth, and the ineffectualness of his stepfather, as starting points for a lifelong witnessing of the moral failure of the American nation—and of Western civilization in general—and the power of love to revive it.

James's stepfather, "the great good friend of the Great God Almighty," was the son of a slave called Barbara who spent the last years of her life, bedridden, in the Baldwin household in Harlem and who filled the young James with awe. One of his first memories was of the old woman giving him a present of a decorated metal candy box that was full of needles and thread. Inevitably, his grandmother was a link to the whispered horrors of what to a child must have seemed like the ancient past. And as the mother of fourteen, some "black" and some—it was said—"white," she would just as inevitably become for James Baldwin, the writer and prophet, the prototype of that ancient forced motherhood that makes black and white Americans "brothers" and "sisters" whether they like it or not.

David Baldwin was a preacher and a laborer who came to the North from New Orleans in the early 1920s and who provided for his family inadequately but as well as he could through the years of the Great Depression. Not only did he take the place for Jimmy of the father he had never known, he too became for him a symbol. He was the archetypal black father, one generation removed from slavery, prevented by the ever-present shadow and the frequently present effects of racial discrimination from providing his family with what they needed most—their birthright, their identity as individuals rather than as members of a class or a race. "I'm black only as long as you think you're white," his stepson was to tell many audiences in later years. The Reverend David Baldwin was living proof of this fact. His bitter subservience to bill collectors, landlords, and other whites led the young James to disrespect him. In "Notes of a Native Son" Baldwin recalls his stepfather's agreeing reluctantly to a teacher's taking him to a play, not daring to refuse permission, the boy believed, only because the teacher was white. This was an outing Jimmy wanted very much, but he wanted much more a father whose word and opinions—however wrong—could be heard and respected.

Today's statistics tell us that fathers in David Baldwin's situation often leave home. But Jimmy's stepfather did not leave home—he went mad. But he did so in stages, beginning in the South before he migrated to New York. If the "white devil" would not recognize him as a man, perhaps God would. He became a preacher, stressing, in the tradition of the pentecostal black church, the hope for a better life after the "crossing over," and calling down the wrath of God on the sinners of the white Sodom and Gomorrah. In the pulpit his bitterness and despair could become righteous anger and power. The subservient wage earner could become the Old Testament prophet preaching the hard and narrow path to self-identity and self-esteem that the economics of real life made impossible: "Choose you this day whom you will serve; whether the gods which your fathers served that were on the other side of the flood, or the gods of the Amorites, in whose land ye dwell: but as for me and my house, we will serve the Lord."

To the people of his house the father's prophecy took the form of an arbitrary and puritanical discipline and a depressing air of bitter frustration which did nothing to alleviate the pain of poverty and oppression. Instead of the loving father for whom the young James so longed—the father he was still trying to create in his very last novel—the Baldwin family suffered the presence of a black parody of the white Great God Almighty so essential to the tradition of the Calvinist American Dream they were not allowed to share.

As a very young child, before the arrival of the eight brothers and sisters, Jimmy had experienced a sense that his stepfather loved him. One of his earliest memories was of being carried by his mother and looking over her shoulder at his stepfather, who smiled at him. And he remembered sensing "my daddy's pride" in him in those days. But as things became more difficult for the Baldwins, the minister's paranoia developed, and young Jimmy often took the brunt of it. His stepfather had him circumcised at about the age of five—perhaps to make him more "Christ-like," somehow less "primitive" and less marked by the "sin" of his illegitimacy. This incident is ambiguously described by Baldwin as "a terrifying event which I scarcely remember at all." He did recall very clearly being beaten for losing a dime he had been given to buy kerosene for the stove—the last dime in the house. It seemed he could do nothing right.

An enduring and ever-present memory was of his stepfather making fun of his eyes and calling him the ugliest child he had ever seen. To the end of his life Baldwin told of an incident related to that memory, an incident that he felt had affected the course of his life. In the streets one day when he was perhaps five or six, he was astounded by the sight of an old drunken woman with huge eyes and lips. He rushed upstairs and called his mother to the window. "You see? You see?" he said. "She's uglier than you, Mama! She's uglier than me!" His mother had the same eyes and mouth that he did, so he assumed she must be "ugly," too, and that she would therefore be interested in what he had seen. Later Baldwin would suggest, with respect to his stepfather's comments on his ugliness, that he was also "attacking my real, and unknown, father." But when as a child he saw that face in the streets it had another significance for him. He knew somehow, without being able yet to articulate it—that would take many years—that his physical appearance need have no effect on what he would do in life, that if his mother was "ugly," then even "ugliness" could be beautiful.

For the young James Baldwin this was an important moment of self-realization. Once again he was playing a significant role in a metaphorical and sociological drama. Children believe what their parents tell them, and oppressed minorities constantly face the danger of believing the myths attached to them by their oppressors. In time Baldwin was to understand that his "ugliness" was his stepfather's problem, that his stepfather's "intolerable bitterness of spirit" was the result of his frustrations, that his need to humiliate those closest to him was, in fact, a reflection of the hatred David Baldwin felt towards himself as a black man: "It had something to do with his blackness, I think—he was very black—with his blackness and his beauty, and with the fact that he knew that he was black but did not know that he was beautiful." And "he was defeated long before he died because, at the bottom of his heart, he really believed what white people said about him."

There were times in Baldwin's adolescence when he nearly came to blows with his stepfather. They fought because he read books, because he liked movies, because he had white friends. For Reverend Baldwin all these interests were a threat to the salvation which could only come from God. But his bitterness and hardness offended even the "saints" of the church, and he became less sought after as a preacher. In his late years he was wary of his own family, going so far as to suspect them of wanting to poison him. His children "had betrayed him by . . . reaching towards the world which had despised him." David, a son by an earlier marriage, had died in jail. That David was to be James Baldwin's model for the many fictional "brothers" who would suffer at the hands of the white "law"—Richard and the first Royal in *Go Tell It on the Mountain,* Fonny in *If Beale Street Could Talk,* Richard in *Blues for Mister Charlie,* for example. Sam, another son by the earlier marriage, had long since left home, and in spite of countless desperate letters from the father, dictated to the despised stepson, he saw his father next only as he lay dead in his coffin.

Sam, too, made a deep impression on his young stepbrother. Baldwin remembered in *No Name in the Street* how as a child he had been "saved" by Sam from drowning, and how he had learned that day "something about the terror and the loneliness and the depth and the height of love." He never stopped longing for a repetition of that love. Sam was re-created metaphorically in several strong protective older brothers to more delicate and artistic characters in Baldwin's fiction: Elisha is an older "brother in Christ" in *Go Tell It on the Mountain,* Caleb and Hall are actual brother-protectors for the autobiographical Leo and Arthur in *Tell Me How Long the Train's Been Gone* and *Just Above My Head,* respectively.

Eventually Reverend Baldwin lost his job, and in 1943 he was committed to a mental hospital, where he died of tuberculosis. It took many years for James's emotions to catch up with his intellectual understanding of his stepfather and his plight. But he never stopped thinking or talking about him, and it is worth noting that his first book and his last were partly dedicated to him. In a late work, *The Devil Finds Work,* he remembers

> the pride and sorrow and beauty of my father's face: for that man I called my father really *was* my father in every sense except the biological, or literal one. He formed me, and he raised me, and he did not let me starve: and he gave me something, however harshly, and however little I wanted it, which prepared me for an impending horror which he could not prevent.

Baldwin came to see that this man, who frightened him so much that "I could never again be frightened of anything else," was a victim of a morally bankrupt religion, a morally bankrupt society, that he was a black parody of that bankruptcy. He was to realize that in the context of such bankruptcy, the life of David Baldwin, Sr.—the attempt he had made to protect his children and to retain his dignity—had been "an act of love." If he was incapable of showing affection, it was because he could not love himself. And if he was hard on Jimmy, he was hard on the other children, too. Tied to an ideological lie that he could not recognize, he was not, finally, to be blamed. And on Sunday morning, dressed in his three-piece suit, his Panama Stroller, his cuff links, spats, and turned-down collar, he was the picture of a longed-for pride and dignity. He was a father from another time, behaving according to another code. If that code could not work for the Baldwin children, if their real father was the one who in his pajamas paced the floor each night mumbling biblical verses—"Set thy house in order . . . as for me and my house, we will serve the Lord"—venting his frustrations as a beaten man, they still longed for his approval, and they still admired the father he might have been.

That Baldwin did manage to come to terms with his stepfather is due in great part to the other significant influence of his early life, his mother. He did not write a great deal about or speak much about his mother, but when he did either, it was with deep feeling and admiration. If, in his use of his own life for metaphorical purposes, his stepfather was the archetypal victim of the "chronic disease" of racism, his mother was the embodiment of the nurturing antidote to that disease. One of Baldwin's very first memories was of his mother holding up a piece of black velvet and saying softly, "That *is* a good idea." For a long time the boy thought that the word "idea" meant a piece of black velvet. He often spoke of her smile—"a smile which she reached for every day that she faced her children (this smile she gave to no one else), reached for, and found, and gave . . . the smile counselled patience." When asked in several interviews towards the end of his life to describe what his mother meant to him, Baldwin usually answered by remembering something she had said to him in his teens: "I don't know what will happen to you in life. I do know that you have brothers and sisters. You must treat everyone the way I hope others will treat you when you are away from me, the way you hope others will treat your brothers and sisters when you are far from them." Berdis Baldwin constantly reminded her children that people must not be put on pedestals or scaffolds, that people have to be loved for their faults as well as their virtues, their ugliness as well as their beauty.

This was important teaching for any child, but especially for one who was to become a witness and a teacher. For Baldwin the love that he learned in part from his mother was to emerge as the central idea in a personal ideology that was to inform his later life.

In Baldwin's eyes his mother was a protector and a maintainer of family unity. One of his childhood memories was a curious parody of that earlier memory of receiving his stepfather's smile over his mother's shoulder. Here again he received a look over his mother's shoulder, but this time she had rushed in from the kitchen to separate and protect the two men from the physical consequences of violent filial hatred.

Emma Berdis Jones came to New York from Deal Island, Maryland, in the early 1920s. Much of her early life's "journey" is suggested in the person and events surrounding Elizabeth in *Go Tell It on the Mountain*. Her mother had died when she was a young child. Berdis was left with her father, rowing out with him as he earned a living fishing on the Eastern Shore. When her father remarried, she moved in with her older sister, Beulah, "the only mother I ever knew." Like so many southern blacks, including her future husband, Berdis Jones traveled North full of hope for a better life. She went first to a cousin in the Germantown section of Philadelphia and then to New York. Life was not easy, and it became more difficult when, in 1924, she gave birth to James. Eventually she found a live-in job with a wealthy family. In 1927, when Jimmy was two years old, she married David Baldwin, a man several years older than she, but a respectable clergyman who seemed genuinely willing to accept her son as his son. And soon there were more children; over the next sixteen years they had George, Barbara, Wilmer, David (named after his father and his father's deceased first son), Gloria, Ruth, Elizabeth, and Paula.

As the oldest child, Jimmy was his mother's "right arm," helping, as she persisted in the "exasperating and mysterious habit of having babies," with the diapers, with walks, with getting them bathed and bedded down for the night. When he was old enough he took his younger brothers by the hand and they would cross the bridge into the Bronx, where they could save money by buying day-old bread from the bakery where it was made. Or he took them to church for the Saturday-night prayer service and for Sunday School before the main service of the week.

An incident that took place soon after the birth of his brother David conveys a sense of the special relationship that existed between mother and son. Mrs. Baldwin wanted to go to Maryland for her father's funeral, but there was no money and her husband disapproved. Baldwin was fond of saying that this was the day he became a thief, that somehow he found the necessary money and gave it to his mother for the trip. Whether this was what the anxious-to-please eight-year-old wished he could have done or whether he actually did it, Baldwin was certain of another memory—of helping his mother and the baby into a taxi before going back upstairs to his stepfather. This was a continuation of his metaphorical role as "native son," this time as part of a matriarchal conspiracy.

The close contact with his mother remained important to Baldwin throughout his life. They corresponded regularly; he always looked forward in particular to his birthday letter from her. The letters were full of advice of the kind that mothers everywhere tend to give sons whose lives are dangerous. Mrs. Baldwin worried about her son's drinking, his smoking, his staying up late. But her concerns went much further than his physical welfare. She was a constant reminder to him of the necessity of "keeping the faith," of not drifting onto the all-too-tempting road of racial or personal hatred.

Sometimes the warnings took the form of somewhat stern letters of reprimand. Once she admonished him for his harsh language. In his answer to that letter Jimmy gently chided his mother, warning her that his work took him beyond the limits of ordinary propriety, that real writers, like real prophets, could not be hemmed in by respectability. To illustrate his point he spoke to his mother's religious side, reminding her that Jesus himself had not in his day been considered respectable, that he had been regarded, in fact, as the "very author of Profanity." Like Jesus, he would rather die than be the victim of the "doom called safety."

In short, there were minor disagreements between mother and son, but there was constructive dialogue as well. And Baldwin always accepted his mother's message of love and tolerance, in spite of ample evidence to support his father's more pessimistic point of view.

The Harlem to which Berdis Jones and so many other black southerners came in the twenties and thirties and in which James Baldwin was raised was in many ways a southern community. Parents knew each other and each other's children, and there was a sense of responsibility for one's neighbor. If Mrs. Smith saw one of Mrs. Brown's children doing something wrong, she applied discipline first and then let Mrs. Brown know about it. And Harlem was still multiracial. There was community in poverty rather than hopeless isolation. This is not to say there was no racial conflict. Baldwin remembered fighting frequently with an Italian neighbor called Tony—a boy of his age—but he also remembered sharing meals with him.

The Harlem of Baldwin's early memory was a place where people still clung to the possibility of a normal life. It was dilapidated, but it had not yet given up. He remembered the grocery store owned by the old Jew who gave the family credit when they could not afford food, the shoe repair shop where the black owner sat in the window, bent over his work, and where they bought their "new" shoes when the old ones were past repair. There was the soda-pop joint and the shoeshine parlor at which he sometimes worked, and the dry cleaners, and Dr. Israel Goldberg's pharmacy, run for the most part by a white pharmacist called "Dr. Martin" to whom the children were sent for fever-curing and skin-soothing homeopathic concoctions made from various exotic roots that were kept in the room behind the main one. The children would help Dr. Martin mix and heat up huge pots of a wax mixture, which they would pour into cans and allow to cool and harden before they attached the "Dr. Martin's Hair Wax" labels. Sometimes Dr. Martin would ask one of the boys to shave him in the morning, as he always nicked himself with the barber's razor he used.

There was also the candy shop run by Reverend Baldwin's sister on 133d Street between Lenox and Fifth. Taunty, as she was called by the children, was the model for Florence in *Go Tell It on the Mountain*. And, of course, there were the stoops which were the centers of restricted areas in which children were allowed to play. There were visits from friends on Sundays, too: Mr. Sinclair, the mover, who was

George's godfather, and Mr. and Mrs. Mickey, who always brought pastrami and who amused the children with a hide-and-seek game in which Mr. Mickey was always hidden from Mrs. Mickey somewhere in the living room.

But this was no middle-class black American paradise. Signs of a worse future were already apparent. Baldwin recalled the images of poverty and decay—"cold slush . . . cooling piss . . . weary sweat," radiators "rusted like dried blood," and the stoned men and boys on the broken stoops, waiting for something that would never come.

As he grew up he became increasingly aware of the racial and economic tension around him, a tension that frequently led individuals to give up their lives rather than continue to suffer. Suicide was a subject that obsessed him throughout his life. He lost several close friends by that route and attempted it himself at least four times. A friend of his tells of his discussing suicide at great length at the age of thirteen as they stood on a rooftop in Harlem one summer night, but his first direct exposure to it occurred when he was nine or ten years old.

In an apartment not far from the Baldwins there was a particularly light-skinned couple with three daughters, the youngest of whom was "scandalously" dark. One of the daughters had a boyfriend who was also blacker than the family would have wished. He was called by the neighborhood "Johnny on the Spot" because he was always on time, particularly at the door in question. Apparently the family caused the relationship to be broken off, and one day Johnny arrived at his "spot" with a pistol, rang the bell, and shot himself in the head as the door was opened. To Baldwin this incident remained a clear example of the agony, in Harlem and elsewhere, that was the result quite simply of the color of one's skin.

In 1929, the year of the great financial crash, Jimmy began school. He was a frail child. A doctor at Harlem Hospital had said he would not live beyond the age of five, but here he was at five in P.S. 24, not dead, but bearing the scars of poverty and perhaps of malnutrition. He remembered a teacher at school taking one look at him and feeding him cod-liver oil. At home they were eating—or trying to eat—the corned beef they picked up each week from Home Relief. His mother would fry it, boil it, bake it, mix it with potatoes or corn bread or rice, "beat it with a hammer." But finally, no culinary magic worked, and the children simply gagged on it.

P.S. 24 was the beginning of a new world for Jimmy Baldwin, a world in which he could survive, not by means of physical strength—

he had little of that—but through his intelligence, of which it quickly became apparent to his teachers that he had a great deal. The principal at P.S. 24 was Mrs. Gertrude E. Ayer, the first black principal in New York City. Years later Baldwin was to say of her, "I loved and feared the lady—for she really was a lady, and a great one—with that trembling passion only twelve year olds can feel." From the beginning Mrs. Ayer recognized that Jimmy was a special child, one she was to remember in her retirement as "a very slim, small boy with that haunted look he has still."

The smallness and the shyness made him a natural victim of his peers, but Mrs. Ayer made sure that teachers helped Jimmy to develop. By the fifth grade it became clear that he had a talent for research and for writing. At home he read and reread *Uncle Tom's Cabin* until his mother, fearing for his eyes, hid it from him. Later *A Tale of Two Cities* became a favorite and led to a lifelong fascination with Dickens. His teachers encouraged him to visit the public library at 135th Street, where he read voraciously in the newly established Schomburg Collection. The library became his sanctuary and, in his mind, as he never went to college, his alma mater—the place where on his deathbed he was to ask that his papers be deposited.

During his pre–high school years young James even gained some acclaim for his written work. He wrote a song for which Mayor La Guardia praised him in a letter, and he won a prize for a short story he wrote for a church newspaper. The elders in the temple were already taking note of this precocious child of the ghetto, and his parents knew they were the guardians of a strange phenomenon. Mrs. Baldwin was "delighted" by what she saw, but her husband said he wanted the boy to be a preacher of the gospel. In time, that would come, too.

CHAPTER 2

Bill Miller

White men don't walk like that.
—a friend's remark

At P.S. 24 Jimmy Baldwin met a young woman who became a significant influence on his early intellectual development and remained a close friend until the end of his life. Later Baldwin described Orilla Miller as "a young white schoolteacher, a beautiful woman, very important to me" whom "I loved . . . absolutely, with a child's love." It was "certainly partly because of her, who arrived in my terrifying life so soon, that I never really managed to hate white people."

Orilla, whom Jimmy always called "Bill," came to New York from Antioch College in 1933. Antioch at the time was under the leadership of Dr. Arthur E. Morgan, the well-known engineer who was responsible for the college's pioneering work-study program in the 1920s and 1930s and who introduced study groups on social issues and economic theories. Antioch and the politics of her father—a Farmers' Cooperative organizer and populist in Illinois—were influential in the emergence of Orilla's left-wing interests. The Millers lost everything during the Depression, and Orilla had to leave Antioch. Not wishing to go "back to the farm," which, in any case, no longer existed, she applied for a job through Antioch and was offered a housekeeping position in Queens.

By 1934 she had saved enough money to start taking courses at Columbia Teachers College and she and a friend cooked for room and board at the Labor Temple on Fourteenth Street in Manhattan. Orilla's sister, Henrietta, came to New York in 1935, and the sisters found an apartment at 124th Street and Eighth Avenue. Joined later by Evan Winfield, a seaman whom Orilla met during a strike action and married in 1937, the two women were active participants in social justice movements—movements in support of labor unions and the

Spanish Republicans and against Hitler, anti-Semitism, and American racism. In 1934 Orilla had been given a twenty-hour-a-week Theatre Project job with the Educational Division of the WPA, a job that took her to the Madison House Settlement and several public schools, including P.S. 24, where James Baldwin was a sixth-grader and not quite eleven years old.

The P.S. 24 in which Bill Miller found herself was a "dreadful ancient . . . school house: dark, dreary and scary at times." In the classes—all boys and almost all black after third grade—there were often as many as fifty children. Most were native New Yorkers or recent immigrants from the South. Nearly all were "hungry and rebellious." The classes were often out of control; many of the teachers seemed to have given up on their charges.

The principal, Gertrude Ayer, was an exception. She was especially supportive of the WPA intern system as a source of enrichment for those students who, either because they were severely limited or because they were unusually talented, needed special attention. Recognizing that the young Baldwin was far ahead of his class, she encouraged the new Theatre Project intern to pay special attention to him.

Bill Miller, delighted to be given a specific charge, took on Jimmy as her "assistant," and they spent time together in the dingy attic where the WPA theater rehearsal room was located. In a comment very possibly made with his later theatrical ventures in mind, Baldwin remembered that Orilla directed his first play and "endured my first theatrical tantrums."

One tantrum, though not uniquely Baldwin's, took place early in Bill's time at P.S. 24. She had been told by Mrs. Ayer never to leave the room when there were children in her charge. This was a school rule. One night she had stayed late for a rehearsal with some fifteen or twenty boys, one of whom was Jimmy Baldwin. Perhaps it was his first play that was being rehearsed. The cast, including young James, got out of control and started shinning on the large old-fashioned heating pipes attached to the high walls. Bill Miller, unable to leave the room or to control the situation, put her head down on the desk and cried. The children, led by Jimmy, were horrified, immediately stopped what they were doing, and gathered apologetically around Bill's desk.

Jimmy and Bill discovered a common interest in Dickens; both were reading him and anxious to exchange views. The young woman from the Midwest was amazed at the brilliance of the boy from the slums. Full of the desire to do good, she questioned him about his life and was distressed to hear that, with the exception of the church and the library and school, he was confined to his apartment, where he helped his mother with the younger children.

She asked James—she always called him that—if she could meet his parents, and he took her home one day after school. The Baldwins now lived on Park Avenue between 132d and 133d—the "other" Park Avenue of the elevated railway. "That day," Orilla said, "we stepped into a kitchen filled with steam because Mrs. Baldwin was doing the laundry by hand. There was a clothesline stretched the length of the room and there in the moist warmth were these many eager small children—his brothers and sisters. I was appalled at the poverty in which he lived." Mr. Baldwin was not at home that day, but Orilla met him soon afterwards, when she returned to ask him permission to take James to a play.

Bill Miller and her sister, Henrietta, visited the Baldwins with some frequency between 1935 and 1939. They often brought clothes for the children, but never in a patronizing manner: "I never felt her pity," Baldwin was to write; it was simply that she "worried about our winters." The Millers had no inkling of Reverend Baldwin's antagonism towards them as whites, only noticing the "quiet dignity" of both parents. They sensed that Mrs. Baldwin approved of their taking Jimmy to plays and movies and museums, which they did regularly after the first permission was given, and that Reverend Baldwin was perhaps unaware of their activities.

The experiences which Bill and Henrietta Miller and later Evan Winfield shared with Jimmy Baldwin provided a formative supplemental education during his elementary and junior high school years. In effect, the Winfield-Millers included him in their family, not only sharing cultural activities but making him a participant in their political discussions. Later Baldwin would often say that his association with Bill Miller gave intellectual support to his instinctive resistance to the oppression he already knew firsthand.

Young James was so much a part of their group that the Millers often forgot about his size—even at thirteen he was still very small. At one May Day parade in which they all participated, he seemed frightened by the police horses, and Evan Winfield "scooped me up" and put him on the subway to go home. Jimmy had, in fact, been "scared shitless." Police on rearing horses might be a thrilling sight for white children. For a black child from Harlem, for whom police were the natural enemy, they were something quite different.

From the example of the Millers and Evan Winfield the young Baldwin learned much about the possibility of political change, and he began to suspect that "white people did not act as they did because they were white, but for some other reason." Bill Miller was someone he could trust. "She, too, anyway, was treated like a nigger, especially by the cops, and she had no love for landlords." Baldwin recalled Bill Miller facing hostile police when she took him and some of his brothers and sisters for a picnic downtown. There was supposed to be ice cream handed out at a police station, but the police were clearly not expecting "colored kids":

> I don't remember anything Bill said. I just remember her face as she stared at the cop, clearly intending to stand there until the ice cream all over the world melted or until the earth's surface froze, and she got us our ice cream, saying, *Thank You*, I remember, as we left.

Movies and plays were the favorite activities of the Millers and their young friend. The outing that meant most to Jimmy was the Orson Welles production of *Macbeth* with an all-black cast from the WPA Harlem theater group at the Lafayette Theater on 132d Street, not far from where James lived. The boy read the play in preparation for the performance. Bill noticed that he "never said a word during the whole show—it was as if he were entranced." Entranced he was, first by the all-black cast and the Haitian setting, and second, and more important, by the phenomenon of theater itself.

The entrancement was to remain strongly with him through the writing and various productions of *The Amen Corner* and *Blues for Mister Charlie*, and was to prevail to the very end of his life. The last writing he did was on a play, *The Welcome Table*. Like Henry James, the writer he most admired, he would have given up almost anything for sustained success as a playwright.

Only the cinema could compete as a preferred vehicle. Movies were infinitely more accessible to poor black children, and from an early age Jimmy had snuck off to see them. Bill Miller gave his moviegoing the stamp of respectability, and from the mid-1930s Baldwin was a film enthusiast. Later he would long to see one of his own works on the screen. In fact, he would write several screenplays, none of which, unfortunately, ever became films, and he was an adept film critic who clearly understood the technological and sociological possibilities of the medium. *The Devil Finds Work*, the book in which his comments on Orilla Miller appropriately appear, and which will be discussed later, is an insightful comment on American cinema.

One of the first films to which Bill took the young Baldwin was *20,000 Years in Sing Sing* with Spencer Tracy and Bette Davis. Davis remained a favorite of Baldwin's. But that first time, what he noticed most was her "pop-eyes popping." He was "astounded" because once again he had "caught my father, not in a lie, but in an infirmity. Here was a rich white movie star, no less, and she was *ugly*" with eyes just like his own. The message was clear and would remain with Baldwin forever. Not only could "ugliness" be beautiful, it could be associated with talent and might even be a source of power.

Of all the films to which Jimmy went with Bill Miller, *A Tale of Two Cities* was the most memorable. This was already a favorite novel. He understood that Bill, social activist that she was, had wanted him to discover in the movie "something of the inevitable human ferment which explodes into what is called a revolution." But the film had a different effect on the child's mind than Bill Miller perhaps expected it would. He wondered where black proletarians—his stepfather, for instance—fit into any American revolution. The union people his stepfather worked with downtown were, after all, proletarians, but as far as David Baldwin, Sr., was concerned, they were "robbers." Later Baldwin was to react similarly to Richard Wright's politics, and he was to develop a general skepticism towards politics in general, and political and social theory in particular.

The Winfields gave up the 124th Street apartment in 1939 and Orilla took a job as a governess on Twelfth Street while Evan went to sea. Sometime during that summer Jimmy was sent by his mother to pick up some dishes and clothes that Bill wanted to give to the Baldwins. Bill remarked that she had not seen him in some time—probably because he was busy now with high school friends. He told his old teacher that day that he was "saved" now, a preacher at the Fireside Pentecostal Assembly, and that as such he could no longer participate with her in ungodly theatrical activities or even see her anymore. Bill was disappointed and disapproving and said so.

Bill and Evan would soon leave New York, and eventually they moved to Los Angeles. For some seventeen years they lost contact with Baldwin. Then, in 1955, Orilla came across "Me and My House" ("Notes of a Native Son") in *Harper's Magazine* and was surprised and pleased to find grateful references to her role in the author's early life. She was also shocked to discover that James's stepfather had greatly mistrusted her and her motives. She wrote to Baldwin in care of his publisher and received an answer from Paris. In that long letter, besides recalling the break with Orilla and describing his eventual departure from the church, and his disillusionment with politics, Baldwin asked his old friend for a photograph and acknowledged her importance to him: "I've held your face in my mind for many years."

In 1963 Evan and Orilla heard that Baldwin was to give a speech for the Congress of Racial Equality (CORE) in Los Angeles. Because of the crowds and the people who were rushing him to another engagement, they were able to speak to him only briefly before his entourage whisked him away, Baldwin protesting characteristically, "But she's my teacher. Don't you understand? She's my teacher." On May 15 Bill wrote a letter full of nostalgia for the P.S. 24 days—the discussions of Dickens, the outings, her "insensitivity" in regard to Mr. Baldwin's hostility. And she gave her former pupil the teacher's blessing:

> James, I want to tell you that the promise of the wonderful child has been fulfilled in the man. I am not referring alone to the development of your writing ability, the incisive use of your intelligence in social commentary. I am referring to the moral you—in the broad sense of one's individual relationship to man around him. That Evan and I had a small part in your life adds to the value of ours. I also say, thank you, that there is this James Baldwin in America in the year 1963.

During a 1976 book signing in Cambridge, Massachusetts, a young man introduced himself to Baldwin as Orilla Miller Winfield's son, Steve. The book in question was *The Devil Finds Work*. Baldwin was moved by this coincidence and wrote Orilla asking if she would appear with him on television to discuss the Harlem days. She accepted somewhat reluctantly but was, in any case, spared when Baldwin became ill and had to cancel the broadcast.

On a trip to Los Angeles later that year, however, he visited the Winfields. When Bill mentioned in passing that the cinema down the street was playing *David Copperfield* and, of all films, *A Tale of Two Cities*, they all agreed that nothing could be more appropriate and spent the afternoon doing something they had first done exactly forty years before.

There were other visits to the Winfields when he was in Los Angeles, and he wrote to Bill in 1982, when he was teaching in the

States, and reminded her again of how she had "helped prepare me for these present stormy days."

Evan Winfield died in 1984 and Baldwin wrote a letter that expressed with great feeling his sense of what both Orilla and Evan had meant to him. He remembered how happy the love between Evan and Orilla had made him as a child, how he had marveled at the way their faces filled with "light" when they looked at each other. He had felt "shy" in their presence but "enormously privileged, too." The love he witnessed between them had helped him to appreciate the depth and the joy of love in his own life.

The final visit was in 1986. Bill had invited him for tea at four; he arrived at six with a bottle of champagne and two friends. The evening was full of laughter and memories. A few days before he died Jimmy spoke of Bill Miller; she was one of those you could depend on, one who knew how to keep the faith. She died in 1991.

CHAPTER 3

Awakenings

And all that heard him were astonished.
—Luke 2:47

Bill Miller could teach the young James Baldwin something about struggle and something about the economics of racism and could introduce him to aspects of "culture" that had been inaccessible to him before her arrival, but she could not help him to understand the ambiguities of his maleness. Furthermore, as Baldwin was to say later, "she could not instruct me as to blackness, except obliquely, feeling that she had neither the right nor the authority." Two African-American teachers at Frederick Douglass Junior High School, which Jimmy entered in the fall of 1935, were able to do a great deal to fill the gap.

Countee Cullen and Herman W. ("Bill") Porter arrived in Jimmy Baldwin's life, as Bill Miller had earlier, at a crucial moment. On the brink of adolescence, at odds with his peers because of his small size and what they perceived as his effeminacy, and denied a father's love or approval at home, young James was desperate for guidance—for love—from adults who were male and black like him.

At P.S. 24 he had learned that he was most likely to win approval by means of his mind. And he knew already that his mind revealed itself most clearly in his writing. For him "writing was an act of love . . . an attempt—not to get the world's attention—[but] . . . to be loved." It was "a way to save myself and to save my family. It came out of despair . . . it seemed the only way to another world."

It was to their great credit that Cullen and Porter, like Gertrude Ayer and Orilla Miller before them, so quickly recognized in the new boy an individual of special value. These were two men who had used their intellects to confront the nemesis of racism and the loss of self-esteem that results from it, and they welcomed Jimmy as a comrade whose schoolboy writing already indicated that he would do the same. They set to work almost immediately giving encouragement and assistance. Cullen brought him into the school's literary club, which he had founded, and spent a great deal of time working with him on both poetry and fiction. Porter, through *The Douglass Pilot*, the school magazine which he advised and of which he eventually made young Baldwin "my editor-in-chief," provided him with a place to publish. The jeers of his classmates soon turned to respect; James Baldwin had found his "profession."

Countee Cullen emerged from the Harlem Renaissance in the 1920s as an important poet. A graduate of New York University, with an M.A. from Harvard, he found his way to teaching jobs in Harlem. He was a minister's son who was living proof for the younger minister's son that a black man could be a writer. And there were other things the boy and the man had in common. Like his young charge, Cullen was oppressed by a sense of his ugliness, a sense that very possibly derived from his own illegitimacy and problems with his stepfather. In spite of all this, Cullen had a certain flair and a kind of elegance that the young Baldwin admired and emulated. He had been to France and he knew French. By his very presence Cullen pointed a way around the mentality of despair and proved that many roads out of the ghetto were possible. Baldwin learned his first bits of French, a language in which he later became fluent, in Countee Cullen's French class at Frederick Douglass, and he always said that his dream of going to France originated with Cullen.

And there was a less tangible rapport that he spoke of—a comforting sense that Cullen and he instinctively understood something about each other, something that prepubescent inexperience would have made it impossible for Baldwin to identify then as homosexuality. Countee Cullen was everything that Jimmy's stepfather was not—a warm man, one who was not afraid to touch, who entered into his students' lives. In some ways he took the place of a father for the young writer, as Beauford Delaney would later. Baldwin "adored" him and his poetry and tried to write like him.

Bill Porter was a different kind of influence. A Harvard graduate, handsome, somewhat aloof, but always fair, he instilled in his students the importance of discipline and self-reliance. And he also took on something of a father's role. Unlike Reverend Baldwin, he was positive about surviving a white-dominated world. Porter was fond of telling the story of the day he took his "editor-in-chief" to the Forty-second Street public library to do research that led to a ninth-grade essay, "Harlem—Then and Now." Porter walked to the Baldwin apartment one Saturday morning to pick up James and was, like Orilla Miller before him, appalled at the poverty he encountered. But unlike Miller, he was well aware of the senior Baldwin's hostility and of the complex reasons for it. Where Mr. Baldwin would not openly confront the white schoolteacher, he had no qualms about insulting Porter, who was "corrupting" his son with books by white devils. The child was so upset by the confrontation that he vomited on the street.

But after Porter got him started at the library it became an important sanctuary during the rest of his school years. Most important, a black man the boy respected and admired had corroborated what Bill Miller was trying to show him, that culture and learning, even when "downtown," were part of his birthright. Porter helped build in his student the confidence to combat his father's skepticism about education and to overcome the white stares and the racial slurs of white policemen, who sometimes actually asked, "Why don't you niggers stay uptown where you belong?"

Baldwin graduated from Frederick Douglass Junior High at the beginning of the summer of 1938, a summer during which he was to be nearly overwhelmed by sexuality and, almost at the same moment, by religion. It was not until several years later, during the writing of *Go Tell It on the Mountain*, that he was able to see some connection between the two forces that possessed him at thirteen and, in their interconnectedness—though in different forms—were to remain central to his life and his work.

The summer was marked by several crucial occurrences. One day Jimmy, still dressed in the shorts commonly worn by somewhat younger boys at the time, was running an errand for his mother when a tall man, probably in his mid-thirties, asked him to go to the store for him. Jimmy agreed, hoping to earn a dime, and went with the man to what he supposed was his house to get the necessary money. On the second landing the man stopped, touched Jimmy on the face, said he was cute, and, before the boy fully understood what was happening, began to caress him sexually. Jimmy was at once horrified and aroused. Frightened by a noise on the landing above, the man gave him some money and disappeared. Jimmy ran home and threw the money out of the bathroom window. He had already realized his alienation from American society as a black; he now experienced a sexual alienation.

His stepfather's frequent references to his ugliness and his own confrontations with prejudice had led him to associate that ugliness with his race. At the age of ten he had been roughed up by white policemen whose insinuations about his body introduced him to white myths about black sexuality. In the context of the self-deprecation that resulted from these events and others like them, the sexual touch of another human being was difficult to associate with beauty or love. Jimmy was, in any case, so frightened by what he later called his "violation" that, after demanding to be allowed to graduate to long trousers, he "found the Lord" in order to protect himself. Religion, he hoped, could mean "safety," safety from himself, who at age fourteen had become, he feared, "one of the most depraved people on earth."

A school friend, Arthur Moore, the model for Elisha in *Go Tell It on the Mountain*, with whom he was "in love . . . as boys, indeed, can be at that age" but without "the faintest notion of what to do about it," took Jimmy to his church, Mount Calvary of the Pentecostal Faith, to meet the celebrated preacher, Mother Horn. Bishop Rosa Artemis Horn was a southerner born of slave parents. She had migrated to Illinois and come to New York in the thirties with her adopted white daughter of Scandinavian descent—later "Bishop" Gladys Brandhagen (the "white angel" or Sister Gladys). "Whose little boy are you?" asked the preacher at that first meeting. And Jimmy's "heart replied at once, 'Why, yours.' "

Baldwin was struck later by the fact that exactly the same question had been asked him by "pimps and racketeers" who wanted him to "hang out" with them. Desperate to be "*somebody's* little boy" and to be free of the adult world's sexual guilt which had begun to overcome him, he chose Mother Horn and the church over the heavy-breathing men in hallways and the pimps on the street, and on a Sunday night when he felt more stained with sin than usual, he responded to the preacher's exhortations by flinging himself onto the threshing floor in front of the altar. After what seemed like hours of wrenching turmoil the "vertical saints" who stood over him brought him "through" with their crying, their singing, and their praying, and when morning came he was pronounced "saved."

Baldwin's brother David, who was always his older brother's favorite, was disappointed one day when he looked into Jimmy's desk and found that the familiar collection of movie programs and modeling clay had been replaced by a Bible. Movies and clay modeling and writing had been Jimmy's means of escape from a dreary existence, and somehow they held out a promise for all of the Baldwin children. Movies, especially, had introduced their brother to a wider world, giving him a sense of human experience beyond his own situation. But now he seemed totally involved in the life of the church, with much less time to spend with his brothers and sisters and no time for the activities that had so fascinated them.

The Moores had a falling-out with Mount Calvary—perhaps associated with Mother Horn's own troubles with her congregation, troubles later given fictional form in Sister Margaret's problems in *The Amen Corner*—and they moved to the Fireside Pentecostal Assembly. By this time Jimmy was spending a great deal of time with them—in fact, he referred to them as his "second family"—so quite naturally, he followed them to their new church. Mount Calvary disapproved and in the boy's accompanying the Moores found reason to accuse him of "walking disorderly." On the last night at Mount Calvary, Sister Gladys, the only white in the church, trapped him on the steps, gripped his arm, and told him—she seemed "to be chewing and spitting out the air"—of the inevitable damnation that faced "boys like me." So it was that even before he became a preacher, Baldwin experienced something of the hypocrisy and intolerance that were eventually to drive him away from the "saints."

But at the age of fourteen he was not yet ready to leave. He had found in the church the "gimmick" he needed to protect himself from himself. It was not, however, enough to be saved. To make the church experience interesting or even possible, he had to do the saving. Late in 1938 he became one of a corps of apprentice preachers, or "young ministers." He quickly demonstrated a gift for preaching and before long was something of a sensation in several Harlem churches.

The church experience was as important to Baldwin's development as a writer and spokesman as were his relationships with teachers like Countee Cullen and Herman Porter and his early reading of Stowe and Dickens. In the pulpit he learned to use rhetoric effectively. And he learned about cadence, about measured speech. Most of all, he was affected—even thrilled—by the sense of the "power and glory" that came with the effective use of "the Word." There were moments when, by "some miracle," he and the church "were one." His experience in the pulpit was a precursor of what he would later feel as a writer and speechmaker.

Jimmy's "second birth" and later his success in the pulpit led to greater self-assurance at home. He began consciously to stand up to his stepfather and side openly against him. He found that Reverend

Baldwin had no choice but to leave him alone more now that he was in the "service of the Lord." When, soon after his fourteenth birthday and after he had finished junior high school, his stepfather suggested that he get a job, Jimmy had the strength to insist that he continue with his education. Fortunately, on Countee Cullen's advice, he had applied to and been accepted for the fall of 1938 into the prestigious De Witt Clinton High School in the Bronx.

A partial list of the more famous Clinton graduates will give some idea of the specialness of this school: Countee Cullen, Richard Avedon, George Cukor, Douglas Fairbanks, Sr., Burt Lancaster, Richard Rodgers, Daniel Schorr, Fats Waller, Charles Rangel, Paddy Chayefsky, A. M. Rosenthal, Neil Simon, Louis Untermeyer, Richard Hofstadter, and Nate Archibald are all alumni of De Witt Clinton.

Across the street from Clinton was a large cooperative-housing development built for the Amalgamated Clothing Workers. Most of the adult inhabitants were Jews of European background. They tended to be left-of-center politically. They were enthusiastic supporters of the social aims of the New Deal, and they were vocal in their support of the black cause. Their children made up the majority of Baldwin's schoolmates. These were young men—Clinton, like most New York schools at the time, was not coeducational—who were more tolerant than other whites and more tolerant than Reverend Baldwin or the "saints" at Fireside. They were bent on academic and social achievement, they were politically active. More interested in Jimmy Baldwin's talent than his race, they admired him for his writing, as most high school students admire their peers for their athletic achievements, and they elected him to the prestigious student court.

Furthermore, at Clinton, Baldwin was exposed to exceptional teachers, some with Ph.D.'s who, because of the Depression and the difficulty in finding university jobs, took on high school positions and provided their students with the luxury of their overqualification. To be sure, not all teachers at De Witt Clinton were "advanced." In one history class, containing not only James Baldwin but boys with names like Capouya, Guerrero, and Cammaro, a perfectly pleasant but naive young teacher revealed her "terrifying innocence" by announcing that America was being ruined by the flood of immigrants from southern Europe. If she thought that of white southern Europeans, what did she think of African-Americans? The young Baldwin could not help remembering his stepfather's constant assertion that all whites were to be mistrusted.

An especially important part of Baldwin's life at Clinton was his work on the school literary magazine. *The Magpie*—"a thing of shreds and tatters appropriate to magpies," as one student put it—was advised by Wilmer Stone, a radical southerner who preached socialism in his classroom, and who took a particular interest in Jimmy, as did students associated with the magazine. These students, all white, almost all Jewish, became Baldwin's closest school friends. They included Richard Avedon, who was to become a famous photographer, and Sol Stein and Emile Capouya, both of whom became publishers. The group would spend hours together in the tower where the *Magpie* room was located, discussing not only future issues of their magazine, of which Baldwin became an editor, but literature, politics, history, and even religion. He did not have such discussions at home or in the church. And the people at the Fireside Pentecostal Assembly would have been scandalized had they been able to watch their favorite boy preacher prancing about with a tambourine in front of several laughing Jewish boys, imitating in song and dance the saints stricken by the power of the Lord at the foot of the cross.

The tambourine scene stands almost as a symbol of the dilemma that faced Baldwin at the time. The three years at the predominantly white but marginally integrated and liberal high school were to coincide exactly with his three years in the pulpit, and this fact caused a terrible mental struggle, which had distinct racial overtones. The trip each day to Clinton was long in terms of time and miles. In terms of landscape, attitudes, and possibilities, the distance was enormous. The world from which the young Baldwin traveled each day was marked by extreme poverty and bleakness and by deprivation, denial, and repression. For him it was a world dominated by an irrational and intolerant stepfather whose rule, because of racism, had no basis in success or socially recognized authority. Religion perhaps held out hope for the future, but it was a sexless, bookless future, ruled by the saints in their white robes and the all-too-likely white god in his.

Yet the world of Harlem was home, the center of his being; the ties of family and church were strong. Clinton was a foreign place from which "the Lord" was apparently absent. Surmounted by its tower and surrounded by the green of Mosholu Park, it seemed to speak proudly of a future in the here and now as opposed to the sanctified hereafter promised by the church.

In later years he would point to the fact that the onset of the demise of his faith during the second year of preaching was simultaneous with his beginning "to read again." At one point Reverend

Baldwin, realizing his stepson's struggle, asked him if it was not true that he would rather write than preach, and Jimmy had answered that it was true. Increasingly, the boy preacher was struck by the arrogance of the ministers with their houses and Cadillacs and the "saints" with their antiseptic holiness in the face of human tragedy. The church even criticized him for helping an old blind woman who was not "walking holy." He was losing respect for himself as he was losing respect for his superiors. He felt he had no right to promise "eternal life" as a payment for the deprivations that marked the lives of his congregation. Furthermore, he began to sense that the passion that overcame him in the church services was merely a mask for his own repressed sexuality, that he was not really escaping from anything. The love he gave his congregation—the love that attracted them—in his sermons and his visitations to the sick was based firmly in his own anguish.

He remembered a "sister" who whenever she was overcome by the Spirit in church would manage to inch as close to him as possible, literally tormenting his body and soul with the presence of her flesh as it moved in the "power of the Lord." One day, towards the end of his ministry, she asked him to make a sick call. He found his way past the leering men on the stoop of her brownstone and climbed the stairs to her door, sensing the whole time that his mission involved more than religion. After the ritual "Praise the Lord," she offered him a lemonade and commented, with a significant edge to her voice, on the heat of the day. As the electricity between them increased, Jimmy became at once apprehensive and excited. The would-be rite of passage was interrupted by the sudden and obviously unexpected entrance of a much older and larger man, who showed him the door. The sister seemed disappointed and never appeared in church again. The men sitting around on the stoop outside laughed to see the young minister leaving so soon.

The problems at church and at home negatively affected Baldwin's work at Clinton. In fact, academic failures would delay his graduation for a year. Nevertheless, he did so well at what he enjoyed—English and history—that he was recognized as a superior intellect. Wiry, nervous, witty, argumentative, and already possessed of the verbal flamboyance that he had learned in part from his preaching, and which would mark his later work, he could not—especially as an African-American—be ignored.

The outcome of the church-school conflict was probably inevitable. A child with Baldwin's drive and ambition, with the hurt he had received from his stepfather and the doubts he had about his vocation as a preacher, would naturally be attracted to the possibilities represented by Clinton. The boy who mockingly "testified" in the *Magpie* tower and who picked up on Mr. Stone's socialism, quickly becoming, at least in his school world, a political radical, was the same one who had stood dreaming on that hill in Central Park not so many years before. Something in Baldwin knew even by the late 1930s that to find the new Jerusalem he would have to leave his home and cultivate the new, admittedly flawed, but challenging world he had discovered at Clinton. The stepson of the Reverend David Baldwin always had doubts about that world, but the artist in him enjoyed playing to it, and the witness in him knew he had no choice.

In any case, by the time Baldwin was doing his tambourine dance for his high school friends, he must have sensed what his real vocation was. A new power or drive possessed him, something that went beyond that old need to write in order to be loved. Next to his picture in the 1941 Clinton yearbook it is stated that his goal was to become a novelist-playwright, that his motto was "Fame is the spur and—ouch!" James Baldwin was beginning to believe in himself.

By his second year at Clinton, Jimmy had become a regular contributor of poems, plays, and stories to *The Magpie*. He even interviewed his old P.S. 139 teacher Countee Cullen, whose advice to him and to all young writers was to "read and write—and wait." The *Magpie* works shed light on the young Baldwin's development as a thinker and as a writer. Not surprisingly, he used his writing to work out the problems with which he was preoccupied. There are several stories, for instance, about the church, in which religious hypocrisy and loss of faith are important themes. Like most juvenilia, the early works tend towards the sentimental, a quality Baldwin had to guard against throughout his career, especially when he treated subjects as close to his heart as father-son relationships and those between male friends or brothers. In the *Magpie* pieces the male relationships provided a vehicle for the transference of the adolescent sexual longings that had been so repressed in the young minister.

The characters in a story called "Peace on Earth," all soldiers in wartime, form the first of the many all-male fellowships or brotherhoods that were to mark Baldwin's fiction. The central character in the story is a boy called John, the name given later to the autobiographical hero of *Go Tell It on the Mountain*. The narrator says of him, "Johnny not only possesses salvation, but he is also a minister. He is friendly, lovable, and Christ-like. We call him the 'Little Minister.' "

The story concerns the death of some of the fellowship and Johnny's steadfast faith in the face of senseless war. The lover here, the source of the boy's longing, is not only the group of young men, it is "the Lord": "Peace like a river. Joy like a flood. I will be with him—always—always—even to the end of the world," says the "Little Minister" of Jesus.

By 1941, in a play called *These Two*, the theme is more secular and the love more profane, if still untainted by sex. Tom, a somewhat criminalized young man, convinces a much gentler boy, David (always one of Baldwin's favorite fictional names), that they should rob a shop. David is an autobiographical character who wants to be a doctor or a priest or anything that will release him from a life of poverty and crime. The police attempt to apprehend the thieves and are shot by them, but not before Tom is mortally wounded. David, torn between guilt over the killing of the police and the agony of his friend, takes his own life as Tom watches helplessly. Weeping, Tom "begins to sink" as he cries out, "Davie . . . oh, Davie boy."

The sexual predilections hinted at in some of the *Magpie* stories were beginning to be expressed in Jimmy's actual life. At about the time he was writing *These Two*, he was spending time with a Harlem "racketeer," a man of Spanish-Irish descent who was in his late thirties and was "in love with" him. Jimmy was "in love," too, but warily so; he was bothered by the obvious conflict between his feelings and the precepts of the church of which he was still the "Little Minister." The obvious attachment of the man and the boy for each other aroused street taunts and rumors, and eventually they drifted apart. But later Baldwin would credit the relationship with bringing to a head the whole question of his association with the church. The positive feelings his love for the older man inspired led him to suspect that real salvation would come from accepting rather than running away from life. He began to sense the sexual roots of the terrifying release he had experienced on the church floor as Mother Horn and the saints had labored over him.

The mid-teens can be treacherous for anyone. For those without the luxury of prospects, they can be devastating. Baldwin always said sixteen was the age at which the child in Harlem can suddenly see the past and the future—his future—in his father's or mother's eyes, in the drunks and pimps of the street. It was the age when people went mad, and he saw madness overtake several of the adolescents in his church. He feared that he would go mad, too, as his stepfather was going mad, if he did not confront his terrors and learn to live with them. He had once cherished the safety of the church; he now valued his self-respect more. The boy preacher had to leave the church to save his soul.

He discussed his problem with his closest school friend, Emile Capouya. Capouya knew something of both the appeal and the hypocrisy of the church, as Jimmy had taken him to hear the famous preacher "Daddy Grace" in Harlem. Capouya, himself a nonreligious Jew, had been moved to a kind of religious experience by the tambourines, the "naked public commotion," and the sense of release that pervaded the church as people testified to their sins before the climactic arrival of their preacher. Daddy Grace, a huge man of some three hundred pounds with shoulder-length hair, clothed in the "splendors of the East," and sporting a pinky nail of amazing length, was carried in an enormous palanquin. Later he lumbered down the aisle as people pinned dollar bills to his robes, chanting, "Sweet Daddy Grace, save my soul; Sweet Daddy Grace, save my soul." Exciting as this was, Daddy Grace clearly was not an appropriate model for James Baldwin. Capouya supported his friend in his desire to leave the church, and the decision was made.

For his last sermon Jimmy chose his stepfather's favorite text, "Set thy house in order." The right topic for nearly every reason, it was a farewell not only to the church but to his stepfather's house and to his old life. One day, late in 1940, sitting on a park bench with Emile Capouya, Jimmy had burst into tears and revealed that he was illegitimate. He had learned this "terrible truth" about himself in a conversation between his parents. What he overheard he had vaguely suspected; it explained much of Mr. Baldwin's attitude towards him. His "father's" house was not *his* house. "Set thy house in order" was a call to the prophet within young James and the essence of the message he would soon carry as the "bastard of the West" into the house that was Western civilization at large, the house that had dispossessed him even as it had dispossessed his ancestors.

After his sermon he left the building, in spite of the objections of the minister in charge, and he joined Capouya on Forty-second Street for a movie. The wider possibilities of the arts and the flesh had won out over the narrowness of the church.

CHAPTER 4

Beauford Delaney

Lord, open the unusual door.
—old song

Baldwin's ability at sixteen to confront his demons and to leave the church and his stepfather's house can be traced in significant part to a friendship that had begun in Greenwich Village in 1940, a year before his last sermon. In the third year of his ministry, already tortured by doubts, obsessed by his newly discovered illegitimacy, torn between his role as a preacher and his growing perception of his own difference and the apparent hopelessness of his situation as a "Negro," Jimmy Baldwin was desperate. His attendance at school was becoming erratic, he was failing some of his courses. There seemed to be nowhere to turn. Emile Capouya suggested that he should meet Beauford Delaney, a black painter he knew who lived in Greenwich Village. Jimmy had an after-school job on Canal Street, not too far from Greene Street, where Delaney lived, so one day after work he took his friend's advice.

In the autobiographical introduction to his final collection of essays, *The Price of the Ticket*, Baldwin points to the significance of his first meeting with Delaney, describing it as a rite of passage. Surprised at his own temerity, he made his way to the Greene Street address, knocked on the door, and was confronted by a "short, round brown man" who, "when he had completed his instant X-ray of my brain, lungs, liver, heart, bowels, and spinal column," invited him in: "*Lord . . . open the unusual door*," Beauford would often sing. Jimmy had come to the right door, "and not a moment too soon."

In Baldwin's personal experience, Countee Cullen had represented a possibility of a black man's succeeding in the arts, but Beauford was the first living exemplar of the black man as functioning, self-supporting artist. When the boy went to Greenwich Village that first day, he was, in fact, on a continuing search for a sympathetic spirit who could understand what made him what he was, someone who could teach him the way a father teaches a son. He had followed his own stepfather by becoming a preacher, and it was not working. It certainly was having no effect on the way the older man acted towards him. He needed a mentor who could understand him and who could guide him in his true vocation.

In Beauford Delaney, then in his thirties, Baldwin found what he was looking for. In fact, he found the person who can probably be called the most important influence in his life. Delaney had the capacity and the inclination to give him something his stepfather or for that matter his mother or Orilla Miller or his other favorite teachers, even Countee Cullen, could not have given him. When Beauford looked through that skinny boy on his doorstep he saw a kindred spirit where Mr. Baldwin, as far as his stepson was concerned, had seen an aberration. Jimmy was not yet fully aware of his own homosexuality or of the demands of his vocation, and Beauford, himself a homosexual, a minister's son, and an artist, was there, as a father in art, to help this younger version of himself through a crucial passage.

From the beginning the young Baldwin sensed a natural connection with Beauford Delaney. He sensed that when he observed him he was really seeing himself as well. Here was a black man, an artist, an outsider, somehow a later version of himself. It was as if Jimmy had found his long-lost father. Beauford was not his father, but he treated the boy like a son. From that first day the man and the boy trusted and believed in each other. Later Baldwin would say of Beauford that he was from the beginning until the last "my principal witness."

Beauford taught his protégé to react to life as an artist. Light and music, for Baldwin, became synonymous with Beauford: "The reality of his seeing caused me to begin to see." Beauford had a barely functional old phonograph on which he played scratchy recordings of music that, for the boy preacher, had been associated with sin and degradation. For the first time, under Beauford's guidance, he began to undergo the "religious" experience of jazz and the blues. Beauford played Ella Fitzgerald, Ma Rainey, Louis Armstrong, Bessie Smith, Ethel Waters, Paul Robeson, Lena Horne, and Fats Waller. And he talked about them, in the soft caressing voice to which Baldwin would turn for comfort and for teaching in the darkest moments of the years to come.

The record player was just one of Beauford's teaching tools. He took Jimmy to galleries and concerts, and he introduced him to his wide circle of friends, many of them successful African-Americans in the world of art and music. Baldwin loved telling the story of meeting Marian Anderson with Beauford after a concert in New York. On their way home Beauford talked about her "smoky yellow gown" and the way it blended with the "copper and tan" of her skin and the roses scattered in her dressing room. Beauford painted that scene later—"fixed it in time"—and he told Jimmy he had painted it for him.

The vocabulary of color and sounds learned in Beauford's presence was to become the basis of Baldwin's art. Delaney was to reconcile for his protégé the music of the Harlem streets with the music of the Harlem churches, and this helped Baldwin to reconcile his sexual awakening with his artistic awakening. Beauford taught his charge how to see beauty even in the metaphorical and literal gutter.

On their outings in New York, Jimmy formed the habit of following his teacher's gaze so that he could see what Beauford saw. There was a particularly memorable moment on Broadway. It was a rainy day in the winter of 1940. The man and the boy were standing at a corner, waiting for the light to change, when Beauford began staring down at the water flowing past the curb. "Look," he said. Jimmy's eyes had already followed Beauford's anyway, but he just saw water. "Look again," Beauford said. Then he noticed the oil on the surface of the water and the way it transformed the buildings it reflected. It was a lesson in complex vision that would remain with James Baldwin the writer.

Forty-three years later Baldwin, pacing one afternoon up and down in his workroom, talked about the deeper meaning of Beauford's lesson. It was not only a question of careful observation, he said; it had to do with a willingness to face ugliness in order to find what the artist has to find. And it had to do with the fact that finding the truth often involves confronting one's own fears. And finally, it had to do with the fact that what one can and cannot see "says something about you."

Delaney was born in Knoxville in 1901, but his family moved to Jefferson City when he was five. His mother, Delia, worked as a housekeeper, nurse, and cook. His father was a minister of the Methodist Episcopal Church and a part-time barber. Far too humble to realize that he might well be describing himself, Beauford spoke of his father as "a man loveable, honest, with a belief in and a need to go among people and bring compassion and love. He gave his life and whatever it offered him to all those close to him."

Beauford remembered a spartan but loving world in which his family, like so many others, survived by virtue of a sense of community and maintained hopes of upward mobility in the face of poverty and segregation.

> Life at home is busy and we find a common interest in the family, the church, and the community. . . . assisting in fund-raising; revivals and concerts of various sorts are constantly under way to provide money. All of these activities are part of the Negro South; it's in the church and home that their world begins and ends.

Baldwin's mother and his stepfather—and, he thought, his real father—had been southerners, and he often spoke of his southern roots. Somehow it was appropriate that his surrogate father should be southern, too.

But for Beauford, as for Baldwin's stepfather, opportunity for advancement was to be found in the North. The Delaneys had moved back to Knoxville in about 1914. There Beauford had found a job in a shoemaker's shop, had attended the Knoxville Colored High School, and had been "discovered" as a painter by a white artist named Lloyd Branson, who gave him lessons and eventually urged him to go to Boston.

In Boston, Beauford flourished. He studied art at the Massachusetts Normal School, went to concerts, met poets and artists, and generally became involved in African-American culture. In 1929 he moved to New York, first to Harlem, which was then experiencing its "Renaissance," and later to Greenwich Village, where he painted W. E. B. Du Bois, W. C. Handy, Marian Anderson, Louis Armstrong, Ethel Waters, Duke Ellington, and many other important African-Americans. He was himself painted by Georgia O'Keeffe.

By the time Jimmy Baldwin walked into his apartment in 1940, Beauford had been featured with other black artists in an October 1938 *Life* article and had had successful one-man shows. He had left the safe world of family and church, and he lived in poverty, but he was on his own, and no one doubted that he was an artist. No wonder the boy saw him as a role model.

In 1945 Henry Miller would comment in an essay, "The Amazing and Invariable Beauford DeLaney [*sic*]," on the contrast between his own world and the world Jimmy Baldwin found in the Greenwich Village studio of his mentor:

> Yes, he is amazing and invariable, this Beauford. It has been storming now for forty-eight hours, here at Big Sur, and the house is leaking from every cement and stucco pore of its being. This is why my mind dwells on Beauford. How is he faring now in the winter of Manhattan where all is snow and frost? Here it is warm, despite the leaks, despite the gale. We have only one problem—to keep the wood dry. A few sticks of wood in the stove and the place is cozy. But at 181 Greene Street, on that top floor where Beauford works, dreams and eats his paintings, only a roaring furnace kept at a constant temperature of 120 degrees Centigrade can combat the chill of the grave which emanates from the dripping walls, floors and ceilings. And of course there will never be such a furnace at 181 Greene Street. Neither will the sun's warm rays ever penetrate the single room in which Beauford lives.

Miller's comments are at once literal and metaphorical. From the light and freedom available to the white American artist he reaches out in his thoughts to the darkness of poverty and racism that oppresses his black counterpart. Beauford would leave that darkness by following other escapees from American racism—Richard Wright, Chester Himes, many friends in the jazz world, and his son in art, James Baldwin—to Paris. But first he would pursue his career in New York. During the eight years between the day the frightened boy from Harlem walked through his door and the day that same James Baldwin left for Paris in 1948, Beauford Delaney watched over his protégé as they both attempted to pursue their careers in difficult circumstances. Over the years the two men would learn to depend on each other more and more. As will become clear, neither would ever betray the bond of the "unusual door."

CHAPTER 5

Probings

Not my father, not my mother, but it's me, oh Lord.
—old song

The end of Baldwin's high school and preaching careers coincided roughly with the entry of the United States into World War II. The draft was a real possibility for him, though he would probably be deferred, as the oldest male child of a family consisting of a jobless father in ill health, a working mother, and eight hungry brothers and sisters.

Clearly, decisions had to be made. He knew now that he wanted to be a writer. He had considered college—City College or the New School for Social Research—but his high school record was marred by some low grades and the delayed graduation, and he had no real desire to pursue further formal education. Countee Cullen, Wilmer Stone, and Beauford Delaney had suggested to him that a writer need not necessarily go to college; the important thing was to respond to one's vocation. But where, and how? Jimmy asked himself.

World War II was already turning Harlem into a true ghetto, a wasteland where white soldiers were forbidden to go, where segregated black soldiers had to go, where commerce was reluctant to go, and where ordinary whites chose not to go. Harlem in 1942 was not the artistic center it had been in the "Renaissance" of the twenties. There seemed to be no reason for the newly liberated ex-minister to remain where he was.

Since the age of fifteen Baldwin had been attracted to Greenwich Village and had found various odd jobs there after school hours. On the surface, the bohemian villagers seemed less concerned with his being "colored" than did white people elsewhere. Greenwich Village was the natural continuation of De Witt Clinton. It was a place for talk, for ideas, for art. And Beauford was there, proving that a black man could live and work outside of the ghetto.

But before he could settle into life in the Village, Baldwin had to earn more money—both for himself and for his family—than he could gain from odd jobs. His stepfather's condition had deteriorated badly. Jimmy had been sent to search for him one evening and had found him sitting on a bench in the 135th Street Lexington Avenue subway station, confused and lost. Now the once seemingly omnipotent minister spent most of his time "locked up in his terrors; hating and fearing every living soul," staring out of the apartment window.

Emile Capouya had found a defense-related job in Belle Mead, New Jersey. In mid-1942 he helped Jimmy get a job there too. The pay was good, making it no longer necessary to live at home, and on weekends there was the Village, where he was making friends, men and women, some black, some white.

Capouya and Baldwin lived in Rocky Hill with an Irish-American couple, Tom and Florence Martin, who shared their interest in literature. Baldwin enjoyed his time in the Martin household, but he did not enjoy working on the tracklaying gang. Capouya was struck by the difference between his own approach to the work and his friend's. For Capouya it was a real job that met the expectations of a young man brought up in a politically ideological subsociety that admired the working class. As for Baldwin, he was simply buying time, "reserving himself," as Capouya saw it, "in the curious way that artists do, to be an artist." The only thing that interested him about the work was listening to the songs the black laborers sang to make their work more tolerable. He was witnessing firsthand the practical use of the sorrow songs in his own culture.

But literally and figuratively he dragged his shovel and had difficulty keeping the job. He disliked the work not only because he was a misplaced artist and because he was small and the work was hard; he disliked it because in New Jersey he was confronted by a level of prejudice that shocked even an exile from Harlem. Most of his fellow workers—black and white—were from the South, and the whites particularly did not appreciate what they considered his "uppity" ways, his sardonic wit, and his lack of "respect." And he found in south Jersey in general a southern attitude that contrasted with the freer ways of his friends in the Village. The Belle Mead year was a traumatic one for the future civil rights leader and activist whose stepfather had warned him about the "white devils."

Years later, in 1965, I was to go with Baldwin to Princeton for dinner at the home of Laurence Holland, a former professor of mine and a fellow Henry Jamesian whom Baldwin wanted to meet. Another professor and novelist, Julian Moynahan, and poet William Meredith were also guests. I was surprised when, although we were already late for our appointment, Jimmy insisted that we stop at a local cafeteria-type restaurant called the Balt for a snack before dinner. He seemed angry as, standing in front of the counter with the usual crowd of Princeton students, he ordered a hamburger, left it on the counter when it was delivered to him, and announced that we were leaving.

That evening at dinner he was particularly argumentative, even abusive towards Moynahan, who suggested a comparison between the problems of Irish-Americans and black Americans. "You might be Irish, baby, but in a restaurant you're just another white man and I'm a nigger," he shouted. Later I asked him why he had been so angry, and he explained it had been the hamburger place more than Moynahan that had got to him. Returning to that part of New Jersey had brought back the memories of 1942. He had insisted on stopping at the Balt because the restaurant had been the location of an incident described in the essay "Notes of a Native Son." Baldwin had come to Princeton once from Rocky Hill and had gone into the Balt for a hamburger. Standing among the students, he had been told after a long wait that "colored boys" were not served there. Baldwin had been surprised and outraged and had literally laid siege to the Balt—short for Baltimore—going there whenever he could, experiencing "some dreadful scenes." Then, on that evening in 1965, he knew he had to make a final push. And, of course, this time, although they served him, he would not, could not, eat the hamburger.

The year in New Jersey was an important test for Baldwin. It marked the closest he ever came to approaching the problem of racism by way of hatred and violence:

> That year in New Jersey lives in my mind as though it were the year during which, having an unsuspected predilection for it, I first contracted some dread, chronic disease, the unfailing symptom of which is a kind of blind fever, a pounding in the skull and fire in the bowels. Once this disease is contracted, one can never be really carefree again, for the fever, without an instant's warning, can recur at any moment. It can wreck more important things than race relations. There is not a Negro alive who does not have this rage in his blood—one has the choice, merely, of living with

> it consciously or surrendering to it. As for me, this fever has recurred in me, and does, and will until the day I die.

In "Notes of a Native Son" Baldwin describes an evening—his last one in New Jersey—during which the fever raged out of control. He had gone with a friend—a relative of the Martins—to a movie in nearby Trenton, a movie entitled, ironically, *This Land Is Mine.* After the movie Baldwin and his friend went to a diner called the American Diner and were told, "We don't serve Negroes here." In terms reminiscent of a sensation that overcame Yank in O'Neill's *The Hairy Ape*, another character condemned to bear the weight of his metaphorical role, Baldwin describes how, when they were back in the street, "all of the people I could see, and many more than that, were moving toward me, against me, and . . . everyone was white."

Something snapped. Baldwin walked ahead of his friend, entered a fashionable restaurant, sat down, and was approached by a white waitress with "frightened eyes" who, after mouthing the by now ritual formula "We don't serve Negroes here," became the necessary object of revenge for a man who had himself become, momentarily, the embodiment of centuries of humiliation and rage. The one object at hand was a water mug, which Baldwin hurled at the waitress, only to hit and shatter the mirror behind the bar.

With the help of his friend he managed to get away, but that evening he was confronted by a war within himself for the domination of his life. As he had so many times before, he wondered whether his stepfather was right. Maybe they were devils. Was violence the only answer? He realized that he could have been murdered in that restaurant. But what worried him more was the fact that he "had been ready to commit murder," the fact "that my life, my *real* life, was in danger, and not from anything other people might do but from the hatred I carried in my own heart." Help came to James Baldwin at this point; it came from the least expected of people, his stepfather, who at the moment of the restaurant incident lay in a mental hospital on Long Island.

Baldwin was fired for the third and final time from his defense job and returned home in early June 1943 to find his mother pregnant. This infuriated him. It was his stepfather's "mocking farewell present," he wrote to a school friend. He took a job in a meat-packing place for twenty-nine dollars a week and went back to living at home. A sense of frustration set in. Here he was, not quite nineteen, back where he had started, at the mercy of his stepfather and his family's poverty. The family waited in limbo between the birth of a child and the death of a father and husband. Baldwin was trapped; it was clear to him that he was in no position to do anything in the immediate future for his family and that as long as he tried to do something for them he would be in no position to help himself and thus help them later.

Mrs. Baldwin urged her son to pay a visit to his stepfather in the hospital, to make things up with him. Having left home partly to distance himself from Reverend Baldwin, Baldwin resisted the deathbed visit: "I had told my mother that I did not want to see him because I hated him." But reluctantly, he accompanied his aunt Taunty to the hospital. Then, when he saw him—"lying there, all shriveled and still, like a little black monkey"—he realized that he did not hate him. "It was only that I *had* hated him and I wanted to hold on to this hatred. . . . I imagine that one of the reasons people cling to their hates so stubbornly is because they sense, once hate is gone, that they will be forced to deal with pain."

It was July 28, 1943. David Baldwin, Sr., would die the next day, on the same day Berdis Baldwin gave birth to their last child, Paula. The funeral, on Jimmy's birthday, August 2 for which, with Beauford Delaney's help, he had raised the necessary money, was disturbing. Jimmy was not altogether sober, and the minister's description of his stepfather had little to do with the man he had known and did nothing to reconcile his feelings of regret and relief.

That night, while he and a girlfriend were downtown "desperately celebrating my birthday," the famous Harlem riot of 1943 started in the Hotel Braddock with the shooting of a black soldier by a policeman. On August 3 the family, including Jimmy, "drove my [step]father to the graveyard through a wilderness of smashed plate glass," a scene that seemed to have been "devised . . . as a corrective for the pride of [Reverend Baldwin's] eldest son," who made the obvious connection in his mind between himself and the biblical figure of the prodigal son. Out of his dead stepparent's bitterness and failure, out of the "folly" of the destruction all around him came a message that Baldwin was never to forget:

> It was necessary to hold on to the things that mattered. The dead man mattered, the new life mattered; blackness and whiteness did not matter; to believe that they did was to acquiesce in one's

own destruction. Hatred, which could destroy so much, never failed to destroy the man who hated and this was an immutable law.

After Mr. Baldwin's death Baldwin realized that the conventionally moral and safe thing to do would be to remain at home to support his mother and his brothers and sisters or at least to work somewhere else and send money home, as he had done from Belle Mead. But he realized, too, that the role of dutiful son and brother would inevitably end the scenario imagined in boyhood on that hill in Central Park and the vocation to which he now felt committed.

During the next few months he continued to live at home, taking the subway each day to work. As he dreaded going back to the apartment he had by now outgrown, he spent hours after work and on weekends on Forty-second Street. Sometimes he sat in Bryant Park until suspicious policemen moved him on. He passed time in the library itself—always a haven since his early adolescence. He also wandered up and down the street, absorbing the relatively brazen sexuality that marked this part of the city even then. But most of all he went to the movies, especially to the Forty-second Street Apollo, which tended to show foreign films.

At this point Baldwin was simply drifting and brooding, struggling with and even against the call of art that was undermining his "duty" to his family. He passed out in the meat-packing factory on the day after his stepfather's funeral and lost his job. He found another position, this one in the garment district, but he began to fall apart emotionally. Worries about finances and his family, and the effect of his stepfather's death, seemed to be closing in on him. One day the sight of the industrial building in which he had spent so many hours that could better have been spent on his vocation "filled me with a choking desire to *scream*." He lost that job and several others. For a while he washed dishes at a place in Times Square. Later he became an elevator boy. In fact, he lost jobs as quickly as he found them. Sometimes he fled without even waiting to be paid. Eventually he stopped looking for work. Things went from bad to worse. He drank a great deal, had a "brief, tasteless, tawdry love affair," and finally suffered the first of what in his lifetime would be several nervous collapses. He would relive this period several years later through the character of Rufus in *Another Country*.

He went to Beauford Delaney, who talked him through his difficulty and convinced him of the importance of coming to a clear decision about his commitments. Baldwin made the necessary break; he decided to leave home definitively for Greenwich Village, whatever the consequences. If he stayed to support his family he would simply end up resenting them, and in the long run they would be more hurt than helped by him. True, there was a good chance that he would not succeed "downtown," but in Harlem he would simply give up, and the thought of exposing his family to the reactions of a man who, like his stepfather before him, had no prospects was more than he could bear. He had no choice; he "fled."

As he would have to find food and a place to live, any earnings would have to be kept for himself. He would hope that his mother and brothers and sisters could survive on their own while he worked to save himself. Perhaps one day he could make their lives better. "I had to jump then," Baldwin always said, "or I would quite simply have died." He was never to live in Harlem again.

Baldwin stayed with Beauford Delaney for a while and then in various rooms around the Village. He found odd jobs until Beauford introduced him to Connie Williams, a Trinidadian who was running the Calypso, a small restaurant across from the Provincetown Playhouse on MacDougal Street. Connie asked him to be her waiter, a job that included good food and good company. Baldwin had disliked working as a tracklayer, but he seemed to take to being a waiter. Connie quickly became a surrogate mother, one of many in Baldwin's life. She offered love and support and she allowed him to give food to his brothers to take home when they journeyed to the Village to see what their mysterious older brother was doing. Often she provided him a place to stay in her loft apartment on Eleventh Street.

Jimmy was not the only person Connie helped. She gave jobs at various times to a whole group of young people, an interracial community of "struggling" bohemians of varied sexual orientation who became Baldwin's close friends during the Village years and provided much-needed stimulation and encouragement. There were seamen, temporarily out of work, who had strong left-wing political interests, would-be artists and writers, and some middle-class exiles and runaways who were simply experimenting with "radical" lifestyles. Relationships between members of the group were intimate and sometimes volatile. They shared what they had, lived at a high pitch, and became very close. At various times one or more of the seamen—Jimmy Callahan, Darwin Dean, Stan Weir, or a black Puerto Rican sea captain called Pepe—gave Baldwin a place to stay, as did a number of the women in the group. Connie's was a meeting place, the Minetta Tavern was a popular hangout and so were the San Remo and Joe's Diner on Fourth Street. And at the White Horse Tavern Baldwin met other "bohemians," of the Beat Generation, people like Jack Kerouac and Allen Ginsberg.

Beauford Delaney, Baldwin, and a young black writer named Smith Oliver spent a great deal of time together. They formed a black triumvirate that "held court" at the Calypso after hours or at the San Remo, where sometimes they took a beautiful teenage Calypso waitress called Ruth Robinson with them. She was of Cherokee, African-American, and African-Scottish descent, had very light skin and long straight hair which they would stroke, much to the confusion and sometimes discomfort of many of the San Remo customers. As for Ruth, she loved being "protected" by the three men. Another frequent companion was Katherine Shipley, a middle-class black teenager intent on experiencing the bohemian life of the Village.

Most important for Baldwin was the Calypso itself. Connie Williams provided the ideal atmosphere for a young man desperate for ideas and for an entrée into the world of the arts. The Calypso became a favorite spot for artists, musicians, actors, and writers in general, as well as for political radicals. Stan Weir, a merchant seaman who took a temporary dishwashing job there and who became a particularly close Baldwin friend, tells of evenings with Beauford Delaney, Henry Miller, and other "radical intellectuals." The Calypso was a place where blacks and whites mixed easily. C. L. R. James and his "Pan-Africanist" friends gathered there. Claude McKay, Alain Locke, and Paul Robeson became regulars, and so did Malcolm X, Burt Lancaster, Marlon Brando, and Eartha Kitt at various times. Weir wrote of his contact with Baldwin at Connie's that it was "the first time either [had] been allowed extended face to face access to a person of 'the opposite race' and the same generation."

Weir perhaps did not know of Baldwin's De Witt Clinton experience, but in spirit what he said was true. The waiter and the dishwasher were encouraged to participate in what must have been stimulating conversations for would-be writers. The young Baldwin, who at the time looked about fifteen, became a somewhat notorious figure at the Calypso. Having left the pulpit, he found a new kind of congregation to whom he could preach. People were amazed at his gift for language and at the power of his arguments. Customers would call ahead to see if "Jimmy" would be there on a given evening. At one of the many costume balls Connie was fond of sponsoring in a hall on Irving Place, she and her friends dressed up Jimmy as a "little preacher." The success of the costume led to an excursion one Sunday by a large number of the Calypso group to Mother Horn's church. One wonders what Mother Horn and the "white angel" thought of this invasion of aliens led by the onetime famous boy preacher.

During this period Baldwin was continuing his search for sexual identity. He had numerous "one-night" relationships with men, and he told Emile Capouya and later Stan Weir that he was homosexual, but he continued to have relationships with women as well. He had for a while been "in love with" a woman called Jessie, a Jewish divorcée, six years older than he, and there were others. But it was never easy with women—especially white women. If they were not trying to "save" him from his homosexuality, they were intent on having their "Negro experience" in the Village, forcing him into the central role as they played out the myths of black sexuality. This was one more obstacle to his birthright as a human being. He did not want to be thought of primarily as a "black stud" any more than later he would want to be thought of as a "black writer."

There was a black woman called Grace with whom he "fell in love," lived with for a while—between late 1946 and early 1948—and "almost married." But he was already twenty-two when he met her, and this was "many light-years too late." By then he knew that his sexuality was predominantly directed towards men, that while he could love women, even be "in love" with individual women, his sexual experiences with them, though possible, were not condoned by his instincts. He knew that for him the best way to love women was not to "make love" with them.

But prejudice interfered with his relations with men as well. From his earliest days in the Village he stood out. He was one of a very small number of African-Americans who actually lived there, and a scoliosis problem caused him to walk in a manner which people saw as effeminate. He was often called a "queer" by men who acted very differently when they were alone with him. Baldwin was well aware then of the agony that plagued the lives of these ostensibly "straight" males who roamed the streets and men's rooms of the Village—"desperate and unimaginably lonely"—searching for "faggots." Not being attracted to men whom he considered to be pretentiously effeminate—men who "pretended to be women"—he inevitably found himself in bed with the more ambiguous sort, and he suffered the abuse that derived from their shame. This was a pattern that was to mark his life from then on. It was a problem he was to treat fictionally in his second novel, *Giovanni's Room.*

When Baldwin did fall in love with a particular man in those days, he sometimes went so far as to avoid any expression of sexual interest in order that the destructive pattern might be avoided and the friendship preserved. The great love of the Village years was Eugene Worth, an African-American who, like Rufus in *Another Country*, "hurled himself" off the George Washington Bridge. Baldwin met Eugene in December of 1943; the suicide occurred in December of 1946. But the two men were never lovers. Worth was evidently heterosexual, and Baldwin, for fear of losing him, made no attempt to consummate the relationship sexually—even when Worth wondered aloud if "I might be in love with you." Later Baldwin considered this to have been an "oblique confession" that was really a "plea," but at the time, he loved Eugene too much and had too little self-esteem to imagine that Eugene could love him in return. And for the rest of his life, especially when he had been hurt by a relationship, he tended to see in the image of Eugene Worth preserved in his memory the model of the perfect love he never found.

Worth was the only person who ever succeeded in getting Baldwin committed to an ideological movement. Baldwin was always suspicious of ideologies—he considered revolutionaries to be sentimental—but under Worth's tutelage, he became for a while a member of the Young People's Socialist League and then, also for a short time, a Trotskyite. He was willing to go very far with Eugene politically. Later he worried often that he might have saved him from his self-destruction had they become lovers as well.

Marlon Brando was another man whom Baldwin loved but did not approach as a lover. He met Brando in the spring of 1944, when he was at the New School taking a theater class as part of a brief flirtation with the idea that he might make a career as a playwright or even as an actor. Brando was studying there with Erwin Piscator. The two became friends quickly and remained so through the civil rights days and after. When Baldwin finally saw Brando in *Truckline Cafe* not long after they had met, he was amazed at his friend's performance. Onstage Brando was a lame, defeated war veteran. Baldwin went backstage after the play and was surprised and pleased to find the familiar confident figure "with that crooked grin on his face." He was even more impressed by his performance in Tennessee

Williams's *A Streetcar Named Desire* in 1947. For Jimmy, Brando was always a "beautiful cat."

Brando and Stan Weir were early embodiments of a type of male who would continue to be important in Baldwin's life, a type to whom he was deeply attracted, perhaps because of a certain toughness, a steadiness of emotions, and an ability to demonstrate love in spite of evident "manliness." This was an ability that made sex less necessary somehow than with the "butch" but frightened and desperate lovers with whom he so hopelessly sought peace of body and mind.

While Baldwin was working at the Calypso, wrestling with sexual, racial, and political identity problems, he was also trying to write. Back in his school days he had begun and quickly discarded a novel about a child in Harlem who wanted to kill his hated church deacon father by poisoning the communion chalice. Still obsessed by the father/son theme, he began working on a novel he called *Crying Holy*. This novel, the title of which he changed for a time to *In My Father's House*, would eventually become *Go Tell It on the Mountain*. He worked at the Calypso at night, stayed there until very late drinking and talking with Beauford and other friends, went home, and, if he was alone, wrote for several hours until he could no longer stay awake. The Baldwin pattern of late-night conversations and hard drinking, followed by writing into the early morning, was established in the Village years.

Contact with friends was then and remained an important priority for Baldwin. His white acquaintances, in particular, were his congregation—listening to his preaching, serving as his witnesses, and directly suffering his anger. Brad and Claire Burch, for example, were old friends at whose apartment on Second Avenue he had dinner on most Thursday nights, after he gave up the Calypso job. Brad had been a De Witt Clinton schoolmate and *Magpie* cohort who had married Claire soon after high school, just before he went off to war. The Burches, and others who sometimes joined them on Thursdays, were the precursors of the well-meaning, committed white liberals who were so necessary to James Baldwin's eventual success in the literary and social world. These were people who were fervent admirers, even disciples. When Claire Burch, in the 1970s, made a short movie about Baldwin in Berkeley, it was distinctly the portrait of a guru-prophet who could do no wrong.

In 1945 the Burches and Baldwin started a little literary magazine called *This Generation* to which Baldwin contributed a chapter from his *In My Father's House*, a short story that would later develop into the play *The Amen Corner*, and several long poems about his stepfather. The venture was short-lived, but it provided a forum for him. On those Thursday nights, discussing the magazine, he was always argumentative, demanding, and sometimes brutally sarcastic. Claire was "Miss Whitey" and the Burches and the other whites present were "bleeding heart liberals." The guru handed out "assignments" to what the group thought of as his "informal army." Once he told them to rewrite the Gettysburg Address to reflect the reality of America. They did, and Claire Burch in 1989 was still rewriting it. Baldwin was persuasive and dominating. His followers "obeyed" him because they believed he was "right." The scenes in the Burches' living room would be reenacted in hundreds of white living rooms in which James Baldwin felt compelled to preach during the forty-two years following the Gettysburg Address assignments.

Sometimes in those living rooms Baldwin would seem to be possessed. In spite of his enjoyment of conversation, good food, and apparent fellowship, something would be said that would transfer Jimmy Baldwin the writer, the homosexual, the fun-lover, the hearty drinker and elegant eater into a whole race. "I toted your barge, baby, I picked your cotton, I nursed your babies, you killed my children, where were you the day Martin was shot?" he would shout as he glared threateningly at stunned dinner guests. He was not a bully, though some of his white hosts and hostesses and their guests sometimes thought he was. It was simply that, as a man with a mission to bear truthful witness, he could not conceive of an evening out with those who, by benefit of their color, possessed power over his people, without reminding them of the real nature of the situation in which they lived.

The Burches learned just how demanding their prophet could be when Brad, desperate for money in the 1950s, took a job writing copy for a pharmaceutical firm, and Baldwin berated him as a betrayer of the cause and essentially dropped him as a friend and associate. "If you can't go all the way," he seemed to be saying, "don't bother at all."

The message was familiar enough. Baldwin had learned it well, albeit in another context, from his stepfather and during his own days in the pulpit, but for people like the Burches, and other white liberals who wanted to be "on his side," it was as difficult a message as the one that confronted the man in the New Testament who loved

Jesus but could not bring himself to give up everything for him. The Burches discovered, painfully, the limitations of their commitment and of the white commitment they represented.

Baldwin would break out of his prophetic explosions as suddenly as he had been possessed by them. The hard angry mouth would smooth out, the enraged eyes would soften, giving way to a smile so welcoming that the victims of the recent harangue would behave as if they had been caressed. There was always the hint of love in Baldwin's anger. Even in cases like that of Brad Burch, he did not hold grudges or deny love. When Brad died in 1967 Baldwin wrote to Claire regretting his loss of Brad in the "storm of my life."

Baldwin was by no means always the confident preacher. The life of the witness usually has its self-doubting, self-searching side. In the Village years especially, Baldwin underwent a period of mental turmoil. He worried about his sexual proclivities and about "abandoning" his family. He struggled to channel his anguish and his message into art. At one point a friend found him a part-time job as an artist's model in Woodstock, New York, and he lived there in a cabin for a while, trying to write. He spent hours weeping and even contemplated suicide. Nothing seemed to be working. The book was not getting written. He returned to New York and spent many a lonely night in cold-water flats "wrestling with my demons." Later he would remember the Village years as his "season in Hell."

Then came the break he had been waiting for. A young woman named Esther, who admired the little bit of *In My Father's House* that she had heard him read aloud, introduced him to the black American writer who had already achieved fame and notoriety for *Native Son*. Richard Wright lived in Brooklyn, and Baldwin visited him there in the winter of 1945. Baldwin was twenty years old, poor, nervous, and frightened. Wright, who had long been Baldwin's "idol," was in his prime at thirty-six. The meeting went well. The two men seemed to take to each other, "as though we were two black boys, in league against the world, and had just managed to spirit away several loads of watermelon." They drank bourbon together, and Baldwin told Wright about *In My Father's House*. Wright was encouraging and asked to see the sixty pages Baldwin, in his enthusiasm, said he had written.

After a few days of furious writing Baldwin sent the sixty pages to Brooklyn. Within a week Wright had read the manuscript, reacted positively to it, and, by way of Edward Aswell, his editor at Harper & Brothers, had recommended Baldwin for a Eugene F. Saxton Foundation Fellowship. The fellowship, including a $500 grant, was awarded in November of 1945. For the moment, thanks to Wright, he seemed to have "made it." He was even taken by Harper's president, Frank S. MacGregor, on the first in a long career of publisher's lunches. When asked where he wanted to go, Baldwin suggested the San Remo, partly because they knew him there and he wanted them to see that he was now on his way.

The lunch was a great success, but the triumph soon turned sour. As the Saxton money evaporated, the book seemed increasingly impossible to write. The style was stiff and the relationship between the father and the son was not working. Even the point of view was somehow wrong. Eventually Harper confirmed what Baldwin feared, that the book was not good enough to publish. Baldwin felt he had let Wright down, but he did see him several times before the older man left for Paris in 1946. By then Baldwin realized that he was not a "second Richard Wright," that, in fact, their approaches to life and to art were very different. The difference would seriously affect their relationship later. But when Wright left in 1946 for Paris, Baldwin admired him as the premier African-American writer of his time and saw in his departure a future path for himself.

Nineteen forty-six was a year badly marred by Eugene Worth's suicide, but through the political associations he had made through his friendship with Worth, Baldwin was able to meet a number of literary "liberals" who would help him during the next three years. Sol Levitas of *The New Leader*, Randall Jarrell of *The Nation*, Elliot Cohen and Robert Warshow of *Commentary*, and Philip Rahv of *Partisan Review* all were particularly supportive. A job as a messenger at the liberal paper *PM* was hardly satisfying. He felt he was a token there. This perception caused him as much "bitter anguish" as the disdain he had generally encountered in his attempts to find work that involved writing. Levitas, Jarrell, and the others were different in that they gave him the chance to succeed on his own as a writer. Levitas suggested a book review per week as a useful discipline, and in fact, Baldwin wrote many reviews for *The New Leader*.

His first professionally published work, however, was a 1947 review of Maxim Gorki's *Best Short Stories* in the April 12 issue of *The Nation*. In this review he hints at ideas that would later become important in his treatment of Richard Wright. Gorki's problem, he suggests, was that he manipulated characters to fit his ideas, that he failed to get inside of them. What was needed in realist fiction was "further exploration of . . . the human heart and mind."

Of the early reviews, only one was chosen by Baldwin for his collected essays, *The Price of the Ticket*, in 1985. This was one he did for *The New Leader* on Ross Lockridge's *Raintree County*, a long novel about the South. The cutting irony that was to be characteristic of the later Baldwin essays begins to surface in this review in such statements as "Mr. Lockridge behaves in the presence of the Word like a child let loose in a well-stocked ice cream parlor" and "Americans are not known for introspection and rather disapprove of it."

The first published essay by Baldwin appeared earlier in 1948 in *Commentary*. "The Harlem Ghetto," which he would include in his first collection, *Notes of a Native Son*, was concerned in part with anti-Semitism in Harlem. It was Warshow, an editor he greatly admired and respected, who pressed him to consider this controversial question. For Baldwin, whose closest school friends and current editors were nearly all Jews, this was difficult enough. It was doubly so because he had to face intellectually certain realities about what was, after all, his home.

Baldwin approached his subject with the chilling clarity of an objective journalist, carefully avoiding the sentimentality or the nostalgia of a hometown boy. The Harlem he depicts is no longer the southern town where mothers watch out for each other's children. It is a community betrayed by its own leaders, its own press, its own religion. Harlem has become a parody of the moral bankruptcy of white society. As for black anti-Semitism, it too was a parody of the nation's anti-Semitism and its general racism.

Jews and blacks, he wrote, have a natural alliance based on racial oppression. The black church has traditionally expressed its longing for freedom in the metaphors of the Old Testament Jews. Yet the realities of racial discrimination—applied to both Jews and blacks—mean that for the child growing up in Harlem, the Jew is often the landlord demanding his payment. The Jew is the white person the black resident of Harlem is most likely to confront and, therefore, to hate, not because he is a Jew but because he is white: "Just as a society must have a scapegoat, so hatred must have a symbol. Georgia has the Negro and Harlem has the Jew."

In the fall of 1948 Baldwin did an essay for *The New Leader* based on a disastrous trip to the South taken by his brother David and three of his friends. The boys—for that is what they still were—had formed a singing group called the Melodeers and had been hired by Henry Wallace's Progressive party to help with its campaign in the South. Baldwin's description of the trip, taken from his brother's journals, became a condemnation of the South, of white liberal-radicals, and of ideologies in general: " 'They're all the same,' David tells me, 'ain't none of 'em gonna do you no good; if you gonna be foolish enough to believe what they say, then it serves you good and right. Ain't none of 'em gonna do a thing for *me*.' "

In the essay's narrative the ruthless irony that will become a Baldwin trademark truly blossoms. As long as the Melodeers behaved and performed as directed, they were "representatives" of the "Negro community." As soon as their humanity surfaced and they wanted things like money, food, and decent shelter, they became "uppity niggers" and were shipped home unceremoniously.

The witness in Claire Burch's living room had gone public. He was challenging the credentials and the morality of the very people who were, in a sense, feeding him. A prophet's job was to remind his nation—all of his nation—of its falling away from truth. Some readers were angry, some resentful. The essay on Harlem, for instance, displeased both Jews and blacks—neither came off particularly well in it—and the Atlanta essay offended white "progressives." But the essays did attract attention, and people wanted to hear more.

But James Baldwin was never intellectually comfortable in his role as essayist. He wanted to be a novelist, and *In My Father's House* sat there in his duffel bag refusing to budge. He tried a new book, *Ignorant Armies*, based on a notorious 1943 murder case that fascinated him. A young bisexual man, Wayne Lonergan, had, allegedly, brutally killed his wealthy wife as a result of their sexual problems. Several facts concerning the personal context in which Baldwin approached this case and began his novel should be kept in mind. Eugene Worth had recently died by suicide, and Baldwin deeply regretted having not admitted his sexual attraction to him. Soon after Worth's death Baldwin had moved in with the woman he "nearly married," and now he had broken up with her and thrown the wedding ring into the Hudson River, not far, as he always said, from where Eugene had jumped. The whole question of sexual dishonesty would preoccupy him until the completion of *Giovanni's Room* some ten years later. Finally, in the wake of the failure of *In My Father's House*, he might well have been tempted by the potential for success that Richard Wright had discovered in the taboo murder in *Native Son*.

Ignorant Armies went well for a while. Baldwin was able to make a good deal of use of his own experiences, especially the confused sexuality that marked his Greenwich Village life. But the characters suddenly stopped speaking, and he lost his sense of the novel's form.

The problem was, apparently, that there were two novels in *Ignorant Armies*: "the bones of *Giovanni's Room* and *Another Country*."

He always said that the failure to complete the novel was also due to the fact that he had not yet come to grips with his own sexuality at the time. He could experience the Village scene he was depicting, and even the Lonergan murder, because the agonies he was depicting were his agonies, but he did not yet have the objectivity—the distance—that could only come with a deeper examination of his own sexuality. In the same way, he would have to confront the relationship with his stepfather more honestly before he could be free to write *Go Tell It on the Mountain.*

In short, Baldwin had gone about as far as he could without facing his "demons" head-on. The Village years had been traumatic and, finally, somewhat productive, but he was still, at best, an "up and coming Negro writer" and, at worst, a confused bisexual black man who had "deserted" his family and who merely pretended to be at ease in what was, in fact, the hostile white world masked by a bohemian life-style. Baldwin had reached another dangerous impasse, and once again he felt chaos closing in.

In July and August of 1948 he spent some time in Shanks Village, a writers' colony near Woodstock, New York. Baldwin's journal from those days reveals just how confused his situation was as he struggled unsuccessfully with his novels and his personal problems. With him was a friend with whom he was in love but whom he feared to "violate." The Eugene Worth syndrome was still in effect: if he really loved a man, sex seemed impossible. Homosexuality involved "violation." It could take place only furtively with other "outlaws" of the night.

The question of his identity obsessed him. What was a homosexual, what was a Negro? Was it necessary to live by these "presumptuous labels"? Like Walt Whitman, whom he was reading at Shanks, he preferred to think of himself as containing all roles, classes, ethnic groups, and orientations. Yet, he was still "fighting with my shame." It was necessary to accept the paradox of himself before he could be "free."

Having reached this Whitmanesque conclusion, Baldwin did succeed in writing and publishing his first fiction in the October 1948 issue of *Commentary*. The short story, "Previous Condition," was a projection of his dilemma. He had written it "in white heat . . . in one night," he told his early biographer, Fern Eckman. Seldom was Baldwin so driven.

The main character, Peter, a black man in his twenties, evicted on grounds of race from his Village apartment, is a thinly disguised voice for Baldwin's frustrations. The apartment becomes a metaphor for white society. The Jewish friend, Jules—a version of Emile Capouya—who had helped him find it, represents the white liberals with whom Baldwin had become so involved personally and professionally. Peter's thoughts are Baldwin's at the time: "I know everybody's in trouble and nothing is easy, but how can I explain to you what it feels like to be black when I don't understand it and don't want to and spend all my time trying to forget it?" Peter makes his way to a bar in Harlem—once home turf but now as foreign as the Village. "What's your story?" an old woman asks him there. "I got no story, Ma," he answers. Peter, like his author, had reached the end of the line.

A former girlfriend said to Baldwin, "Get out—you'll die if you stay here." He knew she was right. Richard Wright had got out and so could he. There was, in fact, a way. In the spring of 1946 Baldwin had met, through his school friend Richard Avedon, a photographer, Theodore Pelatowski, and the two men became close almost immediately. Baldwin referred to "Teddy" as his "first real love," and used him later as the model for Joey, the boy with whom David has his first homosexual experience in *Giovanni's Room*. Baldwin declared his love to Teddy as he had not done to Eugene or to other heterosexual men he loved. In that sense, a barrier had been overcome. The relationship was, however, platonic because Pelatowski was decidedly not homosexual and was secure enough in himself to be Jimmy's friend in spite of the tension the difference in feeling sometimes caused between them. They remained friends whose paths crossed with some regularity for the rest of their lives.

Baldwin and Pelatowski decided on a project that would involve a long essay on and photographs of the storefront churches in Harlem. Baldwin's object was to explore the religion that had been his, to confront verbally and in photographs the "accents of vengeance" in this religion, which would reveal the isolation of the American black as well as the "horrendous dishonesty of the country itself." He and Pelatowski visited and photographed several churches and church services, but the book, which they had planned on calling *Unto the Dying Lamb*, never found a publisher and was never completed. On the basis of a three-page proposal, however, Baldwin was able to win a Rosenwald Fellowship, and this would give him the necessary money to do what he had to do.

Berdis Baldwin brought two of her daughters, Gloria and Paula, to wish Jimmy a happy twenty-fourth birthday on August 2. He had not yet told them that he planned to go to Paris. The old feeling of guilt was surfacing again. Was he betraying them? Could they survive without him? He knew that he really had no choice. It was leave or give in to the impending psychological chaos. When his mother left that night he reminded himself of that other young artist who "denied" his mother and took flight in order to "encounter for the millionth time the reality of experience and to forge in the smithy of my soul the uncreated conscience of my race." He prayed that he might "get beyond my private, incoherent *pain*" so that he might learn to become fully a witness.

He made a few arrangements about future articles with his editors, packed his unfinished writing into his duffel bag, bought a one-way plane ticket to Paris with the last of his Rosenwald money, and on November 11 went to visit his family in Harlem, only then telling them what he planned to do. He was to look back on that day as the most "dreadful" he had experienced. As he got into the cab to drive to the airport bus, "my mother had come downstairs, and stood silently, arms folded, on the stoop. My baby sister was upstairs weeping." That evening, his family's tears and expressions of incomprehension clouding his conscience, he took the flight to Paris. He had his last forty dollars in his pocket.

CHAPTER 6

The Expatriate

> Out of the belly of hell cried I.
> —Jonah 2:2

In fleeing America for Paris, Baldwin was following a long line of Americans—especially black Americans—in the arts. Most important, his old mentor Richard Wright had found refuge and success there. He maintained that he needed distance from the racial realities at home so that he could become the writer he wanted to be. But an equally compelling reason for the move was the need to confront in a new context the personal problems that, since the days in the Harlem pulpit, had undermined his role as a witness.

Baldwin wanted time and new space in which to confront his own inner world. His friend Eugene Worth had left New York by jumping into the Hudson River. Baldwin feared a similar fate. His flight to Paris was a desperate attempt to "cheat the destruction" which he feared would be his fate in New York.

In Paris he threw himself or allowed himself to be drawn into an expatriate life dominated by a frantic search for the kind of companionship that would answer his craving to be loved for himself, not as a son or as a brother or as a black man, but as a human being with flesh-and-blood needs. The end result of his chaotic and unconventional life in Paris during his twenties was a head-on confrontation with his own identity as a man and a writer, a confrontation that occurred with a directness and speed that would have been unlikely in New York. Ironically, one of the first discoveries Baldwin made about himself was that Europe did nothing to change his heritage. He was as much a black man in Paris as he had been New York. In fact, if being in Europe did nothing else, it helped him to better understand "what being a black man meant." He found out just as quickly that Paris was no cure for sexual ambivalence.

Considered in the broad perspective, November 11, 1948, was the day that finally set the course for the violent lifelong conflict that had been brewing within James Baldwin during his first twenty-four years, the conflict between the high school writer and the boy preacher, the relentless prophet-spokesman and the reclusive aesthete who longed for enduring love. This was an inner struggle that surfaced in nearly every conversation he ever had and in every piece he ever wrote. It emerged in essays like "A Question of Identity," where he describes the plight of the black American in Paris in the style of Henry James, or at dinner parties in later years, when the elegantly dressed and mannered expatriate suddenly exploded into the uncompromising and even brutal spokesman for the downtrodden of black America. It would emerge over the years that followed in the fact that Baldwin was torn between his attachments to home and his need to be in Paris, Istanbul, Hollywood, or Saint-Paul-de-Vence.

As the plane circled Paris that first day of his expatriation, with Baldwin overwhelmed by "the absolute certainty of being dashed to death on the vindictive tooth of the Eiffel Tower," four men at the Deux Magots were discussing the imminent arrival of the promising young black writer from New York who, they had heard, had published an interesting essay and a short story in *Commentary*. George Salamos, who had renamed himself Themistocles Hoetis, and Asa Benveniste, a Sephardic Jew from Istanbul and more lately Brooklyn, were entertaining Jean-Paul Sartre and Richard Wright for lunch. Hoetis and Benveniste were starting a new magazine, *Zero*, to which they hoped Wright and Sartre would contribute articles. But the already emerging myth of the defiant and somewhat "crazy" black man from New York was appealing enough to cause Benveniste to leave Hoetis with Sartre and Wright and to go with some friends to the Gare des Invalides to fetch Baldwin. The news of his arrival time had been provided by Mason Hoffenberg, a Paris-based New York friend Baldwin had communicated with during the weeks before he had left the States and who, with Terry Southern, would write the best seller *Candy*. Baldwin was astounded at his welcoming party and delighted to find Richard Wright sitting with the as yet unknown Themistocles Hoetis when he arrived at Saint-Germain.

Wright helped his protégé find a room at the Hôtel de Rome on the boulevard Saint-Michel. Otto Friedrich describes how he and Mason Hoffenberg and a painter called Mottke visited him there on the night of his arrival. Mottke held up a cigarette lighter to find the room number and they banged on the door. They heard "groans and shufflings . . . the clanking of the bolt." The door opened and a small man in "baggy pants and a T-shirt . . . stood blinking in the glow of the cigarette lighter . . . his eyes bulging in his dark brown face, his lips spreading into a gap-toothed smile as he recognized his persecutors [and said,] 'Mason, God, it's good to see somebody.' "

Before long he had no shortage of English-speaking friends in Paris, even running into old Village acquaintances. Among these was Priscilla Boughton, who found him a room in her hotel on the rue de Verneuil not far from the Left Bank of the Seine. The Hôtel Verneuil was physically not much of an improvement over the Hôtel de Rome, but it had become a social center for a whole circle of struggling expatriates, most of them writers, and provided Baldwin with a circle of friends he could depend upon in the difficult times that would follow. Hoetis and Hoffenberg were part of the circle, as were Friedrich, Herbert Gold, and Marty Weissman, a schoolmate at De Witt Clinton. And there were several women to whom Baldwin was introduced by Priscilla Boughton.

Mary Keen was a radical socialist from England who worked for the World Federation of Trade Unions and was eventually expelled from France. Her room became a social center at the Verneuil because she cooked regular meals. And living in an apartment near the Verneuil was Gidske Anderson, a Norwegian with a Dutch-boy haircut and wonderfully bizarre and colorful clothes. Gidske was a journalist who wrote for a socialist paper in Oslo. She and Baldwin met at the Deux Magots, and she became his best friend in the quarter. They shared a concern about sexual ambivalence, and often spent long evenings together, exploring each other's souls.

The Verneuil was run by a Corsican family presided over by a Mme Dumont, who encouraged a certain informality in her establishment and was reasonable about the payment of rent. She invited the tenants in for an occasional social evening with mulled wine in her parlor and tolerated their eccentric behavior to a point. Otto Friedrich remembers a party given by Priscilla Boughton in recognition of the founding of *Zero*. The noise of jazz and shouting went on so late that Madame turned off the electricity. This act had no effect on the party, which continued until well into the morning, when the drink ran out.

People moved around freely at the Verneuil, as they had in Baldwin's Greenwich Village–Calypso set. Relationships were easily formed and just as easily dissolved. There was no problem about bringing a friend home. And if a tenant ran out of money he or she might move in temporarily with another tenant. Mary Keen once left Baldwin her room and her typewriter while she went off on a trip to the south of France. When she returned he not only had failed to vacate the room but had appropriated a duffle coat, which she never got back, and he refused to return her typewriter until he had finished a piece he was working on. On her first night back her guest entertained a lover, leaving her little choice but to move upstairs to the room of another friend. One time she found a boyfriend of hers in Jimmy's arms. Life was casual at the Verneuil. If someone had something—food, a room, a coat, a typewriter, money, alcohol, hashish—it was for all to share.

Baldwin settled into the bohemian life with little difficulty. When he could afford it he had his own room at the Verneuil. Sometimes he ate in Mary Keen's room, or sometimes at a cheap restaurant called Chez Rafi. Every evening he settled in with his notebook at the Deux Magots, the Brasserie Lipp, or, more often, upstairs at the Flore. People from the Verneuil and its periphery passed in and out. By late evening a temporary group had usually solidified and would make its way to the Montana at Saint-Germain or Gordon Heath's Echelle de Jacob on the rue de l'Abbaye for jazz, to Inez Cavanaugh's Chez Inez, where Baldwin once sang "The Man I Love," for fried chicken, or to bars for drinks, deep late-night talk, and the possibility of love. Jimmy and Themistocles could often be seen in berets, leaning over their whiskey, their stories of escapades broken from time to time by Jimmy's "God! God!" or Themistocles' "Wow! Wow!" The group's most popular bars were the Reine Blanche and the more fancy Fiacre, homosexual bars that would later become the models for Guillaume's in *Giovanni's Room.*

The character of the evening would depend upon the amount of money at hand or the odd rich American met or not met. Bistros and tripe soup in Les Halles were a popular early-morning goal. Baldwin was conscious of the Hemingway mystique that pervaded the group; they were reliving the American Parisian myth. He remembered walking through the markets "singing, loving every inch of France and . . . each other . . . the jam sessions at Pigalle . . . the whores there . . . hashish in the Arab cafes," ending at dawn "telling stories, sad and earnest stories, in grey, workingmen's cafes."

Thomas Maltais, a fellow "*ancien combattant,*" memorializes the evening activities of the "American fringe of St. Germain" in an unpublished piece of prose poetry called "Go Tell It at the Metro Bar":

> It is 1948—but which long night of drink and talk—world-changing talk, new freedom, justification? Yes, and it is a first springtime warmth and we sit with others of la bande, cafe-terraced and quite intoxicated by it all including the cheap rouge and people we know are among the crowds passing; laughing, shouting our names from time to time—and often I hear "Salut, Jimmy! Ça va, Jimmy?" And so I learn that much of your name and it is enough for the moment. Then it becomes too late for last metros. And though young, an exhaustion sets in and some begin to make lone ways . . . to wherever they are surviving in the quartier but Jimmy [does not have a place] . . . and we are much into the wine and me living close by just around one corner on the rue Dauphine you trail along with me to number 41 and [the] sign of a firm named Le Coq Hardi. . . . I wake up early to your deep-sleep breathing and to . . . la belle clocharde's rouge-strengthened rendition of *La Vie en Rose* . . . and let you, what's your name, ah oui, Jimmy . . . door-ajar alone . . . free to leave or stay hung-over I could not care less as ever eager for the village life beyond my stairs—though already intrigued by your views or patience for my own weird anarchies. . . . Somewhat later you [come] into view finding your slightly foggy way down our grand boulevard—you pass me and some of the usual frères seated quite deeply again in recovery thirst and the front row of high noon at the Flore . . . but you do not stop though give one surprised to bewildered and delightful smile: "Thanks, it *was* you?" . . . No thoughts of colour . . . in early Paris and our own Liberation time; my next door rue Dauphine haunting of Le Tabou; my meetings with our other local Jimmy—Davis by name as well as Lover Man chez lui off our stage up on Montmartre; the new favorite piano, Arron Bridges and fabled Inez Cavanaugh (also Timmy Rosenkranz and Denmark's Baroness). . . . Our small meeting at the Montana Bar with Truman Capote and one Tony Bower (of the Isherwood friends) and there is talk between you, Jimmy, and Truman about writing and where it should be done—and there is Truman's high-pitched but serious advice to "go back where we all come from . . . and do it there or you are in danger of losing your perspective."

As had been the case in Greenwich Village and as remained the case for the rest of his life, Baldwin maintained non-bohemian friendships as well. The prophet still lived on in the Paris days, and he "preached" at the homes of liberal, white, mostly Jewish middle-class Americans in Paris much as he had done in the Burches' living room in New York not so many years before.

He became a dinner-party celebrity at several of these houses, perhaps most particularly at those of Harold Kaplan and Stanley and Eileen Geist, where he met other American writers such as Saul Bellow and Philip Roth. He especially spent time with the Geists. Not only did Baldwin, often hungry, appreciate being fed by them, he valued conversations with Stanley, a literary historian, who introduced him to the works of Henry James, in whom Baldwin was surprised to discover a kindred spirit and a new model.

For all of his social successes in Paris, Baldwin was sometimes bothered by a sense of his isolation in the American community from French people other than the desperate ones he could pick up at the Fiacre or the Reine Blanche. Several years later, looking back on the early Paris days, he could recognize the irony and the absurdity of the myth that he and other young expatriates were acting out in Paris:

> Paris is, according to the legend, the city where everyone loses his head, and his morals, lives through at least one *histoire d'amour*, ceases, quite, to arrive anywhere on time, and thumbs his nose at the Puritans—the city, in brief, where all become drunken on the fine old air of freedom. . . . More, the legend operates to place all of the inconveniences endured by the foreigner, to say nothing of the downright misery which is the lot of many of the natives, in the gentle glow of the picturesque, and the absurd; so that, finally, it is perfectly possible to be enamoured of Paris while remaining totally indifferent, or even hostile, to the French.

Sometimes Baldwin would set off on his own for another Paris milieu—to the cafés frequented by Algerian workers and African students, which bore no resemblance to those of Saint-Germain. There he would talk for hours with people whose condition vis-à-vis the French reminded him of the condition of his own people in America. But they reminded him, too, of an essential difference: American blacks had been denied identity in a way that Africans had not. Africans had not been alienated from their own people, their own history. The African's mother did not sing " 'Sometimes I Feel Like a Motherless Child,' and he has not, all his life long, ached for acceptance in a culture which pronounced straight hair and white skin the only acceptable beauty."

Baldwin was discovering his American identity. Because of their tragic and obsessive relationship in American history, American blacks and whites could not, finally, deny each other. One day, sitting in the Flore with an American woman friend, he was shocked to hear a Frenchwoman nearby say in regard to the several Americans present, "*Voilà! Regardez les Américains.*" He was clearly included in a group he had come to Europe to escape. In terms of actual heritage he had little in common with the friend with whom he was talking and even less with the more typical touristy Americans who came to Paris. Yet, when he overheard the Frenchwoman's remark he glimpsed the fact that, whatever he might feel about it, he was an American and that it was "impossible" to ignore those people or his "responsibility . . . for them or to them."

During his first Paris years Baldwin traveled in a white American world and basked in the feeling that in Paris, American whites seemed "relieved" at not having to concern themselves with questions of skin color. But although he could relax somewhat in the absence of obvious bigotry in his new surroundings, he did miss the language, the style, the food, the general ambience of the world in which he had grown up. He maintained friendships with black expatriates such as Gordon Heath, a few musicians, and Richard Wright. But he saw Heath only at the club late at night, and the jazz musicians lived in other parts of Paris, far from the little pocket of American writers at Saint-Germain. In any case, the patterns of their lives were necessarily different from those of a would-be writer.

Wright was always cordial with Baldwin, but there was a natural tension between the older black writer and his younger black protégé. Wright perhaps sensed that Baldwin was a rising star whose orbit would not coincide with his. Baldwin rarely spent time with Wright and his friends, who gathered usually at the Café Tournon. He was more likely to be with his younger, more bohemian set or with a homosexual group with which the Wright circle would not have felt particularly comfortable.

And there was another factor. Although Baldwin would have liked more contact with black American Parisians, he discovered that they did not necessarily seek each other out or welcome each other's company. The presence of fellow black Americans sometimes brought joy, but it also brought the memory of "past humiliations."

On the surface, Baldwin seemed at ease in his Paris life; Jimmy

Baldwin the aesthete and lover reveled in the Saint-Germain ambience. But James Baldwin the witness was worried. It was all very well living on alcohol, cigarettes, and good conversation, but he had a mission to accomplish, and there were the people back home trudging through their painful lives. And in any case, was he really happy in Paris? In his sporadic journal entries he wrote of the Verneuil group, suggesting that they were all unhappy, clinging to delusions. He worried that he was essentially lazy and that his life-style was destroying him.

Alcohol was already a problem. One day, walking along the boulevard, he suggested to a friend that they drop in at an AA meeting at the American Church—"We could see what it's all about," he said. Arriving at the meeting, they found well-off, well-dressed "serious" Americans sitting quietly in a fine salon and decided they preferred the Royal Germain Bar.

Baldwin fell ill in January of 1949 and was lucky to be cared for by Mme Dumont at the Verneuil. Madame had taken a liking to him, and she cured him with daily doses of what Baldwin called "gruel." The days in bed were a time for thought and for further depression. In a "Happy New Year" letter to his mother he begged her not to be ashamed of him. Paris would not be his home, he told her, but he had learned a great deal by being there—this after only two months in France. He ended the letter asking her to send him a Bible.

One Sunday morning during his illness he decided that coming to Paris had perhaps been a mistake. Here he was in bed, sick and not getting much done. True, being abroad had allowed him time for self-examination, but what he had discovered, he admitted in his journal, was "not a pretty sight." Still, with perseverance he might learn to accept himself for what he was or was not. Lying in his bed, he reminded himself of the sick Raskolnikov in *Crime and Punishment* or of the narrator in *Notes from Underground*. Dostoevsky had become, for the moment, his favorite novelist. He began several searching essays about his life in Paris. Eventually these would become "Encounter on the Seine," published first in *The Reporter* as "The Negro in Paris," an essay that owes more to Henry James's style than to Dostoevsky's but contains much of the latter's sense of alienation. In this article, which exposed a certain incompatibility between black Africans and black Americans in Paris, Baldwin was expressing his own sense of loneliness during this time of sickness as he meditated on his roots and on his identity as an African-American and as an American. In his determination to relate to his past, he saw himself as peculiarly American; "this depthless alienation from oneself and one's people is, in sum, the American experience."

Baldwin also used his period of recuperation for the writing of an essay that would become the center of a controversy that still rages among scholars of African-American letters. "Everybody's Protest Novel" was his first contribution to *Zero.* It questioned the value of protest literature and seemed to place him in definitive opposition to Richard Wright. In fact, Baldwin was justifying his own refusal—for the moment—to heed the call to protest. It was a brilliant piece, a call for the integrity and freedom of art from the shackles of ideology. Later, in 1951, he would write a companion essay to "Everybody's Protest Novel," an essay called "Many Thousands Gone," in which he would continue the apparent attack on Wright.

In a still later essay called "Alas, Poor Richard," collected in *Nobody Knows My Name,* Baldwin recalls an encounter with Wright on the day the *Zero* containing "Everybody's Protest Novel" appeared. He had gone into the Brasserie Lipp, where Wright was sitting with Chester Himes. Wright had made a scene of sorts, accusing the younger writer of betraying not only him but African-Americans in general by disputing the validity of protest literature.

Baldwin denied that charge then and continued to do so later. The essays in question did remain a subject of strained conversation between the two writers but did not cause a break in their relationship. Until the end of his life Baldwin spoke to friends of his admiration for Wright's work. In a conversation with Wright's daughter Julia a few weeks before his own death, Baldwin told her the rivalry with her father had been grossly exaggerated by others, and only a few days after that he spoke to Wright's wife, Ellen, promising to finish a commissioned introduction to a posthumous novel, *Lawd Today,* which he called Wright's best book, one that was not undermined by ideological "garbage," as *Native Son* had been: "It is full of niggers! It is full of life!"

A rereading of the essays in question suggests that although Baldwin approached his subject with the insensitivity of a young writer determined to shock, he was neither anti-Wright nor anti-black. His criticism of Wright is clearly secondary to larger issues, and an anti-black message does not arise at all.

He begins "Everybody's Protest Novel" by dismissing *Uncle Tom's Cabin,* which had been a favorite novel of his as a child, as "a very bad novel" which, because it is primarily a protest novel, ignores the real, "the carnal man, the man of the flesh." And by extension, Richard Wright's failure is seen to be similar to Harriet Beecher Stowe's. Protest writers are concerned with theories and with the categorization of human beings, and however brilliant the theories or accurate the categorizations, they fail because they deny life.

As critiques of protest literature and of Richard Wright the two essays are of interest, but much more important is what they reveal to us about the development of the young James Baldwin's approach to his craft. In criticizing Stowe and Wright, Baldwin is laying the foundation for his own position as a novelist and spokesperson. The real questions that lie behind the two essays are: What is an artist? What is a "Negro"? and What is morality? As Baldwin sees it, the artist's job is to absorb and re-create not only the deeds of humanity but the motivations for those deeds, which spring from human ambiguity, human complexity: "Only within this web of ambiguity, paradox, this hunger, danger, darkness, can we find at once ourselves and the power that will free us from ourselves."

For Baldwin the obligations of the artist are precisely those of the human being who would be morally free. The protest writer imprisons humanity, as he tells us in "Many Thousands Gone." The co-opting of Wright's Bigger Thomas, that "monster created by the American republic," by socially earnest whites at the end of *Native Son* reflects the all too prevalent assumption "that the black man, to become truly human and acceptable, must first become like us. This assumption once accepted, the Negro in America can only acquiesce in the obliteration of his own personality," in the loss of his freedom to be himself. By the same token, Baldwin insists that what the white American feels about the black American is really a reflection of self-hatred and self-denial: "One may say that the Negro in America does not really exist except in the darkness of our minds. . . . Our dehumanization of the Negro then is indivisible from our dehumanization of ourselves."

In a 1984 interview in the *Paris Review* Baldwin spoke about the books he was constantly asked to review in the late forties—the "be kind to niggers, be kind to Jews" type of book—and he suggested a natural progression to "Everybody's Protest Novel":

> Thousands of such tracts were published during those years and it seems to me I had to read every single one of them; the color of my skin made me an expert. And so, when I got to Paris, I had to discharge all that, which was really the reason for my essay "Everybody's Protest Novel." I was convinced then—and I still

> am—that those sort of books do nothing but bolster up an image. All of this had quite a bit to do with the direction I took as a writer, because it seemed to me that if I took the role of a victim then I was simply reassuring the defenders of the status quo; as long as I was a victim they could pity me and add a few more pennies to my home relief check. Nothing would change in that way, I felt, and that essay was a beginning of my finding a new vocabulary and another point of view.

Perhaps influenced by his new enthusiasm for Henry James, Baldwin suggests in the Wright essays, then, that bad art and immorality have much in common. The artist choosing to deal in truth had better be concerned with articulating the manners, traditions, and rituals through which people have managed to survive in worlds dominated by the myths of others. Certainly the artist treating the African-American situation should bear this in mind along with such complicated questions as the literal and moral "blood relationship" between blacks and whites that is "perhaps the most profound reality of the American experience," a relationship that we cannot possibly understand "until we accept how very much it contains of the force and anger and terror of love." These are themes that took fictional form later in *Another Country, Tell Me How Long the Train's Been Gone*, and *Just Above My Head*.

After his illness and a brief first trip to London in a futile search for magazine contracts, Baldwin turned to an article on homosexuality for the second issue of *Zero*. "The Preservation of Innocence" is his first full statement of a theme that became one of his trademarks. The violence against homosexuals in American life and literature can be traced, he suggested, to our protracted adolescence as a society. Instead of facing and accepting the reality of sexuality that involves "the complexity of human experience," we and our popular authors hide behind platitudes and prejudices and labels that can be "traced to the Rover Boys and their golden ideal of chastity." Reality, in life or literature, "insistently demands the presence and passion of human beings, who cannot ever be labeled."

He had touched on this issue earlier, in August of 1948, when he had reviewed James Cain's *Moth* for *The New Leader* and had criticized the then popular author for his failure to confront reality. He had suggested that Cain's "ruthless protagonists and their fearful sweet-hearts were actually descendants of the Rover Boys and that the only thing wrong with them was the fact that they were still reeling from the discovery that they were in possession of visible and functioning sexual organs."

In the spring of 1949, soon after the *Zero* publication of "Everybody's Protest Novel," Baldwin attached himself to a group of American friends who had money, and traveled for the first time to the south of France. The trip was a *Sun Also Rises* disaster, the group soon disintegrating into factions with which Baldwin, especially given his lack of funds, had little in common. On the train he brooded—Dostoevsky-like—about his inability to fit in. As was usual at the time, his thoughts tended towards the dramatic and the sentimental. He wondered in a journal if he would "never be comfortable in the world." What he saw as the madness of his life frightened him. He longed for a settled kind of existence—a house, regular meals. It was years later, in the south of France, towards which he was now traveling, that his dream of domesticity would come somewhat true.

Soon back in Paris, Baldwin had to face the fact that, in spite of the two recent essays, several well-received book reviews, including an important one for *Commentary* called "Too Late, Too Late" on books about black Americans, he was a penniless would-be novelist with great plans but no novel. Sitting in the Flore with his notebook, he again turned to his despairing *Notes from Underground* mode, beginning a fictional self-analysis called "An American in Paris." The work, which he never published, is thinly veiled autobiography in which the central character is a self-conscious, self-deprecating black Raskolnikov. Although the story does not succeed as fiction, the portrait painted is of interest for what it tells us about Baldwin's lack of self-esteem at the time and for what it reveals of his deft novelist's ability to see himself as he was, an intensely nervous and defensive man with the unpredictable mood change that had already become a Baldwin trademark: "like a flash of lightning . . . naked anger, uncontrolled," and then, just as suddenly, the deeply caring smile. He suggests that those around him might consider his moods—even his smile—"slightly intimidating."

Desperate for money, Baldwin agreed to take a job as a singer in an Arab nightclub. He had been heard singing "Lover Man" for friends there during a particularly boisterous evening in August. A German-American lawyer, Tom Michaelis, whom he met at the Fiacre, saved him from that job by employing him as a clerk. Not surprisingly, Baldwin did not work out as a clerk and Michaelis had to "let him go" in September.

The firing did not seem to bother Baldwin. By then he was well occupied with an actor called Jacques, and Otto Friedrich's published diaries report that he and Themistocles were seen eating and drinking with the likes of Jean-Paul Sartre, Max Ernst, Truman Capote, Stephen Spender, Simone de Beauvoir, "and God knows who else." An American named Frank Price had agreed to advance him money to give him time to write. And he had started a new novel called *So Long at the Fair*, which would eventually evolve into *Another Country*.

Themistocles had recently visited Paul Bowles in Tangiers and suggested to Baldwin that they might both go there to work on future volumes of *Zero* and on their own novels. Baldwin agreed, and he and Gidske planned to accompany Themistocles to Marseilles, where they would all take a ship to Tangiers. Baldwin and Gidske would return to Paris in December.

The relationship with Gidske Anderson had become increasingly important to Baldwin. It appears not to have been sexual—in a letter to a Paris friend who also knew Themistocles and Baldwin, Gidske referred to her two traveling companions as "two small boys"—though Baldwin referred to her as his fiancée for the next few years, and they did travel together when possible. Later Baldwin would speak of Gidske as, like Orilla Miller, a white woman who helped to keep him from hating whites. He remembered telling her once that he hated all the people they had met at a party the night before. When she asked him why and he answered evasively, she suggested that the real reason he hated them was the fact that they were white. It was as if she had "suddenly sprung a trap door at my feet." For a second he hated *her*. But then he had to face the fact that what Gidske had said was true, and in that act of recognition, he said, he became free of the hatred she had revealed to him.

On October 26 a good part of the Verneuil group went with Baldwin, Gidske, and Themistocles to the Gare de Lyon to see them off on their trip to Marseilles. Otto Friedrich describes the scene—he, Baldwin, and the others having a cognac at the bar while Gidske sat in the train compartment guarding the luggage, reading an article in *Horizon* on *The Princess Casamassima*. Henry James fever had apparently seized Gidske, even though her command of English was limited.

The party arrived in Marseilles only to discover that they had missed the boat to Tangiers. Since the cost of the boat tickets was, in any case, too high for their budget, they decided to move inland to Aix-en-Provence, where they would wait at the Hôtel Mirabeau for money to materialize from various sources in New York, Oslo, and

Paris. Gidske wrote to Mary Keen that the weather was fine, that they had had a three-course dinner on October 28 for eighty [old] francs and that they planned to stay where they were for at least three weeks. Then they would go to Tangiers.

Baldwin worked hard, using a secondhand portable typewriter he had bought before leaving Paris. For several days, however, he was asked by the hotel desk clerk not to type because the proprietor was dying in the room next to his. When the man did in fact die, Baldwin returned to his typing, death now being very much on his mind. He managed to complete a story called "The Death of the Prophet," an outgrowth of *In My Father's House*—now again *Crying Holy*—and the precursor of "Notes of a Native Son." Eventually the story would be published by *Commentary* in March 1950. It is an emotional tale that centers on the failure of a boy called Johnnie to come to terms with his father and his subsequent despair over his father's death. The story suggested a family source for much of Baldwin's depression, and he knew that until he could finish *Crying Holy* his stepfather's ghost would hover over him. The last words of "The Death of the Prophet" read: "A cloud uncovered the moon again. He watched it move slowly across the sky, impossible, eternal, burning, like God hanging over the world."

Baldwin now became sick again. Early in November he was hospitalized and underwent an operation for an inflamed gland. During what seemed to be his recovery, he and Gidske decided to stay in Aix rather than travel to Tangiers. Money was short, but through Otto Friedrich and other friends in Paris they were able to raise enough to live on. After a second hospitalization for the gland problem, Gidske sent Baldwin back to Paris at the end of November. She remained behind to wait for sufficient money to pay for the rather large hospital bill.

In Paris, Baldwin found no available space at the Verneuil and moved into the Grand Hôtel du Bac not far away. One of the first things he did was to write his family letting them know that he was back in Paris. In the letter he spoke of his loneliness and of missing the Christmas street decorations in New York. He hoped to come home soon, perhaps with Gidske, "the Norwegian girl who saved my life."

A gloomy place, the Grand Hôtel du Bac would be the scene of an event that was at once terrifying and comical. It was here that Baldwin was arrested in December of 1949 for receiving stolen goods. The incident in question gave him material for one of his best essays,

"Equal in Paris," published in *Commentary* several years later. A careful reading of the piece suggests an inner rite of passage, a journey in the belly of the whale of despair towards a new sense of self that would transform the writer's identity.

The Grand Hôtel du Bac was

> one of those enormous, dark, cold, and hideous establishments in which Paris abounds that seem to breathe forth, in their airless, humid, stone-cold halls, the weak light, scurrying chambermaids, and creaking stairs, an odor of gentility long long dead. The place was run by an ancient Frenchman dressed in an elegant black suit which was green with age, who cannot properly be described as bewildered or even as being in a state of shock, since he had really stopped breathing around 1910.

The hotel was ominous. The owner "looked as though daylight would have killed him," and his daughter, the financial manager, was a crone dressed in black, a *tricoteuse* like the forbidding women who see Conrad's Marlow off on his voyage to the heart of darkness or those women of Greek mythology who spin out the fates of mortals and point the way to death. As she took their money she acknowledged her "guests" with a brief "inclination of the head" that was "chilling and abrupt, like the downbeat of an ax." These were appropriate custodians of a dwelling place for transients which took its name from the word meaning ferry (*bac*) and perhaps suggested to Baldwin the ferry of the ancient underworld that carried the dead and visiting heroes to the land of gloom.

Sometime early in December, Baldwin came across an acquaintance from New York, a young white man "doing" Paris on his parents' money. The man wanted to leave his hotel, the Hôtel des Deux Arbres near the Gare Saint-Lazare—"the hotel of two trees without a tree in sight," as Baldwin was fond of saying after a visit there during the writing of "Equal in Paris." Although he had little in common with his "friend," he missed home and the man was an American. One thing led to another, and Baldwin suggested that he move to the Grand Hôtel du Bac. When he arrived he brought a sheet from the Hôtel des Deux Arbres as a souvenir and gave it to Jimmy, who had been having difficulty getting the staff to change his sheets.

One evening, just before Christmas, police arrived at the friend's room in search of the stolen sheet; the owner of the Hôtel des Deux

Arbres did not recognize the playful American tradition of taking a souvenir hotel towel or, in this case, sheet. Failing to find the sheet in the friend's room, they were directed to Baldwin's room upstairs, and soon both men were under arrest. So began the celebrated case of the *drap de lit.*

Baldwin and the friend were taken to a commissariat and placed in a cagelike cell where they were to spend the night. For Baldwin this was a new and terrifying experience. Here in Paris, where he had come to be free, he found himself facing policemen who were "no better or worse than their American counterparts." Only the fact that he "did not understand these people" made the situation different. He was not able to use the weapons he had learned to apply in the context of American racism. In Paris he was not "a despised black man"; he was, like his sheet-stealing friend, simply an American. He was an "equal in Paris." Deprived of his accustomed role, Baldwin found himself confronting "not *what*" he was "but *who*." This was "what humility must mean." As he stood against a bare wall being photographed for police records, his physical characteristics became exaggerated—including "that color which, in the United States, had often, odd as it may sound, been my salvation"—he felt stripped of the identity with which he had been provided, ironically, by racism itself.

As if to remind him of his nakedness—his mere humanity—and to force him into that confrontation with the "who" rather than the "what" of his being, the police led him handcuffed "downstairs to the bottom of the building into a great enclosed shed in which had been gathered" a sea of down-and-outs—vagrants, beggars, petty thieves—"the very scrapings off the Paris streets." In the center of this modern underworld was "a great hole . . . the common toilet," near which "stood an old man with white hair, eating a piece of camembert"; Baldwin wondered whether he would ever see home again or whether the old man was a shade of his future: "It must have seemed to me that my flight from home was the cruelest trick I had ever played on myself." He had descended "to a lower point than any I could ever in my life have imagined—lower, far, than anything I had seen in that Harlem which I had so hated and so loved, the escape from which had soon become the greatest direction of my life." He had escaped to a deeper hell.

Taken to Fresnes prison outside of Paris, deprived of shoelaces and belt and, therefore, of dignity, Baldwin was placed in a cell with a number of "common criminals" condemned to shuffle about holding up their trousers, and forced, in effect, to undergo several days of a kind of purgatory in which he was faced by a more universal definition of blackness than he had been aware of before. At first he resisted, ironically taking up the role of those who for centuries had denied his humanity in America:

> I was unable to accept my imprisonment as a fact, even as a temporary fact. I could not, even for a moment, accept my present companions as *my* companions. And they, of course, felt this and put it down, with perfect justice, to the fact that I was an American.

On the day before Christmas Eve the case of the sheet came to trial, but the lack of an interpreter caused a postponement until after the holiday that celebrated "the story of Jesus Christ's love for men." The purgatorial period was to be prolonged, leaving Baldwin "hanging in a kind of void" between Christmas memories of "my mother's fried chicken and the cold prison floor."

Hope of release finally came with a visit from Tom Michaelis, to whom Baldwin had managed to send a message by way of a released cellmate. On the twenty-seventh he went to trial again, and the case was dismissed. It was the reaction of the courtroom to the end of his ordeal that finally brought Baldwin to an expanded realization of "what being a black man meant." The laughter that erupted in the court when the sheet incident was "cleared up" reminded him of laughter he had heard at home—the "laughter of those who consider themselves to be at a safe remove from all the wretched," the laughter of those "for whom the pain of living is not real."

Emotionally deadened by the incident, he returned to the Grand Hôtel du Bac, where the landlady greeted him with an ultimatum—the money for his bill in an hour or he was to leave. In his room he tied one of the original dirty sheets to a water pipe, stood on a chair, tied the loose end of the sheet around his neck, and jumped. The only thing that gave way was the water pipe. The hanging had been a desperate act of solidarity with all of those literally and metaphorically imprisoned "blacks" of all races who must bear the agony of not being recognized as human beings. By means of it, the tension and the depression were broken. Rebaptized by the flood of water from the broken pipe, he found himself overcome by a kind of laughter that was more powerful than the laughter in the court. He threw some clothes in a duffel bag and rushed down the stairs into the bright streets. He never returned to the Grand Hôtel du Bac.

Baldwin was obsessed by what had happened to him. The sheet case brought home to him the precariousness of his expatriation as well as the universal pain of the "wretched." In reworking the incident in "Equal in Paris," he made full use of the method that would always mark his essays, that of taking an event from his own life and using it and himself as metaphors for the larger issues that concerned him.

It is clear now that despite his depression, his self-doubting, his illnesses, and his erratic life-style, Baldwin's first year in France had not been wasted. When "Everybody's Protest Novel" had been published in the June 1949 issue of *Partisan Review*, he had become a seriously recognized presence on the literary scene whose short but original list of publications promised much. By the time *Commentary* published "The Death of the Prophet" in 1950, he was described in the identifying remarks as "the most promising young Negro writer since Richard Wright."

Something, however, was missing. By the time he left the Grand Hôtel du Bac in December of 1949, Baldwin knew that he could write, that he might even hope to finish a novel soon, but the real goal of his relocation to Paris had not been realized. He had a better idea of what it meant to be an American, even a black American, but he had still not come to grips with the problem of James Baldwin the individual, the man so desperate for the kind of personal acceptance and commitment he had sought in so many beds. He felt that his failure was representative of the general failure and consequent disillusionment common among the "new lost generation" of which he was a part in the Paris of the late forties and early fifties: "It was because we had failed, after all, . . . to make the longed-for, magical human contact."

Baldwin was overwhelmed by his aloneness. During the many heady celebrations of his release from the French prison he could still be found in the early-morning hours singing a song that had once amused but by now frightened his friends: "Lover man," he sang, "lover man, where can you be?"

CHAPTER 7

Lucien and the Mountain

I abode in the mount forty days and forty nights.
—Deuteronomy 9:9

A few days after his release from the Palais de Justice, Baldwin met a boy of seventeen at the Reine Blanche. Others were there that night, listening to the saga of the *drap de lit*. As on the night David meets Giovanni in *Giovanni's Room*, it was clear to those present that a special kind of meeting had taken place. People left the principals alone as they began their explorations. Baldwin felt as though he was onstage or in a novel, but he did not care. He was to say later that Tom Michaelis became the Jacques in *Giovanni* that night, watching with a mixture of apparent envy and a strange sort of pride as a momentous relationship began. He shared that role with a middle-aged German called Sascha, a habitué of the Reine Blanche and the Fiacre, who gave Jimmy the kind of sensible advice on sexual honesty that Jacques sometimes gives David in *Giovanni*. Jimmy and Lucien went to the Fiacre, where the somewhat arrogant "fancy queen" who owned the club immediately became a character in the play of the moment, reacting to the couple with snide remarks and raised eyebrows. Later Baldwin would re-create him as the fated Guillaume, the bar owner in *Giovanni's Room*. Jimmy was parading his new friend before his entourage even as somewhere, subliminally, he was creating the novel that several years later would allow him to confront so many of the personal problems that had plagued him before Lucien came into his life.

Lucien Happersberger was a Swiss who had left home in search of excitement and success in Paris. In Lucien, Jimmy found the "love of my life." He was a street boy, motivated at first more by the drive to survive in a hostile environment than by any homosexual cravings, but he came to love Jimmy with genuine depth. Apparently oblivious to what people thought of their relationship, he did not mind being called Jimmy's lover even though, during the greater part of their friendship over the next thirty-nine years, he technically was not.

During those first two years Jimmy and Lucien developed an emotional closeness that Baldwin had never experienced before. Lucien was an outsider like himself, and they shared the love of a good time. Their relationship was decidedly not intellectual. They both loved laughter, food, sex, and, above all, drink. Like Giovanni and David in their positive period, they shared whatever they had. Jimmy encouraged Lucien to paint, which he did. Jimmy worked on *Crying Holy*, mostly upstairs at the Flore, finished "The Death of the Prophet" for *Commentary* and "The Negro in Paris" for *The Reporter* in 1950, and a short story called "The Outing" (an outgrowth of *Crying Holy*), a short piece called "The Negro at Home and Abroad" for *The Reporter*, and the second Wright essay, "Many Thousands Gone," all in 1951.

Jimmy and Lucien met every evening, ate where they could afford to eat and drank what they could afford to drink, usually in a little "dive" run by a woman from Brittany. Sometimes they ate sauerkraut with Sascha at his apartment, where, for some months, Jimmy lived. Baldwin's French improved and so did Lucien's English.

The two men became so close that Baldwin's need of an entourage diminished. In any case, the old Verneuil group was disintegrating. It is true that he and Mary Keen were witnesses at the marriage of Otto Friedrich and Priscilla Boughton, that he stayed with Gidske in Gallardon, near Chartres, for a few weeks, and that he continued to see Themistocles from time to time. But Mary Keen was to leave for Vienna in 1951, and Priscilla and Otto would go soon after their marriage. Even Gidske departed for a while to Oslo in 1951, and Themistocles was often away. After the surprise marriage of Gidske and Themistocles in London in 1952, Baldwin saw much less of both of these formerly close associates and traveling companions. The Verneuil group thought the marriage bizarre; he thought it dishonest. Although he continued to see individuals from the group of early Paris friends, Gidske's marriage and his friendship with Lucien effectively ended the Verneuil era for Baldwin.

But there were serious problems in the association with Lucien, problems that surfaced early. Lucien was easygoing and relaxed about the relationship, Jimmy was not. He wanted a mate, Lucien wanted a *copain* who would understand his need for women as well. During the years that they knew each other, Lucien was to marry three times and to produce two children. The first marriage would occur within two years of their initial meeting.

Permanence was all but impossible in Baldwin's love relationships because he was drawn not to other homosexuals but to men who were sometimes willing to act homosexually, temporarily, in response to a need for money and shelter or to what can only be called his personal magnetism and persuasiveness. The nature and length of the given relationship always depended on how much the lover resented or was psychologically unnerved by playing a homosexual role or by being controlled by that magnetism. Baldwin would confront the problem from the point of view of his lovers through the character of David in *Giovanni's Room,* whose need to prove himself a "man" leads to the death of his friend. In Baldwin's own life, the resentment sometimes led to beatings, and in later years to his becoming the victim of outrageous acts of embezzlement and theft.

To do Lucien credit, he never pretended that a permanent relationship was possible. He and Baldwin did not physically live together in the period immediately after their meeting. But Jimmy became increasingly dependent upon him. He opened himself to Lucien in a way he had never done with anyone else. And in spite of the unpleasant turns their friendship was to take, he remained open to him. Every lover he had after Lucien had to compete with the memory of him, the possibility of his return, or his presence down the street, next door, or in the next room. Baldwin remembered as one of the "most tragically absurd" moments of his life lying in bed with a lover in Saint-Paul-de-Vence, many years later, both of them crying as they listened to the sounds of Lucien making love with the lover's supposed girlfriend in the room above.

The first of these other lovers was a young Frenchman who lived in a tiny room near the Port de Vincennes. This was Giovanni's room, and the young man was an ironical, real-life, before-the-fact parody of the central figure of that novel. He was the thoroughly committed Giovanni Baldwin wished Lucien could be. So terrified that he might lose his lover to Lucien, if not to someone else, the Frenchman literally locked Jimmy in the room when he left early each morning to go about his life. Jimmy, always a deep sleeper and a late one, put up with this desperation for a while. As a collector of human oddities he could not help but find it interesting. He was not in love with his

Giovanni prototype, but he liked him well enough. Eventually he managed to get a note to Lucien, who walked to Port de Vincennes and liberated his friend. What he imagined to be his jailer's despair at his departure was later reworked into Giovanni's reaction to David's escape from *his* room. The model for Giovanni, however, overcame his sadness and went on to marriage and a career in the arts.

Liberation from a possessive lover did not solve the problems facing Baldwin. *Crying Holy* was still unfinished. It had been "in the works" for some ten years. Money was still scarce after two and a half years in Paris, and Lucien was still unwilling or unable to be everything his friend wanted him to be. Among other things, Jimmy needed consoling and regular intellectual interaction. He found both of these needs fulfilled by a woman about whom he would later say, "When I realized I couldn't marry Mary Painter, I realized I could marry no one."

Baldwin met Mary, an American embassy economist, at the Montana Bar just after Easter, 1950. Within a week he and Lucien were at her apartment in the rue Bonaparte listening to Beethoven and Mahalia Jackson as the three of them lay on the living room floor drinking PX whiskey and smoking PX cigarettes. Dinner followed. Mary read cookbooks after the meal while they chatted and drank some more. The dinners at Mary's, following this pattern, became a regular part of the lives of Lucien and Jimmy. When Lucien was away Jimmy continued to see Mary often. He loved her more than he had loved or ever would love any woman. They never became lovers physically because by 1950 Baldwin knew well enough that his essential homosexuality precluded a lasting sexual relationship with a woman, and he cared too much about her to lie to her in the way David would lie to Hella in *Giovanni's Room*. Mary remained a supportive center in Baldwin's life even after she married the chef George Garin, encouraging him in his work, exchanging visits with him often in New York and Paris and later in the south of France, where they both lived after the Paris days.

By autumn of 1951 Baldwin was in one of his periodic states of deep depression. His failure to complete *Crying Holy* had become an obsession. He wrote a poem for a magazine called *Janus* about a young man called Johnnie O'Hara. Johnnie was also the name of the autobiographical protagonist of his unfinished novel. And like Baldwin, Johnnie was twenty-seven, dejected, often hungry, and he dreamed at night of "Boys with knives . . . of glory" who "Flogged him under the dripping rod."

Lucien and Mary were worried about Jimmy's state of mind. It was agreed that Lucien should take his friend to Switzerland. Perhaps he could finish *Crying Holy* if he could find some peace of mind and a quiet place to work. This would be the first of several visits to the mountain village of Loèche-les-Bains, where Lucien's family owned a small château. Lucien "blackmailed" his father into giving him money by telling him he had tuberculosis and desperately needed treatment. The two men lived on that money in Loèche-les-Bains during the winter of 1951–52. A girlfriend of Lucien's called Suzy came on weekends with extra food she was able to spirit away from her family's house.

The winter spent in the village was at once disturbing and idyllic. This time with Lucien was the closest Baldwin ever came to his dream of domestic life with a lover, even though Suzy's weekend visits caused him some anxiety. Lucien painted and Jimmy wrote during the day. Bessie Smith was constantly on the small portable Victrola. In the evening the couple strolled through the village to the local café, where they ate sufficiently and drank a great deal. They laughed a lot, told each other stories of childhood, and shared dreams. Jimmy was thoroughly in love with Lucien, and Lucien was fascinated by this magnetic man whose strange eyes commanded attention, and whose touch was gentler and more caring even as it was more demanding than any he had ever known. As he listened late each night to Jimmy's reading aloud of the emerging chapters of *Crying Holy*, now appropriately *Go Tell It on the Mountain*, he barely understood the words, his English being limited, but he fell in love with the voice and he sensed a great talent.

Baldwin was a city person, however, and was always nervous in settings dominated by raw nature. The mountains were, in the end, threatening rather than inspiring. In the city he could blend in; in this village he was an outsider, and as he always did when he found himself in a difficult social situation, he allowed himself to become a symbol, the central figure in an American-European, Western drama that clearly transcended the village of Loèche-les-Bains. The drama took form later in the brilliant "Stranger in the Village," published by *Harper's Magazine* in October of 1953. It was an essay which, like most of the early Paris essays, used a European experience as a means of looking back at America. It was a record of the birth of a new people out of a European past and a history of black and white contact, a birth that paralleled the breaking through on the threshing floor of *Go Tell It on the Mountain.*

Loèche-les-Bains is a tiny Catholic village high in the mountains between Milan and Lausanne. There are a few stores there, and, as Baldwin would write, "no movie house, no bank, no library, no theater; very few radios, one jeep, one station wagon; and, at the moment, one typewriter, mine, an invention which the woman next door to me here had never seen." More important, "from all available evidence no black man had ever set foot in this tiny Swiss village before I came." The villagers had been told that he was American, but to them he was African, like the several Africans the village church "bought" each year for the missionaries. The villagers were friendly enough; they wanted to touch his hair and to rub his skin to see if the blackness would come off, the way it came off the village children who dressed up as Africans each year at carnival time. As he walked through the village streets those same children shouted, in a perfectly friendly way, "*Neger! Neger!*" having no idea of the "echoes this sound raises in me."

The unintentional mistreatment Baldwin suffered at the hands of the inhabitants of Loèche-les-Bains was such as to make the village a model in "Stranger in the Village" for Europe, an extended metaphor in which Baldwin is the alienated black race. The essay is an early example of Baldwin's assertion that America is different, that whatever white Americans might think, the deep and painful association with blacks has changed them forever: "No road whatever will lead Americans back to the simplicity of this European village where white men still have the luxury of looking on me as a stranger." And this is an "achievement," because it means, finally, that "this world is white no longer, and it will never be white again."

Thus, the three months in Loèche in the winter of 1951–52 saw a confrontation not only with his autobiographical novel but with his identity as an American and as a non-European African-American. The two confrontations melded well. The village stay and his sense of alienation as a black in a European setting made him long for home, family, and roots. But he knew that in order to return home he would have to finish the novel that he had gone to Europe to write. With Bessie Smith's musical encouragement and Lucien's support, he accomplished this feat, and on February 26, 1952, he and Lucien took the somewhat battered manuscript down the mountain to a post office and sent it off to New York.

When, several months later, Alfred Knopf expressed an interest in the novel and in meeting the author, Baldwin, with a loan from his old friend Marlon Brando, who happened to be passing through

Paris, bought a ticket home. He could go now, because in *Go Tell It on the Mountain* he had faced something in himself and in his history which made possible at least a partial reconciliation with his stepfather's ghost. And he could go as the novelist he had always said he was. He dedicated *Mountain* to "My Father and Mother"—perhaps to the father he never knew as well as to the stepfather he had known.

The first Paris stage was over. The Verneuil group had broken up, Gidske and Themistocles had already separated, Lucien revealed that he was having a "serious" relationship with Suzy and that as a result of one of her weekend visits to Loèche, she was pregnant. Jimmy was saddened and angered by the news. But he remembered the price his stepfather had exacted for his own illegitimacy, and he strongly urged Lucien to marry Suzy. The love affair of his life seemed to be over.

Nevertheless, he had been able to write *Mountain*. And although the Paris years had been difficult, he had met many people there who had "held on to me" and had believed in him, people who had helped make him a novelist. He sailed for New York in April on the *Ile de France*. It happened that Themistocles Hoetis was booked on the same sailing. According to him, he taught Baldwin "everything he ever knew about jazz" on that trip. In fact, Baldwin had already learned a great deal about jazz from Beauford Delaney in the Greenwich Village days, and he had accumulated a considerable collection of jazz records. What he learned about jazz on the *Ile de France* passage was most likely from Dizzy Gillespie, with whom he spent hours at the bar talking.

It had been three and a half years since Baldwin had seen any member of his family, and now he was returning to arrange for the publication of his first novel. In that novel he had finally come to grips with the reasons for his departure. He could face his family now as one who had successfully taken flight from the labyrinth. But returning to the labyrinth was good cause for anxiety.

Waiting for him on the dock was his brother David. During that short visit to the States in 1952 David was to become his brother's closest friend and confidant. No longer the teenager Jimmy remembered, David immediately sensed his brother's anxiety and took on the role of protector and advisor that he was never to relinquish. The highlight of the return home would be David's marriage on June 27, at which older brother James proudly served as best man.

In the weeks that followed his arrival Baldwin negotiated with Knopf over changes the editors wanted made in *Go Tell It on the*

Mountain. One rather disarmingly asked whether the book would not be better "without all the Jesus stuff." Others understood the book better. He found particular support in William Cole, the publicity director who had originally recommended that *Mountain* be published by Knopf, and he agreed to rewrite parts of the book in return for a $250 advance. Knopf agreed to pay $750 more when the book was finished.

During the next three months Baldwin spent time renewing his relationship with his family. He ate many meals at their apartment, stayed there often, working on the revision of *Mountain* and playing with his nine-year-old "baby sister," Paula.

He took an active role in family affairs. One day his mother showed him a letter from his brother Wilmer, always called "Lover," who had been mistreated by a white officer in the army. She was afraid of the effect this might have on him and suggested that a letter from his older brother might be helpful. Jimmy responded with a letter that reveals the wisdom gained by his having confronted his history in *Go Tell It on the Mountain.* He reminded his brother that racism is based on fear, that when the white racist confronts the black man, what he sees is not the individual man but a "nightmare" of his own creation. Above all, he said, "you must take care not to step inside" his nightmare, his guilt, and his fear, his hatred. To step into the nightmare is to justify it and to relinquish the soul's freedom and the control over one's life. To enter the nightmare is to become a "nigger."

The theme of the destructive fear and guilt at the base of racism would be a Baldwin trademark from this point on. In the letter to his brother he suggests an understanding that will find full articulation in "Notes of a Native Son." It was an understanding that grew, like *Go Tell It on the Mountain*, out of his confrontation with the memory of his stepfather. He was revealing to his brother the means of his own survival.

The summer in New York gave Baldwin a chance to visit old friends and to reassess the whole question of his expatriation. He visited Themistocles briefly on Long Island, taking his old Village crony and fellow writer Smith Oliver with him, and stayed for some days with Beauford Delaney in the Village. Beauford had decided that he too would look in on Paris during a trip to Rome he hoped to be able to make in 1953. Baldwin also gathered a bit of additional money together by selling excerpts of *Go Tell It on the Mountain* to *American Mercury* and *New World Writing*, which they printed as "Exodus" and "Roy's Wound." And through his agent, Helen Strauss of the William Morris Agency, to whom he had been introduced by Smith Oliver, he met other black writers, most notably Ralph Ellison, whose *Invisible Man* was published while Baldwin was in the States and of whom he immediately became and remained a fervent admirer.

The revision of *Go Tell It on the Mountain* was finished quickly and sent off to Knopf in July. They accepted the manuscript as revised and sent Baldwin the balance of his advance. Now he had to decide what to do. The America of 1952 was already experiencing McCarthyism. The "race problem" had certainly not been solved; the great civil rights movement was yet to begin. Baldwin resented the fact that he could still be made to feel uncomfortable in restaurants or on the streets. Paris still represented the possibility of freer movement and a kind of anonymity that he felt he needed. He realized that he had to establish himself more fully as a writer before he could face the political and social tension he felt was brewing in his country.

Using a part of the money he had received from Knopf, he booked passage to France on the twenty-eighth of August. Saying good-bye to his mother again was difficult, but at least this time, unlike in 1948, he could afford to leave some money behind for household expenses. The most wrenching separations were from his brother David, who would soon leave for military service in Korea, and from Paula, for whom he always felt a special responsibility.

Jimmy was enjoying the new role as paterfamilias. It helped him in the crucial process of burying his stepfather's spirit. Soon after he got back to Paris in early September, he was writing to his brother George, in the army in Germany, and to his sister Gloria, who was married to a soldier stationed in England, arranging a get-together.

He felt he had to pay a visit in Switzerland to Lucien and Suzy. In his fatherly mood he felt he should evaluate their relationship, ostensibly in the interest of the child that was to be born. When the child was born in October he was called Luc James, after his father and after his godfather, whose emotions on the occasion were, at best, mixed. The visit with Suzy and Lucien was difficult for everyone concerned, but Baldwin channeled his anxiety into work on "Stranger in the Village" and still another work based on his church experience, a play he had started in New York and which he wanted to call *The Amen Corner*. He had suggested the play idea to Knopf and to his agent in New York. They were not enthusiastic, but he persevered, and by the time he returned to Paris from Switzerland he had made significant progress.

After a brief Christmas reunion in Paris with Gloria and George, Baldwin returned to the chalet in Loèche-les-Bains, this time alone, to work on *The Amen Corner*. He worked sporadically on "Notes of a Native Son" as well. The world of Harlem, church, and family was still very much on his mind.

By April he had still not finished *The Amen Corner*, and he wrote to David to complain about the time it was taking. He hoped to have it done by his birthday—"I'll be 29! What has happened to my youth?" May found him, still penniless, in Gallardon, visiting Gidske. From there he wrote to David again asking for help. It was true, he said, that like most artists he had little sense of money, but that was because he "never [had] any."

In late February, Knopf had mailed an advance copy of *Go Tell It on the Mountain* to Baldwin, just about one year after he had sent off the original *Mountain* manuscript from Switzerland. The copy included a promotional comment by poet Marianne Moore, who praised the book for its honesty: "The verisimilitude is continuous; it does not lapse." With the publication of his first novel in May 1953, Baldwin, still in Paris, still frustrated in his personal life, and still driven to distraction by a lack of money, had nevertheless made the first large step of a climb that would take him in less than ten years to the fame, money, and power he had once dreamed of on his Central Park "mountain."

It was pleasant enough being "famous," he wrote to David. *Time* magazine had even taken his picture one afternoon, and a day later he had been invited to a cocktail party to meet some "Very Important People." But he had had to borrow a suit for the party because his was at the cleaners and he could not afford to "get it out."

CHAPTER 8

Go Tell It on the Mountain

I'm ready, I'm coming. I'm on my way.
—John Grimes

During the last years of his work on what was to become *Go Tell It on the Mountain*, Baldwin had been anxious to avoid the pitfalls he so firmly articulated in "Everybody's Protest Novel" and "Many Thousands Gone." His novel would be autobiographical and would address the African-American condition, constituting a living record of his understanding that "we take our shape . . . within and against that cage of reality bequeathed us at our birth," but he wanted nothing of Harriet Beecher Stowe's "merciless exhortations" and even less of Richard Wright's "curses." Protest writers—black and white—writing about African-Americans too often had written from a political bias, whether abolitionist, like Harriet Beecher Stowe, or Marxist, like Richard Wright. They ignored what is necessarily the basis of any realist fiction, the "complex intragroup dynamic, 'that depth of involvement and unspoken recognition of shared experience' " without which the given author seems to suggest "that in Negro life there exists no tradition, no field of manners, no possibility of ritual or intercourse." The problem was "not that the Negro has no tradition but that there has as yet arrived no sensibility sufficiently profound and tough to make this tradition articulate."

Baldwin felt that he possessed such a sensibility. His novel would go to the heart of the reality of life "in my father's house," a house that was his family's apartment on one level, Harlem on another, America on still another, and the "deep heart's core" on another. *Go Tell It on the Mountain*, then, as the launching of the young writer and as his first full attempt to articulate through the traditions of black culture "the uncreated conscience of my race," was James Baldwin's *Portrait of the Artist as a Young Man*, a parable that could illustrate the ideas contained in the early essays concerning the question of self-identity.

It is of interest to note that Baldwin read James Joyce's work in Paris in 1950. The connections between Joyce's flight from Ireland and his own from Harlem were certainly not lost on him. As Horace Porter suggests, Baldwin's hero, John Grimes, is "like Stephen Dedalus—both are young artists, both troubled by their religious heritage." Furthermore, both Joyce/Stephen and Baldwin/John had sought escape from adolescent sexual awakening and guilt by turning to the church. *Portrait* is the metaphorical record of Joyce's coming to grips with the threefold threat to his art of family, nation, and religion even as it is also the record of his recognition that family, nation, and religion were necessarily the basis of his art. Precisely the same can be said of Baldwin's relationship to *Mountain*.

The process that culminated in *Go Tell It on the Mountain* had been a difficult one for Baldwin. The early work on *Crying Holy* had been a constant source of pain. It had haunted him as it lay neglected in various rented rooms while its author talked of other things or worked on other projects in the bars of Greenwich Village or Saint-Germain-des-Prés. It had been easy enough to record, through the characters in the novel, the literal facts of his early life in Harlem, and the autobiographical elements are evident enough. Baldwin's childhood, like John's, was dominated by the church and by a stepfather's relentless disapproval. Obsessed by guilt, Jimmy and John were fascinated by the story of Noah's son's sinful viewing of his father's genitals, and were tuned to the rumors of sexuality in the church and the clear signs of it on the streets outside. Both, having discovered their illegitimacy, were constantly curious about the circumstances of their conception. Both were "saved" with the direct help of young male "saints" with whom they had fallen in love.

But for many years the novel had simply refused to coalesce around the mere facts of autobiography. It was as if it resisted being born of the kind of hatred and despair found in "The Death of the Prophet," as if such a birth would have been a negation of the philosophy of love that was taking form in Baldwin's mind. To succeed, the novel would have to be a true representation not only of the essence of events in 1938 but of the mind and soul of the man telling the story in 1952, a man living in France, searching for cultural and personal identity, and wrestling with sexual ambivalence, who had chosen Paris over Harlem. The novel would have to tell the story of a "birth" even as it recorded the "killing" of a father.

Later Baldwin was to say he could not finish *Go Tell It on the Mountain*, or continue writing at all, until he was able to understand his stepfather's agony and therefore "forgive" him. Of John Grimes's stepfather, Baldwin would say he was "John's first apprehension of history, and . . . history is brutal."

In the novel, as the struggle for John's soul occurs on the "threshing floor" that takes its name from the floor described by that earlier John, the Baptist born of another Elizabeth, John is forced to confront not so much his own sin as the historical source of the misery of the saints who watch his agony. Once again we must see John here as a metaphor for the real story—the inner story—of James Baldwin. John's night down at the cross is less the struggle for the soul of John Grimes than it is a metaphor for the struggle in the twenty-eight-year-old James Baldwin between the instinct that said, "I have escaped my heritage; I can be free of it now," and the instinct that told him he must journey to the very depths of the sorrow of his people before he could "climb the mountain" and be free.

In the second part of *Go Tell It on the Mountain*, in which John's stepfather, mother, and aunt make their own "night journeys" into the past, Baldwin prepares us for John's descent into history. Each of the family members in *Mountain* is a part of that great migration of southern blacks to the North in search of the "American Dream." The hopes of each have been dashed by the failure of the American nation to see through its own myths, by the dominance of the myth of racial inferiority over the reality of what it is to be human. Florence and Elizabeth, and even Gabriel, have been denied the salvation of love, not, ironically, because they were unable to say yes to love, but because the nature of racism was such as to preclude the kind of self-respect that viable relationships require. Richard, Elizabeth's lover and John's biological father, is driven by racism to suicide, thus effectively ending Elizabeth's dream as well as his own. He will not be the last Baldwin character to die in this way for the same reason. Florence's relationship with Frank is destroyed by a self-denigrating hatred of her own blackness, and Gabriel's mistreatment of his wife and the mother of his first son can be traced clearly to society's racist denial of his manhood, a denial that leaves him no place to turn but to a reverse racism and self-hatred masked by his hypocritical religious vocation.

John Grimes does not know the contents of his family's reminiscences, of their "prayers," but James Baldwin the writer does, and in his novel gives metaphorical life to the specific sources of the agony that prevailed "in my father's house." Florence, Gabriel, and Elizabeth are based on members of Baldwin's own family, but, more important, they are historical figures in a "house" that is the historical condition of African-Americans.

Later, John, too, experiences this history in the visions that precede his salvation. "Who are these? Who are they?" he cries upon discovering the multitudes during his descent into the darkness of the threshing floor. "They were the despised and rejected, the wretched and the spat upon, the earth's offscouring; and he was in their company, and they would swallow up his soul."

John's instinct said to escape, to get off the floor and to leave, but a voice called to him to "go through," to face the agony of his vision. "He wanted to rise—a malicious, ironic voice insisted that he rise—and, at once . . . leave this temple and go out into the world." But the Baptist prophet had warned his people of one who would baptize "with the Holy Ghost and with fire. Whose fan is in his hand, and he will thoroughly purge his floor, and will gather the wheat into his garner."

"Then John saw the Lord" and broke through to discover the midwife of his second birth in Elisha, the seventeen-year-old piano player whose voice had been with him on his whole journey. And when he heard that voice as he rose from the floor, "a sweetness filled John." This was the voice of love and the metaphorical birth of the main tenet of Baldwin's prophecy: salvation from the chains and fetters—the self-hatred and the other effects—of historical racism could come only from love. In John's heart "there was a sudden yearning tenderness" for his guiding saint; he felt "desire, sharp and awful as a reflecting knife, to usurp the body of Elisha, and lie where Elisha lay; to speak in tongues, as Elisha spoke, and, with that authority, to confound his father." Here John acts out a reconciliation of sex and religion. Love, including physical love, is a sacred trust and one means by which Baldwin could be saved from the hatred represented by his stepfather. Elisha's body fills John with "a wild delight" as, while cleaning the church, they wrestle playfully on the evening of John's conversion. The wrestling perhaps recalls Jacob's wrestling with the angel on the night he is given his new name, Israel, and his life's mission. It is the vision of the beautiful Elisha among the saints praying over him, the sound of his voice, that brings John through the passage between his old life and his new one. "It was you," says

John to Elisha, ". . . who prayed me through." And in the last pages of the novel John turns to Elisha as the primary support for that new life as he begs his new "brother" to pray for him:

> "I been praying, little brother," Elisha said, "and I sure ain't going to stop praying now."
>
> "For me," persisted John, his tears falling, "for *me*."

And Elisha kisses him on the forehead—"a holy kiss." After that the sun rose, and "it fell over Elisha like a golden robe, and struck John's forehead, where Elisha had kissed him, like a seal ineffaceable forever." The imagery is of initiation and transfiguration. With the rising sun, the newly born James Baldwin, through his character John, can now say, reminding us of any number of young prophets, "I'm ready, I'm coming. I'm on my way."

The history—his stepfather's history and the larger history it represents—that Baldwin faces metaphorically in John Grimes's salvation experience and in the flashbacks to earlier days in the lives of John's family he confronts in more intellectual terms in the essay "Notes of a Native Son." It is no mere coincidence that Baldwin began work on "Notes" during the years he was finishing *Mountain* or that the original titles of the essay and the novel were respectively "Me and My House" and *In My Father's House.* The problem relating to his stepfather that he addressed in "Notes" he had originally treated fictionally in that early story about the boy murdering his deacon father and later in "The Death of the Prophet." These had been stories marked by bitterness and a sense of failure, characteristics that do not apply to *Mountain* or "Notes." As John Grimes is saved against his father's will in the novel, the persona of the essay is saved on his way to his father's burial by a revelation that if he cannot transcend it, racial hatred will destroy him, as it had destroyed his father. It was only through the death of the old prophet of doom that the new prophet of love could be born, just as the Reverend David Baldwin's last child was born on the day of his death, a point emphasized in "Notes."

In other words, once he had put his stepfather into historical and cultural perspective in the essay, once he had lifted him and his relationship with him out of the merely personal and had assimilated him intellectually, Baldwin was able to treat the subject metaphorically in the novel and to create a fictional hero of aesthetic and moral integrity who could emerge as the first fictional embodiment of what

Eleanor Traylor has called "the Baldwin narrator-witness" (he might also be called the Baldwin artist-hero or poet-prophet) on his long quest for love, recorded fictionally in six novels, several short stories and poems, and three plays. Looking back on it later, Baldwin was well aware that *Mountain* was the beginning of this autobiographical quest. "The morning I typed *the end* to my manuscript," he wrote, "I knew that I had come through something."

The critical reactions to *Go Tell It on the Mountain* were generally positive. *The Saturday Review* noted Baldwin's ability to discover the inner worlds of his characters: "His penetration of the mind of John," a skill which Baldwin credited to his reading of Henry James, ". . . is as valid as anything in William James's *Varieties of Religious Experience* and as moving as the interior monologues in Faulkner's *As I Lay Dying*." Emerson Price in the *Cleveland Press* called it an "almost perfectly executed story," and John K. Hutchens in the *New York Herald Tribune* praised it as a work of "insight and authoritative realism."

But the book was somewhat misunderstood. Some reviewers saw it as a work that was concerned primarily with ethics and religion. Orville Prescott, for instance, in *The New York Times*, while praising the book, found it "almost as remote as a historical novel about the Hebrew patriarchs and prophets."

And a note of dissent was expressed privately by Langston Hughes in a letter to Arna Bontemps. He seems to have reacted primarily against what he considered to be Baldwin's tendency to place art before truth: *Go Tell It on the Mountain* was "a low-down story in a velvet bag."

Whatever the reaction, Baldwin himself knew he had overcome a great hurdle. When, years later, he discussed the characterization of John Grimes, the words he used might well have applied to himself. John's conversion, he said, marks "his first step out of his father's house." On the church floor he has confronted the "anguish of his ancestors, and the price paid for him." From then on his "responsibility" is clear. He must, no matter what the cost, "keep the faith." This was the charge to John Grimes, and it was James Baldwin's pledge to himself for the years to come.

CHAPTER 9

The Search for Giovanni

The misery of which the jewel of life is formed . . .
—Beauford Delaney

Nineteen fifty-three found Baldwin mostly in Paris. One friend described him during the months immediately following the publication of *Go Tell It on the Mountain* as "looking gracious, almost regal." He spoke a great deal about future contracts, future novels, and about his play. But he remained essentially penniless, depending on small loans by mail from his brothers and the generosity of friends like Themistocles, Sascha, and writer Fred Moore, whose apartments he sometimes used.

When he did have a bit of money he attracted people who did not. Friends from whom he had once borrowed now expected repayment or asked for loans themselves. He was, after all, a success, as he so often reminded them. Keeping to budgets was never a Baldwin interest, keeping friends was. By the fall of 1953 he felt trapped by poverty and was unable to write. It seemed that publishing a novel did not lead to happiness or the kind of inner stability for which he so longed. The demands of creditors became so overwhelming that he escaped for a while to Bilbao, Spain, where he visited a friend. He worked more on *The Amen Corner*. But no money was forthcoming, and his agent and his editors at Knopf urged him to write another novel, preferably a sequel to *Mountain*, or at least another Harlem novel. There was no future in a play. This attitude alienated Baldwin from them. He had already written his Harlem childhood novel, he now wanted to write a Harlem play, and there was the "Notes of a Native Son" essay to polish up, and then there would be other novels, but not necessarily Harlem novels; he was not a protest writer or a "Negro writer," he was a writer.

Then there was the natural letdown that followed two momentous endings. Without the novel he had worked on for over ten years and without the lover with whom he had hoped to achieve domestic stability, he began to experience the kind of deep depression that had plagued him before. He knew that he had not faced something in himself, something that had to do with love, his need to be loved, and the relation of that need to his own identity.

One night he had a terrifying dream. He stood in the midst of a number of family members who were scolding him for being so intransigent in regard to his stepfather. His mother, who sat at the edge of the room trying to soothe her son, appeared at once frightened, appalled, and guilty. She was suddenly very old, with a tooth missing. The dream persona wanted to remain calm because he knew how much his filial attacks hurt his mother, causing her to blame herself for bringing an unloving stepfather into her son's life. But he was so unnerved that he suddenly found himself standing in front of her, clenching his fists in the air and shouting at the others in the room that his mother had never realized the extent of his hatred for her husband.

In *Go Tell It on the Mountain* and the work already done on "Notes of a Native Son" Baldwin had confronted the historical sources of his stepfather's hostility, but he still had work to do in terms of assimilating him emotionally. He felt in 1953, and was to continue to feel throughout his life, that the rest of his family, including his mother, resented his consistently unfavorable remarks about the man whose wife and children they were and whose biological child he was not. Since for Baldwin his stepfather's house was a metaphor for society itself, his position as (in the biological sense) an outsider in the family extended into the larger social vision of the witness who saw himself as a "stranger in the village."

Another aspect of Baldwin's makeup contributed to his sense of being an outsider, even an "outlaw." As a homosexual who had only obliquely announced his sexual orientation, he was still concerned about what people might think of him on that score. The second part of the 1953 dream suggests this insecurity.

The dream scene changed from the room in which Baldwin had been under attack from his family to a street in Spain where he and a lover and another friend, Bernard Hassell, found themselves in the midst of a revolution. The "noble" but "cruel" and "impersonal" revolutionaries were projections of the kind of man with whom Baldwin so often became sexually involved and by whom he was so often "punished" for his affection. When one of them cocked his rifle, the dreamer experienced something "deeper than fear."

As the violence increased, it became clear that Jimmy's lover, Robert—in reality, as well as in the dream, a French policeman—was distancing himself from Jimmy and Bernard. They screamed and ran from the crowd. Bernard disappeared down a hole and Jimmy approached a house in which two people were having a conversation about the imminent arrival of an old woman who was coming home to die. The old woman was somehow himself. Once again the dreamer was an outsider. Often in his dreams and in his later writing, Baldwin would create the persona of a woman to express his own inner struggles.

The third part of the dream follows thematically from the other two. The dreamer now found himself visiting Grace, his "fiancée" of the Greenwich Village years. And then he was back in Spain trying to find Robert when he saw a running male figure machine-gunned against a wall. The scene shifted again to his walking with Grace, who had apparently become a prostitute, to her next place of assignation. There was great sadness in their conversation, and as they separated, her strong, confident face expressed the knowledge that men have always betrayed women and always would. The dreamer, overcome by guilt, ran terrified through a mob, still looking for Robert, still an outsider.

The dream reflects concerns deep within Baldwin that would influence events in his own life during the coming years and which would be confronted directly in *Giovanni's Room*, a novel that was beginning to take preliminary form in his mind and which he would begin writing in earnest two months later.

Bernard Hassell, who plays a significant role in the three-part dream, was a dancer at the Folies Bergère, an African-American Baldwin had met at the Montana Bar just after his return to Paris from the States in 1952. Hassell had recently arrived in France and was surprised to be introduced to the author of "Roy's Wound," which he had recently read in *New World Writing*. The relationship between Baldwin and Hassell never became a sexual one, but it was among the most important associations in the lives of both men. Hassell was a central figure in the change that took place in Baldwin's life in Paris beginning in 1952. From then on black Americans would to a great extent take the place of the primarily white bohemian set with whom Baldwin had associated during the first years of his expatriation. He spent a good deal of time at Gordon Heath's club as well as at the Mars Club, where Bobby Short, a new friend, was performing. And he continued to see Inez Cavanaugh at her club. He met Maya Angelou at about the same time; she was dancing in a production of *Porgy and Bess*. The writer Richard Gibson was also an acquaintance, though the two men tended to clash. At the Montana and elsewhere he often ran into the composer Howard Swanson, and at the Café Tournon, where he went occasionally, he saw Chester Himes and Richard Wright, who still resented the criticism of *Native Son* but was willing to argue with the younger writer over the odd café dinner.

By far the most important personal event in Baldwin's life in 1953, the event that cemented and formed the core of his African-American connections in Paris, was the arrival of Beauford Delaney. When, in New York in 1952, Beauford had talked of visiting Europe, Jimmy had not thought he would actually do it. It was with amazement, then, on September 3, 1953, that he looked across the street from the Flore, where he and his friend Mary Painter were sitting, and saw Beauford Delaney standing on the corner. He was looking down into a puddle. The memory of the incident years before, when Beauford had shown him light and reality in that Greenwich Village puddle, flashed through his mind. At first he could not believe his eyes, but he "leaped" from his seat, "screamed" his friend's name, and within seconds he and Beauford, in the middle of the boulevard, oblivious to astonished pedestrians and honking traffic, were locked in each other's arms. Always one to concentrate on inner significance rather than literal fact, Baldwin was to say later of Beauford's "dogged and splendid" life's "journey" to Paris from Tennessee—via Boston and New York—"I have the impression that he walked and swam."

In fact, Beauford had come by ship. A fellow African-American and painter, Herb Gentry, had also been on board. Gentry knew Paris and he and another black friend, cartoonist Ollie Harrington, settled Delaney into a hotel in Montparnasse. Most of the rooms were used by prostitutes, but some on the top floor were rented by artists. Later he would move to the slightly better Hôtel des Ecoles in the rue des Armes. The friends told Beauford where he would be likely to find Jimmy, and it was in the course of searching for him around Saint-Germain that he passed by the Flore, where Mary and Jimmy were sitting.

Baldwin introduced Beauford to Bernard Hassell on that first day. It was Bernard who, with his friend Richard Olney, arranged for the painter to move near them into an old house surrounded by a garden in Clamart. The house was watched over by the landlady, Mme Martine, who wore lots of makeup and exotic hats and obviously had designs on Beauford. This would be his home for many years and would serve as a refuge for Baldwin, much as the Hôtel Verneuil had during the first years in Paris. Baldwin and Beauford saw a great deal of each other; they would sit for hours on the window seat in the Clamart studio, from which they could look through the branches of a large tree to the garden. Baldwin wrote of Beauford's window that it was "a kind of universe," containing every imaginable human experience, as reflected by the changes in weather and light that it framed. Sitting there, Baldwin and Delaney meditated on and discussed the larger questions of life itself.

Clamart was good for both men. Jimmy noticed that his friend's work "underwent a most striking metamorphosis into freedom" there. And Beauford's understanding of light took on a deeper significance. It seemed to "illuminate" for the younger man corners of his life that he had had difficulty facing. It was as if Beauford's light had the "power . . . to redeem and reconcile and heal." His art drove the viewer, spiritually as well as physically, "to a new confrontation with reality."

Baldwin and Beauford became increasingly dependent on each other, and when Baldwin spent time on a fellowship at the MacDowell Colony in New Hampshire in 1954 they corresponded regularly, as they continued to do throughout their lives. In his letters Baldwin took the tone of a devoted son worried about a father in delicate health and shared his loneliness and feelings of depression as he wrestled with the problems associated with *Giovanni's Room* and Lucien. Beauford responded like the loving father the younger man dreamed of having. He advised, he sympathized, he chided, and he caressed. Most of all, he preached the importance of love. Love could protect against anything. It was the ultimate source of inner strength that made possible the honesty and the insight without which there could be no art. Beauford's teaching was essential to the James Baldwin prophecy. His was a Bessie Smith blues lesson: he spoke of sadness and pain that was also joy, of the "misery of which the jewel of life is formed." It was the lesson first taught in that Greenwich Village street several years earlier.

There was profound depression, as well, in Beauford's letters.

By the mid-1950s he was already falling prey to a psychological condition that would eventually destroy him. He confided to Jimmy that there was a certain vacantness at the center of his being but that he depended on his art as a barrier to insanity. Through his art he could confront the many sides that "make up Beauford" and try to "merge them into some sense of composition." Implicitly, he was suggesting a path for Jimmy to follow as well. Art was the only hope, and art, he said, required a recognition that one's friends were oneself. In his letters to Jimmy, Beauford referred frequently to "our" work, "our" friends, "our" way. One senses from his letters that although Beauford accepted his fatherly role, he would have preferred to have been Jimmy's lover.

In October "Stranger in the Village" appeared in *Harper's Magazine*. Once again Baldwin had a small sum of money, and he decided to spend some of it on a working vacation. He had reestablished a relationship with the actor Jacques, whom he had met in 1949 and with whom he now arranged to rent a house called the Villa Lou Fougau in Les Quatre-Chemins, near Grasse in the south of France. There he planned to do some more work on *The Amen Corner*, add some things to the "Notes of a Native Son" essay, and give some thought to a study of post–Civil War African-American literature. He foresaw this project's involving a trip to the American South in 1954. He also talked of writing a primer "on being a Negro" in America, which would be done in the form of a "Letter for My Younger Brother." The trip to the South would take place and the letter would become, several years later, the "Letter to My Nephew" segment of *The Fire Next Time*.

But the time with Jacques was not at all tranquil. Baldwin was, quite simply, still in love with Lucien and he constantly thought of the all too recent times with him in Loèche-les-Bains. The more he brooded, the more he was forced to face questions of his own emotional needs, his own failure to achieve a viable domestic situation, his sexual ambivalence, and the apparent failure of the one great love affair of his life. What was he doing with Jacques when he belonged with Lucien? He feared that like all of his relationships after Lucien, this one was a dishonest evasion.

In danger of drifting into another of his depressions, he confronted his agony by channeling it in earnest into the beginning of a new novel for which he already had some notes. He would call it *One for My Baby*, *A Fable for Our Children*, and later *Giovanni's Room*. The seeds for the work were in the manuscript called *Ignorant Armies*, which he had started some years before, and in time, much of the early work on that novel would lead to *Another Country*.

The work Baldwin did in Grasse was an autobiographical meditation on love and the payment incurred for the denial of love. The surface of the novel that became *Giovanni's Room* developed from Baldwin's own life in Paris. Now the Villa Lou Fougau and the dishonest love affair it housed would serve as an appropriate setting for the brooding of David at the beginning and end of the novel.

Just before Christmas Jacques left Grasse for a while. There had been a harsh disagreement, and Jimmy felt particularly upset. Christmas, in any case, always made him homesick. He thought of his mother and he looked at his life. He wrote her a letter, hoping it would get to New York in time for her birthday. He longed for home, for her, for the children. He told her giving birth to novels was like giving birth to children. As both mother and father of his "children," he watched them with anxiety as they went out "into the world."

As he often did, he used the letter to his mother as a vehicle for the working out of an idea. He talked of his obligations as a writer in terms that closely paralleled his feelings about his own relationships and the lessons on love and art that he had learned from Beauford. It was the "faith and love of a few people" that made life supportable. And it was necessary for the artist to live up to that faith and love. To betray it was to betray one's reason for being. *Giovanni's Room*, as a novel about the requirements of love, would serve as a vehicle for Baldwin's feelings about his mission as an artist.

The Grasse arrangement with Jacques having failed, Baldwin returned to Clamart in March with the intention of going back to the States as soon as possible. But first there were things to do. There was a renewed need for money. He had had to borrow some from his mother in February. He wanted to pay her back, and he required funds for his ship passage. There were some possibilities. He had been asked by *Partisan Review* to do a piece on Americans in Paris. This would become the essay "A Question of Identity," a work that spoke in part to the issue of the destructive aspect of American "innocence" that he was facing in the writing of *Giovanni's Room*. He looked forward to the French and English publications of *Mountain*, and he dreamed of a simultaneous publication and Broadway production of *The Amen Corner*, on which he still had some revisions to make. He was sure this would solve his financial problems and leave him money to spare to free his family from poverty.

Finally, he had to see Lucien again before leaving Europe, even if that meant threatening the integrity of his friend's new family. He had seen Lucien with Suzy and with Luc James, and he doubted the honesty of that relationship; he would try to get Lucien back.

In Paris he gave act 1 of *The Amen Corner* to Themistocles for publication in *Zero.* Most important, he was informed that his application for a Guggenheim grant had been successful and that the paperback rights for *Mountain* had been sold. He now had enough money for his trip home.

After an emotional meeting in Paris, Jimmy and Lucien agreed that they would share a place in New York beginning later in the fall. Baldwin always had trouble leaving for anywhere, and as much as he longed for home, he delayed his departure several times before finally sailing on the *Ile de France* at the end of June. The "native son" was returning for the second time.

CHAPTER 10

Notes of a Native Son

I want to be an honest man and a good writer.
—James Baldwin

Arriving in New York early in June of 1954, Baldwin carried with him the completed manuscript of his play and most of the essay that would become "Me and My House" ("Notes of a Native Son"). In both works, directly in the essay and indirectly in the play, he had continued the process, begun in *Go Tell It on the Mountain*, of exploring the effect of his relationship with his stepfather on his own ability to overcome the isolation imposed by race and sexual ambivalence.

One of the first things he did upon returning was to visit Mother Horn's church in Harlem. He took Bill Cole from Knopf, as well as an old school friend with whom he had an idea of making a movie about Holy Rollers. He enjoyed being back in church, joining energetically in the singing and celebrating. Part of facing his stepfather's life in "Notes" involved returning to the world in which it had been played out. The renewed church interest was also related, of course, to his work on *The Amen Corner*. He wanted to get back into the atmosphere that he had tried to recapture in the play.

The Holy Roller movie project died quickly, just as the Baldwin-Pelatowski church venture had failed years before. But Baldwin was not, in any case, seriously committed to it. He had some money, so he could spend time with friends in the Village. He lived for a while on Greenwich Street and then borrowed Bill Cole's apartment while he and his wife were away on vacation. And in August he was awarded a fellowship at the MacDowell Colony to do work on his new novel. While there he also revised "Notes of a Native Son" and "Equal in Paris" and completed an essay called "Gide as Husband and Homosexual."

The Gide essay would be important for Baldwin, one he would

later include in the collection *Nobody Knows My Name* as "The Male Prison." It was important because it tackled the same problems Baldwin was dealing with fictionally in *Giovanni's Room.* Through Gide, he told his first biographer, Fern Eckman, he was "accusing" himself "of a certain fear and hypocrisy." For all of the ambiguity of his feelings about Gide's homosexuality and its effect on his life and work, Baldwin emphasizes his belief that the real question here is the creation of "prisons" of various sorts, not necessarily homosexual ones, that make love impossible. Mickey Spillane's heroes, for example, are imprisoned "because their muscles, their fists, and their tommy guns have acquired such fantastic importance." We should be "humbled by Gide's confession as he was humbled by his pain and make the generous effort to understand that his sorrow was not different from the sorrow of all men born." The alternative to this understanding might well be strangulation by a "most petulant and unmasculine pride."

As protective as the time at MacDowell was, New Hampshire reminded Baldwin of Switzerland and of Lucien, and when he left the colony late in the year it was with a sense of relief at being able to return to the city. When Lucien arrived in December—his first trip to America—Jimmy was at the airport to meet him. The memory of that arrival was the source for the scene at the end of *Another Country* when Eric meets his French lover, Yves, at the airport in New York. Baldwin was still under the delusion that Lucien and he could make a life together, and the couple moved into a small apartment on Gay Street in Greenwich Village after a brief stay with the family uptown.

But soon old problems resurfaced. There were many fights as Lucien chafed under what he considered Jimmy's lugubrious approach to their relationship. Nothing really had changed; Jimmy wanted a lover to end all lovers, Lucien wanted a friend. When several women came into Lucien's life, Jimmy was hurt.

Relief came in the form of an invitation to spend time at Yaddo, the writer's colony in Saratoga Springs, New York. A particularly thrilling moment marked that stay. He watched on television as his childhood cinema idol Bette Davis presented his friend Marlon Brando with the Academy Award for his performance in *On the Waterfront.* Inspired by Brando's success, he made great strides at Yaddo with *Giovanni's Room,* and he worked on the collection of essays that would be called *Notes of a Native Son.*

The idea for the collection had come from his old school friend

Sol Stein, now an editor at Beacon Press. At first Baldwin had resisted, telling Stein he was "too young to publish my memoirs." Baldwin realized all too well what it would mean to retrace his steps as an essayist from 1948 to 1955. It would force him to stand back from his work and, by examining it, examine himself and his contribution. He doubted whether he was ready for this exercise. But Stein, seeing the makings of a book, persisted, and a work emerged that was much more than the sum of its parts. It is a book that, to be given its due as a classic, must be considered as a whole.

With the publication of *Notes of a Native Son*, Baldwin staked a large claim in an area of American literary territory inhabited by such masters of the essay and autobiography as Ralph Waldo Emerson, Henry David Thoreau, and Frederick Douglass. Combining the powerful rhetoric of the Old Testament with a style that was highly polished and bitingly ironical, the prophetic voice that emerged from this collection could not be ignored.

Notes of a Native Son can be said to constitute a James Baldwin manifesto, an overture to the story he was to tell during the rest of his life. Each of the major Baldwin themes is touched on here: the search for identity in a world that because of its racial myths cannot recognize reality, the acceptance of one's inheritance ("the conundrum of color is the inheritance of every American") as one claims one's birthright ("my birthright was vast, connecting me to all that lives, and to everyone, forever"), the loneliness of the artist's quest, the urgent necessity of love.

Notes of a Native Son maintained the autobiographical approach that had been set in *Mountain* and which would color all of Baldwin's work—fiction and nonfiction. The special circumstances that confronted him from the day he realized he was black made the autobiographical voice inevitable. He had to write specifically about being a black man "because it was the gate I had to unlock before I could hope to write about anything else." In the mid-1980s, as he wrote *Evidence of Things Not Seen*, he was still trying to unlock that gate, a fact indicative at once of the beauty and the tragedy of Baldwin's life and work and of the moral failure of the society that held the key to the lock.

The essays contained in *Notes* had been published between 1948 and 1955 in *Commentary*, *The New Leader*, *Partisan Review*, *The Reporter*, and *Harper's Magazine*, all leading "liberal" journals that, like Alfred A. Knopf, the publisher of the first novel, had recognized in Baldwin a voice that could penetrate old mental barriers, that could carry the message of African-American deprivation into the living rooms of white America.

The liberals were right. *Notes of a Native Son* was the "making" of James Baldwin in white America. It was also the source of a misconception which was to plague him throughout his career. "Why don't you write more essays like the ones in *Notes of a Native Son*?" he was constantly asked by whites, who appreciated and were subtly comforted by the fact that in the *Notes* essays, when he is not speaking directly from a first-person autobiographical perspective, Baldwin tends to assume the point of view of "one of us" (white Americans) looking objectively and honestly at "them" (black Americans): "What it means to be a Negro is a great deal more than this essay can discover; what it means to be a Negro in America can perhaps be suggested by an examination of the myths we perpetuate about him." In "The Harlem Ghetto" Baldwin writes, "we" watch black people "with a kind of tolerant scorn," without realizing that when we do so "it is ourselves we are watching, ourselves we are damning, or—condescendingly—bending to save."

Baldwin's method is to reach consciences by way of minds. He seduces the reader by delivering his message without resorting to the violence or the harshness of a work like Richard Wright's *Native Son*—a work which, ironically, influenced his own title. He leads the white consciousness through the horrors of the black dilemma, not without passion, but with the subtlety and elegance of a Henry James. A second source for the collection's title, Baldwin always said, was James's autobiographical *Notes of a Son and Brother*.

African-Americans have not always been approving of the white persona that seems to pervade much of *Notes*. In his review of the book in *The New York Times Book Review*, Langston Hughes suggested that "Baldwin's viewpoints are half American, half Afro-American, incompletely fused." Others have asked why the white man's hand should be held at all. Baldwin's own prose from *The Fire Next Time* on increasingly suggests that he asked himself this question as well.

The problem of point of view in *Notes of a Native Son* must be confronted by anyone concerned with the question of appropriate audiences for "minority spokesmen." It seems obvious that Baldwin's choice of perspective can best be understood through a consideration of the context in which the essays were written. These were the first essays of an escapee—an escapee from a repressive religion and an oppressive stepfather, from the ghetto itself, and from the restrictions placed on him as a man and as a writer by the very existence of the ghetto and the reasons behind it. Rightly or wrongly, at this juncture in his career Baldwin felt that he must reveal his experience not in the form of protest literature, not as a "Negro writer," but as a writer. In order to achieve this goal he had to reach out beyond the ghetto for his audience. The "liberal" journals were the logical place and the uninvolved objective point of view followed just as logically. "I want to be an honest man and a good writer," he wrote, and this is what took him first to Greenwich Village and then to Paris. In both places he could continue his experience of an integrated life-style—albeit first with bohemians and then with expatriates—that was particularly uncommon in the first half of this century, an experience that had begun with his friendship with Orilla Miller in the early thirties and developed in close friendships with schoolmates such as Richard Avedon, Sol Stein, and Emile Capouya.

Baldwin's expatriation and his attempt to reach the minds and emotions of the white world did not mean that he had denied or broken away from his ethnic roots any more than he dropped his white friends when in later years he became more Afro-centric. And Baldwin's approach to white America was never humble or self-denigrating; neither in the *Notes* essays nor elsewhere was he obsequious or apologetic. Baldwin often said that he left the pulpit to "preach the gospel." Whatever his technical point of view in *Notes*, he used those essays to bring to white America a prophetic message concerning the perilous state of a nation of blacks and whites—a nation he, the "native son," dared to call his own.

Furthermore, even in the Village and Paris years he never lost sight of his need to confront his "inheritance" as an American black in order to achieve his "birthright" as a man. In the "Autobiographical Notes" in *Notes of a Native Son*, for example, he speaks admiringly of Ralph Ellison for being able to "utilize in language, and brilliantly, some of the ambiguity and irony of Negro life," and this achievement was always a Baldwin goal as well.

Notes of a Native Son is divided into three parts. The first is concerned with the identity of the "Negro" and with the African-American as artist. The second contains three essays on black life in America, culminating in the great autobiographical essay "Notes of a Native Son," which is the record of a painful search for self as well as for ethnic identity. The last part is made up of four essays written to America from the expatriate in Europe.

Part 1 begins with the two *Partisan Review* essays, "Everybody's Protest Novel" and "Many Thousands Gone," originally written in

1949 and 1951. It ends with a more recent article, a review of the film *Carmen Jones* written in 1955 for *Commentary*. In "Carmen Jones: The Dark Is Light Enough," as in nearly all of his comments on films, Baldwin is torn between an almost childlike love of the silver screen and the necessity of seeing in the movies themselves—particularly American movies—the reflection of social realities. As an all-black film, *Carmen Jones* had to be a thrilling experience for an African-American brought up on Lana Turner and Gary Cooper. But the astute social critic was quick to recognize that white Hollywood was using the beautiful "Negro bodies" in the film to perpetuate white myths of black sexuality. And once again Baldwin found an opportunity to articulate one of his major leitmotifs: "What is distressing is the conjecture this movie leaves one with as to what Americans take sex to be. . . . The most important thing about this movie . . . is that the questions it leaves in the mind relate less to Negroes than to the interior life of Americans." The idea that white myths about black sexuality reflect a perversion that follows inevitably from one race's dehumanizing another is an idea that would be explored fictionally in such works as *Blues for Mister Charlie*, "Going to Meet the Man," and *Another Country*.

The second part of *Notes of a Native Son* speaks directly to conditions in black America. The two 1948 essays "The Harlem Ghetto" and "Journey to Atlanta" serve as prefaces to the title essay. Baldwin had been working on that essay for several years; Stein encouraged him to finish the piece for the book, and it was published first by *Harper's Magazine* in November 1955 under its earlier title, "Me and My House."

Often called the greatest of his essays, "Notes of a Native Son" has been discussed earlier as the story of the return of the "native son" to his stepfather's "house"—Harlem—and as a metaphor for the thirty-year-old James Baldwin's attempt to discover his stepfather's legacy within himself and to rework that inheritance into something universal that will open the gate to his birthright as an artist and as a man. The final section treats the narrator's attempt to learn from the message in his stepfather's favorite text: "Choose you this day whom you will serve." In the essay Baldwin had continued the process of burying David Baldwin, Sr. In later years he would learn even to love him.

The four essays that make up part 3 of *Notes of a Native Son* grow directly out of Baldwin's life in Paris in the 1950s. "Encounter on the Seine," "A Question of Identity," "Equal in Paris," and "Stranger in the Village" also have in common the fact that they are records of an expatriate's attempt to discover from a distance what it means to be an American. In this search Baldwin has much in common with Henry James.

"A Question of Identity" is perhaps the most Jamesian of Baldwin's essays. James certainly would have agreed that "from the vantage point of Europe [the American] discovers his own country." Listening to Baldwin, one feels at moments as if one were in the presence of a mid-twentieth-century Lambert Strether discussing the problems of Americans—in this case students—living abroad. The essay, in fact, is a revisiting of the problems James takes up in *The Ambassadors*. And it was written at a time when Baldwin was particularly occupied with a reading of James. Lambert Strether might himself have spoken of "the moment, so to speak, when one leaves the Paris of legend and finds oneself in the real and difficult Paris of the present" or of the "American confusion seeming to be based on the very nearly unconscious assumption that it is possible to consider the person apart from all the forces which have produced him."

But it is the style that more than anything else must remind us of James—the elegant and complex sentences that attempt to reveal so much at once, and always the irony:

> What the European, in a thoroughly exasperating innocence, assumes is that the American cannot, of course, be divorced from the so diverse phenomena which make up his country, and that he is willing, and able, to clarify the American conundrum. If the American cannot do this, his despairing aspect seems to say, who, under heaven, can?

In "Equal in Paris" and "Stranger in the Village" Baldwin uses the autobiographical events described in both essays to reveal the alienation of the African-American in the Western landscape and to treat, as he had in "Encounter on the Seine" and "A Question of Identity," the uniqueness of the American experience and identity.

The last pages of *Notes of a Native Son*, which are the closing pages of "Stranger in the Village," were written during a stay in a small village near Chartres. While he was there Baldwin visited the great cathedral several times and read Henry Adams's *Mont-Saint-Michel and Chartres*. "Stranger in the Village" and, in a sense, the whole collection of which it is a part are Baldwin's answer to Adams and the "civilization" he represented:

> The cathedral at Chartres . . . says something to the people of this village which it cannot say to me; but it is important to understand that this cathedral says something to me which it cannot say to them. Perhaps they are struck by the power of the spires, the glory of the windows; but they have known God, after all, longer than I have known him, and in a different way. . . . I doubt that the villagers think of the devil when they face a cathedral because they have never been identified with the devil. But I must accept the status which myth, if nothing else, gives me in the West before I can hope to change the myth.

These are the words of the stranger in the village of Western civilization. Whereas Henry Adams finds in the great cathedral a symbol for a European-based unity in a disintegrating world, Baldwin finds in his reaction to it a sense of community with his own countrymen, for whom it represents an alien if beautiful force, a force that cannot speak to the new order that will inevitably emerge from the uniqueness of the American experience.

Henry Adams bemoans the passing of an earlier age, Baldwin welcomes that passing. Out of the agony of the black-white experience—however negative—says Baldwin, a new understanding, one that transcends the old European dualities of God and the devil, light and dark, love and lust, is taking form. It is an understanding that will eventually change the world.

In light of this prophecy, it is of interest to note that only a few weeks before Baldwin's arrival in New York, the nation's schools had been desegregated by law in the Supreme Court's *Brown* v. *Board of Education* ruling, and the civil rights movement of the fifties and sixties was just getting under way. In ten years' time Baldwin would be a celebrity and *Notes of a Native Son* would be commonly assigned in college English courses.

Baldwin dedicated *Notes* to his sister Paula. The book did not sell well and was soon remaindered. But when it reappeared in paperback in 1957, after the publication of *Giovanni's Room*, it sold briskly and has continued to be among the most popular of Baldwin's works. In spite of the reservations of Langston Hughes, the reviews were largely enthusiastic. One reviewer went so far as to see in *Notes* proof that Baldwin was "the most eloquent Negro writing today."

CHAPTER 11

The Amen Corner

It's a awful thing to think about, the way love never dies.
—Sister Margaret

Early spring 1955 found Baldwin at Yaddo longing for the city and ready for still another try with Lucien. He returned to the New York apartment, but Lucien now had a life of his own there. He had begun painting, he had a circle of friends, and he was decidedly not interested in playing the role of lover to Jimmy. One day he brought home a drinking buddy, an African-American musician named Arnold. Arnold and Jimmy immediately related on a level that excluded Lucien, and before long they became lovers. Anger at Lucien and desperation as well as physical attraction motivated Baldwin. Arnold enjoyed Jimmy's company and, like so many of his lovers, was willing to accept a sexual relationship to keep it. The two men fought a great deal even in the early stages of their relationship, but for the moment Jimmy was "in love" and began to think of ways to send Lucien back to Suzy. His presence in the apartment with Jimmy and Arnold created a strain that was becoming intolerable. Meanwhile, the opportunity for a change of scene developed.

Owen Dodson, a writer and the director of the Howard University Players in Washington, D.C., was looking early in 1955 for a play by a black playwright to be performed by his players in May. A friend told him about *The Amen Corner* and he contacted Baldwin at Yaddo. Although an amateur group, the Howard Players had a professional reputation, and Baldwin liked what he heard about Dodson. He had been trying without success to sell the idea of a professional production of *The Amen Corner*, but there was "no market" for a play about a storefront church in Harlem. Now at least there would be an opportunity for the play to be performed. He accepted Dodson's invitation to assist in the production, and in May he went to Washington, began attending rehearsals, and revised the play for the stage. It ran from May 11 to 14 at Howard's Spaulding Hall and was attended by such notables as E. Franklin Frazier, Sterling Brown, and Alain Locke. The Baldwin family came from New York in a car rented and driven by Lucien.

The plot of *The Amen Corner* centers on the struggle of a pentecostal minister, Sister Margaret, and her wayward musician husband for the soul of their son David. On the surface, Sister Margaret has a direct autobiographical source in Mother Horn, the minister who presided over Baldwin's own "salvation." An outsider as a female in a male-dominated profession, Mother Horn—like the famous Mother Robinson in Philadelphia—ran a highly combative ministry, "praying" a neighboring pool hall and a nearby liquor-dispensing shop out of business and struggling to keep her congregation—perhaps especially the men—in line. Her first husband, Mr. Artemis, a musician, died of tuberculosis. The connections between Mother Horn and Sister Margaret are clear enough.

In the course of the play Margaret loses her church, her husband dies, and David steps out into the world against his mother's will. Margaret is confronted by the terrible cost of choosing safety over engagement in life. The "saint" is forced to acknowledge the presence in herself of a longing for the love of another individual that years of marriage to "the Lord" have not stamped out.

The Amen Corner stands with "Notes of a Native Son" as a continuation of the story of the Baldwin hero begun in *Go Tell It on the Mountain.* John Grimes in *Mountain,* the narrator in "Notes," and David in *Amen* all embody the inner world of James Baldwin, wrestling with the significance of his heritage. Through John's struggle in *Mountain,* Baldwin had successfully turned a hated stepfather into a vehicle for his own awakening to prophecy. Baldwin develops this theme in "Notes," using his relationship with his stepfather as the determining factor in his own escape from despair and self-destruction. In *The Amen Corner* David faces his father's experience, learns from him as from a prophet, and accepts his love; and it is this experience, this lesson, and this acceptance from which he draws the strength to challenge the safety of a prolonged childhood and to step into the dangers of life as an artist.

In his introduction to the published version of *Amen* in 1968, Baldwin looks back at the days of the play's composition. He remembers that the first line he wrote is now one spoken by Sister Margaret in act 3: "It's a awful thing to think about, the way love never dies."

This is a line, he suggests, that, like the whole play, "says a great deal about" its author. In writing it, he was concerned with "the terrifying desolation of my private life" and also with "the great burdens carried by my father." Baldwin was able, "at last, to recognize the nature of the dues he had paid."

As he assimilated his stepfather's larger cultural significance into the role of Luke, Baldwin expressed the significance of his mother's life in the character of Sister Margaret, taking off where he had left Elizabeth in *Mountain*. Margaret's situation is in a sense that of the ghetto mother in general. In creating her, Baldwin recognized "the stratagems [his mother] was forced to use to save her children." Berdis Baldwin's dilemma, like Sister Margaret's, was "how to treat her husband and her son as men and at the same time to protect them from the bloody consequences of trying to be a man in this society."

In the character of David, Baldwin clearly is considering his own condition as a teenager vis-a-vis the church and home. David, like his author at age seventeen, leaves the church and home on the same day. He leaves with the intention of becoming a musician. Baldwin had left to become a writer. In his act 2 scene with Luke, David describes the struggle between the church and his need to express himself sexually and artistically. Baldwin had had such conversations with friends like his schoolmate Emile Capouya at a similar stage in his own life.

But on an autobiographical level, it is not so much his early departure that Baldwin is recording in David's rebellion as it is his later departure for Paris. In the introduction to *Amen* Baldwin himself makes this connection by bringing the whole question of his "exile" into his discussion of the genesis of his play. In the course of this discussion he uses words to explain his flight to Paris that apply as well to his and his character David's reasons for leaving home: "I left because my homeland would not allow me to grow in the only direction in which I could grow."

Baldwin had felt a great deal of guilt, first about leaving the church and later about leaving his mother with the burden of a large family. In letters during the 1950s to his mother and his brother David, he repeatedly attempts to justify what he fears must seem like his desertion of his family.

In act 3 of *Amen* David says it all in a speech to his mother, Sister Margaret, who cannot understand his desire to leave the church and home for a dubious career as a musician: "If I stayed here—I'd end up worse than Daddy—because I wouldn't be doing what I know I got to do. . . . I love you both!—but I've got my work to do."

And then David says something that seems to tie his new life as a musician with a larger mission. He articulates the connection between his author's need to write and the prophetic quest reflected in such scenes as the flashbacks of *Go Tell It on the Mountain* and the incidents recorded in "Notes of a Native Son": "Every time I play," he says, "every time I listen, I see Daddy's face and yours, and so many faces—who's going to speak for all that, Mama? Who's going to speak for all of us?"

It is David's father, Luke, who brings his son to this realization. He is another, more benevolent and sympathetic expression of the lesson that had emanated from the dead stepfather in "Notes." David's deathbed conversation with Luke is the one Jimmy wished he could have had with his stepfather in that hospital on Long Island. Luke's story dramatizes a conflict that by the 1950s has become Baldwin's primary concern, the conflict between safety and love.

In the larger organism that is Baldwin's overall literary output, Luke prepares us for the next major work, *Giovanni's Room*. The crucial moments are during the conversation in act 2 when Luke and David confront their relationship. Luke lectures David on the necessity of engagement with life: "Son—don't try to get away from the things that hurt you—sometimes that's all you got." David responds with an outcry against the safety of the church. When he discovered music and his ability to make music he began to realize that safety was smothering him, rendering him dysfunctional: "Even when I tried to make it with a girl—something kept saying, Maybe this is a sin."

The Baldwin message is clear: to be safe is to deny the emergence of one's music, one's own song, one's self. "I don't care what kind of life he lives," says Luke to Margaret about their son, "—as long as it's *his* life. . . . I ain't going to let you make him safe." And Luke adds another essential Baldwin ingredient: No one ever became himself "without somebody loved him." The Lord, for Luke, is not in the church, but in the people, the pain, the struggle, the sheer messiness of real life—in the love of one person for the other in mind, soul, and body. Sister Margaret learns this lesson when Luke dies and she realizes the emptiness of the safety she has so desperately nurtured as a "saint," when she realizes that all she ever really wanted was Luke: "It's a awful thing to think about, the way love never dies."

The play was a success, but people complained of its language.

Baldwin overheard one person suggest, "This play will set back the Speech Department for thirty years." He was, if anything, pleased with that particular criticism. It made him popular with those at Howard who felt there was such a thing as "Negro English" and that such English had a place on a college campus. And he was thrilled by the experience of immediate public recognition and reaction. Reviews in the Washington papers were enthusiastic. Baldwin felt he could be a playwright now and began again trying to make arrangements for a professional production of *Amen.*

The Howard interval was of great importance to Baldwin. Not only did the university provide him with his first experience in the theater, it gave him his first taste of academic life. Howard was, in fact, the first American university Baldwin had ever visited, and as a child of the ghetto and a habitué of bohemia, he was surprised at how much he enjoyed the experience. He especially liked the people he encountered in Washington, among them LeRoi Jones (later Amiri Baraka), a student at Howard, and the scholar Richard Long, whom he met at Owen Dodson's apartment. Long would become a close friend and confidant, with whom Baldwin usually stayed when he traveled to Atlanta in the 1970s and 1980s.

He was deeply and favorably impressed by two Howard faculty members who befriended him and became for the moment his primary mentors. E. Franklin Frazier, the sociologist, and Sterling Brown, the poet and literary critic, were well-known scholars who treated the young playwright as a serious voice who could be a positive influence on the academic community as well as in the world at large. Baldwin reacted well to these two men because, like Beauford Delaney, they gave him moral support, but more important, he admired and respected them for the power of their minds, and he felt a special connection with them. They were not white intellectuals admiring his "surprising" ability to articulate his condition, they were not followers who enjoyed the whirl of days and nights in his presence, and they were not white liberals who urged him to stay on in America writing books that would improve the image of "his people." They were black intellectuals who had, as he liked to say, "paid their dues" and who demanded intellectual rigor.

Sterling Brown, especially, became for Baldwin during those weeks in Washington, and continued to be until he died, an intellectual father substitute for whom Baldwin had an almost adulatory admiration. He remembered long sessions in Brown's office at Howard: Brown, professorial, pipe in mouth, surrounded by books, lecturing the younger man, who sat sometimes on the floor—literally at his feet. Baldwin always said that Sterling Brown made him "see" what his stepfather, another southerner, could not articulate about the South—the gun-toting streetcar conductors, the fear on summer nights, the lynchings.

Baldwin's feelings had been briefly hurt by some people at Howard who suggested that as a northerner he could not possibly understand the problems of Washington, D.C., let alone the South. Brown reassured him but suggested the importance of his visiting the South, something Baldwin would do after more visits with his mentor during his next trip to the States, in 1957. At the same time, it was Brown who encouraged Baldwin to live in Paris if Paris was a place in which he felt comfortable, a place in which he could write.

Brown supported his young friend against those who accused him of "setting back the Speech Department" with his use of African-American speech patterns in *The Amen Corner*. He had incorporated such patterns into his own poetry and understood what Baldwin was doing. Find your own way, he advised; don't be anyone's "spokesman"; give us real books—a "five-foot shelf" of them, not "a pile of slogans and manifestoes." This was just the kind of advice the writer of "Everybody's Protest Novel" wanted.

After the *Amen* production Baldwin asked Owen Dodson if, joined by Arnold, he could stay on for a while to do some revisions on *Amen* and to make some last-minute changes on "Notes of a Native Son." He wanted to work on a new short story, "Sonny's Blues," too, which was based in part on Arnold, who was himself, like Sonny—and like Luke and David in *Amen*—a musician. He needed Arnold's company, ostensibly to serve as a catalyst for the composition of the story, and to work as his typist on the *Amen* rewrites. Dodson agreed to put both men up temporarily, but was surprised when Arnold arrived with a guitar and two footlockers and announced, "I'm here to stay."

A very private and somewhat fastidious man, Dodson soon began to chafe under the constant presence of Arnold and Jimmy. The guitar playing was entertaining, and he and his friends enjoyed hearing Baldwin read aloud from portions of new works, especially "Sonny's Blues" and *Giovanni's Room*, but his guests' irregular hours interfered with his life, and their lack of funds for household expenses was placing a strain on his own pocketbook. In addition to food, Arnold drank two quarts of milk a day, and Baldwin required a daily fifth of vodka. After a particularly unpleasant scene in which

Dodson shouted at the top of his lungs, "Get out! You niggers leave my house. I don't care whether you are going to be the greatest writer in the world, I am finished," Jimmy and Arnold left for the Dunbar Hotel, where they lived for several weeks on hot dogs.

Baldwin understood Dodson's irritation and knew he should leave Washington, but he felt trapped. He had no money and now no apartment in New York. Lucien was surviving there by "crashing" with acquaintances in the Village and with Baldwin family members uptown. Baldwin had made progress with *Giovanni's Room* at Yaddo, but he still had work to do on it and knew that it would be no easy matter selling it to a publisher. He also had doubts, later confirmed, as to whether he would be able to sell *The Amen Corner* in any form. He sent the revised manuscript to Gordon Heath in Paris—he hoped Heath would play Luke in a professional production—with instructions that he take it to a British producer for consideration. Heath's mission came to nothing.

In desperation Baldwin wrote his close friend Mary Painter requesting that she send Lucien money to return to Switzerland. He wrote to his mother wondering whether a Washington woman she knew might be willing to put him up in return for odd jobs, and asking her to get David to send him five dollars.

He tried to concentrate on *Giovanni's Room*, but money problems and fights with Arnold made work difficult. He turned, as he was to do with increasing frequency during the rest of his life, to his brother David. He wrote to him suggesting that they buy a house on Long Island through a GI loan, since David had served in Korea. It would be a house where anyone in the family might live, but especially Jimmy, his mother, and Paula. Jimmy, of course, would spend much of the time abroad in order to remove himself from the pressure of friends who did not seem to understand the fact that he had a mission that rendered him lonely and vulnerable and neither safe, respectable, married, well employed, nor happy: "I'm not really interested in being what Americans call 'happy.' " All that was important was his commitment to his art. For Baldwin, pursuing his mission meant, for the time being, living in Paris; he was not yet ready to face America squarely.

There was also a more personal reason for returning to France. Arnold was more restless than ever. In fact, he did little typing and found the penniless days in Washington not particularly exciting. Like most of Jimmy's lovers, he began to make his own friends, many of them women, whose company he seemed to prefer to that of a man, who spent most nights at the typewriter. Baldwin wrote to David of his longing—once associated particularly with Lucien—for domestic stability. What he most wanted was someone with whom he could be simply himself: not James Baldwin the author, but "a scared little boy from Harlem who's out here scuffling."

Jimmy hoped a change of scene would help matters. The lure of foreign travel might rekindle Arnold's interest. Perhaps he would become the domestic lover of his fantasies. He would take Arnold to Paris.

Mary Painter did send money, and Lucien left for Switzerland in September. Jimmy and Arnold returned to New York, where Baldwin managed to finish a very rough draft of *Giovanni's Room*. His friend Bill Cole, the publicist, was away when the manuscript arrived at Knopf, and two editors, apparently in consultation with Alfred Knopf himself, decided that the book's homosexual theme would make it too controversial. A black writer was one thing; a black homosexual writer was simply too much for the public to bear.

Still, the delivery of *Notes of a Native Son* to Beacon and the sale of the title essay to *Harper's Magazine* brought in a little money, and in September, Baldwin, with Arnold, set sail once again for France. From the ship he wrote to David apologizing for a somewhat abrupt departure: for him, crossing the ocean was "beginning to be rather like going to Brooklyn."

CHAPTER 12

A Period of Transition

I can't live there no mo'.
—old song

Baldwin's return to Paris in October of 1955 was mildly triumphant. He did not have Lucien, but he did have Arnold, he had some money, and soon the positive reviews of *Notes of a Native Son* began to appear.

Through a friend, Baldwin found a small apartment of his own at 119, avenue de Versailles, and at first things went well. Jimmy took a genuine interest in Arnold's career. He always felt more comfortable introducing his lovers as fellow artists and did his best to see that they were in some way productive. Lucien was encouraged to paint, as were several later friends. One lover was provided with a camera and became a reasonably successful photographer. Another was supported in his interest in mime. Often the ambition was Baldwin's rather than the lover's.

It was Jimmy's hope that Arnold would succeed as a jazz musician in the Paris clubs. But Arnold had left his vibraphone in New York at his family's house, having learned to prefer the guitar, an instrument in no particular demand at jazz clubs. Jimmy was persistent; he wrote home asking David to retrieve the vibraphone and to send it C.O.D. to Paris. Arnold did make an attempt in the club world but, musical talent aside, he had emotional problems—traceable to a ghetto childhood, drugs, alcohol, and mistreatment in the army, and a resentment of his benefactor—which made perseverance difficult.

Plans for *The Amen Corner* were progressing. Owen Dodson, friendly again, wrote Baldwin that *The New York Times* had announced a fall production of the play in New York. This was a production that had been talked up by a friend who had connections with the Phoenix Theater. It did not materialize, but for the moment Baldwin was hopeful. He foresaw a London version, too, and planned a trip there to pursue that matter and the possible publication of *Giovanni's Room.*

The London visit took place in November. Mary Painter accompanied him for moral and financial support. But by November the optimism of the month before had begun to wane, and Baldwin was once again edging back towards his chronic depression. He wrote to David from London generally bemoaning his situation. People in America seemed to consider his work immoral or offensive, and the English would probably agree.

He goes on in the letter to reveal another source of his depression. The old guilt about having deserted his family is still with him; he apologizes for not having seen more of David and the family before leaving New York and goes to great lengths to explain the fact that he is not ashamed of his family or his Harlem origins. He assures David and the others of his love. Although it might appear that his intention has been to exclude his family from his seemingly "glamorous" Greenwich Village/Paris life, nothing could be further from the truth. When he had left home originally, he had believed he could succeed quickly as a writer and that his family would benefit. He was sorry that things had not worked out as planned and that he was causing pain to his family, but he had to keep trying.

And there was another issue. In New York he was increasingly recognized as a homosexual, and Baldwin still had enough of the preacher's outlook to want to "shield" his mother from the "details of my peculiarly lonely life." Baldwin hoped that David would understand the connection between his being true to his sexual nature and his being true to his vocation. David could be a loving buffer between his ostensibly disreputable life and his family's love and respect. This was always to be one of David's roles. Baldwin's concern about his family's feelings towards him worried him particularly now, because he feared they might be embarrassed by the forthcoming novel *Giovanni's Room.*

In a letter to his mother his tone was equally apologetic but also much more explanatory. Baldwin tended to use letters to his mother as a vehicle to explain to her and to himself the inner reality of the writer's mission. He was born, he said, to translate the painful human experience into art. He might not be a saint of the church any longer, but his mother could be reassured that he was still in the service of some power for good beyond himself, that his mission was sacred. He begged her to believe in him and his mission. He was "swimming . . . in this deep, red sea," burdened by a "dreadful responsibility" that had literally consumed his being, as the whale—and God—had consumed the prophet Jonah. It was a responsibility that had isolated him from his friends and his family and from simple "peace."

In London things suddenly took a turn for the better. *The Amen Corner* failed to interest publishers or producers, but Michael Joseph, the publisher of *Mountain*, liked and agreed to bring out *Giovanni's Room* in spite of the risk of public outcry. Michael Joseph himself had so much faith in Baldwin that he pledged to publish not only *Giovanni* but anything else he might write. The association with his British publisher was to remain the most congenial of Baldwin's professional relationships. Finally, almost immediately upon his return to Paris he received a letter from Helen Strauss announcing that *Giovanni* had been accepted in New York by a small publishing house called Dial Press. This publishing relationship, though less congenial than the one with Michael Joseph, was to play a significant role throughout Baldwin's career. He would react with particular favor to James Silberman, his first editor at Dial.

In spite of some success, however, the first months of 1956 were difficult. Increasingly nagged by a sense that he was wasting his life in Paris, Baldwin was acutely aware of the developing civil rights movement in the States and of his distance from it. On the thirty-first of May the year before, the Supreme Court had reinforced its *Brown* ruling by ordering school integration "with all deliberate speed." The racist murder of fourteen-year-old Emmett Till in Money, Mississippi, had taken place just before Baldwin left New York. The lynching and the acquittal of the killers would fester in his mind until the writing of *Blues for Mister Charlie*. In December 1955 a black seamstress and NAACP official, Rosa Parks, had been arrested for refusing to give up her seat to a white man on a Montgomery, Alabama, bus, thus triggering a massive bus boycott led by a twenty-six-year-old black minister named Martin Luther King, Jr. In January, King's home had been damaged by a bomb. In February, Autherine Lucy, a black woman, had been admitted to the University of Alabama and then expelled after a riot. The struggle between the new White Citizens Councils and King's nonviolent, passive-resistance movement was obviously having a profound effect on the American scene. It was hard not to be there, and to make matters worse, the fights with Arnold created an atmosphere not conducive to writing. And he missed Lucien again.

Baldwin began to face the American problem by making tentative plans to return to the States to work on a biography of Booker

T. Washington and a "slave novel" tentatively entitled *Talking at the Gates*. Later he would describe this novel in outline form in an application for a Ford Foundation grant. It would address the so tragically denied bonds between black and white Americans, a subject he had treated in the essays of *Notes of a Native Son*.

Baldwin also had commissions to write two articles, one a long review for *The Nation* of Daniel Guérin's *Negroes on the March* and J. C. Furnas's *Goodbye to Uncle Tom*, and the other an essay for *Partisan Review* on William Faulkner and racism. He turned to the review and the essay with enthusiasm, and both appeared later in the year.

In "The Crusade of Indignation," the review article, Baldwin once again takes up the question of *Uncle Tom's Cabin* and suggests that in its sentimental portraits it "has set the tone for the attitude of American whites towards Negroes for the last one hundred years." He then merges the question of racism with the question of self-identity, which had always been his concern and had been most fully treated in the context of homosexuality in *Giovanni's Room*. The African-American has been regarded in stereotype rather than as a human being, and, says Baldwin, one can only begin to recognize another's humanity "by taking a hard look at oneself."

"Faulkner and Desegregation" was written in answer to an unfortunate March 1956 interview in *The Reporter* in which Faulkner, a man Baldwin greatly admired as a writer, made his famous remark about having to side with his fellow white Mississippians in a hypothetical war over desegregation "even if it meant going out into the streets and shooting Negroes." Baldwin's response is an attack on the "middle-of-the-road," "go slow" mentality that he felt Faulkner represented:

> Faulkner—among so many others!—is so plaintive concerning this "middle of the road" from which "extremist" elements of both races are driving him that it does not seem unfair to ask just what he has been doing there until now. Where is the evidence of the struggle he has been carrying on there on behalf of the Negro? . . . Why—and how—does one move from the middle of the road where one was aiding Negroes into the streets—to shoot them?

Baldwin was returning to his form as a spokesman. He was shedding what he now saw as sentimental literary preferences in favor of judgements based on the role of art as an agent of social change. In some sense he was preparing for the trip to the American South that Sterling Brown had suggested he must finally make if he was to understand the civil rights movement. The major part of the Faulkner essay is not so much an attack against Faulkner as a preliminary examination of the South itself. The problem with the South—and the South is only an extreme version of the American nation—is that "it clings to two entirely antithetical doctrines, two legends, two histories." The southerner is "the proud citizen of a free society and, on the other hand, is committed to a society that has not yet dared to free itself of the necessity of naked and brutal oppression." The liberal "middle-of-the-road" southern position asks for time.

> But the time Faulkner asks for does not exist—and he is not the only Southerner who knows it. There is never time in the future in which we will work out our salvation. The challenge is in the moment, the time is always now.

This was a prophecy that made sense in the context of the nation to which Baldwin would soon return, the South to which he would travel, and the novel he had just completed. It might be safer to remain in the middle of the road in regard to sexuality and race relations, but the middle of the road was not an honorable place.

Having committed himself to a return to America in 1957, Baldwin would like to have enjoyed what he thought would be his last year in France, and he hoped to finish the new novel he was working on before turning to what he knew would be a totally new existence for him in America. The novel would become *Another Country*.

The spring of 1956 brought several good things his way. On April 8 he sent off the final version of *Giovanni's Room*, and on May 23 he was awarded a grant by the National Institute of Arts and Letters in recognition of his creative work—"for the excellent directness of his prose style and for the combination of objectivity and passion with which he approaches his subject matter," as the certificate signed by Malcolm Cowley announced. He asked Knopf friend Bill Cole to take his mother and David to the ceremony to receive the award for him. That night in Paris, Beauford Delaney, Arnold, Mary Painter, and Jimmy had dinner together at Mary's to celebrate the occasion. Baldwin's satisfaction with finally being properly recognized was heightened by still another prize, this one a support grant from *Partisan Review*. He suddenly had some $4,000—more than he had ever possessed. He wrote to his mother announcing that some of the money would be sent to her.

Another bright spot in Baldwin's life—although a temporary one—was a friendship with Norman and Adele Mailer that began at the Paris apartment of the novelist and translator Jean Malaquais. The Mailers and Baldwin saw a lot of each other during the summer of 1956, Baldwin acting the part of Parisian guide, especially to late-night clubs. The Mailers enjoyed meeting Jimmy's and Arnold's jazz musician friends, and Mailer helped his new friend by writing a favorable prepublication comment about *Giovanni's Room*. But Mailer criticized Baldwin for being an expatriate, thus touching a particularly sore point. The tension between the two men would increase over the years.

By late summer of 1956 Baldwin had an emotional relapse of sorts. He was sure now that the relationship with Arnold could not last. In a 1961 *Esquire* article, "The Black Boy Looks at the White Boy," he describes how he spent his nights that summer drinking in "low-life" bars looking for sex, how each morning he returned home to the new novel that refused to take form. Real despair seemed about to overtake him. He had achieved some success, but the prospect of the money he had sought for so long now seemed dull, because his "private life had failed." Not only was the affair with Arnold about to end, but love itself seemed to be "over." He could foresee only a series of "fantastically unreal alternatives to my pain," a desperate loneliness and obsession with self, with sexual and racial isolation. Appropriately, Baldwin would include the *Esquire* essay in a volume called *Nobody Knows My Name*. He wondered whether it was all worth it: "*How*, indeed, would I be able to keep on working if I could never be released from the prison of my egocentricity? By what act could I escape this horror?"

As he looked back on this period, Baldwin saw this crisis as signifying the death of his early idealism about love and success. He had had success and he had had love and he was still a prisoner of his particular condition, his particular inheritance. For an artist at this point in his life who saw despair and inactivity where there had once been optimism and action, this was the most terrible of moments, a time for insanity, or "suicide"—or "good works" and "politics."

Baldwin would eventually take the path of good works and a kind of politics by returning to America for some of the major events of the civil rights movement. But first he chose suicide. One evening, after a particularly unpleasant fight with Arnold, he took an overdose of sleeping pills. Almost instantly horrified by what he had done, he phoned Mary Painter, who rushed to the avenue de Versailles with a friend and forced him to vomit before the doctor got there.

Suicide formed a strange leitmotif in Baldwin's life, extending back to that rooftop conversation when he was thirteen, and there had been the "hanging" in the Left Bank hotel in 1949. There would be other somewhat halfhearted attempts later. The suicidal tendency usually emerged during long periods of depression, and the incidents were in almost every instance preceded by a major fight with a lover.

The 1956 suicide attempt had a temporary cathartic effect. Jimmy had given full voice to his depression, and Arnold, frightened by what Jimmy had done, responded with what at least seemed to be love. Jimmy decided on a trip to Corsica, where he would try to finish *Another Country*. He knew that he would have to send Arnold away to lead his own life. But, having made these decisions, he felt better.

Before leaving for Corsica late in September, Baldwin covered the Congrès des Ecrivains et Artistes Noirs (Conference of Negro-African Writers and Artists) for *Preuves* and *Encounter*. The conference was essentially an expression of an intellectual movement called *Négritude*, a movement dominated by two African poets, Léopold Senghor from Senegal and Aimé Césaire from Martinique. Baldwin's essay on it was called "Princes and Powers."

Baldwin found the conference a disappointment. It was ironical that in their emphasis on African originality the speakers were so clearly French in their approach. Senghor talked nostalgically about the creative interdependence between the African poet and his audience, yet here he was in Paris, speaking French, composing poetry in French. By this time Baldwin had faced the irony of his own connections with France while Rosa Parks and Martin Luther King and black children were challenging racism in the streets, schools, and buses of the American South. In fact, it seems clear that much of the pique that is evident in "Princes and Powers" can be traced to Baldwin's own feelings of inadequacy and guilt in the face of the looming racial struggle. A message to the conference from W. E. B. Du Bois, who had been denied a passport by the State Department, elicited irritation: "Any American Negro traveling abroad today must either not care about Negroes or say what the State Department wishes him to say," wrote Du Bois.

For Baldwin, and probably for Richard Wright, John Davis, and the other members of the American delegation, to whom Wright had introduced Baldwin, the message from Du Bois was "ill-considered."

Not only did it undermine the American presence at the conference, it contributed to the already deep African misunderstanding as to the nature and situation of African-Americans. The failure of understanding was evident, Baldwin felt, when Senghor in his speech stressed the African heritage of Richard Wright's *Black Boy*: "In so handsomely presenting Wright with his African heritage, Senghor rather seemed to be taking away his identity." *Black Boy* descended from Africa rather in the way *A Tale of Two Cities* derived from Aeschylus. The connection in terms of the real experience revealed in the book "did not seem very important." *Black Boy* was "one of the major American autobiographies" and could be understood only in the context of the peculiarly American experience. The leaders of the conference were trying to assimilate black American experience into the theory of *Négritude*, and Baldwin resented the attempt.

For him, even Wright was guilty of putting theory before common sense. In his speech, Wright defended the questionable political means that Africans would use to unify their countries, claiming that eventually dictators, having accomplished their missions, would voluntarily give up power. "He did not say what would happen then, but I supposed it would be the second coming."

After the conference Baldwin traveled to the village of Ile-Rousse in Corsica, the hometown of Mme Dumont from the Hôtel Verneuil. Here he stayed, but for a few short trips to Paris, for some six months at the home of a friend, Mario Garcia. His arrival in Corsica coincided with the publication of *Giovanni's Room* in New York.

CHAPTER 13

Giovanni's Room

Set me as a seal upon thine heart . . .
for love is strong as death.
—Song of Solomon 8:6

The novel for Baldwin was as appropriate a vehicle for prophesying and witnessing as the essay was. The method in his novels is consistent. In each of them Baldwin uses clearly traceable events from his own life as a basis for fictional explorations of and sometimes almost allegorical depictions of his philosophy of life. The novels are best described as modern parables—or as segments of a long parable—in which the central figures are tortured perpetrators or victims of those personal limitations and larger social problems that are the author's particular concern.

In a 1974 interview Baldwin spoke of the connection between the characters in his novels. Johnny in *Go Tell It on the Mountain* becomes both Giovanni and David in *Giovanni's Room*, he suggests, and he notes links between such characters as Richard in *Mountain*, Rufus in *Another Country*, Richard in *Blues for Mister Charlie*, and Giovanni in *Giovanni's Room*, each of whom is a victim, a symbolic cadaver in the center of the world depicted in the given novel and the larger society symbolized by that world. Other characters, like Leo in *Tell Me How Long the Train's Been Gone* and Fonny in *If Beale Street Could Talk*, he sees as related victims who have nonetheless found some reason for remaining alive in the social prison in which they find themselves.

By the time he wrote *Giovanni's Room* the parable had already been established as Baldwin's fictional vehicle. In *Go Tell It on the Mountain* he had used a set of autobiographical characters and situations to develop a metaphor for the emergence of his identity as an artist and for the emergence of the African-American's identity through the necessary confrontation with and assimilation of his history. *Mountain* is a portrait of the young artist reaching for identity in his own ethnic environment. In that novel of adolescent life there is a clear sense that religion is merely to be a stepping-stone for the Baldwin hero, as it had been historically for the African-American. And the potentially alienating sexuality that foments below the surface of John's feelings for the seemingly heterosexual Elisha points to a larger social problem still to be confronted, the whole question of the social effects of sexual dishonesty or the denial of love.

Love is at the heart of the Baldwin philosophy. Love for Baldwin cannot be safe; it involves the risk of commitment, the risk of removing the masks and taboos placed on us by society. The philosophy applies to individual relationships as well as to more general ones. It encompasses sexuality as well as politics, economics, and race relations. And it emphasizes the dire consequences, for individuals and racial groups, of the refusal of love.

Giovanni's Room takes up this question. It is a novel about safety as opposed to honor, about the innocence that fills the vacuum of noninvolvement as opposed to the freedom that comes with the loss of such innocence. It is a story of the search for identity in the context of social alienation. The fact that the particular type of alienation in question has a homosexual base and is placed in a Parisian context with "all-white" characters should not deter us from an understanding that alienation can, for example, be racial and American. Where, through Johnny in *Mountain*, Baldwin tells us the story of his own and black America's confrontation with heritage and history, in *Giovanni's Room* he uses David as a vehicle for his confrontation with himself, and he uses Giovanni as a metaphorical or symbolic vehicle for his and black America's confrontation with the white world. *Giovanni's Room* as an "all-white" novel is not a bastard among the literary offspring of James Baldwin; it is one of the more impassioned expressions of the story he told all his life.

The point of view in *Giovanni's Room* is that of David, a young American who, during the temporary absence of his fiancée from Paris, becomes involved, through the Saint-Germain homosexual set, with a young Italian barman named Giovanni. The attraction of Giovanni is for David a calling, something he cannot at first resist, a "ferocious excitement that burst in me like a storm," and Giovanni is revealed in words that suggest religious power. He is the vehicle of the Baldwin Word. Later, after Giovanni is dead, David remembers the man he has betrayed:

> Until I die there will be those moments, moments seeming to rise up out of the ground like Macbeth's witches, when his face will come before me, that face in all its changes, when the exact timbre of his voice and tricks of his speech will nearly burst my ears, when his smell will overpower my nostrils. . . . I will see Giovanni again, as he was that night, so vivid, so winning, all of the light of that gloomy tunnel trapped around his head.

These are the words and memories of a Judas, and Giovanni's room itself is a symbol, a symbol of the paradoxical gift offered, the enveloping and overpowering gift of freedom that is so hard to accept. David's fiancée, Hella, understands the paradox and is willing to accept it through marriage with David: "I began to realize . . . that I wasn't free, that I couldn't be free until I was attached—no, *committed*—to someone." David, however, attempts to attach himself to Hella not to achieve real freedom but to avoid it by refusing the call of Giovanni and his room: "Nothing is more unbearable, once one has it, than freedom. I suppose this is why I asked her to marry me."

David is right to fear this freedom, but wrong to refuse it. It is true that the room is confining and demanding. In it one cannot escape the dirt of life, the vulnerability of love. *Giovanni's Room* tells of a man who cannot accept his own feelings, his own self, who fears the "room" towards which he is drawn and denies the figure who gives it life and could give him freedom. To freedom he prefers the safety of relationships that do not touch the soul. David is incapable of treating Hella as a woman or Giovanni as a man. As David leaves Giovanni to go off with Hella, Giovanni preaches to him in words that are as much the author's as his own. They are words that apply not only to David but to the larger world he represents:

> You are not leaving me for a *woman*. If you were really in love with this little girl, you would not have had to be so cruel to me. . . . You do not . . . love anyone! You never have loved anyone, I am sure you never will! You love purity, you love your mirror—you are just like a little virgin. . . . You will never let anyone *touch* it—man *or* woman. You want to be *clean*. You think you came here covered with soap and you think you will go out covered with soap—and you do not want to *stink*. . . . You want to leave Giovanni because he makes you stink. You want to despise Giovanni because he is not afraid of the stink of love. You want to *kill* him in the name of all your lying little moralities. And

> you—you are *immoral*. . . . Look, *look* what you have done to me. Do you think you could have done this if I did not love you? Is *this* what you should do to love?

David's denial of love is horrendously expensive. Indirectly, Giovanni becomes the sacrificial victim of David's inability to accept the taste, the smell, the touch of love, merely because Giovanni is a man and he is a man. And David's "punishment," his hell, is depicted in the last lines of the novel. In the south of France, where he has gone with Hella to escape himself, and his own ambivalence, he tears up the letter that contains the news of Giovanni's fate. Hoping that somehow all of this will blow away, he watches the pieces of the letter "dance in the wind. . . . Yet, as I turn and begin walking toward the waiting people, the wind blows some of them back on me."

David is doomed to relive Giovanni's death—the death of his own real self, his own soul—in every relationship he will ever have. His friend Jacques had warned him: "You play it safe long enough . . . and you'll end up trapped in your own dirty body, forever and forever." *Giovanni's Room*, Baldwin always said, is "not about homosexual love, it's about what happens to you if you're afraid to love anybody."

The relevance of *Giovanni's Room* to subjects other than homosexuality is evident. David is above all an American: "My ancestors conquered a continent, pushing across death-laden plains, until they came to an ocean which faced away from Europe into a darker past." His is the story of a young man who cannot accept the love of an outsider, a dark-skinned man who contains the traces of that "darker past." Asked once if his message was the New Testament commandment "Love your neighbor as yourself," Baldwin replied with a still newer commandment: "If you really love one person, you will love all people."

In later works Baldwin would continue to take up the theme of David's hell. The ability to touch and to love will be the black American weapon against white American self-denial in the novels that follow *Giovanni's Room*. David is representative of the outlook and the failure of white America, and Giovanni is just as clearly the embodiment of what Baldwin sees as the outlook of the black man. "The Americans" are funny, Giovanni says to David.

> You have a funny sense of time—or perhaps you have no sense of time at all. . . . Time always sounds like a parade *chez vous*—a

> *triumphant* parade, like armies with banners entering a town. As though, with enough time . . . and all that fearful energy and virtue you people have, everything will be settled, solved, put in its place. And when I say everything . . . I mean all the serious, dreadful things, like pain and death and love, in which you Americans do not believe.

This is an attack on the white American myth embodied in such terms as the "American Dream," "upward mobility," the "melting pot," the "middle of the road," "Manifest Destiny," and the "work ethic." It will be echoed by any number of black American characters in the later segments of Baldwin's parable.

"I am the man, I suffered, I was there," wrote Walt Whitman. Baldwin chose these words as the epigram for *Giovanni's Room*. They can, of course, be applied to David after the fact of Giovanni's death as well as to Giovanni. The David who speaks to us has achieved wisdom of a sort. He is Judas returned, analyzing his motives and his actions. He is the Ancient Mariner condemned to relive the great tragedy of his life, and he is well aware of his sin and of its source in American values:

> For I am—or was—one of those people who pride themselves on their willpower, on their ability to make a decision and carry it through. This virtue, like most virtues, is ambiguity itself. People who believe that they are strong-willed and the masters of their destiny can only continue to believe this by becoming specialists in self-deception. . . . Perhaps, as we say in America, I wanted to find myself. This is an interesting phrase, not current as far as I know in the language of any other people, which certainly does not mean what it says but betrays a nagging suspicion that something has been misplaced. I think now that if I had had any intimation that the self I was going to find would turn out to be only the same self from which I had spent so much time in flight, I would have stayed home.

In these last words, of course, there is something of the man who would soon write an essay called "The Discovery of What It Means to Be an American," who was examining his own motives for having spent most of the past eight years in France and whose personal life was in a state that made him wonder about the value of his having left home to begin with.

In a letter to Bill Cole, Baldwin takes up the question of *Giovanni's Room* as a book about America and American "loneliness and insecurity" rather than homosexuality. In fact, he had chosen as a main character the most stereotypical of Americans, "the good white Protestant."

As in the case of all Baldwin novels, there is a recognizable and specific autobiographical dimension to *Giovanni's Room. Mountain* grew out of the author's Harlem childhood and his church experience; *Giovanni* is a direct product of the ten years following his leaving home. Baldwin himself said that the novel emerged from his experiences in Greenwich Village and Paris in the forties and fifties. Specifically it reflects his own wrestling with sexual ambivalence. Like David, he had been engaged or nearly engaged. He too, with Grace in the Village, and to a lesser extent with Gidske Anderson and Mary Painter in Paris, had tried to convince himself of his essential heterosexuality. But unlike David, he had willingly accepted the reality represented by Giovanni's room when it came to him in the person of Lucien, to whom he dedicated the novel. Ironically, it was Lucien who married and who, several times over the years, rejected the room to which Jimmy called him and who, in Jimmy's eyes, became David to his Giovanni.

In terms of physical reality, Lucien was Giovanni. Dark-haired and somehow alien, he talked like Giovanni and liked wine and food and love the way Giovanni did. But the soul of Giovanni was Baldwin himself—the man who longed for a lasting relationship and had what can only be called sentimental visions of domesticity with several lovers in the course of his life, but especially with Lucien. Love for Baldwin was contained in the image of the person who would willingly "hold me . . . if I am vomiting . . . if I am dying."

There are, of course, many other autobiographical facts that lie behind the incidents, characters, and situations of *Giovanni's Room.* The catalyst for the homosexual murder at the end of the novel was a newspaper story that had fascinated Baldwin in 1943–44. It involved a Columbia undergraduate named Lucien Carr, who had stabbed and killed an older male friend who had approached him sexually. The adolescent sexual incident between David and Joey is based on a similar encounter the young Baldwin had with an even younger Italian boy in Greenwich Village in the forties. As has been noted earlier, the house in the south of France where David goes to try to begin a life with Hella, only to be confronted by Giovanni's death and his own lie, was inspired by the house near Grasse where Baldwin and his friend Jacques tried unsuccessfully to cement a relationship.

But the autobiographical aspects of the novel are merely bits and pieces, images and faces that Baldwin uses to tell the much deeper story which had raged within him and which he saw raging within the American society of which he felt himself inevitably a part. Ready now to return to America, Baldwin was determined that he would avoid Giovanni's fate, that he would do what he could to turn white America away from David's sin.

Years later, writing about the trip to the American South that followed closely on the publication of *Giovanni's Room*, Baldwin would emphasize "the devastating effect" of the "private life" on "American public conduct." His trip to the South was to bring home to him in unveiled terms the truth he had known all his life and expressed metaphorically in *Giovanni*, the fact that the black American in the context of the so-called "Negro problem" was the scapegoat for the "white problem," and that those who have made him the scapegoat, who have castrated him and hanged him on the trees of the southern roads, "pay for what they do . . . by the lives they lead." Baldwin's subsequent words echo Giovanni's own assessment of David and his nation and suggest the connection between sexuality and public social conduct. They point, as well, to the connection between *Giovanni's Room* and his journey into the social struggle that was beginning to unfold in the America of the mid-1950s: "the South was a riddle which could be read only in the light, or the darkness, of the unbelievable disasters which had overtaken the private life."

Baldwin would explore the still larger ramifications of the riddle explicitly in *Blues for Mister Charlie* and in the short story "Going to Meet the Man." In *Giovanni's Room* the question lurks below the surface of the text.

To Baldwin's great relief, the reviews of *Giovanni's Room* that arrived in Corsica were all good, and no one in his family criticized him for his subject matter or seemed shocked by the sexual preference that he felt the novel revealed. In *The New York Times Book Review* Granville Hicks noted that Baldwin had taken on a highly sensitive subject and had managed to avoid sensationalism in the process, writing "of these matters with . . . dignity and intensity." Mark Schorer went even further, calling the novel "nearly heroic." Others were just as positive. In *The Nation* Nelson Algren wrote, "This novel is more than another report on homosexuality. It is a story of a man who could not make up his mind, one who could not say yes to life. It is a glimpse into the special hell of Genet, told with a driving intensity and horror sustained all the way." With *Giovanni's Room* Baldwin had produced his second successful novel and had proven his ability to treat a variety of subjects with sensitivity and intelligence. Some said he was now a homosexual writer rather than a black writer. But he felt that he was simply a writer. In his next novel he would bring together the two worlds with which he had been associated. He was well into that novel now, but before leaving France, the author of *Giovanni's Room* had to face the reality of a failed love affair.

CHAPTER 14

End of an Era

Just a room and an empty bed
—Bessie Smith,
"Empty Bed Blues"

Baldwin had known for some time that the relationship with Arnold had to end, but he had thought that it was he who would terminate it. Once in Corsica, in October of 1956, however, he had succumbed to the delusion that life with Arnold was, after all, possible and even desirable. Without the distractions of Paris they seemed to be growing close again. Mario Garcia's house, where they were staying, was beautifully located by the sea; the three men enjoyed the same food, the same music, and the same general routine, one that was much less hectic than the life Jimmy and Arnold had lived in Paris. The day began with lunch at noon or so, Jimmy worked in the afternoon, dinner was late, followed by Billie Holiday and Bessie Smith songs on the record player and good brandy, and then a night of work. There seemed a reasonable chance of getting a good portion of the new novel done before returning to the States.

Then Arnold himself announced only a month after their arrival that he had had enough. He wanted to study music in Paris; there was nothing for him in Corsica or, for that matter, anywhere else with Jimmy; he did not want to be anyone's possession.

At first Baldwin reacted defensively, and the fighting was emotionally brutal on both sides. Then a noncommunicative coldness prevailed, and it was during these days that Jimmy thought once again of suicide. But by thinking of it in writing, he somehow deflected the impulse.

The writing in question was a long, confessional journal entry that was as carefully constructed as a draft for a short story. It even had a title, "The Last Days," and it worked for Baldwin as a kind of bridge between David's agony at the end of *Giovanni* and the parable on relationships of various sorts that is *Another Country*. The voice in the piece would find fuller expression in the suicidal Rufus in *Another Country* as well as in the various striving couples of that novel. "The Last Days" also provides direct insight into Baldwin's confrontation at this pivotal moment in his life with the fact of his own personal unhappiness. It is among the most explicit and revealing of his self-examinations.

The writer describes how on an October evening, after learning of Arnold's plans, he left the others listening to Billie Holiday in the living room and went upstairs with his brandy. Still somehow holding on to the glass, as to an anchor, he climbed along the roof of the living room, swung down onto a stone wall, and made his way with difficulty through a patch of briars down to the sea. He finished the brandy, threw the glass into the water, and thought of Virginia Woolf and her walking into the water to her death. He compared the death agony of drowning to the agony of his love affair. The death itself might be rather like the goal that seem unattainable in life. The sea seemed willing to embrace and accept him in a way that the "world" and "life" and "love" had not. Holding his shoes in one hand, he advanced until the water reached his hips, and then he decided to wait. That night's encounter with the sea, he thought, could serve as an appointment for a later, more final meeting when there would be only the sea and Jimmy and no chance of rescue. The sea might digest him and then vomit him up some place where "nobody knew my name." Out of these suicidal thoughts, then, came the title of his next collection of essays.

The most depressing aspect of his current breakup was the fact that although in all likelihood he would, with spiritual and emotional recompense, get over the loss of Arnold, his life seemed to promise a sordid pattern of many Arnolds. In time, he would in all likelihood meet someone else, fall in love again, and find himself sooner or later in some room alone facing the fact of his new lover's desertion. And between the discoveries of love, there would be all the others, the one-night boys brought home to fill the empty spaces in the heart and the bed. These boys would "not matter." But what did it mean to become a man "to whom nothing matters"?

Finally, the writer of "The Last Days" recognized another, related pitfall. He could build a wall around himself made of fame and money. This, he realized, would be the worst possible of options. Perhaps he should not wait for this kind of demise. The sea might be better. Suicide was a clear tendency in Baldwin's personality. It grew out of an essential loneliness that was in turn related to his sexuality and to his mission. On that fateful night in Corsica, however, the call to witness asserted itself at the last minute, and he stepped out of the sea and turned back to *Another Country*. Five days after the abortive suicide, having given Arnold a good deal of money to pursue his studies in Paris, he was writing the Guggenheim Foundation for a grant application.

For the first time in his life, Baldwin lived alone for several months. Arnold was gone, and Garcia spent much of the time away in Paris and elsewhere. Baldwin knew that the Corsica days would mark the end, for the time being, of his expatriation. His thoughts turned often to New York and to his days in the Village. He remembered Grace, he relived the confusing relationships of the forties—the gay lovers, the straight lovers, the women he had slept with. He wondered about himself and he regretted not having pursued the relationship with Eugene Worth. More and more he recognized in Eugene a kindred spirit, and he began to suspect that the route to full recognition of his own agony would come through a confrontation with Eugene's agony. Eugene would be the primary instrument for a central portion of *Another Country*. Baldwin also spent a great deal of time wondering how he could best contribute to the American civil rights struggle. He was, of course, discovering what *Another Country* had to be about. And he was saving himself from despair.

Garcia and a friend came down for Christmas, and Jimmy cooked a turkey for them and two or three villagers. He was always a good cook and took a playful pride in that fact. He announced to his mother that the meal was "a great success." But he was lonely, and once again his mind was on Lucien, who had called from Switzerland with Christmas greetings. Things had been going badly with him, and Jimmy saw the glimmer of a hope that somehow they might someday get back together. The delusion that he could "save" Lucien was never far from his mind.

By the end of the month Jimmy felt he had to get to Paris. There he stayed with Beauford, who was surviving well enough in Clamart under the watchful care of the amorous landlady, Mme Martine. Richard Olney and Bernard Hassell were still nearby, Gordon Heath was at his club, and Jimmy saw Arnold as well. The meeting was not rancorous; Jimmy sympathized with his friend's lack of progress as a musician in Paris. The big disappointment of the Paris visit was the absence of Mary Painter, whose job had taken her to Washington for a time. Also, Paris itself, or at least Jimmy's Paris, had changed. The race problems there had been complicated by the French colonial wars, and they reminded him continually of his need to get home.

Back in Corsica he received news that *Giovanni's Room* had sold six thousand copies in six weeks, was still selling, and was in another printing. As his advance had by now been made up, he was actually in line to earn more money from the book. In March he went back to Paris for the publication of *Giovanni* in French. Meanwhile, he had been approached by theater people in New York about a dramatic version of the novel and by movie people about a treatment he was doing with Sol Stein of "Equal in Paris."

Another Country was moving slowly: the characters in the novel were "hanging around" doing nothing, he told David. He did not like them much but "I suppose I had better face them." Face them he did, but he found that in this novel—more so even than in his earlier work—he was constantly having to face himself, and what he saw he did not much like. The characters in the novel seemed to be insisting on holding back the truth, and he realized this was partly the result of a certain cynicism he knew was developing in himself. It really was time to go home, if for no other reason than to avoid the arrogance that might come with isolation in his European tower. To his mother he wrote of his "responsibility . . . to learn the humility" that would make it possible for him to "publish the truth, sparing no one," including himself.

Philip Rahv at *Partisan Review* wrote to suggest a long piece on the American South, to which Baldwin readily agreed. He promised to be home as soon as *Another Country* was done, and he spoke of his slave novel, for which he now had chosen a new title, *Lead Me to the Rock,* on the theory (though the song the title comes from refers to Christ) that "freedom is a rock."

In June, Baldwin left Corsica for good and returned to Clamart with the intention of leaving for New York. Originally he had planned to sail in the fall, but it was clear now that *Another Country* was a long way from being finished, and there were too many projects waiting in New York for him to simply while away the summer in Paris. Lucien turned up but returned to Switzerland after some inconclusive talk about eventually visiting Jimmy in New York.

Beauford was particularly upset when Jimmy announced his decision to leave. He had begun to drink a great deal and to hear "voices." He became obsessed by the fact that a portrait he had painted of Jimmy in the Village years—the first portrait of Baldwin—

was missing. For some reason Jimmy had left it at Owen Dodson's home in Washington in 1955, while he was working on *The Amen Corner*. Now Dodson seemed unwilling to return it. Beauford was insistent, and Jimmy wrote to David, asking him to intervene. David, too, was unsuccessful, and the portrait has always been the basis of a *cause célèbre* among friends of Dodson, Delaney, and Baldwin. When Baldwin and Dodson had a falling-out over Dodson's belief that Baldwin should have asked him to direct *Blues for Mister Charlie* in 1964, any chance of the picture's being returned was lost. It turned up among Dodson's possessions after his death.

After a brief visit with Edith Piaf, whom he hoped to interview for *Esquire*, Baldwin sailed for New York in July. The early years were over. The prophet had served his apprenticeship; he was returning as a somewhat notorious but clearly successful writer to the place where one of the central dramas of the twentieth century was being played out. He felt anxiety, but he experienced a strange joy as well. He even sensed the attraction of fame.

CHAPTER 15

The Journey South

Lord, you brought me from a long ways off.
—old song

Baldwin's arrival in New York coincided with the *Partisan Review* publication of "Sonny's Blues," a story written mostly in Washington. "Sonny's Blues" can be seen as the prologue to a dominant fictional motif in the overall Baldwin story, the relationship between two brothers that takes much of its energy from the close relationship between James and David Baldwin. The brother motif would be treated later in such novels as *Tell Me How Long the Train's Been Gone* and in *Just Above My Head*, which is in some ways an extended version of "Sonny's Blues."

Like David Baldwin, Sonny's brother, the narrator in "Sonny's Blues," has been in the army, is a married man who struggles to maintain his own life while feeling a strong commitment to save his brother from the precariousness of his life as an artist. Sonny, the jazz musician, is, of course, an aspect of the story's author, a man driven by the need to avoid mental and emotional suffocation in the ghetto so that he can give rein to a "voice" that is desperate to be heard. The struggle Sonny has with addiction is suggestive of Baldwin's with alcohol and Arnold's with drugs. The emotional cost of prophecy is high: "It's not so much to *play*," says Sonny to his brother. "It's to *stand* it, to be able to make it at all. On any level . . . In order to keep from shaking to pieces."

And when the narrator observes Sonny playing in the Village he realizes what it is that the artist faces. Here the narrator serves, in effect, as a mouthpiece for Baldwin's own feelings about the creative process and its cost to the creator:

> Sonny moved, deep within, exactly like someone in torment. I had never before thought of how awful the relationship must be between the musician and his instrument. He has to fill it, this instrument, with the breath of life, his own.

Sonny's brother has a revelation; he sees that the artist, especially the black artist, is a prophet of freedom, not only of freedom for his own race but of freedom for all those suffocating under the repressive blanket of emotional safety and innocence—the Davids of the world of *Giovanni's Room*, the lynchers of the South, to which Baldwin was returning home to visit. For Baldwin the artist was a victim and a savior who "plays" for his very life and for ours. As his brother listened to Sonny, he

> seemed to hear with what burning he had made it [the song] his, with what burning we had yet to make it ours, how we could cease lamenting. Freedom lurked around us and I understood, at last, that he could help us to be free if we would listen, that he would never be free until we did.

The last vision of Sonny is a link to the sense of mission and prophecy that the young Baldwin had felt on his Central Park hill and in his Harlem pulpit. Sonny, reflecting Baldwin's sense of his own role, is a new victim-savior with a new gospel. The narrator watches Sonny take a sip of his drink.

> Then he put it back on top of the piano. For me, then, as they began to play again, it glowed and shook above my brother's head like the very cup of trembling.

During the summer, as he waited for the funding that would make the trip South possible, Baldwin himself was experiencing something of Sonny's agony and was adjusting to the kind of savior-victim persona represented by Sonny. He became moody and withdrawn and underwent one of his many periods of self-examination. He had to confront the fact that, as far as he knew, his expatriation was over. It was in America that he would have to act on what his "journey" to this point had made him. He stayed at his mother's apartment or with friends in the Village. Arnold was back in New

York and that friendship was renewed at a less volatile level than in the Paris days. He spent time with old friends and made new ones. He socialized with Irwin Shaw, Budd Schulberg, James and Gloria Jones, with William Styron, and with composer Lonie Levister, with whom he planned a collaboration on an operatic version of "Sonny's Blues."

Having been disappointed by the negative reaction of Helen Strauss to *Giovanni's Room,* he had hired a new agent, Bob Mills, with whom he stayed sometimes. In the Village he ran into John A. Williams, who was also represented by Mills. Mills later showed the manuscripts of *Night Song, Moody's Squad,* and *Sissie* to Baldwin, who composed a favorable publicity quote for the jacket of *Night Song.* In a letter to Williams both praising and criticizing his work, Baldwin speaks as an established writer lecturing a colleague with an almost professorial air. He reminds Williams that he "knows" the *Night Song* and *Sissie* "scenes," and the people in them. He suggests that Williams's attitude towards his fictional world is ambivalent, that he does not seem to have faced his own feelings about black people. Williams had all the necessary talents to make him a fine writer, but one's writing is a reflection of one's "private life," and the writer can only reveal to the world what he is "willing to face about" himself.

Baldwin was writing to himself as well as to Williams. Something that had long preoccupied him was the writer's responsibility to the "private life." It was a preoccupation that colored his approach to his southern journey.

During the summer of 1957 Baldwin talked incessantly about the South, his fear of it and his sense of his own vulnerability in relation to it. James Silberman, his editor at Dial, a man Baldwin respected for his intelligent suggestions by mail in connection with *Giovanni's Room,* was surprised when he met the author for the first time at a Dial function that summer. Baldwin sat alone in a corner looking worried and distracted. In his first conversation with Silberman he spoke of the fact that he was almost thirty-three and reminded him that this was the age at which Jesus had been crucified.

By September he had backing from both *Partisan Review* and *Harper's Magazine* for pieces on the trip South. The *Harper's* essay would be called "The Hard Kind of Courage" and would be included in *Nobody Knows My Name* as "A Fly in Buttermilk." The *Partisan*

Review article, "A Letter from the South: Nobody Knows My Name," became the title essay for the same collection. Still later, in the seventies, Baldwin would comment on the southern trip in the long autobiographical essay *No Name in the Street.*

These were extraordinary days in the South. Not only had the Supreme Court ordered the desegregation of schools "with all deliberate speed," in November of 1956 it had declared the segregation of buses unconstitutional, and the Montgomery boycott had finally ended. Because of that boycott, Dr. Martin Luther King, Jr., had emerged as the dominant figure in the southern struggle, becoming the first president of the Southern Christian Leadership Conference, founded in February. In May there had been a major civil rights demonstration in Washington, and June marked the beginning of the Tuskegee boycott of city stores in protest against a redistricting that effectively barred blacks from municipal elections. On August 29 Congress passed the first significant civil rights legislation since Reconstruction. In September, when schools were to open, there was open resistance to the Supreme Court's ruling. Everywhere in the South there were demonstrations and bombings. A new elementary school in Nashville was destroyed by a blast after accepting one black child. President Eisenhower would have to send troops to enforce the ruling in Little Rock after white mobs turned on blacks and threatened the safety of the nine black teenagers attempting to go to school at Central High.

Baldwin had been away a long while and realized that before leaving for the South he needed to get a better grasp on the movement than he had been able to gain through the newspapers. He was fortunate, therefore, to have the opportunity to meet and to spend a great deal of time with one of the great African-American intellectuals of his time, Dr. Kenneth Clark. Clark had been moved by *Notes of a Native Son.* Later he would say of Baldwin's work for civil rights, "He impressed me as resembling an Old Testament prophet . . . he was concerned about the future of America. He saw a lack of concern or an inability in this nation to deal ethically with the problem of race." Clark recognized Baldwin as potentially a productive figure in the civil rights movement and provided him with invaluable information on the issues confronting the movement and the prominent figures in it. He told him what he knew of those figures and suggested people he might meet.

On September 9, 1957, Baldwin flew to Washington, D.C., beginning his southern trip with a visit to Sterling Brown. For Baldwin, Brown, like Clark, was a "teacher" whose judgement was completely trustworthy. He went to him as to a father who could connect him somehow with his southern roots and who could help him thus to find his proper place in the struggle for freedom.

Brown was a link to a nightmare world about which Baldwin knew only a little, from bits and pieces of conversation overheard in his childhood, before it had begun to change into another, more modern nightmare. Baldwin had only "seen the photographs," the records of an almost mythological past. Brown recalled the "Negroes hanging from trees" and "might have been one of them." He remembered hearing Booker T. Washington, he remembered the Scottsboro Boys case and followed "the rise and bloody fall of Bessie Smith." These had been "books and headlines in music" for Baldwin, "but it now developed they were also a part of my identity."

Brown cautioned Baldwin to "remember that Southern Negroes had endured things I could not imagine." He warned him of the tension that might exist between blacks of the South and the black reporter from the North. Visit the barbershops and the bars, he urged. And the churches, Baldwin, true to his own past, thought to himself. Finally, Brown suggested somewhat ominously that it might be a good idea to arrive in Charlotte, North Carolina, the first stop on the itinerary, during the day rather than at night.

Baldwin was drawn to Charlotte because of a photograph he had seen of a fifteen-year-old black girl called Dorothy Counts being harassed by an unruly crowd as she attempted to enter a segregated white high school in Charlotte. He was moved by the mixture of pain and pride in the girl's expression as she faced her ordeal "with history, jeering, at her back" and saliva dribbling off the hem of her dress.

The stay in Charlotte had been arranged in part by Brown through acquaintances at Johnson Smith, a black university there. Baldwin sensed in the officials at Johnson the kind of resentment that Brown had warned him about. People at Johnson were proud of what they felt they had accomplished and were in no hurry to leap into integrated higher education or to stir up what they seemed to consider satisfactory "race relations."

Unable to get a sense from these people of the real conditions of the African-American in a city in which he had heard black men could be neither electricians nor plumbers, Baldwin turned to newspaper people to whom he had introductions, especially to Harry Golden, the editor of *The Carolina Israelite*. From Golden he gathered facts about the emergence of white supremacy organizations in the face of the school integration rulings, and he learned about the school situation, including details about the integration effort of which Dorothy Counts was a part. Golden emphasized that integration in Charlotte meant that four high schools took in one black each. The Reverend Mr. Counts, a prominent black minister, fearful for his daughter's life, had, in fact, given up and placed Dorothy back in one of the "separate but equal" schools.

Among the most advanced white people he met in Charlotte was Julian Sheers, an editor at *The Charlotte News*, but even with Sheers he felt uncomfortable talking as "freely" as he did; it was "as though I were giving away atomic secrets."

Baldwin was directed to the home of Gus Roberts, who was one of the four blacks integrating the high schools. He learned firsthand the horrors of Gus's experience—the taunts, the threats, the anonymous phone calls, his having to sit alone in the lunchroom—and was impressed by his stoical reaction: "Pride and silence were his weapons." But he wondered, and he knew Mrs. Roberts wondered, about the psychological and emotional effects of the struggle on the boy. Baldwin's perspective throughout his trip to the South was as much that of the novelist as of the reporter or social activist. What did racism do to the inner lives of people—black people and white people?—was always his question.

He interviewed the principal of Gus's school and received at least a partial answer to his question. A quiet, somewhat formal southerner, the principal had been supportive of Gus Roberts, but he admitted to Baldwin that his traditions and beliefs did not include a commitment to integration; separate but equal was his philosophy. Baldwin suggested that the principal's actions had been based on a simple morality that transcended his heritage of prejudice; surely he had supported Gus because he could not bear to persecute an innocent child. The black interviewer from the North watched the very human reaction of his southern interviewee to this interpretation. The principal's "eyes came to life," expressing "anguish . . . pain and bewilderment" and he "nodded his head" in agreement. It was typical of Baldwin that he came to like this man—a racist—because he recognized in him a complex and redeemable humanity.

Just before a speech by Harry Golden at the public library, he met several "dedicated Southerners"—presumably liberals if they were attending Golden's antiracist speech—and he sensed above all else how nervous they were about shaking his hand, touching his flesh as equal flesh to theirs. This was especially true of the women. He felt he was a sexual object, the living version of a myth.

Baldwin's preoccupation with the private lives behind the public revolution and counterrevolution became stronger as he traveled farther South. The handshaking incident was a real-life indication of the validity of his concerns about the connection between sex and racism, a concern expressed fictionally, for example, in the relationships of the southerners Leona and Eric in *Another Country*, and in the predicament of the white sheriff in the short story "Going to Meet the Man." As his plane "hovered over the rust-red earth of Georgia," his mind "was filled with the image of a black man . . . hanging from a tree, while white men watched him and cut his sex from him with a knife."

The sexless black victim on the tree was a fascinating and somehow ominous image for Baldwin at this moment. It spoke to his own sense of vulnerability both as a black man and potential victim engaged in a dangerous movement and as a homosexual whose sex could become an instrument of love between men, regardless of race.

In Atlanta, as elsewhere on his trip, Baldwin perceived the widespread sexual aspect of racism, a paradoxical hatred and fascination with the black man's sex that had its origins in the violation of black women by white slavemasters who, naturally enough, mythologized and when possible removed the would-be instruments of revenge. When, one evening, a white man of some authority—one of those who might traditionally have participated in his castration had he been a lynch victim—made sexual advances towards him, "we were both, abruptly, in history's ass-pocket."

That history—that obsession with the black man's sexuality—had at its center a terrible curse. Everywhere he went he sensed an atmosphere of secret desire mingled with fear and guilt. The constant fear expressed by whites in Atlanta, as in Charlotte and in Little Rock, was that their girls would inevitably be violated by black flesh if the schools were integrated. Baldwin found himself in a heightened, racially motivated version of *Giovanni's Room*. "What passions cannot be unleashed on a dark road in a Southern night!" he thought. And his novelist's mind created the scenes that could depict the strange paradox of erotic hatred:

> The youth, nursed and raised by the black Mammy whose arms had then held all that there was of warmth and love and desire, and still confounded by the dreadful taboos set up between himself and her progeny, must have wondered, after his first experiment with black flesh, where, under the blazing heavens, he could hide.

The point was he could not hide. His progeny or his slaveholder father's or grandfather's progeny by his black slaves was everywhere to be seen. Like it or not, most "white" men had unrecognized "black brothers," most "white" women unrecognized "black sisters." This, of course, was true in the North as well, but in the South it was more immediate and literal, because the day-to-day physical proximity between blacks and whites was so close.

It is appropriate that it was in Atlanta in September of 1957 that Baldwin met for the first time the central martyr in a modern story that would have several. As he tells us in "The Dangerous Road before Martin Luther King," he met King in the latter's hotel room in Atlanta, where the minister was taking a few days away from his activities in Montgomery to work on a book. And that evening he encountered him again at a party.

In his reactions to these and later interviews, Baldwin still revealed himself as the novelist masquerading as reporter, with a primary interest in motivation and inner complexities:

> The questions I wanted to ask him had less to do with his public role than with his private life. When I say "private life" I am not referring to those juicy tidbits, those meaningless details, which clutter up the gossip columns and muddy everybody's mind and obliterate the humanity of the subject as well as that of the reader. I wanted to ask how it felt to be standing where he stood, how he bore it, what complex of miracles had prepared him for it.

But King talked little about himself, and Baldwin had to glean what he could by observation. It is clear that he liked what he saw, the "restless, intuitive intelligence," the certain sadness about him, as if he sensed the real possibility of personal failure, the curious

Connie Williams at the Calypso in Greenwich Village in the 1940s

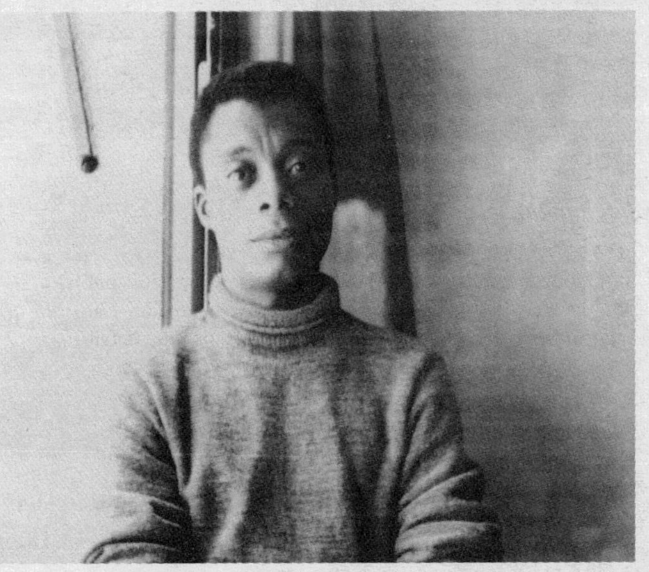

James Baldwin in his twenties

Orilla "Bill" Miller Winfield
in New York, c. 1938

The Melodeers in a
Harlem church, 1948

An "Elisha" plays in a Harlem church, 1948

In Paris in the 1960s

With Beauford Delaney and Lucien Happersberger in Paris, 1953

With Lena Horne, 1963

Having tea on the Bosphorus in the 1960s

In the pulpit, 1963

With a child in Louisiana, 1963

In the South, 1963

Cooking for Bertice Redding in Istanbul, 1966

With Engin Cezzar in Istanbul, 1965

combination of gentleness and power. Baldwin was impressed by his air of authority and by his eloquence and his obvious spirituality.

Of course, Baldwin did his work as a reporter, too. In these first interviews King was subdued but informative. Desegregation was what concerned him now. Integration was something for the future. Ultimately, he felt that the fate of America rested on the moral decision about integration. He suggested that southern politicians were well aware that segregation was finished but that for political reasons they hoped to delay it as long as possible: "The sin of the South" is that of "conformity," he said.

From Atlanta, Baldwin flew to Birmingham, Alabama. Here his main contact was the Reverend Fred Shuttlesworth, a civil rights leader and nemesis of the racist sheriff "Bull" Connor. Shuttlesworth's church and home had already been the targets of bombs and bullets. This was "a marked man in Birmingham." He visited Baldwin's hotel for an interview late one night, and Baldwin noticed that he kept looking out of the window to check that his car was not being booby-trapped. As Shuttlesworth left for home Baldwin said something about the danger that might face him, and he thought he saw a response in the sadness that the minister's expression reflected. He sensed that Shuttlesworth worried as much about the spiritual self-destruction of his oppressors as he did about his own physical safety. Again, then, Baldwin's primary concern was the inner world of the "private life."

King had suggested that Baldwin visit Montgomery to observe the results of the bus boycott firsthand. He promised to have him met at the airport by a representative of the Montgomery Improvement Association, the group directing the boycott. The car was late, and Baldwin underwent the first of several Montgomery experiences that would bring home to him the dangerous reality of his own position as an "intruder" from the North as well as the daily humiliations faced by southern blacks. Wanting to phone the MIA office, he had to pass, typewriter in hand, a line of hostile white men. It was strange and sad to think that these men, in effect, could not allow themselves to respond to him as a fellow human being. Even at this moment Baldwin was fascinated by what was going on in the minds of those responsible for oppression.

That night in Montgomery he explored the town and for the first time was pleased to be in the South. He felt strangely comfortable walking the night streets; the atmosphere here reminded him of the fried chicken and biscuits and music—the southern heritage—of Harlem. He realized that in Paris he had missed the world of his roots. He rested for a while on the thought that he might have been born in such a city had his mother not moved North.

Without considering what he was doing, he stepped into a restaurant, and suddenly he was in a southern version of the northern restaurant experience he had described in "Notes of a Native Son": "the arrival of the messenger of death could not have had a more devastating effect than the appearance in the restaurant doorway of a small, unarmed, utterly astounded black man."

After the momentary silence Baldwin was approached by a woman with "eyes like two rusty nails—nails left over from the Crucifixion. . . . What you want, boy?" she "barked." Directed to the "colored entrance" by a white man who watched him "with a kind of suspended menace," he soon found himself in what to him was not only a very real situation but one emblematic of the reasons for the current struggle. He was in a tiny cagelike room on one side of which was a window that looked through a kind of wire screening onto the back of the counter at which the white patrons were being served only a few feet away. The mesh made it so that he could not be seen by these white people. He was, literally and sociologically, an invisible man.

When a black man joined him in the cubicle and received his order through the cage opening, Baldwin watched his patience with admiration, realizing that in the face of such strength the whites had something to be frightened of. Montgomery was no longer "down home." Baldwin recognized that he did not have the other man's patience or, therefore, his strength. He was an outsider. Walking out of the restaurant, he dropped his uneaten hamburger in the weeds and walked back to his hotel in an agitated state.

The next day he took a ride on a Montgomery bus to observe the situation after the recently ended boycott. What he noticed most was the silence, which "made me think of nothing so much as the silence which follows a lovers' quarrel." Most interesting to him was the psychological question of the attitude of the whites, who, "beneath their cold hostility, were mystified and deeply hurt. They had been betrayed by the Negroes, not merely because the Negroes had declined to remain in their 'place,' but because the Negroes had refused to be controlled by the town's image of them."

On Sunday morning Baldwin attended the services at Dexter Avenue Baptist Church, where he heard Martin Luther King, Jr., preach. An expert on the subject, he pronounced King a great preacher. He took note of "a feeling in this church which quite transcended anything I have ever felt in a church before. . . . The Negro church . . . had acquired a new power. . . . The joy which filled this church . . . was the joy achieved by people who have ceased to delude themselves about an intolerable situation, who have found their prayers for a leader miraculously answered, and who now know that they can change their situation, if they will."

After church Baldwin met Coretta King for the first time at the dinner in the church basement. He described her as "light brown, delicate, really quite beautiful," and later he would come to know her much better. For now it was her husband who commanded his attention. He overheard King "explaining to someone that bigotry was a disease and that the greatest victim of this disease was not the bigot's object, but the bigot himself. And these people could only be saved by love." To Baldwin it was as if he were hearing the message of "Notes of a Native Son"; he had for some time preached the "gospel" of love as an antidote to hatred and bigotry. He could not help but be impressed by the success of this gospel in the face of the bombs that had damaged the very church in which King preached.

But now, having seen something of the South for himself, he wondered if nonviolence would be enough. As much as he found admirable about King, there was something in him he did not like. Having gone the church route himself and rejected it, Baldwin was naturally uncomfortable with the idea of a clergyman's leading a revolution. And perhaps he sensed some aloofness in King's attitude towards him. What could this educated, middle-class, southern clergyman think of the author of *Giovanni's Room*?

Baldwin had other memorable experiences on that first southern trip. He visited Nashville and Little Rock and once more was struck by the heroism of the black children who, in the struggle for equal education, were confronting not only the white power structure but history itself. These children were a new version of those Crusader children "marching on to war" and perhaps to slaughter.

That the whites of Little Rock could not see the heroism before their very eyes underscored the fact that "the nation has spent a large part of its time and energy looking away from one of the principal facts of its life. This failure to look reality in the face diminishes a nation as it diminishes a person, and it can only be described as unmanly." The failure of the South was symptomatic of a national failure, a national lie, the lie Baldwin had cast in metaphor in *Giovanni's Room*. The American nation was in desperate need of honest self-examination: "If we are not capable of this examination, we may yet become one of the most distinguished and monumental failures in the history of nations."

At one point in the trip Baldwin flew to Tuskegee, Alabama, where he stayed at the Tuskegee Institute, made famous by Booker T. Washington. There, in what might be called a center of the myth of black progress, he wrote a letter to his brother expressing, with the personal intensity always reserved for David, his feelings about his trip South. Once again he is more a student of human nature than a protester, more a prophet than a politician. What he had encountered in the South, he said, was deeply troubling. What he was witnessing was the "birth-pangs" of a "new order." Before that order was born there would be immense suffering, not only among the oppressed blacks but among the naive whites who were destroying their souls with hatred and fear. In a sense, he told his brother, it was exhilarating to be a black in the South; something was finally happening; there was a noticeable growth of self-esteem. But whites were caught in their own myths; they were blind to the inevitability around them. When he looked at these people he wondered, "like Ezekiel . . . 'Can these bones live?' " One could only hope for a repeat of the biblical miracle. "Nobody Knows My Name," would be difficult to write, he said. He prayed that "the Lord" would "touch my pen."

Back in New York in late October, his suitcase, stuffed with notes, pamphlets, and books, burst in Grand Central Station. After tying up the bag with his belt, he made his way to a friend's apartment in the East Village. There, having fallen into a deep depression brought on by the terror he had suppressed in the South, he retreated for several days until one afternoon, walking along Sixth Avenue, he ran into his friend Lonie Levister. Lonie bought him a drink and welcomed him back to at least a moment of his old life. But Baldwin knew that his life would never be the same again. He was committed to the lonely existence of the witness. Whatever he did, however he laughed or played, wherever he found himself—in a pulpit, in someone's bed—he would always have that commitment in mind and he would always come back to it.

If he feared his life in Paris had been a Jonah's life, he knew now that he had been brought back to his mission "from a long ways off."

CHAPTER 16

The Call of the Stage

How did you feel when you come out the wilderness?
—old song

In New York Baldwin met Engin Cezzar, a young Turkish actor and protégé of Elia Kazan who had recently come to Lee Strasberg's Actors Studio from the Yale Drama School. The two men took an immediate liking to each other, and Baldwin envisioned Cezzar as Giovanni in a workshop version of *Giovanni's Room* planned by Strasberg. They read the Studio-prepared script with this in mind and agreed that it needed to be completely rewritten, this time by Baldwin himself. Cezzar agreed to help, and in a few days they had restructured the play. Baldwin would spend the next several months doing the actual writing.

The collaboration with Cezzar extended in later years to other projects and gave rise to a friendship that continued to the end of Baldwin's life and led to his spending several years in Turkey. The relationship was platonic but profound. Whatever the basis of Baldwin's original interest, he respected Cezzar's intelligence and his abilities and was more than willing to maintain the friendship without a sexual component. They referred to each other as "my brother," and meant it.

The plans for a Studio production of some sort having been agreed upon, Baldwin withdrew once again to his favorite writing sanctuary, the MacDowell Colony. By early December he had the first act of *Giovanni* completed and took it to New York for his new friend to see. While there he signed a lease for an apartment at 81 Horatio Street. This was to remain his home for several years. He paid $100 a month for three large rooms and was happy to discover that there were "a couple of Negroes in the building already." He had to borrow $50 from David to pay the security deposit.

Back at MacDowell after Christmas, Baldwin continued work on the *Giovanni* script. He also spent a good deal of time on *Another Country* and on the two southern essays, "The Hard Kind of Courage" and "Nobody Knows My Name," and he finished a short story, "Come Out the Wilderness," which *Mademoiselle* would publish in March.

The surface of "Come Out the Wilderness" reflected both the "downtown" office work experience of his sister Gloria and his own experience of broken love affairs. But the story is really about the failure of a man to accept a woman's love. Ruth, the black heroine, senses the imminent end of her relationship with a white artist called Paul. She comes to the realization that he cannot accept the demands of a full commitment to her and that part of the reason for this is her race.

Ruth and her situation are closely related to Ida and her dilemma in *Another Country*. Her story actually emerged from work on that novel. On the level of Baldwin's continuing parable, Ruth's story, and to some extent Ida's, is about that "army of boys—boys forever!"—who, like David in *Giovanni's Room*, lacked the ability or the will to say yes to life, to the "stink" of love. And as in the case of *Giovanni*, the question of the failure to accept love in an individual relationship is a metaphor for a larger social failure, the failure of the white world to move beyond the level of guilt, stereotyping, and the boyish need for sympathy in its relations with the black world. The inevitable result of that failure is the black world's unwillingness to forgive:

> The sons of the masters were roaming the world, looking for arms to hold them. And the arms that might have held them—could not forgive.

Baldwin's use of his fiction to reinforce the thought contained in the essays is clear here. In "Nobody Knows My Name," the essay he was writing during the same period, he speaks, as we have seen, of the youth "nursed and raised by the black Mammy . . . confounded by the dreadful taboos . . . [who] must have wondered, after his first experiment with black flesh, where, under the blazing heavens, he could hide." "Come Out the Wilderness" is in part the story of that young man's desperation and his need to hide. More important, it is also the story of the effect of that desperation and that need on the soul of the "black flesh" he has so callously used but not accepted.

"Come Out the Wilderness" is the first work in which the Baldwin voice assumes the female role. It would do so again to some extent in *Another Country*, in *If Beale Street Could Talk*, and in his final work, *The Welcome Table*. In his female persona Baldwin found a disguise that made it possible for him to confront some difficult questions about himself.

Early in March, Baldwin had a dream in which he was joined by a beautiful, very young black woman who, after performing a song and cakewalk with him, seemed to merge with him—"her breasts digging against my shoulder-blades." The dance became perilous and the dreamer experienced fear. And on March 25 Baldwin wrote a poem in which he refers to painful visions of himself as a child "wrestling in the darkness." The poem bemoans the loss of an earlier Jimmy, questions the identity of a new Adam and Eve "struggling" to unite, and generally conveys a sense of overwhelming original sin, brokenness, and alienation, ending with the prophet Ezekiel's cry to God "Can these bones live?"

On April 13 Baldwin dreamed about another building with a dance floor and of a series of unsatisfactory encounters between himself, Arnold, the actor Rip Torn, whom he had met in New York, and a young woman. At one point he escapes the whole scene of sexual encounters and makes his way down a long dark alley, which the "voice" with him "calls 'Adam's nightmare.' " He makes his way and breaks through the barrier in the alley, thus reaching the door to the building he wishes to enter.

The question of primal relationships, between blacks and whites, homosexuals and heterosexuals, was the basis of *Another Country*, the novel Baldwin was working on at MacDowell. And, of course, it was an essential question in Baldwin's own life. The struggle between Paul and Ruth, the dancing dreamer and his other—female—self, the Adam and Eve figures "struggling" to come together in the poem, and the complex sexual relationships from which he feels he must escape in order to enter the house where the dance—the creative endeavor—can take place are all related elements of Baldwin's agony, his own version of "Adam's nightmare."

He returned to New York in April, having more or less finished the *Giovanni* script, and the Studio workshop production was staged in May. It was directed by Eli Rill, and it starred Engin Cezzar as Giovanni and Mark Richman as David. Baldwin was especially pleased by Cezzar's interpretation; he presented a Giovanni who, true to Baldwin's ideal and vision, "was a man, whatever he did in bed."

There is a scene in the play in which Giovanni spits on a crucifix. In spite of his having turned away from any kind of formal Christianity, this was a difficult scene for the ex-preacher to watch. He was impressed by how well Engin executed it, remarking wryly that "only a Moslem could have done it so well."

The play was received relatively well by the Studio members and interested friends who saw it. Lorraine Hansberry, whose *Raisin in the Sun* would be produced on Broadway the next year, was complimentary. Lee and Paula Strasberg were less than enthusiastic, but they saw sufficient promise to encourage Baldwin to write another play for the organization. Baldwin's real hope was for a full-scale stage or film production of *Giovanni*, starring his old friend Marlon Brando as David, but Broadway and Hollywood producers were not yet ready to invest in a script such as *Giovanni's Room.*

The Studio experience was useful, if for nothing else, in that it led to Elia Kazan's suggesting to Baldwin that he learn more about the mechanics of the theater by working as his assistant on productions of Archibald MacLeish's *J.B.* and Tennessee Williams's *Sweet Bird of Youth.* Baldwin accepted the offer, hoping this would lead finally to the fulfilment of his Broadway dreams.

The apprentice work with Kazan would not begin until fall, but Baldwin saw his mentor several times during that spring and summer. One night Jimmy, with David and Lonie Levister, took Cezzar and Kazan—their Turk and their Greek—on a tour of Harlem night spots. This was a useful outing because he and Kazan were able to relax together and it helped him overcome some of the negative feelings he had about what he considered Kazan's capitulation during the McCarthy anti-Communist "witch-hunt" of a few years before.

Baldwin settled into his Horatio Street apartment in April. He finished the first southern essay, "The Hard Kind of Courage," and turned back to *Another Country.* He wrote to a friend in Paris that he planned to have the novel finished by the end of the summer. He also confided that he had booked a ticket on the *Liberté* for the end of June. Paris, it seems, was not completely out of his system. He felt he would be able to finish the novel more easily there. New York always involved pressure for Baldwin. His social life was becoming unruly, as it always did when he stayed in the city for any length of time. And there was still the constant presence of racism, the reminders that it was impossible to escape labels and stereotypes. The South was certainly cursed, but so was the liberal North. When he considered America he became "sad." France had its "terrors," he wrote to his Parisian friend, but nothing as bad as what, "in a hideously hidden fashion, is happening here." Something of the American dilemma would be in *Another Country*, he said.

It was with some relief, then, that he arrived back in Paris. As usual, he went directly to Beauford in Clamart. He knew it must seem strange to his family that he had returned to Paris so soon after he had apparently settled in on Horatio Street, and he wrote to David trying to explain his position. He had to come to Paris to face the end of an era in his life. He realized that he had changed a great deal in the years since his first arrival in Paris. Paris was no longer home, but it had been an important place in his life and seemed an appropriate place to return to in order to reassess that life. Now that he was there, he realized that he had become an outsider even among those who had known him in the old days. He was struck by his own loneliness and aware that this was a condition essential to his life and personality, a condition he would have to learn to accept, wherever he eventually decided to live. In fact, he told David, he would have to learn to be "happy with it," to make it "give me what it has to give."

Ostensibly, Baldwin had returned to Paris with the idea of doing a commissioned article on Paris for *Holiday* magazine, to get a feel for the city as it was now. The article took form quickly as "Paris 1958," but it was clearly not *Holiday* material. His work on it led to an article for *The New York Times Book Review* called "The Discovery of What It Means to Be an American," which became the opening essay of *Nobody Knows My Name*, the essay in which Baldwin stresses the necessity of freeing oneself from the myths of America in order to face the reality of the American experience and the American identity. It suggests that black and white Americans know much more "about each other than any European ever could."

The original essay, "Paris 1958," eventually submitted to and refused by *The Reporter* rather than *Holiday*, was, in its many unpublished versions, a recapitulation of his French experience and an important element in his "discovery of what it means to be an American." In the essay Baldwin takes note of the fact that in one sense the old Paris is still very much there: the sheer beauty of it, the "incredible light," the bookstalls "with their sullen vendors," the painters and writers on the Pont des Arts, and, of course, the cafés. He is sad to hear that the market area, Les Halles, is about to be torn down. Returning there, he loves the sounds and smells and the old late-night bistros. The changes in Paris, he reminds himself, are the business of the French. It is to America and its problems that he has turned, and France serves him in 1958 more as a reminder of American problems than of anything else.

These were the days of the reemergence of Charles de Gaulle. The violence in Algeria was coming to a head and was spilling over into Paris. Here, in the place to which he had once come to escape bigotry, where people had been so universally critical of American racism, he now discovered in the treatment of Algerians all the elements of prejudice he had so recently encountered in the South. Like the Americans, the French appeared to be victims of their own myths. De Gaulle was calling for a revival of French glory, but this did not seem a possibility until the French could free themselves from their "myths" and "illusions" about their history and themselves. Baldwin would take up this theme in "This Morning, This Evening, So Soon," a short story that would be written in 1959–60. And what he said about French myths and illusions might just as well have been said about the American South. In fact, he was completing the *Partisan Review* article on the South, "Nobody Knows My Name," even as he was working on "Paris 1958."

For all of its difficulties, however, France remained France, and Baldwin loved being there, eating the food, walking the streets, spending time with Beauford. The house at Clamart was relatively quiet, and he began to make progress on *Another Country*. In August he heard that "Come Out the Wilderness" had won an O. Henry Award and was to be included in *The O. Henry Best Short Stories of 1958*. "Sonny's Blues" had been included in *Martha Foley's Best for 1957*, and now *Esquire* wrote asking him if he had another jazz story to publish. The short story seemed to be a viable genre for him, and he hit upon the idea of writing about a black jazz singer returning home to America after several years in Paris. This would eventually become "This Morning, This Evening, So Soon."

In a letter to Engin Cezzar dated August 12, however, Baldwin reveals that in Paris he tended towards the same kind of chaos that made his "flights" from New York so necessary. He speaks of working well until a combination of his "perverse self-will" and would-be friends led him to a series of dinner parties, bars, strange beds, and promises of future engagements. He complains of the "sense of futility" that overwhelms him when he wakes up in an unfamiliar place, "nearer to my end," because of excessive alcohol and tobacco, and lonelier, than before. Still, he assures his friend, this kind of life has helped him to solve certain problems related to the writing of *Another Country*.

During the summer Baldwin did not finish the novel, but he did complete the final draft of the "Equal in Paris" screenplay, which he called *Dark Runner*. The scenario opens with an attempt to put the sheet incident into a larger social perspective. The narrator tells us that the story could have begun in Harlem when he was born or in Africa before the slaves were brought to America, or when his father had first read to him from the King James Bible. Billy, the Baldwin hero, a young black would-be writer, meets Maurice Portnoy, a lawyer based on Baldwin's Paris patron Tom Michaelis, and a young white musician named Square Watson. Portnoy suggests that the young men go to Paris. Before they do they experience the restaurant scene described by Baldwin in "Notes of a Native Son," in which Baldwin is refused service and considers killing the waitress. There is also a tender scene between Billy and his mother, during which he announces his intention to go to Paris. The rest of the play involves Paris life and the sheet incident itself. The final scene is a somewhat sentimentalized, heterosexual version of the relationship with Lucien, which had begun soon after Baldwin's release from jail in 1949, but it also owes something to Baldwin's association with Gidske Anderson. *Dark Runner* is considerably less effective than either "Notes of a Native Son" or "Equal in Paris." Baldwin understood this and never put much effort into getting it produced.

In September, Martin Luther King, Jr., was stabbed by a black woman while autographing books in Harlem. It seemed to be a signal that it was time to go back. Once again Jimmy had to convince Beauford that he was really planning to return to the States in October, and once again Beauford began to hear voices. He had perhaps hoped that everything would return to the way it had been in the early fifties, when Lucien was in Paris with Jimmy. If so, the hope was probably kindled by Lucien's arrival in Clamart late in September.

Lucien's life with Suzy, by whom he now had two children, had deteriorated, and he was desperate for a change. He had a brother in Peru but lacked sufficient money to travel there. He knew that Jimmy, with whom he had continued to correspond, was staying with Beauford, and he knew about his friend's recent successes. He asked for a loan, and Baldwin felt compelled to find the money. He even went so far as to convince himself that his reason for coming to Paris in the summer had been to help Lucien arrange a move. Lucien remained somewhere at the center of his being, and he still hoped for a future with him. If he could go to Peru he could eventually come to New York. Jimmy extracted a promise of sorts that Lucien would do just that, and by selling an option to *Giovanni's Room* to a French producer, an option never taken, he raised the money for the passage to Lima. He wrote to David that by buying the ticket, he supposed he was giving back "something which was once given to me" by Lucien. Fortunately, Baldwin could not dwell on the Lucien question for long in New York because he quickly became involved in his work with Elia Kazan and threw himself into planning for still another Actors Studio production of *Giovanni*. There was a reading in November, an option for a Broadway production was taken, and Baldwin busied himself trying to contact Montgomery Clift, his choice to play David. Marlon Brando had already indicated he would not be available. Rip Torn and Christopher Plummer were also possibilities. Baldwin pursued the *Giovanni* project without success well into 1959.

Sitting in on rehearsals of MacLeish's *J.B.* as "production observer" for the New Dramatists group and notetaker for Kazan, contributed to Baldwin's already strong love for the theater. But he disliked *J.B.* with a passion, finding it pretentious and unsuitable for any kind of serious communication from the stage. He also resented what he considered to be MacLeish's patronizing attitude towards both Kazan and himself, another J.B. Kazan would say later that it was "a case of two different cultures, Harvard and Harlem."

The production of *Sweet Bird of Youth* was much more to Baldwin's liking. He did not admire the play particularly, but he developed close friendships with members of the cast, especially Geraldine Page and Rip Torn, and he respected Tennessee Williams and almost everything he had written. The two men had in common homosexuality, a propensity for long nights of drinking and talking, and a curiosity about the "private lives" of their characters and their friends. Baldwin was interested in what he considered Williams's "gothic" side, particularly as it related to the South.

During the March 1959 pre-Broadway tour of *Sweet Bird*, Baldwin attended a preview performance of *A Raisin in the Sun* in Philadelphia and renewed his acquaintance with Lorraine Hansberry. The friendship was always an explosive one that both of them enjoyed. Hansberry would be an important ally in later civil rights activities. Through her Baldwin came to know Lloyd Richards, who would later direct a production of *The Amen Corner*, and Sidney Poitier, the star of *Raisin*.

Poitier seemed to like Baldwin and asked for a copy of *Go Tell It on the Mountain*, which he had heard about but not read. Immediately Baldwin thought of him as a possible star in a Baldwin play or film. In 1959 and later Baldwin and Poitier had conversations about the sexual politics behind the treatment of a black matinee idol, a subject Baldwin had first touched on in the *Carmen Jones* essay in *Notes of a Native Son* and would treat again in *The Devil Finds Work*. He would also discuss it in connection with Poitier in a *Look* magazine article in 1968, speaking there of "a quality of pain and danger and some fundamental impulse to decency" in Poitier "that both titillates and reassures the white audience . . . black men are still used in the popular culture as though they had no sexual equipment at all."

At the end of the *Sweet Bird* work Kazan suggested that Baldwin write a play of his own based on his evident concern with the "private lives" of blacks and whites in the context of the civil rights struggle. Conversations with Rip Torn, Sidney Poitier, Tennessee Williams, and Lorraine Hansberry fueled this idea, and eventually *Blues for Mister Charlie* would be born of it.

CHAPTER 17

Sermons and Blues

This train is bound for glory.
—old song

Early in 1959 the essays "The Discovery of What It Means to Be an American" and "Nobody Knows My Name" appeared and did a great deal to establish Baldwin, not only as a reliable commentator on racial conditions in America but as a witness to the whole dilemma of what it meant to be American in the context of those conditions.

His accomplishments were bringing honors and financial benefits as well. He received word that he was to be awarded a two-year Ford Foundation grant of $12,000 for work on *Another Country*. There were countless speaking invitations, and he was often asked to comment on literature, especially African-American literature; his judgements were taken seriously and he spoke with authority.

Nineteen fifty-nine brought an opportunity to react publicly to the work of a boyhood hero who had been sometimes complimentary and sometimes critical of Baldwin's efforts. As a Harlem child, Baldwin had grown up knowing of Langston Hughes's reputation as one of if not the leading black American writer. For the young would-be writer, the older poet was inevitably an important model. Baldwin often said that Hughes's poetry had helped him to understand his father's rages and his mother's passivity, as well as the people in the churches and on the streets of Harlem: "Hughes gave voice to the people who had no voice," and this was what Baldwin, too, longed to accomplish.

On March 8, 1948, Hughes had written to Baldwin praising "The Harlem Ghetto" as "a most beautifully written and effective" piece, and on March 7, 1953, he wrote a letter praising "Everybody's Protest Novel." Baldwin answered on March 25 of the same year, speaking of the "butterflies" in his stomach as he waited for the publication of *Go Tell It on the Mountain* and telling Hughes how Countee Cullen had once accused him of writing poetry that was "an awful lot like Hughes's." In the same letter he expressed a desire to meet Hughes and Arna Bontemps, who, he had recently learned, had endorsed him in his application for a Rosenwald Fellowship in 1948. On July 25 Hughes sent Baldwin copies of the reviews of *Mountain* and commented that he had particularly admired the "beautiful" treatment of Richard's suicide. Baldwin wrote Hughes to thank him for his support. But later he was hurt by Hughes's negative comments about his point of view in *Notes of a Native Son*, and the publication of Hughes's *Selected Poems* in 1959 gave him the opportunity to express reservations about the poet's work.

The Baldwin review appeared in *The New York Times Book Review* of March 29, 1959. Whenever he read Hughes, Baldwin wrote, "I am amazed all over again by his genuine gifts and depressed that he has done so little with them." It has become commonplace to see the Baldwin review as an act of revenge or as an attack on a "father figure." But when he wrote at the end of the review that Hughes "is not the first American Negro to find the war between his social and artistic responsibilities all but irreconcilable," he clearly saw himself as one of that company. As far as he was concerned, he and Hughes, like all black writers, were engaged in the same struggle. What he found lacking in Hughes was the ability to make what might be called Jamesian use of the private nuances of black speech, which, like black music, had developed complexities that made it possible "to express . . . the private or collective experience." From Baldwin's point of view, Hughes used black speech photographically, as it were, to create local color, rather than as a vehicle for the revelation of the inner world of black society.

The Baldwin review hurt Hughes. In response to it he wrote this note:

> Hey Jimmy:
>
> Ain't you heard?
> RACE and ART
> Are far apart.

Whatever the nature of their dispute, Baldwin maintained no ill feelings at all towards Hughes. On April 20, 1960, he and author Kay Boyle wrote him a friendly postcard from the MacDowell Colony.

On May 10 of the same year Hughes requested some copies of Baldwin's books for an African project, and Baldwin responded in a friendly first-name-basis letter and sent the material.

Even after a somewhat sarcastic reaction to *Nobody Knows My Name* in a letter of May 4, 1961, in which Hughes refers to Baldwin as "a sage—a culled sage—whose hair, once processed, seems to be reverting," Hughes maintains a light note: "Jimmy: I fear you are becoming a 'Negro' writer—and a propaganda one at that! What's happening???? (or am I reading wrong?) Hope it makes the best sellers list. You might as well suffer in comfort."

In 1961 the two writers participated with Lorraine Hansberry, Alfred Kazin, Emile Capouya, and Nat Hentoff in a symposium on WBAI-FM, New York, printed in *Cross Currents* as "The Negro in American Culture," about art versus social responsibility in the creative works of African-Americans. During the discussion they did not seem particularly to disagree. Hughes reacted favorably to Baldwin's remark—an articulation of his anti–protest literature stance—to the effect that "the Negro writer is not as interesting a subject to me as the Negro in this country in the minds of other people—the Negro character . . . and the role that he's always played in the American subconscious."

On the few occasions they met or corresponded between the 1959 review and Hughes's death in 1967, Baldwin and the poet spoke as friends and with what appeared to be genuine interest and respect on both sides. Late one night in 1964, Baldwin took me with him to a little restaurant in Harlem called Jenny Lou's. After we ordered porgy and grits, the specialty of the house, at the counter, Baldwin suggested that if I looked at the man in the corner of the booth nearest the back wall I would be looking at one of the great poets. At about the same moment Hughes saw Baldwin, smiled, and made a wide gesture of invitation with both arms. We joined him at his booth, and a long relaxed conversation followed, first about Jenny Lou's and the welcoming "Negro ambience" that prevailed there and in Harlem generally, then about race and art. About the latter they disagreed, but the discussion never became rancorous.

From different perspectives, each accused the other of being "hung up on race." Hughes resented what he considered Baldwin's negative exposure of black life. Harlem was home to him, while for Baldwin it was only a place in which to collect material for "prophecy." He teased the younger writer about still being a preacher. Baldwin took this in good humor, but when I asked him later what he really thought of Hughes he said he was a great poet who ignored the inner life at his peril as an artist, that he oversimplified and sentimentalized issues that needed to be confronted more thoroughly and directly. Hughes needed to "get out of Harlem" so that he could look at it. He did not say these things to Hughes himself. In fact, an observer such as myself could only have come to the conclusion that Baldwin stood in awe of Hughes as one of the real giants of African-American culture.

He was thrilled to receive a telegram of support from Hughes on the opening night of the Broadway production of *The Amen Corner*. And during the same year he would invite the older writer to an *Amen* cast party in Paris. When Hughes died Baldwin wrote a note to a friend of the poet speaking of him as the pathfinder for writers who came after him. Baldwin said he would especially miss Langston's smile, "which always welcomed and always forgave."

Continuing to live on Horatio Street, Baldwin worked hard during the winter and spring of 1959 on *Another Country*, and gradually developed an entourage. Mary Painter, who had been transferred from Paris to Washington, sometimes visited. Lonie Levister came by often and so did Engin Cezzar. Sam Floyd, a young black schoolteacher-journalist recently arrived from the South, lived nearby and became one of his closest and most trusted friends. Baldwin and other friends, including, over the years, black artists, writers, and entertainers such as Lorenzo Hail, Paule Marshall, Nina Simone, Rosa Guy, Maya Angelou, Max Roach, Abbey Lincoln, and Nikki Giovanni, would often meet at Floyd's for drinks and talk. Bill Weatherby, a British journalist living in New York, met Baldwin at 81 Horatio. He describes the general scene there in his biography. Dan Wakefield, another writer friend, tells of afternoons there drinking bourbon, listening to Bessie Smith and the Modern Jazz Quartet, and sharing a love of Henry James and an aversion to the Beats. An addition to Baldwin's life at this time was Tony Maynard, who would work as his "man Friday" for a time and would eventually become involved in a racially tinged murder case from which Baldwin would help to extricate him. Still another new black acquaintance was Jimmy Smith, who would also serve as an assistant to Baldwin.

As much as Baldwin enjoyed having people around him, there came moments when neither his finances nor his emotions could stand the strain. This was especially so when racism broke through the mask of liberalism that the world around him often wore. One occurrence in the spring of 1959 especially frightened him and convinced him that once again he would have to flee New York if he hoped to get any work done.

It was an incident that might well have ended in his and his friend Engin Cezzar's death. He and Engin, another white friend, and Engin's girlfriend were out for a late-night drink at a small bar called the Village Paddock, not far from the Horatio Street apartment. Sitting at a table, they were not particularly concerned with the several men who sat at the bar itself. The evening had been particularly successful. The dinner at Jimmy's favorite restaurant, El Faro, and drinks after dinner at the White Horse Tavern, had been even more lively than usual. At the Paddock the group was having a mildly noisy good time, laughing a lot and singing blues songs. At one point Engin's girlfriend, who was white, put her head on Jimmy's shoulder in the course of laughing at something he had said. A remark was made from the bar and within seconds the table was attacked. Chairs were broken over heads, Engin was badly beaten up, Jimmy received a gash across his nose and was hit over the head. The police arrived, did little about the offenders, but did send Cezzar to the hospital, where he had to remain for several days. At one point he awoke to find two men standing over him discussing where a Moslem could be buried. A black man on a trolley next to him laughed and said, "Don't worry, baby, they have a real good Moslem cemetery in Harlem." Jimmy refused to be hospitalized but was taken by a friend to a doctor for treatment the next day.

The fight hurt and upset Baldwin as much as anything in the South had. He had gone through the South without undergoing any physical harm; here he had been badly beaten, and one of his best friends had nearly been killed. He apologized some days later for missing an appointment with another old friend. He had got into a fight and he wasn't up to seeing anyone, he said: "My emotional troubles [have] descended on me."

Leaving Tony Maynard in charge of the Horatio Street apartment, Baldwin took himself to Fire Island to the Cherry Grove Hotel and later to a friend's house there. This pattern of behavior, involving immersion in a time-consuming, money-consuming, emotionally draining social life followed by an escape into isolation was already firmly established.

As was usual in his periods of isolation, Baldwin wrote and read a lot while he was in Cherry Grove. He finished yet another stage version of *Giovanni's Room* and worked on *Another Country*. Among the books he read was Warren Miller's *The Cool World*, which he reviewed for *The New York Times Book Review*, praising Miller's sophisticated use of the "argot of the Harlem streets" to reveal the private lives of black children. These are children who "watch their contemporaries and their elders dying by the hour. And we ignore this world at our own peril, for as long as they are dying, we are dying, too."

Not only was Baldwin restating a position in this review, he was expressing an interest in the fictional uses of black English, which would become increasingly important to his work in the later years. He was also preparing himself to address further a subject that he had touched on in *Go Tell It on the Mountain* and articulated more explicitly in the first southern essay, "The Hard Kind of Courage," namely, the effect of racism on the hearts and minds of children. This would become a prime Baldwin theme in such works as "Fifth Avenue, Uptown," the first section of *The Fire Next Time*, and the late work on the Atlanta murders of the 1980s, *Evidence of Things Not Seen*. In a letter to Miller's agent he asserted that "the crimes committed against the children" were the "most unforgivable" ones.

Baldwin was never comfortable being alone, and as often happened when he was, his thoughts turned to his family. The channel for those thoughts was almost always his brother David. He discussed in some detail the fact that he needed to alter his erratic life-style. His hope was to start a savings account and eventually to rent an apartment for his mother and other members of his family. He also confided a growing need for legal and financial assistance. An agent was no longer enough. His commitments to publishers, to colleges for speaking engagements, to landlords, and, now that he was actually making money, to the Internal Revenue Service, were complicated and time-consuming. He had hired an accountant and a lawyer, and somewhat embarrassed, he admitted to David that he had also hired a "secretary" and "man Friday," Tony Maynard. He sensed that his life was about to change radically, and he was trying to get ready for that change. In some ways he felt "helpless" when faced by the realities of both his private and public life. One consolation was the fact that he had a brother to whom he could "write long, incoherent, confused letters." He knew that his remaining afloat depended more on David than on the various protectors or raiders of his pocketbook.

It also depended on his being true to what he saw more and more as his mission. This meant public appearances as well as novels and essays. Baldwin would present papers and participate in symposia at Bard College, the University of Notre Dame, San Francisco State University, Kalamazoo College, and several radio stations during the next months. On June 3, 1959, he delivered what was perhaps his most important speech of the period, a paper entitled "Mass Culture and the Creative Artist," at the Tamiment Institute in Pennsylvania. He was extremely nervous about the paper and typed it out in full to be read aloud. As the engagements became more frequent, and as he gained confidence as a public speaker, Baldwin would depend only on brief notes and adrenaline.

The mass culture speech is a Jeremiah's speech; it cries out to the nation, condemning its drift away from truth into false myths. Mass culture reflects the conflict between America's "official" values and its actions; it avoids the truth "about ourselves." The "serious" creative artist has little to do with mass culture. The artist's role is to be a witness to the truth. He must "rob us of our myths and give us our history, which will destroy our attitudes and give us back our personalities." Mass culture "can only reflect our chaos." The role of the artist is necessarily a lonely one. Remembering T. S. Eliot's famous line, Baldwin reminds his audience that "people can't bear an awful lot of reality," which is to say, truth. It is the artist who must tell the story of what happens below the level of "the eternal conundrums of birth, taxes, and death." And this necessity, this burden, isolates the artist and sometimes causes people to "hound or stone" him "to death" before they honor him.

The Tamiment speech was at once prophecy and confession, sermon and blues. This was the Baldwin method, that of a man torn between the calling to preach the Word whatever the cost and the man longing for the stability represented by a perfect love between two people in domestic isolation. The summer came, and Baldwin returned to Paris, in part, at least, in search of the latter.

He thought that this trip might well be a mistake. He seemed unable to shake the Paris nostalgia, even though he had publicly and privately decided that he must live in the States. Arriving in Le Havre on July 3, he immediately telegraphed David, who had been worried about what he saw as his brother's gloomy state of mind, assuring him that everything was "OK," and later he explained, as he had so many times before, that he had come to France to "take stock of my life." He took the train to Paris and then directly to Clamart, where once again he leaned on his spiritual father. He spent the first few days in France sleeping and eating under Beauford's care. Then he began to work.

He wrote an essay for *Commentary* called "On Catfish Row," originally a review of the Otto Preminger *Porgy and Bess*, rewritten, as he told his brother David, "around the death of Billie Holiday—comparing the Hollywood lies" to reality. The essay was a logical extension of the Tamiment speech and Beauford's wisdom, stressing the mass culture's ability to smother truth in myths and sentimentality. Placed against the Preminger film, "heavy with the stale perfume of self-congratulation," was Holiday, the consummate "serious" creative artist destroyed by the very society that so desperately needed her prophecy. *Porgy and Bess*—especially the Preminger version—is designed so that the white man's vision of himself might be maintained. But those who attempted to "define" a Billie Holiday or a Bessie Smith as a "coarse black woman" were enslaved by their own "definitions," their own myths. The truly free people were the Smiths and Holidays, who in their art had transcended definitions and become themselves. Now in death Holiday had "escaped forever from managers, landlords, locked hotels, fear, poverty, illness, and the watchdogs of morality and the law . . . and no one has managed to define her yet." Baldwin, on his own quest for identity, was well aware of the dangers inherent in his own relationship with landlords, agents, tax collectors, lawyers, contracts, and prevailing morality.

Another Country, too, would speak to many aspects of the struggle between mass culture and individual integrity. The novel continued to progress, but slowly. After a month at Clamart, Jimmy felt the need of the boulevards and old street friends. He went to Saint-Germain, borrowed a friend's apartment, and settled in. Less fortunate friends began to settle in, too. Paris was becoming increasingly like New York as Baldwin achieved more fame. He wrote to David complaining that it was as if "all the homeless and unhappy people" of Paris and New York were living with him. What he left out was the fact that he often encouraged them to do so. Earlier in the year, for instance, he had met and fallen in love with a young man in New York who had grown up in the streets of the Lower East Side and made a living essentially as a hustler. Baldwin, for all his anxiety about the complexity of his New York life, took his "juvenile delinquent," as he liked to call his new friend, to Paris with him. Once there, the boy proved to be anything but the faithful, attentive lover Jimmy had hoped he might be, and so began once again the familiar saga of the personal tragedy he had foreseen on that fateful night by the sea in Corsica. The boy was there and then he was not there. When money was needed he came by, when it was not he was more often in someone else's bed. All of this was depressing and demoralizing.

On September 21 a disturbing letter arrived from David that

contributed to the depression. A former lover with whom he had remained close in spite of a tumultuous breakup some years earlier had been committed by his parents to a mental hospital after a serious nervous breakdown. Baldwin's immediate reaction was to blame himself, but he came to the conclusion that what had happened had its sources in an experience that transcended any single personal relationship. He might just as well blame himself for his father's insanity or for Beauford's potential for insanity. All three personal tragedies were dues paid to that larger social tragedy of racism to which he was a witness, a tragedy that constantly threatened his own sanity. Frustrated by his not being able to learn details of his friend's condition, Baldwin asked David to visit the hospital, wrote Mary Painter in Washington asking her to do what she could, and wrote Congressman Adam Clayton Powell to see that the young man was not treated "simply as one more penniless black patient." He suggested to David that he try to raise money for the hospital bill by contacting Nat Hentoff at *The Jazz Review.*

Meanwhile, there were two important projects to complete. *Esquire* magazine had proposed two interviews, one with Ingmar Bergman and one with Charlie Chaplin, two examples of serious creative artists who stood out against the bland mass culture Baldwin had so strongly castigated in his Tamiment speech. He liked nothing better than talking and writing about the movies. He would become and remain friendly with Bergman, and he would later make close friends of the directors Joseph Losey and Costa-Gavras. Several of his fictional characters—the hero of the story "This Morning, This Evening, So Soon," which was in progress at the time of the Bergman interviews, Leo Proudhammer in *Tell Me How Long the Train's Been Gone*—are film actors. He would do a book, *The Devil Finds Work,* on American films and, of course, he always dreamed of writing for the screen himself.

Charlie Chaplin was a longtime hero whose work Baldwin had followed since the thirties. Not only did he admire his films, he respected Chaplin for his political stand against McCarthyism. He had always wanted to meet him and had recently met his son Sidney in Paris. As it turned out, in spite of two trips to Switzerland, the encounter proved to be impossible to arrange. The two men would get together for the first time several years later, in London.

Arriving in Stockholm in early October, Baldwin had much more success making contact with Bergman and, in fact, had several interviews with him at the Filmstaden. He had only recently seen *The*

Seventh Seal, and in the Stockholm studio, before he actually met with the director, he would view for the first time *The Magician, Summer Interlude*, and *Wild Strawberries*. The meetings between the two men are described in detail in "The Precarious Vogue of Ingmar Bergman," which was included in *Nobody Knows My Name* as "The Northern Protestant."

Baldwin and Bergman liked each other immediately. They discussed the realities of modern Stockholm, their relationships with their preacher stepfathers, the role of the artist, and Bergman's films. *The Magician*, Baldwin suggested, was "a long, elaborate metaphor for the condition of the artist," and Bergman agreed; the artist by definition was always on the brink of "disaster." Baldwin understood this situation perfectly. Somehow, he thought, this Northern Protestant, so obsessed with the darkness of existence, with the private life of the human being, thought the way he did. Both were concerned with the problems of overcoming "our . . . loveless and ominous condition." Each found in art the means both for social commentary and the inner search for identity.

On his way back to his hotel after the first interview, Baldwin fantasized a film that would be *his* version of *The Seventh Seal*. It would be, in effect, a version of the slave novel he had long planned on writing, to which he now again planned to give the title *Talking at the Gates*. Full, like Bergman's, of symbol and metaphor, his film would be a study in white and black—a white ship, black slaves, white masters, black sea. The ship would be called the *Jesus*. Yet Baldwin realized that because of his "black Protestant . . . unwieldy, unaccepted bitterness," he would not be likely to make a film based on his collective past as easily as Bergman made films about his. Turning in his mind to the hero of his film, he saw his former lover who had been committed to the insane asylum as a symbol of the condition to which his people had been condemned. His protagonist would in all likelihood be an addict. But more important, his own "bitterness might be turned to good account if I should dare to envision the tragic hero . . . as myself." The survival of artists depended, after all, on their facing the truth; it was necessary to "vomit the anguish up."

In these thoughts lurked the character of Rufus in *Another Country*, Sonny in "Sonny's Blues," the black singer protagonist of "This Morning, This Evening, So Soon" (which he had just begun), and Baldwin himself. In order not to fall, like Rufus, in order not to be swallowed by the mass culture, the artist, as Beauford had always taught, must literally sing of the agony of his life. Only in this "blues" way could life be preserved.

Not surprisingly, then, between visits with Bergman and screenings, Baldwin found that *Another Country* was flowing again. In Paris he had begun to think it was a disaster and that he would never finish it.

In late October, in Paris, he met another "serious creative artist," Jean Genet, and saw the opening of *Les Nègres* (*The Blacks*). It was an important play for him in that it gave him new ideas as to methods of conveying on the stage the merging private and social realities that concerned him as a black man and an artist in the white world. The Genet play depends for its success on the confrontation between black characters acting out a ritual of resentment and a white audience facing, through that ritual, a vision of itself. Baldwin would remember *The Blacks* in the early 1960s when he was writing *Blues for Mister Charlie*, a play that depends on the same kind of tension and has a similar purpose. He would see *The Blacks* again several times when it had its New York production and would discuss it extensively with the American members of the cast—especially Maya Angelou—with whom he became increasingly friendly during the years that followed.

In Paris, Baldwin wondered whether he should stay where he was or return home to face the problem of his hospitalized friend and other commitments. For a while he even considered a trip to Istanbul, where Engin Cezzar, who was playing *Hamlet* there in Turkish, had invited him. As it turned out, a complex social life and work on *Another Country* kept him in Paris for a while longer. His developing friendship with James and Gloria Jones was especially important to him, and he worried that Beauford's condition was getting worse. And there were several fleeting love affairs, one with an old friend of Lucien's who kept horses and who, when he met Mary Painter, insisted on describing to her in detail how horses mated. One of his horses was a black stallion whom he named Black Boy after Baldwin. Not surprisingly, the name had connotations that upset the man so "honored." But there were more important problems with the lover; he was married, had several children, and was consumed by guilt as he carried on the affair. Clearly, he was not the answer to Baldwin's dream of tranquil domesticity.

The main reason he could not bring himself to return to New York, in fact, was a kind of inertia stemming from his obsession with that dream. After Stockholm he had gone to Switzerland to try again to contact Chaplin. While there he found himself nearly overwhelmed by the memory of Lucien. "It's an awful thing to think about, the way love never dies!" he wrote to David, quoting Sister Margaret in *The Amen Corner*. Back in Switzerland again, in January he wrote to David that there was nothing there that was not "stained with the one real love story of my life."

He was tired of running, tired of personal disasters. In three letters to David at the end of 1959 he speaks of the pain that these disasters have brought. He reveals that he had even had relations with several women during the summer, that he had considered the picture of himself married, with children, living a thoroughly ordered and domestic life. Yet, he knew well enough that love was a state of "perpetual danger" rather than safety, that the "mutual need" of love can easily lead to mutual destruction. Baldwin had found that as a famous man he was seen as a "catch." But he was lonelier than ever. Perhaps, he suggested, loneliness was part of the artist's burden and personal disasters were necessary fuel for the kind of work he did.

Baldwin's plans to be home by Christmas were deferred by still another failed attempt to find Chaplin in Switzerland. The Bergman story, which he had sent to *Esquire* in November, was received with enthusiasm, and they hoped not only for the Chaplin profile but for a Harlem essay.

He began working on "Fifth Avenue, Uptown: A Letter from Harlem" almost immediately and finished a first draft, which he called "All Up and Down That Street." In the *Esquire* essay, which he would include in *Nobody Knows My Name*, he revisits the Harlem of his first essay, "The Harlem Ghetto," no longer wearing the mask of an objective voice of no particular color, but as a black man who knows all too well that Harlem is "occupied territory." "Negroes want to be treated like men," he tells his reader. Let northerners not think that racism is a southern problem or that there has been real progress for ordinary people in the North. And let people not forget the effects of racism on both victim and perpetrator: "It is a terrible, an inexorable, law, that one cannot deny the humanity of another without diminishing one's own: in the face of one's victim, one sees oneself." It was only necessary to "walk through the streets of Harlem and see what we, this nation, have become."

The Harlem essay was important because it turned Baldwin's attention back to the details of the civil rights struggle. He made an agreement with *Harper's Magazine* for the article on Martin Luther

King, Jr., ("The Dangerous Road before Martin Luther King"), which would necessitate another trip to the South. His last weeks in Paris that year were spent in a small apartment a few blocks away from Beauford in Petit Clamart. To cheer up his old friend and mentor he threw a huge Thanksgiving dinner in the restaurant under his apartment run by a couple he liked to call Pierrot and Pierrette. Their closest Paris friends were invited. Robert Cordier, a Belgian cohort of Baldwin's who was to remain close to him during the sixties, described the scene to biographer Fern Eckman as a "banquet," noting that Jimmy, a "gourmet, a connoisseur of wine," had "supervised" everything and that it was "a great night!"

As if to convince himself of the necessity of leaving France, Baldwin returned to "This Morning, This Evening, So Soon," a story about history, about being an American, about the painful necessity of "singing" in one's own land. The autobiographical elements of the story point clearly to its function as a personal parable as well as a public one.

Finished early in 1960, the story relates directly to Baldwin's Paris experience. The black singer protagonist had first come to Paris, like him, twelve years before. His first trip home coincides with Baldwin's 1952 trip. The description of the hero's first visit South takes its energy from Baldwin's own initial trip there, emphasizing the emasculating process so basic to southern racism. The character of the singer's sister, Louisa, plays a role in the protagonist's life that suggests the role of David Baldwin in his brother's. She is there to meet him at the ship in New York, in 1952, as David had been there to meet Jimmy; she serves as a protector and as a source of strong solace in his agonizing struggle between the commitments of art and those of personal love. The singer's white European wife, Harriet, embodies the Baldwin dream of domestic bliss. Their declaration of love on the bridge in Paris is based on the 1949 meeting with Lucien, another white European. The memories of the singer are Baldwin's, too. Discussing his past with the film director Vidal, he speaks of his father as Baldwin had spoken so many times about his stepfather—most recently, with a real-life film director, Ingmar Bergman—and in nearly identical words:

> How could I *know* what he had borne? . . . However he had loved me, whatever he had borne, I, his son, was despised. Even had he lived, he could have done nothing to prevent it, nothing to

> protect me. The best that he could hope to do was to prepare me for it; and even at that he had failed. How can one be prepared for the spittle in the face?

The singer has a son of his own. Returning to America to pursue his own career, to answer the call of prophecy which is the call of the serious creative artist, might well place his white wife and his "mixed-blood" son in jeopardy. Safety versus honor is the prime Baldwin theme. It takes another metaphorical guise at the end of the story, when some young black acquaintances of the singer, who in Paris are somehow American innocents rather than African-Americans, are robbed by a down-and-out North African friend. The singer finds himself caught between the safety of conventional morality and the honor that transcends that morality; he finds he understands the North African's need in a way that mere conventional morality cannot. This incident serves as a parable in itself, to elaborate on some of the issues discussed in such essays as "Princes and Powers" and "The Discovery of What It Means to Be an American," questions related to the paradoxes involved in being an African-American among Africans in a European world.

In Paris the singer and his family, like other people, can "live their own lives, *their private lives*," whereas in America the black man is a category: "I always feel that I don't exist there, except in someone else's—usually dirty—mind." In America, in short, "nobody knows my name." When he is confronted by the expectations of other Americans—including black Americans—in Paris, he is reminded of the struggles which await him at home, for, as the film director reminds him, America is, like it or not, home.

"This Morning, This Evening, So Soon" is a story about the American artist's responsibility—specifically, the African-American artist's responsibility—to redeem his nation. In this sense, it is a descendant of "Sonny's Blues." As the young man Pete sings the old church songs in a Parisian café, the singer narrator comments, "the song has come down the bloodstained ages. I suppose this to mean that the song is still needed, still has its work to do." Earlier, in a discussion with Vidal, the singer had complained, "I've never understood why, if *I* have to pay for the history written in the color of my skin, *you* should get off scot-free!" Vidal answers, giving voice to Baldwin's concern not only with black protest but with the fate of the oppressors: "What makes you think I *do*? . . . I am a Frenchman. Look at France [the France of 1960, the France of the Algerian "problem"]. You think that I—we—are not paying for our history?" This was the history of the European, the history of the white race, that Baldwin had discussed in his notes for "Paris 1958."

As the hero of "This Morning" wrenched himself away from Paris, so did Baldwin himself. In January he wrote to David asking him to get someone to fix up the Horatio Street apartment and to solicit Mary Painter's and his sister Gloria's help in organizing an "office" for him. On January 27 he sailed on the *Cristoforo Colombo*. He was coming home to the call, because "I can't fool myself any longer: this train is bound for glory."

CHAPTER 18

In Search of a Role

And I will give them one heart, and one way.
—Jeremiah 32:39

Early in 1960 Baldwin delivered a speech at Kalamazoo College that gave new life to a theme he had treated earlier and would set the tone for his work and his life during a period that would include the publication of *Nobody Knows My Name*, *Another Country*, and *The Fire Next Time*. In the speech, later included in *Nobody Knows My Name* as "In Search of a Majority," Baldwin argued that the solution to the race "problem" and, therefore, to the American problem, was in the hands of those who could realize that majorities had nothing to do with numbers and everything to do with moral influence. The only majority that could save America was one that could create a place in which there were no minorities. What is happening to blacks in America, he told his primarily white Kalamazoo audience, is also happening to whites. The oppressor destroys himself as he destroys the oppressed. The only identity Americans—black and white—have has been achieved through their shared experience as *Americans*.

In considering the African-American's role in that relationship, Baldwin turns, with the religious fervor he had acquired in the pulpit, to the question of love. It is the African-American who must teach the white American about love, "because he has had to . . . bear you, and sometimes even bleed and die with you, ever since we got here . . . and this is a wedding." A wedding needs love, and real love—God's real love—is, for Baldwin, a power learned in the trials of his life: "Love is a battle, love is a war, love is a growing up."

Even as he was addressing the students of Kalamazoo, Baldwin was exploring ideas about love in the complex relationships that form the basis of *Another Country*. The struggle of the races was analogous to the struggle of sexual union. Out of the struggle could come a breakthrough to real communication, to a recognition of the love bond, to real "growing up."

After a thorough tour of Harlem, of the streets he had walked as a child, of the blocks on which he had been raised and educated, and of the churches in which he had worshipped and preached, Baldwin returned to the MacDowell Colony, where he worked desperately on *Another Country* and finished the Harlem article, "Fifth Avenue, Uptown," for *Esquire*. By early April he had turned in an excerpt of *Another Country* to *Partisan Review*; it appeared as "Any Day Now" in the spring issue. He also began preliminary work on *Blues for Mister Charlie*, the play that would preoccupy him for several years to come.

While at MacDowell this time, Baldwin made the acquaintance of a woman with whom he was to visit and correspond throughout the activist days of the sixties and seventies. Kay Boyle, who had developed a reputation since the late twenties in Paris as a radical writer, shared Baldwin's love-hate feelings towards what he considered his cursed and she her philistine homeland. Both were concerned with the relationship between the breaking down of personal barriers associated with love and the breaking down of public barriers associated with social injustice. In Baldwin, Boyle found a new inspiration. She loved watching him and listening to him. One night he gave her a copy of *Notes of a Native Son*; she read it and immediately saw its importance. In a note to Baldwin she spoke admiringly of the honesty and precision of his writing, which is "exactly your voice speaking." Like several of Baldwin's female friends, she took a somewhat maternal line with him, begging him to beware of drinking, reminding him of his youth and of the fact that "we need you terribly."

Boyle took to walking Baldwin to his cabin after dinner each night. Always a "city boy," he was uncomfortable in the night woods and welcomed her company as well as her conversation. One night, as she was walking him home, she pointed out that she too was afraid of the dark, so after a few drinks he accompanied her back to her cabin only to realize, of course, that now he would have to return to his own cabin alone. After much laughter about the dilemma Jimmy had another drink and waited for dawn. Kay was always to remember him as he was that night in the New Hampshire woods, dancing about in the snow in his fox-fur hat, laughing, and singing.

Later they would meet from time to time—at Rowayton, Connecticut, where Boyle's husband taught, and still later at Wesleyan University, where she spent time at the Center for Advanced Studies in 1963, and in San Francisco, where she moved after her husband's death. In an introduction to a 1963 television address that would later be published as "Words of a Native Son," Boyle summarized her admiration for Baldwin, speaking of him as having "established a spiritual climate which now stands in real and vigorous opposition to the material climate of our country." Like all "men of genius," he was an "Aeolian harp on which is played the longing of all men." In 1969 she sent her friend a poem in which she called him "Witch doctor for the dispossessed" who had "said it all."

In May of 1960 Baldwin took his second trip to the South, again on assignment. Since his 1957 trip the movement had continued, concentrating on school and public-facility desegregation. Sit-ins, demonstrations, arrests, and bombings were common. In March police arrested thirty-five students on the Alabama State University campus. Tear gas was used on students in Tallahassee, Florida. The Associated Press reported that over one thousand blacks had been apprehended in sit-in demonstrations. A student movement, more radical than King's Southern Christian Leadership Conference, was beginning to take shape. In mid-April the Student Nonviolent Coordinating Committee (SNCC) was founded. In early May a second Civil Rights Act was signed.

Baldwin's trip is described in a journal and in two essays: "They Can't Turn Back," a piece on the student movement in the South, and "The Dangerous Road before Martin Luther King." Arriving at the Atlanta airport on May 19, with a one-hour wait for his flight to Tallahassee, Baldwin was faced once again with a reality that still had the power to amaze and horrify him. What he noticed first was the sign on a lavatory door that read "Colored Men." He entered that room but found that his body refused to "function" there, almost as though it were waiting to be "released." He resisted the temptation to order a Coke at the soda counter, wondering if he would have been served, and still thirsty, he took the plane to Tallahassee.

At the Tallahassee airport he again confronted a "Colored" sign, this one posted over a place that was more like an alcove than a waiting room, and to which the white travelers were oblivious. He noticed a black chauffeur, leading a small dog, meeting a "middle-aged" and "powdery-faced" white woman who was obviously "delighted to see both the beings who make her life agreeable." He imagined how he might quite naturally have extended his hand in response to the woman's radiant expression and how "panic" and perhaps "the threat of death" would have resulted from such an act.

Once again he found himself fascinated by private lives, the inner conflicts he perceived in the South. What effect, he asked himself, was the protest movement having on the psychology of those southerners facing the reality of protest against a system that had bred the airport "Colored" signs and the moment between the chauffeur and his "mistress"? The Tallahassee protest had been in large part student-led, but the administrators and students to whom Baldwin talked were by no means unanimous in their support of it. It was difficult to break free of the myths of inferiority and superiority that had fed racism. Then there was the question of personal conservatism and practicality—the question of safety as opposed to honor. Trained to "respect their elders" and to be grateful for the chance to be educated, many of these students resisted the call of the more radical students led by the Congress of Racial Equality (CORE), a biracial national organization committed to passive resistance. It was in Tallahassee that Baldwin became directly involved in CORE, which had been supporting civil rights since 1942. Later he would become a CORE member and, later still, a member and supporter of SNCC.

In the taxicab from the airport to the university, Baldwin had wondered about the feelings of the white cabdriver, who seemed benevolent enough and on the verge of a willingness to discuss the "situation" in Tallahassee. When there turned out to be no room in the university guesthouse (surprisingly, since he had been expected), he began to feel that he was not wanted. The cabdriver took him to a motel on the outskirts of town. Baldwin noticed the driver's casual and friendly way with the black woman who ran the place. He wondered what their true feelings towards each other were.

In the motel he had a crisis of sorts. Feeling ill at ease because of the lack of reception, he began to muse on other immediate problems, such as the struggle he was having with *Partisan Review* over the language in the *Another Country* excerpt. He began reading *Pornography and the Law*, and then to consider an old concern, the sexual aspect of racism. The false morality of racism and the false morality of the censor really have nothing to do with reality: a person's physical being cannot "*be* dirty, it can only be lied about." One of the results of this kind of lying is an illusion of innocence and cleanliness and a hatred of those different from oneself. Baldwin was instinctively making the connection between the conclusions he had reached in *Giovanni's Room* and the sexual basis of racism.

The next day he was taken to a protest meeting by an enlightened music professor at the university. If many students and administrators and teachers preferred to avoid the confrontation, there were also plenty who were committed to the struggle. On May 27 the activists decided to hold a biracial prayer meeting on the Tallahassee capitol steps. Baldwin had decided to go with them. In the planning sessions for the meeting, he watched the faces and listened for the inner voices of the students who spoke. The daughter of a segregationist was indirectly denying her father's criminality by suggesting that the group could depend on the police for protection. The black students would have none of this. Baldwin was aware of a new self-confidence in the black students and was reminded of the changes that had taken place in the South and of how long it had taken him to cleanse himself of the "filth I'd been taught about myself . . . before I was able to walk on the earth as though I had the right to be there."

The students were impressive. They were products of the successful meeting of a challenge that faces black parents: how to develop in the young a basic disrespect for the white world's "definition" of them. These students were standing against a people "ignorant of its history and enslaved by a myth"; they were on the march "in search of a majority." They were the missionaries of a kind of love that mattered, a love nurtured in agony.

As it turned out, the planned meeting was canceled. On his last night in Tallahassee Baldwin spoke to a small audience on campus. His theme was once again the role of the African-American as savior of the nation. Only black Americans contain the true history of America, he said. And only that history can "redeem" the false history and release Americans from the "tyranny" of their myths. And only after such release can the nation survive in the context of its stated ideals.

It was appropriate that Baldwin should go next to Atlanta to again interview Martin Luther King, Jr., the recognized leader of the nonviolent movement in the South and the spiritual leader of the movement everywhere. The interview took place in an office in the Ebenezer Baptist Church, where King was now co-pastor with his father. Baldwin's concern was still the man behind the public persona. They discussed the challenges facing King, his recent acquittal in

Montgomery on charges of tax evasion, perjury, and misuse of funds, his troubles with his followers and with more radical leaders. People wanted him to move faster; they questioned his abilities as a leader, and this bothered him. Baldwin wanted to know how he would bridge the gap between the old revolution and the new—the revolution of the bus boycott days and that of the new student revolutionaries he had met in Tallahassee. To some extent the old revolution, represented by the nationally recognized "Negro leaders" such as King, was based on Christian and bourgeois values and traditions borrowed from the white world. The new revolutionaries "have never believed in the American image of the Negro . . . for the myth of white supremacy is exploding all over the world." They recognized that the white man on whom the bourgeois African-American has so long modeled himself was "himself, very largely a mythical creation."

What Baldwin looked for in the King interview but did not find was the Negro leader's position at this crossroads. But there were hints in the subjects King chose to talk about. The nation as a whole was on his mind and he had developed, as a result of a trip to India, a religious and philosophical understanding that transcended even national and Christian boundaries. Baldwin was struck by King's apparent sense that the management of the details of the movement, management for which he had been criticized, should be left to others. It was his role to be a symbol as well as a day-to-day leader. The symbolic role both fascinated and disturbed the interviewer. Symbols were all too visible objects of persecution.

It was the relationship between King and his father that perhaps most interested Baldwin. Like his own stepfather, he had once been a preacher, but the Reverend David Baldwin had failed to prepare him for or protect him from the realities of racism. The idea of their sharing a pulpit would never have arisen, given the resentment and hatred that marked their relationship. Yet here were a father and son working in apparent harmony at the same task. Baldwin both admired them and envied them for their accomplishment. He wondered at the battles that must have been fought by the elder King to so successfully protect his son from the power of racism, a power that debilitated the mind and undermined self-esteem. Whatever he had suffered in a society that tried to deny him his manhood, he did much to create a son who, as he said, "never went around fighting with himself, like we all did." In this sense, King and his father were both symbols. The father represented the old quiet revolution still based in old values and the son represented the self-esteem Baldwin had seen in the student activists at Tallahassee. Whether Martin Luther King, Jr., himself, would join and/or lead the new revolutionaries was still open to question.

Baldwin visited the scenes of his earlier trip to Montgomery and Birmingham, but by mid-June he was back in New York, where he finished "They Can't Turn Back" before making a quick trip to Paris as an antidote to America, and particularly the South. But there was no escape from racism in Paris. The Algerian struggles were affecting life in the city, and Baldwin's mode there was no longer that of the down-and-out bohemian scratching about for a meal or a drink. He was already a "mythic" figure in Saint-Germain. A longtime friend, Bill Belli, remembers his first meeting with Baldwin in Paris one day that summer. Belli was walking past the Brasserie Lipp in Saint-Germain when the friend he was with, who knew Baldwin, said, with a certain sense of awe, "There's James Baldwin and Beauford Delaney." Belli knew some of Baldwin's work, and he asked to be introduced.

Baldwin and Belli connected immediately. Belli wanted to be a writer himself; he had met several of the Beat writers and he had read and been impressed by *Notes of a Native Son*. He had identified somehow with the photograph on the book's cover. Baldwin looked alone and alienated, and Belli at twenty-three admired the alienated, the "outlaws," a category in which he included the Beats, himself, and Baldwin as well. Baldwin liked Belli for many of the same reasons Belli liked him; he too was attracted to "outlaws" and, in spite of his growing fame, considered himself an alienated individual. *Nobody Knows My Name* would be the title of his next book.

Baldwin worked on *Another Country* and the Martin Luther King article while he was in Paris, and he started choosing and arranging a collection of essays for *Nobody Knows My Name*. He saw something of the Joneses and William Styron. The Styrons, the Joneses, and Baldwin spent long nights in the cafés, arguing about politics and race, and drinking heavily. Baldwin sometimes stood behind the pulpit bar at the Joneses' preaching mock sermons on the evils of drink. Sometimes the group drove around in the Jones Mercedes, living a latter-day version of Hemingway's Paris.

Early in the fall Baldwin left for New York and traveled almost immediately to San Francisco. He had agreed to participate with John Cheever and Philip Roth in an *Esquire*-sponsored symposium on "the role of the writer in America" at Stanford, Berkeley, and San Francisco State, where, on October 22, he delivered an address which he entitled "Notes for a Hypothetical Novel" when he included it in *Nobody Knows My Name.*

The address was enthusiastically received. Students always responded well to him. The speech served as a pretext for Baldwin's putting his own life in focus and for relating the job of the novelist to that of the witness-spokesman. The hypothetical novel he outlined was a novel about his own life, but it was also about the trap in which he found himself. One could write novels about one's life, but not without recognizing that one was a part of a larger reality—in this case, America—with its own peculiarities, its closeted "skeletons," about which we hope we can but obviously cannot avoid talking. The writer's problem, said Baldwin, was "to describe things which other people are too busy to describe." As a writer, therefore, he could not, in the light of the upheaval within the nation, remain aloof from the fact that "this country is yet to be discovered in any real sense." The writer has no choice but to confront and dispel the myths which are the barrier to that discovery. "We made the world we're living in, and we have to make it over." Baldwin's role, like any true artist's, was to take the lead in that process of remaking. His novel need not be a protest novel, but it must speak to the identity of the nation, it must open the forbidden closets, reveal the inner secrets of sexuality, racism, and history.

Among the most important events that occurred in San Francisco were the friendships that Baldwin developed with Roth and Cheever. With Cheever, especially, he discovered a great deal of affinity—a love of talk, of drink, and of literature. The homosexual connection was perhaps felt as well, though apparently it was not discussed by the two men. Baldwin began reading Cheever's stories in San Francisco and remained an enthusiatic admirer of his prose style and his sensitivity to the inner dynamics of the human experience.

The time in San Francisco made possible the renewal of two old friendships he valued greatly. Theodore Pelatowski, the photographer with whom he had collaborated back in 1948 on the aborted Harlem church project, lived in the Bay Area, and so did Stan Weir, his longshoreman-dishwasher companion from the Connie Williams/Calypso days. Baldwin stayed for several days with the Weirs, and several with the Pelatowskis.

With Weir he attended a predawn longshoremen's meeting and began a twenty-year involvement with the struggle of rank-and-file longshoremen against the union and the maritime industry's discriminatory practices. He joined the Longshoremen's Defense Committee, which praised him for his "exemplary courage" in support of "these almost forgotten workers, more than 90% of whom are Black [and who] must be vindicated and restored to . . . employment."

The stay with the Pelatowskis was more emotional, both because of Baldwin's particularly deep feelings for Pelatowski—he once called him the man he loved better than anyone else in the world—and because of the dislike he developed for his wife, Marjorie. Unlike Mary Weir, who became a close Baldwin friend, Marjorie complained of being kept up all night during his stay. She resented the drinking and what struck her as endless haranguing. For his part, Baldwin resented what he considered Marjorie's interference. It was particularly important that he have free access to individuals such as Pelatowski in whom he had complete trust. Later he would react in a similar way to the wives of friends Bill Belli and Lonie Levister and of several others to whom he was emotionally attached.

Baldwin returned in early November to Horatio Street, where he found a letter from Lucien announcing that he planned to leave Peru and, as promised, to meet him in New York. The letter served as a catalyst for the further development of the character of Yves in *Another Country*, the French lover who returns to Eric in the novel.

At the end of November came news of the death of Richard Wright. He had died in the American Hospital of a heart attack and under what Baldwin and many of Wright's friends considered strange circumstances. It was said that he had been visited not long before his death by an American intelligence agent. Some sort of foul play was suspected. *Preuves* in Paris and *Encounter* and *The Reporter* asked Baldwin to write essays on his old mentor, which he eventually did, incorporating them into a single essay, "Alas, Poor Richard," in *Nobody Knows My Name*. He convinced Dial Press, which was to publish the collection, that he needed a trip to Paris to research and write the Wright essays and they agreed to advance him more money. In Paris he completed the King article for *Harper's* and the Wright essays.

The pieces on Wright presented an opportunity to relieve the guilt Baldwin felt about never having properly made up with his onetime benefactor. Now "the man I fought so hard and who meant so much to me" was dead; "he had survived exile on three continents and lived long enough to begin to tell the tale."

In "The Survival of Richard Wright" Baldwin briefly sketches Wright's career, concentrating on the stories in *Eight Men*, of which the article was ostensibly a review. He criticizes Wright for playing to white American sexual paranoia by making use of gratuitous violence without examining the sexual roots of that violence—"the rage, almost literally the howl, of a man who is being castrated." But more important, in taking stock of Wright's work as a whole, Baldwin is impressed by "an ability to convey inward states by means of externals." He seems intent on closing the gap between himself and his old mentor:

> It is strange to begin to suspect, now, that Richard Wright was never, really, the social and polemical writer he took himself to be. . . . It had not occurred to me, and perhaps it had not occurred to him, that his major interests as well as his power lay elsewhere.

The *Encounter* essay was a more personal reassessment, going back to the first meeting and subsequent ones in Greenwich Village in the forties and moving up through the difficult period of their argument over protest literature in Paris. He calls Wright's work "an irreducible part of the history of our swift and terrible time" and, in his own way, acknowledges a great debt: "Whoever He may be, and wherever you may be, may God be with you, Richard, and may He help me not to fail that argument which you began in me."

In the final section of what developed into the three-part Wright essay in *Nobody Knows My Name*, Baldwin delves still further into the personal, regretting the failure of what could have been for both of them an instructive reconciliation, "nothing less than that so universally desired, so rarely achieved reconciliation between spiritual father and spiritual son." The failure, he felt, was not traceable to a personal problem or even personal dislike. Wright's rejection of his filial overtures was based in the price he paid for the "illusion of safety" in his "acceptance" as an African-American in Paris. The price was a kind of self-hatred that resulted from the struggle within between "whiteness and blackness," between the "dark . . . erotic past" and the European world that had taken him in on the condition that he "bury" that past. For Baldwin his failure to achieve reconciliation with Wright was, in this light, inevitable. It is only through reconciliation of the division within ourselves that we have any hope "of surviving the wilderness which lies before us now." Wright "found himself wandering in a no-man's land between the black world and the white," oppressed by the myths of each about the other. Hope lay in the kind of fusion of "blackness and whiteness" that would make neither condition relevant. Baldwin had seen the early stages of such fusion reflected in the obvious self-esteem of those students in Tallahassee.

CHAPTER 19

Nobody Knows My Name

To walk in Jerusalem, Just like John
—old song

In January of 1961 Baldwin's Belgian friend Robert Cordier organized a Greenwich Village "funeral party" for the Beat Generation. Baldwin was there with Tony Maynard and David. A somewhat reluctant guest, he did not participate in the "funeral march," complete with mock coffin, that took place in the street after the party. Other guests included William Styron and Norman Mailer.

Baldwin had not seen Mailer in some time. They had got along reasonably well in Paris during the few weeks their paths had crossed there, but Baldwin had been angered by Mailer's writings, beginning with comments on the black basis for white "hip" culture in the 1957 piece "The White Negro." Furthermore, he resented the derogatory comments about Jones, Styron, and Ralph Ellison in the 1959 book *Advertisements for Myself*, and was insulted and hurt by Mailer's dismissing him in the same book as being "too charming to be major."

In spite of several meetings over the years, including a visit to the Mailers in Provincetown, Baldwin, who admired some of Mailer's fiction, never really changed his essentially negative assessment of the man. Their meetings were nearly always, in one way or another, rancorous. Baldwin seemed to think of Mailer more as a rival than a colleague. He was once purposely late to an Actors Studio reading of Mailer's *The Deer Park*. At the Beat party he accused Mailer of being obsessed with his public image, and when both men were commissioned late in 1962 to cover the Floyd Patterson–Sonny Liston heavyweight championship fight for different magazines, they nearly came to blows. Mailer's interest in the fight was that of an avid boxing fan, Baldwin was preoccupied with the inner life of the fighters and the symbolic significance of the fight in relation not only to the world at large but to his "fight" with Mailer.

Both fighters were black, but Liston was tough and uncompromising—rather like Mailer—while Patterson was a shy man who seemed to carry the suffering of his race on his shoulders. Baldwin identified with him; he even bet $750 on him. As he watched Patterson jumping rope in a gym, he saw a "boy saint hopelessly dancing and seen through the steaming windows of a store front church." At a party the evening before the fight Baldwin and Mailer exchanged harsh words. People there said that Mailer reduced Baldwin to tears. Sonny Liston did much the same thing to Floyd Patterson the next night.

In a 1961 *Esquire* article, "The Black Boy Looks at the White Boy," Baldwin had given public voice to his feelings about Mailer. Mailer did not understand love, he was obsessed with power. A writer of potentially great vision, he was adolescent in his outlook. Furthermore, in his "beatnik" aspect, he was representative of the white man's naive and arrogant perversion of black culture—a culture centered in pain and deprivation—for bourgeois "hip" purposes without understanding it.

The *Esquire* article summarizes the Baldwin-Mailer "friendship" to 1961 and conveys the ambiguity of a relationship between two very different individuals who were fascinated by each other's differences. Mailer was perhaps curious about Baldwin's homosexuality and by the myths associated with his race. He also enjoyed sparring with him verbally. Baldwin was attracted by Mailer's "macho" characteristics even as he disapproved of and was suspicious of them. He was even "a little in love" with Mailer, rather in the way he was a little in love with Marlon Brando. Like Brando, Mailer exuded an aura of confidence that Baldwin envied. Even as he attacks Mailer in "The Black Boy Looks at the White Boy," suggesting that his understanding of the world of the late fifties lacks focus, he gives him credit for his sure sense of "ourselves as we are."

The generosity of the last remark did not prevent Mailer from criticizing *Another Country*, and the Mailer-Baldwin relationship would continue to deteriorate. When they met professionally, as they frequently did, a general coldness prevailed.

William Styron was a different matter. A southerner, the grandson of a slaveowner as Baldwin was the stepgrandson of a slave, he was nevertheless "serious" in his attempt to enter the black experience in his work. Styron and Baldwin had met several times before—first at a Manhattan dinner party given by George Plimpton and later at the Joneses' in Paris. Early in 1961 Robert Silvers, who was soon to become the editor of a new journal, *The New York Review of Books*, had learned that Baldwin was in financial difficulty and in need of a place to work. He suggested that the Styrons invite him to go with them to Connecticut, where he could have the use of their guesthouse. Styron agreed, made the invitation, and in early February he drove Baldwin to Roxbury.

The Connecticut stay, which lasted off and on until July 4, was remarkably successful. Baldwin and the Styrons seem genuinely to have enjoyed each other's company. The privacy afforded by the guesthouse and the relaxed attitude of his hosts made it possible for Baldwin to settle down and to work.

Meeting for lunch and dinner, Styron and Baldwin would discuss their work. Baldwin read aloud from *Another Country*, and Styron from *The Confessions of Nat Turner*. Later Baldwin would write to Sidney Poitier praising Styron and urging Poitier to get involved with a film version of *Nat Turner*. He respected Styron's attempt to present reality from what had to be, for a white grandson of slaveowners, a wholly novel point of view. Baldwin had, after all, taken a similar risk by working through the mind and "history" of the white David in *Giovanni's Room*. He felt that a writer should be encouraged in any attempt to enter new and foreign territory. When it was published in 1963, he would courageously defend *Nat Turner* against what he considered the unfair attacks of some black critics. In this support he demonstrated a commitment to art over politics or political correctness.

Eventually, what always happened to Baldwin when he sought to retreat from the world happened to him at Roxbury. Friends discovered where he was, and they began to visit. Connecticut liberals discovered him, too. Baldwin took a certain pleasure in "setting these liberals straight" about the "Negro problem," which he reminded them was a "white problem." "Mr. Baldwin," they would say, "are you saying we can expect trouble?" "Yes, baby," he would answer. "They're going to burn your house down." One young guitar-playing married woman was so impressed that she asked to move in with him.

The arrival of Lucien, after several years' absence in Peru, brought Baldwin back to New York. In any case, his second collection of essays, *Nobody Knows My Name*, was to be published in July, and he wanted to be in New York in time for that. The collection was less a manifesto than *Notes of a Native Son*. As Baldwin indicates in his introduction, it is a collection of pieces written over the six previous years "in various places and in many states of mind." The essays are the thoughts of a former expatriate who has decided he must return home, of a man represented fictionally by the returning singer in "This Morning, This Evening, So Soon." The six years in question seemed to the writer to be, "on the whole, rather sad and aimless."

Yet the essays indicate the opposite; these were, in fact, years in which Baldwin had faced the question of identity as a man and as a writer in such articles and papers as "The Discovery of What It Means to Be an American" and "Notes for a Hypothetical Novel." The politics of race had also been tackled in "Princes and Powers," "Fifth Avenue, Uptown," "East River, Downtown," "A Fly in Buttermilk," "Faulkner and Desegregation," "In Search of a Majority," and in the title essay, "Nobody Knows My Name." If the issue of race seemed to take up so much space in the book, said Baldwin, "the question of color . . . operates to hide the graver questions of the self." It is this theme of the "graver questions of the self," questions of the inner effects of racism and other masks, that concern Baldwin in *Nobody Knows My Name*. You don't know my name because you can't see me, these essays say. You see only the mask you have made me wear.

In the essays on Gide, Bergman, Wright, and Mailer, which make up the second half of the book, Baldwin attempts to discover his "name" by examining the inner worlds of other artists: "One can only face in others what one can face in oneself. On this confrontation depends the measure of our wisdom and compassion."

Nobody Knows My Name is at once a self-examination and an example of prophecy at its best. Baldwin calls on America to look at itself, to tear down its myths and to regain an ability to see things as they are. In "East River, Downtown," a 1961 essay that appeared originally in *The New York Times Magazine* as "A Negro Assays the Negro Mood," he admonishes the nation to end the great "division in our house."

The book was an immediate success, moving quickly to the *New York Times* best seller list. The reviewers were full of praise. Terms such as "masterly" and "major literary talent" were applied to it. Alfred Kazin's review in *The Reporter* was particularly searching and perceptive: "This is the book of a deeply troubled man," wrote Kazin, "the spiritual autobiography of someone who hopes, by confronting more than one beast on his way, to see whether his fear is entirely necessary."

The quest for "beasts" had taken Baldwin to many strange and distant places during the six years of the "composition" of *Nobody Knows My Name*, and he was now in a sense the most cosmopolitan writer of his day, at home with William Faulkner, André Gide, Richard Wright, Ingmar Bergman, Norman Mailer, and Martin Luther King, equally familiar with Lenox Avenue, Christopher Street, the Deep South, and the boulevards and alleyways around Saint-Germain-des-Prés. Baldwin knew the theater and the cinema well, was well read in the "classics" as well as in contemporary literature. He gave the impression of knowing everyone and knowing about everything. His education, self-directed and constructively encouraged by such wise men and women as Orilla Miller, Countee Cullen, Beauford Delaney, Sterling Brown, and Kenneth Clark, achieved a kind of fulfilment in the collection so ironically entitled. By July of 1961 almost everyone knew James Baldwin's name.

Awards, including a Certificate of Recognition from the National Conference of Christians and Jews, and speaking engagements followed the publication of the essays. Baldwin participated in a June 2 forum sponsored by the Liberation Committee for Africa on nationalism and colonialism and United States foreign policy. His picture was in *Time* magazine, and he was interviewed by Mike Wallace on television. *Ebony* did a long piece called "The Angriest Young Man" in which Baldwin spoke of his love-hate relationship with America. "I love America," he said, but "I'm angry about America calling itself the leader of the free world while there are 20,000,000 captive people living within its borders."

Friends who needed money or Baldwin's time arrived in droves. Horatio Street became impossible, and his publisher, Richard Baron, was urging him to complete *Another Country*. He had hoped rather naively for a quiet time in which to renew connections with Lucien, and there were, in fact, several reunions at Horatio Street that involved Jimmy, Lucien, Mary Painter, and Baldwin's sometime secretary, Jimmy Smith. But fame spoiled any hope of domestic tranquility. At one point things became so bad that Baron hid him away at his home in Westchester. But the followers found him there.

In mid-July, Baldwin went to Chicago on a book tour for *Nobody Knows My Name*. While there he appeared on Studs Terkel's radio show. In that interview, while explaining the constant strain of being a black man in a white man's world, he predicted that violence was around the corner. And he placed the civil rights movement in the context of the anticolonialism that had been rocking the old empires and was changing the Western world.

A month later, back in Chicago, where he had been called to deliver a talk at the University of Chicago and to appear on television, he was invited to dinner by the leader of the Black Muslims, Elijah Muhammad, who had been impressed by Baldwin's effectiveness on radio and television, especially by an April radio discussion with the Muslims' second-in-command, Malcolm X. In that program, hosted by Princeton professor Eric Goldman, Baldwin and Malcolm had appeared, in spite of their differences on the subject of integration, to understand each other well, and it seems likely that Malcolm suggested the dinner meeting to the leader of the Muslims.

By 1961 Elijah Muhammad and the Nation of Islam were an established part of black American life. Muslim speakers had been on Harlem street corners for some thirty years, so Baldwin had grown up with them. Elijah, with his prophet's name, had first been seen as merely an eccentric, but now, in the context of the struggle between assimilationists and separatists in the civil rights movement, he was being taken much more seriously. For one thing, the Muslims were achieving concrete successes: they cleaned up neighborhoods and cured criminals and addicts, and most of all, they seemed to be able to provide the African-American with a pride that the Christian church had failed to furnish. If their claim that all whites were "devils" was racist and extreme when it came to individual cases, it could certainly be supported by the overall facts of black life in white America. When Elijah called for a separate nation and preached a new religion, there was something in the African-American that inevitably said, "The white God has not delivered them; perhaps the Black God will." Baldwin was moved when, after his August television interview in Chicago, a young man shook his hand and said, "Goodbye, Mr. James Baldwin. We'll soon be addressing you as Mr. James X."

In discussing the meeting he had with the Honorable Elijah, as Baldwin does later in *The Fire Next Time*, he is careful to give a fair and detailed version of the tenets of the Muslim movement, but it is clear from the outset that his real interest is that of a novelist. Entering the "stately mansion" on Chicago's South Side and finding Elijah among his followers of white-robed women and black-suited men was like entering a myth and encountering a real prophet. It was only of secondary importance that the house, the life-style of the followers, and the doctrines of the prophet were in direct opposition to his own beliefs. Baldwin was "frightened" when he arrived at the house, "because I had, in effect, been summoned into a royal presence." He knew that his fears were a reflection, too, of the struggle within himself between his longing for a life based on love and his sense that power was necessary in a world that valued only power. Intellectually, he knew, in short, that the Muslims had a point.

He entered their house, a half hour late, very conscious of being the James Baldwin who drank, smoked, and had a great deal of sex, and he "felt as deserving of a scolding as a schoolboy." When Elijah greeted him "with that marvellous smile," he was carried back to the day when Mother Horn had asked him, "Whose little boy are you?" And "he made me think of my father and me as we might have been if we had been friends. . . . I felt I was back in my father's house."

In fact, Elijah's viewpoint was eerily close to that of the Rev. Mr. Baldwin, the "good friend of the Great God Almighty." All whites were devils, even the ones who seemed to be otherwise. He said he had decided to invite Baldwin "home" since "it seemed to him that I was not yet brainwashed and was trying to become myself." At each word of the leader, the followers cried, "That's right," just as his stepfather's words—and his own—in the pulpit had been greeted by the inevitable "Amen." At first Baldwin was overcome by the same kind of force that had nearly stifled him as a child. What were his beliefs, asked Elijah.

"I left the church twenty years ago. . . ."

"And what are you now?". . .

"I? Now? Nothing. . . . I don't . . . think about it a great deal." And Elijah said to the whole room, "I think he ought to think about it *all* the deal." Baldwin was humbled: "My weak, deluded scruples could avail nothing against the iron word of the prophet."

"I've come," Elijah said, "to give you something which can never be taken away from you."

Something in Baldwin longed to be a follower, a witness. Here was a man whose father, it was said, had been lynched in the South: "I felt that I knew something of his pain and his fury, and, yes, even his beauty." Yet, what he knew of life and of himself would not allow for a conversion to Islam. He and the old prophet were doomed to be "strangers, and possibly, one day, enemies."

Somewhat dazed, Baldwin was provided with a driver to take him to his next appointment. "We take the responsibility of protecting . . . [a guest] from the white devils until he gets wherever he's going," said Elijah. Baldwin "was, in fact, going to have a drink with several white devils on the other side of town."

Increasingly, however, he turned to the black world for "running buddies." Soon after the Muslim dinner he met a young man called Marc Crawford at the home of Gwendolyn Brooks. Crawford, an editor at *Tone* magazine, had talked to Baldwin on the phone in connection with a negative piece written by Nelson Algren about *A Raisin in the Sun*. A mutual friend informed Crawford that Baldwin had said he would like to answer Algren, who had favorably reviewed Baldwin in the past and who was Crawford's mentor. Through correspondence, Baldwin agreed to do the piece, a strong defense of Hansberry and her play, for *Tone* ("Is *Raisin in the Sun* a Lemon in the Dark?"). He was so late turning it in that Crawford had to take the article down by dictation over the phone, no easy task. In describing the phone conversation later, Crawford was reminded of a remark attributed to Alex Haley: "I like those Baldwin sentences with all them commas 'n' shit."

When Baldwin and Crawford met, they found they had a lot in common, and Crawford introduced Baldwin to a friend of his, Francis M. Mitchell, who worked for the Johnson Publishing Company, the owners of *Ebony* and *Jet* magazines. Mitchell, Crawford, and Baldwin were all ministers' sons, and they all loved to drink and talk. It was Mitchell and Crawford who were with Baldwin in the airport scene described in *The Fire Next Time*. A bartender refused to serve the three "boys"—all over thirty, Crawford a Korean War veteran—because they looked "too young," and an altercation ensued. Baldwin saw the scene as the American problem in microcosm. When a young white man at the bar, who had been a witness to the argument, asked the men if they were students, Baldwin reacted angrily, and Crawford asked the man why he had not intervened on their behalf, pointing out that the fight in the bar "had been his fight, too." The young man's reply said it all: "I lost my conscience a long time ago."

Baldwin liked Crawford so well that he suggested he join him in Paris later in the year. Crawford agreed, and it was soon arranged that he should accompany Lucien and Baldwin's eighteen-year-old sister, Paula, on a September ship to Europe. Baldwin had long wanted to do something special for Paula; besides, he was worried about the growing racial tension in New York and decided now was the time to get her "out of America." She could go to design school in Paris.

Baldwin, too, felt he must get away. *Another Country* was still not finished, and he had been commissioned by *The New Yorker* to do a travel piece on Israel and Africa. As he had preparations to make for Paula's visit, he flew to Paris alone in early September, after leaving it up to his brother David to conclude the lease on the Horatio Street apartment and to make the final arrangements for Lucien, Marc, and Paula to follow on the SS *Olympia* via Lisbon and Naples. This they did, and then they traveled to Paris by way of Lausanne, where they visited with Lucien's family.

Meanwhile, Baldwin had reestablished himself in Paris for the moment. He wrote to David speaking of his relief "now that the . . . pressure of New York [is] off me." His "juvenile delinquent" friend was there and Jimmy Smith had come over. Mary Painter was back, and Bernard Hassell and Richard Olney were in residence again after a stay in New York. And there was a new friend, a black expatriate photographer called Emile Cadoo. Beauford was there, too, but he somewhat mysteriously announced that he was about to go off on a trip to Greece.

Paris, however, was by no means paradise. The Algerian problem had become even worse than it had been the year before, and Baldwin worried about bringing Paula from one trouble spot to another, in some ways, even more complicated one. The old night life seemed less appealing, too: "I just want to work . . . and grow old beautifully," he wrote to David. He arranged for Paula to attend classes at the Alliance Française and stay for a while at the Joneses'.

When Paula, Marc, and Lucien finally arrived, the social life did pick up. There was a memorable day in the Joneses' Mercedes with Tennessee Williams when the car was stopped by gun-toting police. There was a reunion at the Abbaye with Gordon Heath, who greeted Baldwin with the words, "Well, you're still ugly." "But I don't *feel* ugly," he answered. And there were the nights with the Joneses, with Jimmy "preaching" from their pulpit-bar. One evening a particularly noisy party took place at the Paris home of *Playboy* artist Leroy Nieman. Bill Belli was there, as were Marc Crawford and Lucien. Crawford and Baldwin engaged in a "heated conversation" with Belli and several other white men. Baldwin was finding it less possible to be patient with arguments like Belli's that Italian immigrants had had as difficult a time as black Americans in gaining acceptance in America. Belli later admitted that his argument was based more on resentment and a sense of his own lack of identity—his own feelings of alienation—than anything else. Baldwin seemed to realize this and homed in on Belli as if his life depended on his converting him. Belli was a potential disciple as much as he himself had been a potential convert to Elijah Muhammad.

Baldwin left for Israel feeling some anxiety about "abandoning"

Paula and even more about Beauford's state of mind. Things were not going well for Beauford. It was true that he had had two relatively successful exhibitions in recent years and that he continued to live and work near Richard Olney and Bernard Hassell in Clamart. Mary Painter saw him often, too, and he had many other friends. But Beauford was increasingly oppressed by his "voices" and by a dependency on alcohol that only aggravated the problem. As his letters indicate, his art grew out of an inner agony, out of the role that the great American curse had foisted on him and on his young "son" in art. It grew out of what Baldwin called the "darkness . . . full of sorrow" that had driven his stepfather insane. And if, as Baldwin also said, the light in Beauford's paintings "held the power to illuminate, even to redeem and reconcile and heal," it also was a light—a confrontation with reality—that cost Beauford *his* sanity.

Sometime in October, Beauford took the train to Brindisi to catch the boat to Greece. On the train he was accompanied by the menacing voices. They called him "nigger" and "queer," and urged him to give his money away to the people on the train who were "trying to get" him. The voices followed him around Brindisi. They plotted to castrate him and then to murder him. He wandered the streets aimlessly—a living expression of the black man's fear in an unseeing but nevertheless hostile white world—scolding the voices, waiting for sailing time. The voices were relentless. He would quiet them by killing himself. Beating himself on the head with a rock only caused a scene. The voices laughed. The police put him on the ship.

The voices were quiet while he was drinking at the bar, but when the ship got to Patras they were waiting for him. Beauford gave in to them. He threw his coat, his apartment keys, and other belongings off one side of the ship—perhaps as a decoy—and when the voices still laughed he walked slowly to the other side and jumped. Almost miraculously—he could not swim—he was rescued and placed on the bus for Athens. In his hotel the voices tormented him again, and he attempted to cut his wrists; he was hospitalized and flown back to Paris for treatment at a clinic in Vincennes. He was then put in the care of an American couple called Charley and Gita Boggs, before being moved by friends some months later to his last home, 53, rue Vercingétorix.

Meanwhile, Baldwin was in Israel. He would record his reactions, not in *The New Yorker* as originally planned, but in a series of letters to his agent, Bob Mills, later published by *Harper's* as "Letters from a Journey." The trip to the Holy Land for the former child preacher, steeped in the language and mythology of the Old Testament, was an extraordinary experience, but one tempered by modern political realities. In several weeks of "wandering up and down Israel," he visited bazaars, art colonies, kibbutzim, and, most of all, holy places. Places like Sion, the Negev, the Dead Sea, the river Jordan held a metaphorical significance for Baldwin that was associated directly with the history and aspirations of his people.

And when the onetime boy preacher visited Jerusalem, something of the old religious fire arose in him. He sat for a while in the Garden of Gethsemane and then stood on the Mount of Olives and looked down over the ancient walls, the golden dome where the Temple had once been, and at the streets where Jesus, John, and the prophets may have walked. He thought of the old song his father had so often sung, "I want to be ready to walk in Jerusalem,/Just like John." And his own John Grimes came to mind, that early ghost of himself on the hill in Central Park. Later he would visit the "upper room," the scene of the Last Supper, and there he remembered the songs of Mahalia Jackson and Marian Anderson singing "Go Down, Moses" at the concert Beauford had taken him to all those years before.

And then he put his feelings and memories into perspective: Was he ready, like John? He thought not. Here he was in a place that had helped to shape his identity, the model for the "promised land" of the old songs. The meaning of being a Jew was somehow involved with the meaning of being a black man. Yet the Holy Land was a battleground between Arab and Jew, and Baldwin could not help but feel his own "homelessness" in a land that had become a "homeland to so many faces from so many corners of the world." He took notice, too, of the "tremendous gap" between European and Asian Jews, and he was "saddened" by the whole idea of men fighting wars over national flags. Fewer rather than more nations would be better. He was resigned to the fact that some people would think his writing on Israel was anti-Semitic.

Baldwin had intended that Israel would be the prelude to Africa—another "homeland" which had "given me my identity." But he found he was not able to travel and work on *Another Country* at the same time. He decided to put off Africa temporarily and to make the long-promised visit to Engin Cezzar in Istanbul. Arriving in October in the middle of a party for Engin and his wife Gülriz Sururi, Jimmy was literally and figuratively embraced by the entire Istanbul intellectual world. Engin and Gülriz already had reputations as successful actors, and their friends were the leading theater people, journalists, writers, painters, and academics of Istanbul. Baldwin was amazed at the people he met that night, including, especially, the painter Aliye Berger and the novelist Yasar Kemal, both of whom could justly be called legends in their own time.

Yasar was a huge, gruff peasant from the southern mountains, who had escaped from and documented in several novels—most notably *Memed, My Hawk*—the oppression of his people by a deeply embedded and unfair economic and class system. He would spend many years in jail for his political views, and Baldwin would become his great friend, supporter, and defender.

Aliye Berger was one of an extraordinary family group that included her famous brother, the "Fisherman of Halicarnassus," a poet who had been exiled to Bodrum years before for having shot his aristocratic father in a quarrel, it was said, over a mistress of the son's whom the father had expropriated during the son's stay at Oxford. Aliye had left home at nineteen and formed a relationship with a Hungarian Jew (whom she later married), who was the violin teacher to the last sultan. After her husband's death she taught herself engraving and through that medium explored forgotten corners of the Turkish world. She was also famous for her bathtub full of home-made vodka, which Baldwin occasionally enjoyed in her apartment in the bohemian quarter of Istanbul called Pera.

A woman purported to be a mistress of the great Turkish leader Mustafa Kemal Atatürk was also at the Cezzar party, as well as a painter whose compositions, on close inspection, could be seen to be made up of tiny penises. Istanbul was clearly a cast of characters for a man with Baldwin's instinctive interest in social and personal complexity. The city would quickly become his third home. Exhausted by his journey and his welcome that first night, he fell asleep with his head on the lap of a well-known Turkish actress, but not before learning several Turkish folk songs and singing them with Yasar Kemal.

The next day Engin gave his guest three letters that had arrived while he was in Israel. Charley Boggs and Beauford, who had heard from Paula of his plans to visit Istanbul before Africa, had written about the disastrous Greek trip, and Paula wrote expressing discomfort with the political problems in Paris. During his time in Israel, Baldwin had been unaware of his sister's misery or of Beauford's suicide attempt. The Boggs letter about Beauford was upsetting in the extreme, but it was clear that Charley and Gita had things well under control. Beauford's letter, dated October 15, the day after Charley's, was reassuring. He was happy to be staying with the Boggses; he knew that at the moment he could not care for himself. The mental breakdown even had a positive side; he was trying to rework the Greek tragedy in painting: "Life has so many ways of teaching and preparing us."

Paula's situation was of more immediate concern. He suggested to her in a letter that they go to Loèche-les-Bains for a holiday with Lucien. She answered that he did not have to rush back, that she was all right. Still he worried. He wanted to stay in Turkey, where he felt he could work, but he wrote to David that he felt guilty about abandoning his sister. He wrote as well to Mary Painter, to whom he would dedicate his new novel, to the effect that he was unwilling to take "*Another Country*, unfinished, into yet another country." And there were also two other pieces on which he was beginning work, "The New Lost Generation," on his generation of Paris expatriates, for *Esquire* and "They Will Wait No More," on the impending explosion in the black ghettoes, for *Negro Digest*. Finally, there was the promised play, *Blues for Mister Charlie*, which he hoped to present to Elia Kazan by February.

He apologized to David for leaving him with the responsibility of cleaning up his "mess" with the landlord at Horatio Street. There had been a story in *Jet* about the landlord denying rentals to other blacks after Baldwin's departure. Once again he found it comforting to open himself to David in ways he could not open himself to anyone else: he sensed he was "surrounded by trouble," he wrote. He knew he was impractical by nature and that he caused inconvenience to his family and friends. But unfortunately, "the other side of . . . strength is infirmity."

As Engin was doing his obligatory military service and could not stay in Istanbul, Jimmy moved in with Engin's sister, Mine, and brother-in-law, Cevat Capan. I was teaching at Robert College in Istanbul at the time and was a friend of the Çapans. It was at a party at their apartment on the Bosphorus that I first met Baldwin. When I came into the house, someone said I should go into the kitchen to meet Jimmy; "He's finishing his novel, and he wants to see what Americans in Istanbul are like." The setting into which I then strolled consisted of a kitchen counter covered with seemingly disorganized papers mingled with glasses and Turkish hors d'oeuvres at which, on a high stool, sat a small black man with huge eyes who paid no attention to me as he scribbled furiously on one of the pieces of paper until he abruptly stopped and stared for some time at what he had written. "God," he said, "it's finished." As it turned out, he had just written the last words of *Another Country*. For the first time, he looked at me. "Hey, baby," he said, "I'm Jimmy." "I'm David," I said. He looked at me quite seriously for what seemed a long time before breaking into a large smile. "I like that name," he said, "it's special to me. Let's have a drink."

On several occasions during that visit and during his other times in Istanbul in the next two years, I went with Jimmy to various night spots in Istanbul and we talked. Or rather, for the most part, Jimmy talked. The night he finished *Another Country* we spoke hardly at all about his novel and a great deal about American literature. He was thinking of his work now in that context.

Baldwin wrote to an American friend during the period of these first conversations about "the crippling power of the American myth." And in a 1962 article called "As Much Truth as One Can Bear," which he was also working on in Istanbul, Baldwin speaks of the "giants" of American literature—Hemingway, Faulkner, Dos Passos, Fitzgerald, et al.—having in common a "way of looking at the world, as a place to be corrected, and in which innocence is inexplicably lost." The real problem reflected in American literature, however, was contained in the question "How shall we put ourselves in touch with reality?" The essence of the American classics was a conflict between nostalgia for a lost innocence and an "ironical apprehension of what such nostalgia means." In the innocent world of the Garden of Eden the Tree of the Knowledge of Good and Evil stood as a temptation. "What is meant by masculine sensibility," says Baldwin, is "the ability to eat the fruit of that tree."

When Baldwin was not talking about literature during our early meetings, he was discussing the condition of the black American in the context of American history and Western culture. It was as if he was saying, "Learn what I know quickly or I won't have the time or the patience to be your friend." The gap between us was, after all, considerable, and this was a period—soon after the visit with Elijah Muhammad—during which Baldwin was becoming impatient with the consequences of such gaps. We were both Americans, but I was white and he was black. We were both preachers' sons, but my father was High Church Episcopalian and his stepfather had been storefront Baptist. We both liked music, but he had grown up with gospel and moved into blues; my music then was Bach and Mozart. Both of our families were the "stuff" of American myth; my maternal grandfather was of self-made Quaker stock and my paternal grandfather was a European immigrant, and Jimmy's grandparents were slaves. I would understand the nature of Baldwin's urgency when I read these words by him in May 1963: "There is a very grim secret hidden in the fact that so many of the people one hoped to rescue could not be rescued because the prison of color had become their hiding place."

The trip to Africa was put off once again, in spite of a concern he voiced in a letter to his agent, Bob Mills, about what the black press would say when he returned to America before visiting "the land they so abruptly are proud to claim as home." Baldwin worked in Istanbul until just before Christmas, when he flew to Paris to spend the holiday with Mary Painter, Beauford, and Lucien. Paula had already returned to New York.

During the Istanbul period and the months in Paris after Christmas, Baldwin came to a decision. He could not give up America, and he could not give up Europe. He would be neither an expatriate nor a full-time American resident. He was doomed to juggle his prophetic mission as an American with his deeply complex and confused state as James Baldwin the individual. He would from now on resign himself to becoming a "transatlantic commuter . . . a stranger everywhere."

After Christmas, Baldwin was compelled to face not only a large number of unpaid bills but the fact that a friend had sold his winter clothes. Walking around Paris without an overcoat and trying to cope with the financial problems left him exhausted and in bed with a severe case of flu. As he had in the past, Lucien came to the rescue and took him off to Loèche-les-Bains, where he had finished *Go Tell It on the Mountain.* There Baldwin worked on a new essay, first called "Down by the Levee" and then "Down at the Cross," which would become the major portion of *The Fire Next Time.* He also did a Swiss television movie of "Stranger in the Village," and a short, highly complimentary piece on Geraldine Page before returning to the States for speaking engagements.

He began at Howard, where the students he had become close to in 1960 in connection with the founding of SNCC had asked him to speak. There he pledged his loyalty to them: "As a black writer I . . . represent you . . . brothers and sisters." He was determined to remain a part of the cutting edge of the movement.

In April of 1962 Baldwin was invited to the White House for a dinner in honor of American Nobel Prize laureates. He was not at all sure of the Kennedys' commitment to civil rights, but he felt that as a "spokesman"—a role he found himself assuming even against his will—he had no choice but to accept the invitation. Perhaps the Kennedys could be influenced. Then, too, there was the personal sense of achievement that came with being invited to the White House with the likes of William Faulkner, who, much to Baldwin's disappointment, refused the invitation, and Katherine Anne Porter.

Baldwin was an admirer of Porter. She was one of several white women writers, including Lillian Hellman, Mary McCarthy, and Carson McCullers, with whom he developed friendships. In a letter to Glenway Wescott, Porter describes two incidents relating to Baldwin at the White House:

> I met James Baldwin again after ten years, and we talked and he beamed, he was enormously shining-eyed and excited already. . . . later in the evening as we were waiting for the President and Mrs. Kennedy to pass on their way to the stairs, [he] came leaping back, seized both my hands, put his face very close to mine and shouted, "I LOVE YOU!" and leaped away, leaving me a little surprised to say the least. . . . [A] few days later I met someone else who had been to that party, and he told me that James Baldwin had discovered Admiral Morison, and simply haunted him for the rest of the evening. . . . And the Admiral later asked . . . in great annoyance, "Who WAS that ugly little dinge who pestered me all night?"

Porter was amazed at Samuel Eliot Morison's reaction, wondering, as a southerner, "about a Southerner who should so far forget himself as to make such a remark[.] But from this justly famous member of a fine old New England Abolitionist family, it was not only well received, but with hilarious enjoyment!" Neither the remark nor the reaction would have surprised Baldwin; he had no illusions about the liberalism of the North, whether the North was represented by Morison or the Kennedys.

Yet, as was the case with Morison, Baldwin was surprised to find that he rather liked, or at least was interested in, John Kennedy, not particularly as a politician, but as a man. In the president he sensed a sadness which he found appealing. From the moment he met Robert Kennedy, he did not like him. This fact would play an important part in his encounters with him during the following year.

A month after the White House dinner Baldwin flew to Spain with the intention of nominating Porter for the Prix Formentor in Majorca. The Formentor Prize process, supported by a group of publishers, consisted of several days of discussion culminating in a vote and the award of $10,000. The American delegation had counted on Baldwin's help, but he did not arrive in Majorca until the very last minute, too late to be successful in the attempt to gain the prize for Porter. He did get there soon enough and dramatically enough to deliver an impassioned nominating speech and cause a considerable stir.

After a brief meeting with Lucien at the home of mutual friends in Lisbon, Baldwin traveled to London, where various publishers were negotiating with his agent for future contracts. The negotiations took several days, during which one publisher attempted to woo him away from Michael Joseph by giving him a flat and an unlimited supply of whiskey and cigarettes. Baldwin enjoyed the attention, but a lunch meeting with his editor, Raleigh Trevelyan, convinced him that he should remain loyal to his first British publisher. Baldwin respected few people more than Trevelyan, yet two people could not have been more dissimilar on the surface. Trevelyan was quiet, sober, "very British," but he liked Baldwin from the start and understood clearly that his job was to "take care of Jimmy" whenever he was in London. This he did admirably over the years, sometimes allowing himself to become involved in situations quite foreign to his own temperament.

It was clear by mid-1962 that James Baldwin was the rising "star" on the international literary scene. But he was not elated by his successes. Loneliness and dissatisfaction with his personal life plagued him. In a public lecture in New York on "the creative process" he stressed the artist's need to "conquer the great wilderness of himself" and to accept his prophetic responsibility "to illuminate that darkness . . . and to make the world a more human dwelling place" as he carries on a "lover's war" with society.

He retired to Bob Mills's home in Westchester and then to Sam Floyd's apartment on Horatio Street, trying desperately to work on "Down at the Cross." Literally chased from hiding place to hiding place by friends and petitioners for whom he seemed almost compulsively to leave a trail, he finally decided he could put off Africa no longer. He felt that perhaps the issues he was facing in "Down at the Cross" were somehow connected with Africa and had better be traced to their source. But first there was the publication of the long-awaited *Another Country*.

CHAPTER 20

Another Country

Come and drive my blues away.
—Bessie Smith,
"Do Your Duty"

In February of 1968 a young teacher at Montana State University wrote to Baldwin complaining that he had been called a "smut peddlar" for attempting to teach *Another Country*, and describing how his university had banned the novel from his classroom. He asked the author what he had intended in the book.

Baldwin responded with a candor rare in artists asked to explain their work. The very shapelessness of *Another Country*, he said, was a reflection of the "incoherence" of life in America. Its characters are on desperate searches for the self-knowledge and self-esteem—the identity—without which real love is impossible. Without such love people are unable to learn to see real human beings behind the categories, labels, and prejudices created by the loveless, and the horrifying results of such blindness are evident in the history of the twentieth century. *Another Country*, said Baldwin, is not pornographic; rather, it is an attempt to break through cowardly and hypocritical morality. It is a novel which suggests that love is refused at one's peril. It celebrates its author's belief—one that he knows is anathema to the standard-bearers of conventional morality—that human beings are not by nature sinful unless they ignore the call of love, which is to say, of life itself. This, Baldwin said to the Montana teacher, was the essential message of Conrad, James, Joyce, Dostoevsky, and Shaw, "my models."

What Baldwin's letter makes clear is that, once again, he had used fiction to illustrate ideas he had articulated in essays and speeches. "Love does not begin and end the way we seem to think it does. Love is a battle, love is a war; love is a growing up," he had said in his "In Search of a Majority" speech. Following from this and his other nonfiction of the period, *Another Country*, like *Giovanni's Room*, is a commentary on love and the cost of the failure to love, on the relationship between racism and sexuality, on the necessity of honor and the dangers of safety. Its subject is characteristic of a Jeremiah or an Ezekiel, namely, "the spiritual state of our country."

The first part of the novel is the story of the demise of Rufus Scott, a jazz musician. Like Sonny in "Sonny's Blues," Rufus has been deeply wounded by the realities of racism. He is an embodiment of the curse that lurks in the American soul. Rufus, said Baldwin, is "the black corpse floating in the national psyche"; he and what he represents must be squarely faced if we are to find peace in ourselves and our society. In "Nobody Knows My Name" Baldwin had written, "The nation, the entire nation, has spent a hundred years avoiding the question of the place of the black man in it." Rufus is that man. Although denied, he is an integral part of the identity of Americans. Without the recognition of Rufus, wholeness is impossible and the love that breaks through barriers is impossible. The presence of Rufus, then, is at the source of all the relationships in *Another Country*. Each character has been touched in one way or another by him, by his agony. Rufus Scott is the Christ figure—the sacrificial victim—in this parable of James Baldwin's "gospel." Like Arthur in the later novel *Just Above My Head* and Richard in *Go Tell It on the Mountain*, Rufus "got boxed in, fought out his life, and died."

We know just how much of a victim Rufus is and just how much he has been hurt when we discover that he is too broken to accept love or to give it. Society has taken away his freedom to find *his* individual identity and in so doing has removed the self-respect and respect for human life that, for Baldwin, make love possible. Rufus can only assume the worst even of those who mean well. When he makes "love" to the white southern woman, Leona, he does so as an instrument of history: "He cursed the milk-white bitch . . . rode his weapon between her thighs." Sex was a "beating" that produced "venom." Rejecting the help of a would-be friend, the young writer Vivaldo, rejecting the love of Leona, and even the adoration of his sister, Ida, and the support of his family, Rufus follows in the path of Eugene Worth, Baldwin's friend of the Village days, and leaps off the George Washington Bridge.

On the autobiographical level, Rufus Scott is much more than a fictionalized version of Eugene Worth; he is the embodiment not only of the collective tragedy of racism but of the personal crisis

James Baldwin left America to escape. In a sense, all of the characters in *Another Country* are versions of their author. It is through Rufus's sister, Ida, the surviving witness, that Baldwin carries the message of Rufus's tragedy to the "white liberal" world represented primarily by her white lover, Vivaldo. Like Baldwin, Ida sees herself as a voice in "another country." Again like him, she stresses that she can trust the love of that country's white inhabitants only if they can afford to know her "name," her history, her condition: "How can you love somebody you don't know anything about?"

Baldwin is also Vivaldo, the struggling writer determined to suffer for the success that eludes him and at the same time longing romantically for an exclusive love that will spare him from pain of any sort: "Can't we step out of this [racial] nightmare?" Vivaldo asks Ida, as Baldwin had so often asked himself.

Even the "successful" white writer, Richard, who has betrayed his own talent by producing potboilers, represents an aspect of Baldwin, or of his worst fears about himself. And Richard's wife, Cass, in her frustration over the loveless trap in which she finds herself, with a husband she cannot respect, sounds strangely like Baldwin in his darker moments. "This isn't a country at all," she says at one point, "it's a collection of football players and Eagle Scouts. . . . We're doomed."

The most directly autobiographical character in *Another Country*, although he is white and southern, is the actor, Eric, who, like the hero of "This Morning, This Evening, So Soon" and Baldwin himself, leaves France, and the safety of an idyllic love affair, in order to accept the challenge of artistic expression and "risk it all" in a country that has only brought him pain. Eric is another Baldwin mouthpiece; he is one of those "who did not believe in the vast, gray sleep which was called security . . . and this meant he had to create his standards . . . as he went along."

The main body of *Another Country* takes place after Rufus's death. It concerns the attempts of the five principal characters, who, directly or indirectly, had been witnesses to Rufus's destruction, to accept the deeper call of life beyond prejudice through relationships with each other. Each of these relationships is burdened by American myths of race, sex, or money that serve to deny that call.

As a boy, Eric has challenged the prejudices of race and sexual preference in a relationship with a young black friend in the South. In a current relationship with a young European lover, Yves, he challenges the differences of age and cultural background. Still another challenge has been met in a very brief affair with Rufus himself. With Rufus he had suffered, "but Rufus had dared to know him." If nothing else, Eric has discovered the peace that comes from self-acceptance and openness to the needs of others. Sounding very much like his creator, he suggests that all we can finally do is "love and be each other's witness."

Cass comes to Eric as a lover to break out of the bourgeois/bohemian trap in which she finds herself in her marriage with Richard, an American "innocent" who has failed to understand that the real reason for his writing second-rate books for money is the fact that he is "afraid of things . . . deep" within himself. It is clear that Richard's lack of concern for Rufus's plight or for his death is based in this fear.

Finally, Vivaldo's brief affair with Eric is a metaphor for the shedding of the kind of innocence that prevents him from knowing Ida. Since Eric had once made love with Rufus, Vivaldo's night with Eric was for Vivaldo a love act, by proxy, with Rufus. With Eric, Vivaldo shared something which his own desire for security and regard for emotional safety had prevented him from sharing with Rufus. He tells Eric of his feeling that he might have "saved" Rufus "if I'd just reached out that quarter of an inch between us on that bed." Baldwin always felt the same thing about himself and Eugene Worth.

But it is really Ida and Vivaldo who are at the center of Baldwin's novel. The meeting of anger and guilt, knowledge and innocence, honor and safety, in these two characters, is basic to the American dilemma as Baldwin sees it. "The principal action" in *Another Country*, he said, was "the journey of Ida and Vivaldo toward some kind of coherence." In some sense Vivaldo's love for Ida is based on an attempt to make amends for his failure to save Rufus, while Ida's love for Vivaldo is marred by a deep need to avenge what she considers her brother's murder at the hands of white racism.

Ida's anger is as evident in her singing as Rufus's was in his drumming. It gives shape to her identity and life to her art. She sings with a "sense of the self so profound" that "it transforms and . . . gives life, and kills." Vivaldo believes that Ida sings to "flaunt before him privacies which he could never hope to penetrate and to convey accusations which he could never hope to decipher, much less deny." In a long session, after Vivaldo returns to her from Eric, Ida reveals her infidelity with a white entrepreneur from whom she had hoped for help in her career. Through this revelation Ida forces Vivaldo to take a further step towards an understanding of Rufus's tragedy and the reality of Rufus's tragedy in her own life. Vivaldo's anger is the anger of a man whose girlfriend has cheated on him. Ida's reaction is that of the black woman who carries the burden of her history and cannot afford the luxury of a sentimental relationship with a white man or, perhaps, any man. Being with Vivaldo is "fun," but Vivaldo is of no permanent consequence until he can shed his innocence and be willing to "know" the truth: "Vivaldo didn't want to know my brother was dying because he doesn't want to know that my brother would still be alive if he hadn't been born black," Ida had said earlier to Cass.

Ironically, it is only through the relationship with the homosexual Eric and Ida's revelation of infidelity that Vivaldo is finally able to know something of Rufus's experience and in so doing to know the woman he loves. As Vivaldo had said earlier to Eric, "if you can accept the pain . . . you can use it, you can become better." This is, of course, the essential message of the blues. When we last see Ida and Vivaldo, they are "like two weary children. And it was she who was comforting him. Her long fingers stroked his back, and he began, slowly, with a horrible strangling sound, to weep, for she was stroking his innocence out of him."

Here Ida acts out the role for black Americans that Baldwin had so often described in his essays and speeches. She becomes, not a Faulknerian "Mammy," but a Madonna of the Baldwin gospel, administering the power of the blues and bringing the white man through to a vision of himself that takes into account the fact that "what is happening to every Negro in the country at any time is also happening to you."

On the level of parable, then, *Another Country* has at its center the observing artist-mediator played by Eric, who preaches and practices a lesson of acceptance and love among a group of Americans who are "victims" of the incoherence of American life, who must find their own identity before they can love and be whole. These Americans, like the nation they represent, are haunted by the spectre of Rufus and Rufus's agony. Their lives are, necessarily, a blues song of longing.

As for Eric himself, the focus of the autobiographical point of view in the novel, he can only hope that his life with Yves will be grounded in truth rather than innocence, but he is not altogether optimistic. Yves arrives at the end of the novel "more high-hearted than he had ever been as a child," seeing New York as a New Jerusalem, "the city which the people from heaven had made their home." But Eric, like Baldwin, knows that hell was also the home of "people from heaven." Yves, wrote Baldwin, is representative of "*all* the innocent Europeans" who "came seeking another country," and "I spent a whole book trying to convey what this innocent European was going to get himself into." As Eric sits with Cass one evening listening to Bessie Smith sing the blues—"The blues has got me on the go"—it comes to him that he will lose Yves in America, as Baldwin had, and would, in fact, again, lose Lucien there.

On June 25 *Another Country* appeared in the bookstores, and on the twenty-eighth Dial Press threw a party for Baldwin at his favorite nightclub, Wilt Chamberlain's Small's Paradise, in the neighborhood where he had been born and brought up. The Small's Paradise party was a homecoming, and it was a great success. Baldwin had invited not only childhood friends from Harlem, later friends from the Village, Paris, and the publishing world, but the celebrities—black and white—who had touched his life from the 1940s on. The party epitomized Baldwin's dream of success, of racial harmony, of human contact. Dial editor James Silberman turned to his wife at one point in the party and said, "It doesn't get any better than this." Baldwin had finally achieved the goal of those daydreams on that Central Park hill years ago. He was being celebrated; his voice was being heard; he was on the verge of becoming one of the most famous men in America.

The reviews of *Another Country* in the black press were positive. White reaction was mixed. Charles Poore, in *The New York Times*, suggested that "forty years after T. S. Eliot published 'The Waste Land' in verse Mr. Baldwin has given us a prose version of human desolation in a very different manner and with far less obscure symbolism." Lionel Trilling in *Mid-Century* praised it for its "power," and many critics, including Mark Schorer and Norman Podhoretz, were complimentary. Stanley Edgar Hyman, Elizabeth Hardwick, Paul Goodman, and Whitney Balliett were all negative in their assessments, but strangely inconsistent. The novel was "conventional" or too erotic or a cheap attempt to fabricate a best seller. It was too unrestrained or it left out too much. It was, some said, badly written. But nearly all of the reviewers spoke of Baldwin as one of America's most important writers.

Another Country became a best seller and, with *The Fire Next Time*, one of Baldwin's two most successful books in terms of sales. But Baldwin was hurt by some of the reviews, and he tried to explain what he had attempted. In a note in *The New York Times Book Review* he suggested that he was "aiming at what Henry James called 'perception at the pitch of passion,'" but that he had modeled himself on jazz musicians rather than other writers—especially on Miles Davis and Ray Charles—who "sing a kind of universal blues." His goal had been to "try to write the way they sound." Furthermore, he had confronted sexual and racial issues that had been virtually ignored in American literature. He suggested in his *Times* comment that perhaps Americans found *Another Country* worth reading because they were more like the people in the novel than they had dared admit to themselves before, that they responded as well to the book as they did because it had the same kind of effect on them that the sounds of Ray Charles had.

Baldwin's public argument with his negative reviewers marked the beginning of what became, in effect, a war between him and those who believed he should have continued in the mode set by *Go Tell It on the Mountain* and *Notes of a Native Son*. Baldwin was most angered by people who implied or suggested outright that he confine himself to the essay form. Yet, as if to oblige them, his next major work would be his longest essay.

CHAPTER 21

Africa and *The Fire Next Time*

I will make my words in thy mouth fire.
—Jeremiah 5:14

On July 7, 1962, Baldwin, accompanied by his sister Gloria, arrived in Africa. For some time he had felt he "should see Africa" but had resisted the trip because of a persistent feeling, expressed, for example, in the "Princes and Powers" essay, that he had infinitely more in common with his compatriots, even his white compatriots, than he did with Africans. He was frankly skeptical of the interest among American blacks at the time in their African "homeland." He had, for instance, been almost scornful of Richard Wright's movement in that direction. An important part of Baldwin's message to this point, as indicated in speeches like "In Search of a Majority," was based on the idea of unbreakable, if painful, "blood ties" between white and black Americans and the notion that the unique American experience, for all its problems, was the best hope for the future. To "return" to African roots was to return to a distant past and to a relationship that was based on shared color rather than on shared experience. He had written to a friend from Israel that he knew instinctively what he might experience in Africa, that this frightened him, and that this was why he had put off the trip for so long. To Fern Eckman he confessed that he was "afraid" of being looked down upon as an American and afraid that something American in him might look down on Africans.

At first it seemed as though such fears might be justified. In the usual confusion surrounding his travels, Baldwin had forgotten about visas. Arriving at the airport passport control in Dakar, he was confronted for the first time by official bureaucracy wearing a black mask. In front of him in line was a white European being dealt with somewhat harshly, and this "rattled" him. When his turn came he could not understand the official and attempted to explain who he was by showing him a picture of himself in a magazine. The official told him he would have to buy a ticket for some other destination before he could be issued a temporary transit visa. Where did he want to go? Baldwin suggested Brazzaville, having no plans beyond Dakar. The policeman laughed and suggested Conakry. Eventually, with the help of a taxi driver, he and Gloria were able to negotiate the visa problem, and soon they found themselves in downtown Dakar.

One pleasant surprise was their being mistaken at first for Africans. A small child had left her mother's side and presented herself to Gloria to be lifted up. Gloria complied and the mother watched with evident pleasure and pride. When the father came over to Baldwin and asked if they were from Dahomey, he suddenly had a sense that he belonged in the scene, that he had roots here and need no longer be "afraid." The style of the people on the streets even reminded him of Harlem. The robes, the colors, the turbans, the colorful caps, the women wrapped in cloths of bright prints, their babies tied to their backs, were at once wildly exotic and oddly familiar. Dakar was strange, a European city surrounded by a culture it had worked so hard to undermine. The people he saw seemed at once at home and out of place; he began to identify with them and perhaps to wish he were somehow more like them in appearance. He found that his external "white consciousness," his sense of the appropriate instilled in him by a long history as a minority race, was challenged by a physical representation of a way of perceiving that had its source in prehistoric times, before humans began to think about who or what they were. The visitor from America longed for the easy unselfconscious self-assurance he thought he saw in the streets of Dakar.

Baldwin was experiencing his version of *The Heart of Darkness* and he found in it—its exoticism, its marketplace scents and sounds, its beggars, its lame, its colors, its emotional expressiveness—something of the depth, the ability to touch, the willingness to accept the "stink of love" that he had chastised his nation for suppressing. Africa in all of its turmoil, in all of its pain, was teeming with the essence of what it was on the most basic level to be human, and Africa was, above all, black.

During the time in Africa he made a point of talking to whites—especially white Americans—in the diplomatic and information services as well as to Africans. He had dinner with the American ambassador to Senegal, went to the beach with other white diplomats, and got to know United States Information Service officials. When one USIS man suggested to Baldwin that Africans had all of the Western vices but none of the Western virtues, he listened, but he wondered whether the USIS's ideas of the nature of vice and virtue would be his.

A few days after his arrival in Dakar, Baldwin was asked to speak at the U.S. cultural center. He talked on a favorite theme—the goal of "liberation" for whites as well as blacks in the American civil rights struggle. When a white USIS officer asked whether whites or blacks in America would be liberated first, a young Senegalese answered for Baldwin in a manner that coincided completely with his point of view. The fact that a white American could ask a black American such a question was itself an answer to the question.

After a seminar on Senghor and *Négritude* on another day, Baldwin was taken out for dinner by a prestigious, wealthy, and rather intoxicated African man through whom he was exposed to an aspect of Africa that somewhat undermined the appealing qualities he had noted in the public marketplace and among students at the cultural center. The man talked of nothing but money, the quality of various scotch whiskeys, and the laziness of his "help." The rich African was a horrifying parody of "white consciousness" and a living representation of those black slave-trading middlemen who were so much a part of his history.

The Baldwins were met in Conakry, where they went next, by the head of USIS, and they were introduced to President Sekou Toure, who seemed to Baldwin to be proud, impressive, but unsympathetic. The atmosphere in Guinea was markedly different from that of Senegal and contributed to his negative attitude towards its president. Escaping from his hosts, Baldwin wandered the streets and was struck by their relative barrenness and by the attitude of wariness that prevailed in the city. He sensed he was being watched. Later, back among the American officials, he heard stories of the influence of the Russians and Chinese. One USIS man told of the mysterious arrest of his houseboy. The American center had been closed, and there were very few books to be found in Guinea. Christianity and capitalism were not the only white ideologies to have left their painful marks on Africa

It was with some relief that Baldwin and Gloria arrived late in July in Freetown, Sierra Leone. This was to be the most important stop on the African tour, primarily because of an introduction to Frank Karefa-Smart, a USIS employee who became, in effect, their guide and host. Frank was the younger brother of Dr. Joseph Karefa-Smart, a leading politician and the head of one of the most influential families in Sierra Leone. Baldwin took an instant liking to both Karefa-Smarts, especially to Frank, in whom he saw the kind of complexity to which he was invariably attracted in another human being —sensitivity and intelligence combined with a certain sadness and skepticism, an essential "privacy." He could not have known then that in a few years Gloria would marry Frank Karefa-Smart.

Through their new friends the Baldwins learned a great deal about the Sierra Leonean version of the peculiar legacy of colonialism. The Karefa-Smarts were English-speaking people of the old British protectorate, while the majority of Freetown's citizens were Creole descendants of the original settlers of the Freetown colony. The gap between the colony and the protectorate was evident in all areas of life in Sierra Leone, not least in the parliament itself, a session of which Baldwin attended with Frank Karefa-Smart, where the protectorate-based Speaker wore a British judicial wig, carried a mace, and exhibited pure arrogance in relation to the much less sophisticated parliamentarians from the colony. Baldwin was finding that "discovering" Africa would mean sifting through not only the ancient tribal differences but the modern ones artificially created by the white oppressor. Color could not in itself make a "nation."

The rest of the African trip included stops in Monrovia, Abidjan, and Accra. But everything after Freetown was anticlimactic, and Baldwin realized he did not want to write the article on Africa commissioned by *The New Yorker.* As was the case with his trips to the South, he was uncomfortable in the role of reporter. The pages of notes on the diamond trade in Sierra Leone left him cold, and an agricultural station outside of Monrovia had something of the same effect. His interest was always in the inner workings of people, and he was finding himself more and more the captive of American officials whose company he enjoyed well enough but who could provide him only with a predictable outlook on Africa. Throughout the notes he kept on Africa there are indications of the things that really attracted him but which he was unable to pursue in any depth. He comments frequently on the sheer beauty of the landscape, the farms, the people—"especially the children, the openness and gentleness. . . . *The Children.*"

Baldwin left Africa glad he had been there but with his eyes firmly focused on America. What he had seen—the political turmoil, the poverty, the pride, the physicality, the failure of the whites in Africa to understand—led him directly to the essay that he had left unfinished before the trip and which he knew now he must finish before he could do anything else. "Down at the Cross" would, he thought, be his consideration of Western culture from the perspective of the people oppressed by that culture. In it he would expose the real "moral history of the West." After Africa he was more convinced than ever that America's—and the West's—only hope of survival lay in a liberation from the hypocrisy that had made oppression and subjugation in the name of democracy and religion possible. It was time for a "redefinition" of our myths in the context of our deeds. Africa had cemented his belief that to be of African descent in the West was "to be the 'flesh' of white people—endlessly mortified."

Baldwin had gone to Turkey to finish *Another Country*. Now, a little less than a year later, after picking up Lucien in Paris, he went back there to finish "Down at the Cross." Several years before, Baldwin had promised an article on the Black Muslims to Norman Podhoretz at *Commentary*, at about the same time he had committed himself to writing the African piece for William Shawn at *The New Yorker*. As there was no African travel essay, he decided that *The New Yorker* should be offered "Down at the Cross," which, in any case, since it included a long segment on his early life in the church, had developed into something more than an essay on the Muslims. Podhoretz considered, with some reason, that he had been treated badly, but Baldwin also wanted a wider audience than *Commentary* would provide, and short of money, as always, he needed the higher fee that *The New Yorker* could pay.

The twenty-thousand-word essay, unlike anything *The New Yorker* had ever printed before, was published as "Letter from a Region in My Mind" and almost immediately became, literally, the "talk of the town," causing the magazine's sales to soar. *Time* magazine called it "compelling" and "bitterly eloquent." There were also detractors—and friends—who resented Baldwin's placing such a work in *The New Yorker* among the elitist ads for expensive cars and clothes. Many of the same people complained of his selling serious articles to *Playboy* and *Mademoiselle*. Baldwin's not altogether tongue-in-cheek reply was always that his audience were the "publicans and tax-collectors" as well as the righteous.

Meanwhile, in commemoration of the one hundredth anniversary of the Emancipation Proclamation, he wrote an open letter to his nephew James, his brother Wilmer's son. This was published in *Progressive* as "A Letter to My Nephew." Both pieces were received with enthusiasm. It was James Silberman at Dial who recognized the larger importance of the two articles and their essential connection. Against the advice of Shawn at *The New Yorker*, he suggested using the "Letter to My Nephew" as an introduction to the longer essay. *The Fire Next Time*, then, became a book which contained "My Dungeon Shook: Letter to My Nephew on the One Hundredth Anniversary of the Emancipation" and "Down at the Cross: Letter from a Region in My Mind."

The "Letter to My Nephew" is an impassioned cry to the African-American youth represented specifically by Baldwin's nephew and more generally by the young people challenging the old guard in the rights movement. It is a direct and clear articulation of the Baldwin philosophy, as much a manifesto as *Notes of a Native Son* had been in 1955, but a much angrier one.

The idea for the open letter had taken hold during a visit to an elementary school classroom in Dakar on the second day of Baldwin's recent trip. When he entered the room the children were reciting in unison from a history textbook. The words seemed to have little to do with the lives of those in the room, and upon reading the opening passage of the book (published and written in France)—"Our ancestors, who came from Gaul . . ."—he was enraged by the irony. These children were being denied their own heritage; the object was to turn them into absurd replicas of their colonizers. He thought of the analogous situation of millions of black children in American classrooms reading about "our ancestors," the Europeans, the pilgrims, the writers of the Constitution, and the pioneers. African-American children must not be "educated" into the myths of the oppressor; they must not be denied their own identity.

The greatest danger, Baldwin announces to his nephew, is "believing that you really are what the white world calls a *nigger*." As for the white oppressors, their greatest crime is their "innocence"; they "have destroyed and are destroying hundreds of thousands of lives and do not know it and do not want to know it." Ida had told Vivaldo in *Another Country* that he had no right not to "know." Baldwin reminds his nephew of the results of the failure to know, the results of this white innocence: "You were born where you were born and faced the future that you faced because you were black and *for no other reason*."

Then Baldwin turns to the question of the role of black people in reeducating whites. Integration does not mean that you have to become like white people, he tells his nephew, or that they must accept you. The point is that "we, with love, shall force our brothers to see themselves as they are, to cease fleeing from reality and begin to change it. . . . We cannot be free until they are free."

In "Down at the Cross" Baldwin considers the question of the relationship between religion and the love he had spoken of in the letter to his nephew. He begins with a wonderfully vivid description of his own church experience, emphasizing that his desire to be saved as a teenager was in reality a desire to be saved from the call of the body and from the agony of racial oppression. He describes how he began, however, even in the church, to recognize the importance of *sensuality*: "To be sensual . . . is to respect and rejoice in the force of life, of life itself, and to be *present* in all that one does, from the effort of loving to the breaking of bread." But finally there had been no choice but to leave the church. Christianity was more concerned with the soul than the body, "to which fact the flesh (and the corpses) of countless infidels bears witness."

In Africa he had found the same struggle between the sensual and the repressive that he had found in his own church. It was as evident in the African colors, sounds, and smells surrounded by the French and English buildings of Dakar and Freetown as it was in the saints in their Sunday best "down at the cross" of the white God. And once again he had come to an anti-Christian position. "Whoever wishes to become a truly moral human being," Baldwin writes,

> must first divorce himself from all the prohibitions, crimes, and hypocrisies of the Christian church. If the concept of God has any validity or any use, it can only be to make us larger, freer, and more loving. If God cannot do this, then it is time we got rid of him.

Having disposed for the moment of the old religion of the black diaspora, Baldwin turns his attention to the new religious hope of the black dispossessed, the religion of Elijah Muhammad. This was a religion that had in many ways succeeded where Christianity had failed. It had reached out to junkies, to drunkards, to prostitutes, to the poor, and had inspired pride, self-respect, and the possibility of material achievement. Yet, behind these achievements was a parody of a familiar point of view: "God is black. All black men belong to Islam; they have been chosen. And Islam shall rule the world. The dream, the sentiment is old; only the color is new."

During his visit to Elijah Muhammad, Baldwin had felt "I was back in my father's house," back in a set of puritanical taboos and totems that could not speak to the real nature of our problems as a nation, that, like all ideologically based forms, could only serve to imprison us further, to keep us from the "sensuality" which is an acceptance of life: "Perhaps the whole root of our trouble, the human trouble, is that we will sacrifice all the beauty of our lives, will imprison ourselves in totems, taboos, crosses, blood sacrifices, steeples, mosques, races, armies, flags, nations, in order to deny the fact of death, which is the only fact we have. . . . One . . . ought to *earn* one's death by confronting with passion the conundrum of life." To accept death—and, therefore, life—in this way is to be free, but "freedom is hard to bear." The Nation of Islam's call for a separate nation is no less ironical or dangerous than the de facto establishment of exactly that by the white power structure in America.

At the end of his essay Baldwin points, as he had elsewhere, to the power of love as our only hope, love "not in the infantile American sense of being made happy but in the tough and universal sense of quest and daring and growth," the sense represented metaphorically in *Another Country*. The final words are a Jeremiah-like last-chance charge to a nation on the brink of disaster; they are James Baldwin's "I have a dream":

> If we—and now I mean the relatively conscious whites and the relatively conscious blacks, who must, like lovers, insist on, or create, the consciousness of the others—do not falter in our duty now, we may be able, handful that we are, to end the racial nightmare, and achieve our country, and change the history of the world. If we do not now dare everything, the fulfillment of that prophecy, re-created from the Bible in song by a slave, is upon us: *God gave Noah the rainbow sign, No more water, the fire next time!*

The reviews of *The Fire Next Time* were highly favorable and the book went to the top of the nonfiction best seller lists all over the country, and for the first time Baldwin became an internationally recognized writer. The reception in England was especially enthusiastic. In *The Guardian* Marcus Cunliffe wrote, "James Baldwin has become world-famous . . . he speaks with an appalling authority, as one at the head of a multitude." Ved Mehta, writing in *The Observer*, said "*The Fire Next Time* is an extraordinary human document—a classic." Most important was a letter from Beauford Delaney, in which his old mentor summed up what Baldwin had hoped would be the reaction of black Americans: The work "reveals for all of us so much that we feel but cannot put into words." The prophet had been heard by the *whole* nation.

CHAPTER 22

The Activist

I've been here 350 years but you've never seen me.
—James Baldwin

During the second half of 1962 two events that occurred in Oxford, Mississippi, caught Baldwin's attention. William Faulkner died; and a young black man, James Meredith, enrolled at the all-white University of Mississippi after being denied admission by the governor of the state and only after twelve thousand troops sent by Washington prevented the realization of Faulkner's nightmare of black and white Mississippians killing each other in the streets of Oxford and Jackson. It was this nightmare—and Faulkner's role in it—to which Baldwin had so strongly reacted in "Faulkner and Desegregation."

The South was still the arena for events that would change the nation. The great curse that Faulkner described so often, the curse glossed over for so long by American myths, was as operative as ever—only more explosively so than usual—in Birmingham, in Greensboro, and in the prototype for Yoknapatawpha County itself.

A month after Meredith entered "Ole Miss," "Down at the Cross" appeared in *The New Yorker*. Where Faulkner had lamented and cajoled, Baldwin was the prophet of "the fire next time." He had become the most articulate witness of his nation's agony: "There's a bill due that has to be paid," he cried. He had returned from Africa with his eyes once again on the movement and its most public battlefield, the Deep South.

After a New Year's Eve party in his honor at the New York apartment of June Shagaloff, an NAACP official, Baldwin left early on the morning of January 1, 1963, for Jackson, where he had an appointment with James Meredith before beginning a whirlwind lecture tour of the South for CORE.

Even after the two earlier long visits he was appalled and frightened by the power of the South's myths and the overtness of its hatred. Furthermore, he was well aware that the resistance to desegregation had entered a new, more violent phase since his last visit. White administrators had closed public parks rather than allow them to be integrated, white businesses had been badly hurt by black boycotts, white children were being sent to segregated private schools set up to isolate "integrated" public schools, and churches and houses were being bombed even more often than they had been before. Demonstrations, in which marchers confronted police, with their clubs, their dogs, and their fire hoses, were a regular occurrence now, and as always, there were the black bodies found mutilated in ditches or hanging from trees. This was the time of the freedom riders, who were attacked and beaten as they rode through the South for justice.

The president, John Kennedy, and his brother, the attorney general, seemed unable or unwilling to take sufficient action to uphold antisegregation laws. When two students supporting voter registration in Ruleville, Mississippi, were wounded by bullets fired into a house, James Forman of SNCC demanded presidential backing. Verbal support came in a September statement from the White House against church burnings and in favor of voter registration. Such gestures would not be adequate. The beatings and the burnings went on, and particular resentment was directed at "meddling" northerners. There was good reason to be afraid—especially if one was a black celebrity from the North.

Baldwin arrived in Jackson in time for a New Year's Day party, complete with "hog jowl, black-eyed peas, cornbread," and plenty of music and dancing. James Meredith was amused at Baldwin's version of the twist and was surprised to hear later that his guest had been frightened. He suggested that the fear might have explained Baldwin's surprising "quietness" during his three-day visit in Oxford and Jackson. In fact, if he did not talk much it was probably more because he had little in common with Meredith. He did like him, however, and he was impressed by his courage. Meredith was "very gentle" and "one of the noblest people I have met."

He met a man in Jackson on January 4 who impressed him even more and with whom he traveled around the state. Medgar Evers was the chief NAACP officer in Mississippi. Baldwin was drawn to him immediately. Later he called Evers "a *great* man . . . a beautiful man" and sensed in him a resignation that sprang from an inner knowledge that he was "going to die." Evers was looking into the backcountry murder of a black man with the idea that it was in all likelihood a racially motivated act that might allow for the application of federal as opposed to local jurisdiction. He was a "troublemaker," and therefore in constant danger; the time he spent with Baldwin was characteristic. The two men visited people mostly at night "behind locked doors, lights down." It became clear that the murdered man had been the victim of a white storekeeper who had been attracted to the black man's wife.

Baldwin quickly lost interest in the details and took in the scene as if for a novel or a play. He gave up note taking and began to concentrate on "the climate . . . and Medgar." He was moved by the sight of a small church he and Evers came across; it struck him that his stepfather had probably preached in such a church before coming North, and when they looked in the window, he saw immediately a stage set—the piano, the pulpit, the worn benches, and most especially the "*peculiar, horrible* and moving painting of our Lord and Savior, Jesus Christ, *on* the stage."

For some time *Blues for Mister Charlie*, the play based on the Emmett Till murder that he had promised Elia Kazan back in 1959, had been on his mind. Now the trip with Evers was bringing the play into focus. The murder of a black man by a white storekeeper and the little Mississippi "colored" church were parts of the puzzle along with the Till case itself.

The CORE trip involved some dozen appearances—primarily in New Orleans and in Durham and Greensboro, North Carolina. Baldwin was followed by Jane Howard, who documented the trip for the May 23 issue of *Life* magazine. The article is memorable for a series of fine photographs, including one of Baldwin in Durham holding an abandoned child under a garish picture of a white Jesus, and one of him doing the "Hitchhike" with a CORE member in New Orleans.

Baldwin's lectures often were presented in churches. Speaking in his stepfather's hometown, New Orleans, was both strange and exhilarating. He was in his stepfather's pulpit—"in my father's house"—as it were, but he was preaching his own gospel, one full of the old Baldwin motifs and the Baldwin irony, but characterized by a new anger and frustration.

The primary device, whether the given speech was directed at white liberals or black students, involved the speaker's use of himself and his audience as rhetorical actors in his nation's history. The "sermons" were marked by vivid images of the Baldwin message, some taken from the "Bible" of his own speeches and essays, some created on the spot. Whites were driven by a "fantastic desire to be safe." He as a black man had the right to marry a white man's daughter but was not likely to want to do so, "knowing the family as I do." True, he personally had not been bought as a slave, but "you still treat me as if I had been."

Everywhere he went, people asked about the Muslims. Yet angry as he was, and fascinated as he had become by Malcolm X, and as skeptical as he sometimes felt about the methods of Martin Luther King, Jr., Baldwin could neither give up on King's nonviolent program nor at this point turn to the more muscular approach of the followers of the Honorable Elijah. As far as he was concerned, the single "useful function" of a "racist organization" such as the Muslims was to "scare white people." For the moment, the students of CORE and SNCC seemed the best hope. Baldwin's struggle to reconcile "Martin's" view with "Malcolm's" would be reflected in the coming year in *Blues for Mister Charlie*.

Back in New York, Baldwin threw himself into the movement there. He joined Lorraine Hansberry, Linus Pauling, David Dellinger, Conrad Lynn, and others in a demonstration outside the office of the Anti-Defamation League to protest its having conferred the "democratic legacy" award on President Kennedy in spite of his disappointingly weak record on civil rights. The rally would also protest the prosecution of black journalist William Worthy, who had received a three-month sentence for returning home from Cuba "without a passport."

After *The Fire Next Time* appeared in bookstores at the end of January, Baldwin became more familiar than ever on television talk shows; soon he was recognized everywhere. He lived simply, if tensely, with Lucien in a two-room walk-up on West Eighteenth Street, and he tried to work on *Blues for Mister Charlie*. But the apartment became, as he himself said, a den of thieves and parasites, all wanting something—money, promises of collaboration. He still had the "poor boy's" fascination with the "rich and famous," too, and they were just as fascinated by him. He found it difficult to refuse their frequent invitations. In short, the work was not getting done, and late nights out were financially draining and damaging to his health. In February Baldwin fled once again to Turkey. It was understood that when he returned, Gloria and Lucien, who would become his "business manager," would try to organize an office/home for him. He needed a larger place and he hoped to find a better apartment for his mother as well. Meanwhile, he would try to finish *Blues*.

But the continuing explosion in the South, particularly Birmingham, Alabama, that brought Baldwin home after three months. Dominated by the almost mythic Bull Connor, the prototype of the racist southern sheriff, Birmingham, as *Time* magazine put it, was the "toughest segregation town in the South." Since December, Martin Luther King, Jr., had led the protest there, holding nonviolent workshops, prayer meetings, and demonstrations, heading delegations that attempted to integrate white churches, directing a 90 percent successful black boycott of white businesses, going to jail, demanding that those in jail for demonstrating be released; twenty-five hundred blacks, including many children, had been incarcerated.

Attorney General Kennedy sent his assistant, Burke Marshall, to attend secret meetings between white and black leaders. On the streets, Connor and King, the most visible symbols of the two sides in what even then was recognizable as a historic struggle, faced off against each other. Baldwin had already probed for the real Martin Luther King when he had interviewed him on his southern trips. He was just as fascinated by the consciousness of Bull Connor; later he would explore that consciousness in the figure of the white sheriff in "Going to Meet the Man," whose sexuality is tragically imprisoned in the myth of black sexuality that dominates his psychic world. In California, Baldwin spoke to an audience of "the guilty imagination" of whites who project "their hates and longings" onto blacks. The black man, he said, all too often bears the burden of the "sexual paranoia" of white people.

Baldwin was watching the "real-life" version of *Blues for Mister Charlie*. The challenge to King's nonviolence that was represented by his arrest and the arrest of two thousand others on April 3, as well as the bombings and riots that followed in early May, must, he thought, have been severe. During the riots Baldwin's friend the Reverend Fred Shuttlesworth was slammed against a wall of his church by a seven-hundred-pound-pressure "blast" of water as he "yelled helplessly" at the rioters to remain nonviolent. King himself vowed, "We will turn America upside down in order that it turn right side up." Meanwhile, the Kennedy administration still used few of the powers available to it to stop the rioting and to support the just demands of the blacks. Eisenhower had done more at Little Rock.

Again traveling around the country for CORE, Baldwin, as always, pleaded for an end to racism and warned the nation of the price it would have to pay for not facing the plight of black Americans.

At the University of California at Berkeley he reminded his primarily white audience, "I hoed a lot of cotton. . . . You wouldn't have had this country if it hadn't been for me." The real American history had yet to be taught in American schools; he was determined—was duty-bound—to change that.

Real history, Baldwin said, was taking place in Birmingham, where blacks were being struck down by the unwillingness of whites to see or know them as human beings. And history in Birmingham was not unrelated to history in the North. Whites in the South made blacks their victims, but at least there was physical proximity between the two races. In the North blacks were either shunted off to ghettoes and ignored or treated by white liberals as "wards." The North needed to change as much as the South did.

By "change," Baldwin meant inner change: the giving up on the part of whites of the deep-seated, guilty, and arrogant belief that black people want to be white. To liberate themselves from the curse of racism and the damage it inflicts upon white souls as well as black souls and black bodies, whites must in a sense "become black," must become involved in a process of "liberation of the blacks . . . in the cities, in the towns, before the law, and in the mind."

Baldwin's face appeared on the cover of the May 17, 1963, issue of *Time*, and the magazine's lead article on the Birmingham situation was followed by one on Baldwin—Baldwin the spokesman, Baldwin the prophetic witness who cried out across the gulf between the races, whose "bolts of intellectual lightning" illuminated that gulf. "I've been here 350 years," he told his audiences, "but you've never seen me." But with his help, the voice of the African-American was finally being heard, if not listened to.

Baldwin's opinions were now constantly sought. What did he think of education, of politics? What were his favorite books? And most of all, "What do you want us to do?" In San Francisco he was the central figure in a documentary called *Take This Hammer*, in which he walked through the city commenting in a gurulike manner on its possibilities and its inequities.

On May 20, just before he left California for the East Coast, Connie Williams, his surrogate mother from the Greenwich Village days, threw a party for him at her Haight-Ashbury restaurant. The restaurant was closed to the public, but after Baldwin arrived, with a large entourage, literally hundreds of people struggled at the windows of the restaurant to get a glimpse of him. By midnight friends and fellow CORE workers had filled all the tables, and the room rocked to Jimmy's own record of Mahalia Jackson singing "Didn't It Rain?"

On the twenty-second, accompanied by Bob Mills, Baldwin kept a speaking appointment at Wesleyan University in Middletown, Connecticut. Kay Boyle, on a resident fellowship at the university, had made the arrangements. After dinner, a speech in the university chapel, an hour of talk with students at a fraternity, several nightcaps at Boyle's apartment, and two hours of sleep back in New York, Baldwin flew with Mills from La Guardia to Washington, D.C., to keep another appointment, this one with Attorney General Kennedy and Burke Marshall.

On May 12 Baldwin had sent Robert Kennedy a telegram from Los Angeles taking him and the government to task for allowing the Birmingham situation to occur. It was the political establishment, including President Kennedy, which had made possible the actions of Bull Connor. The crisis was beyond region and race; it went to the core of the nation itself. Nothing would be solved until Americans were willing to recognize that the black race was composed of real human beings.

Robert Kennedy's reaction to the telegram was to invite Baldwin to breakfast on May 23 in McLean, Virginia. In a home setting, interrelating easily with his children, Kennedy impressed Baldwin much more than he had in the White House or on television. Baldwin responded to his questions: "What do Negroes want?" Kennedy asked, and "Which Negroes will other Negroes listen to?" Baldwin tried to convey the fact that black Americans wanted to be treated as Americans, that they wanted their president to treat civil rights militantly, as a "moral issue" rather than as a political one. Negroes would listen to people like Lena Horne, Harry Belafonte, Lorraine Hansberry, Kenneth Clark, and the freedom riders.

Kennedy suggested that Baldwin gather a group of such people for a meeting with him in New York on the next day. Baldwin agreed, and after a dinner that night at El Faro in the Village with Mills, his brother David, a freedom rider named Jerome Smith, Rip Torn, and Geraldine Page, he returned to his apartment for a strategy session/party with his dinner guests and several other close associates, including his sister Gloria and Frank Karefa-Smart. By early morning he had arranged his cast for the now famous meeting with Robert Kennedy.

Baldwin's immediate group gathered at Mills's office and walked to Kennedy's apartment at 24 Central Park South. Kennedy and Burke Marshall arrived at about the same time. When everyone was present, there were Baldwin, Kennedy, Marshall, David Baldwin and a friend, Thais Aubrey, Mills, Harry Belafonte, Lena Horne, Lorraine Hansberry, Kenneth Clark, Rip Torn, Baldwin's friend Eddie Fales, Edwin Berry of the Chicago Urban League, Clarence Jones (a Martin Luther King, Jr., associate who sometimes acted as Baldwin's lawyer), Henry Morgenthau III (the producer of a WGBH television program Clark and Baldwin would appear on later in the day) and Jerome Smith, the twenty-five-year-old scarred veteran of the "Mother's Day" freedom ride who had been badly beaten during the attempt to desegregate interstate buses and bus terminals across the South. Dr. King could not or would not attend; he asked Dr. Clark to represent him.

On the surface, the meeting was not a success; it crystallized a problem that was basic to the civil rights movement of the sixties. The white liberals, represented by Kennedy and Marshall, were still pledged to reform the existing system. The blacks at the meeting saw the race problem as having moral dimensions that transcended the particular concerns of the day and went to the heart of what it was to be American. They wanted something from the Kennedys that went beyond civil rights laws. They wanted the president, for instance, to escort a black child into a Deep South school. Kennedy rejected this as a "meaningless moral gesture." To Baldwin and the others it would have represented a moral commitment. With the president there, the point would be made, as one of the participants put it, that anyone who "spits on that child will be spitting on the nation."

The Baldwin faction was represented most forcefully by Jerome Smith, who, as a freedom rider working in the field, was, Lorraine Hansberry announced, "the most important person here." Smith began by expressing his disgust at the necessity of such a meeting in the first place in a country that espoused equality for all. After what had happened to him in the South, after the failure of the federal government to protect him from racial beatings, Smith said, he could not conceive, for instance, of "fighting for my country."

Kennedy expressed shock at this lack of patriotism, and Clark and Baldwin and their group were just as surprised that he could not understand Smith's point of view. Kennedy suggested that he, too, as a descendant of Irish immigrants, could point to a background of oppression. But his family had pulled themselves up. With luck, a black man could be president in forty years.

Here Baldwin, who had been quiet at the beginning, broke in. What the attorney general had said was absurd. It was true that the ancestors of the Kennedys had come to America as immigrants, but long after blacks had arrived, and the point was, a Kennedy could already be president while the black man, as the present meeting illustrated, was "still required to supplicate and beg you for justice."

These remarks seemed only to further alienate Kennedy, and the meeting never led to any real discussion. Kennedy and Marshall presented facts and statistics to support their contention that the administration was doing the best it could. Smith countered with facts about the mistreatment he and his wife and children had suffered. The blacks at the meeting, especially the two Baldwins, Smith, and Hansberry, were not there to hear statistics; their concern was to convey to Kennedy that time for compromise, for nonviolence, was running out. Theirs was the message of *The Fire Next Time*. The Bible and peaceful protest would give way soon to the methods of those who would wait no longer and who would use the gun if necessary, even if it meant they would lose their lives. Baldwin remembered Lena Horne turning to Kennedy and suggesting that he go to Harlem with his record on civil rights: "*We* ain't going . . . because *we* don't want to get shot."

When Baldwin looked back on the Kennedy meeting years later, he especially remembered Hansberry; it was the last time he was to see her on her feet. For Baldwin, she towered over the meeting as a moral force. Baldwin was fascinated by Lorraine's face as it changed, reflecting her longing that the attorney general might understand and her gradual realization that he would not. In his mind Baldwin compared that face to Sojourner Truth's; it was "still," "beautiful," and "terrifying," the way it must have been a year later when, just before she died of cancer, she said into her tape recorder, "My Lord calls me. . . . I ain't got long to stay here."

As Baldwin remembered it, the Kennedy meeting ended with Hansberry's comment that she was deeply concerned about the state of a civilization which could produce the now famous photograph of a white policeman standing on the neck of a black woman in Birmingham. She had smiled then in a way that had made Baldwin glad she was not smiling at him, and she had shaken Kennedy's hand, said, "Good-bye, Mr. Attorney General," and left the room. Everyone else had followed her, feeling "devastated."

Baldwin and Clark were late for their interview and left quickly. In their car they passed Hansberry, who was walking in the opposite direction; she did not see them. Baldwin took note of what appeared to be her emotional pain—her "twisted" face, her eyes "darker" than any he had "ever seen."

For both Baldwin and Clark the Kennedy meeting illustrated a conflict between "Negro urgency" and a "need to protect the image of liberal concern within the context of political realism." Later Clark would suggest that the group had failed to "communicate . . . that this was not a group of Negroes begging the white power structure to be nice to Negroes." Rather it was a group that was "trying to say that this was an emergency for our country, as Americans."

Baldwin was disappointed, too. Yet he felt the meeting had been useful and that it might even lead to concrete action. A dialogue is better than no dialogue, and he hoped Kennedy had absorbed something of what it might be like to be an African-American. Besides, as he told M. S. Handler of *The New York Times*, "despair is a sin. . . . there are people who have proved to me that we can be better than we are." In his television interview with Clark he indicated his determination to continue the struggle: "I think one has got to find some way of putting the present administration of this country on the spot," he said.

The government apparently thought it was important to keep Baldwin on the spot. For several years after the Kennedy meeting he was watched carefully by the FBI, which compiled a considerable file (no. 100-146553) on his activities. A reading of the file reveals the ineptness of the investigators. There is a fixation on Baldwin's support of the Fair Play for Cuba Committee in 1960 and on his homosexuality. One memo captures much of the tone of the FBI's pursuit:

> Nothing is known about the current location of JAMES BALDWIN, the Negro Aughor [sic] and Playwright. Baldwin was at an affair held for PAUL ROBINSON [read Robeson] at the Americana Hotel. It has been heard that BALDWIN may be a homosexual and he appeared as if he may be one.

Baldwin never saw the FBI files, but he knew he was often followed and he spoke of the clicks on his phone line. Later, after the assassinations of the Kennedys and Martin Luther King, Jr., and Malcolm X, he took the FBI's activities very seriously and often spoke of fearing for his own life.

Whether it was Robert Kennedy himself who ordered the FBI surveillance or whether J. Edgar Hoover alone was responsible is not clear. It is known that Kennedy believed Baldwin used the New York meeting with him to generate personal publicity. In retrospect, however, it seems possible that the meeting was at least in part responsible for the Kennedy administration's apparent awakening one month later to the importance of civil rights. Baldwin and his group had repeatedly asked for a commitment on *moral* grounds, and on June 11 President Kennedy addressed the nation on radio and television on the question of civil rights, stressing that segregation was morally wrong. And he would soon send to Congress the most comprehensive civil rights bill ever drawn up by an American administration.

One of the happier moments of 1963 for Baldwin was an early June celebration in his honor at his old school, the Frederick Douglass Junior High School in Harlem, where he had been taught by Countee Cullen. He told the children there that there was "no moral value to black or white skin." Clearly there were adults who did not agree. Only a few days after the school appearance and the day after the Kennedy speech on the immorality of segregation, Medgar Evers was shot on his front porch in sight of his family. The first of a series of assassinations of public figures had taken place; the killer was a segregationist, the motive was color and the negative moral value attributed by segregationists to people with black skin. On July 5 Baldwin was back in a Harlem pulpit prophesying racial conflict in New York. The race problem was not confined to the South, it was rampant, and time had just about run out.

After the Frederick Douglass School celebration Baldwin and Lucien had gone to Puerto Rico for a working vacation. In spite of the news from Mississippi, this was perhaps the most successful holiday Baldwin ever had. He enjoyed touring the island and being with Lucien. And his outrage at the Evers murder spurred him on in his work on *Blues for Mister Charlie*.

It was in Puerto Rico, too, that he began work on a book with photographer Richard Avedon called *Nothing Personal*. Avedon, a De Witt Clinton schoolmate and *Magpie* cohort, had photographed his friend earlier in the year for *Harper's Bazaar* and had suggested at the time that Baldwin might do the text for a series of photographic portraits of the American scene. The photographs somehow captured Baldwin's anger and depression resulting from the Evers case. Avedon joined Baldwin in Puerto Rico and on June 23 they began putting the book together. Avedon said of their collaboration that it was just the way it had been back in the *Magpie* days at De Witt Clinton. They discussed the general theme of the book, which was to be "despair, dishonesty, the . . . things that keep people from knowing each other."

Nothing Personal contains some of the most lyrical prose Baldwin ever wrote. It forms, with the remarkable photographs, a meditation on the Baldwin gospel:

> One must say Yes to life and embrace it wherever it is found—and it is found in terrible places. . . . For nothing is fixed, forever and forever, it is not fixed; the earth is always shifting, the light is always changing, the sea does not cease to grind down rock. Generations do not cease to be born, and we are responsible to them because we are the only witnesses they have. The sea rises, the light fails, lovers cling to each other, and children cling to us. The moment we cease to hold each other, the moment we break faith with one another, the sea engulfs us and the light goes out.

Nothing Personal was at once a eulogy for Medgar Evers, a love song to Lucien, and a celebration of his love for his family.

Baldwin invited his mother and brothers and sisters to visit him for his birthday. In spite of the fact that she had never flown and had a real fear of doing so, Mrs. Baldwin accepted the invitation and she and Jimmy's brothers and sisters flew to Puerto Rico for what Paula called "a wonderful week," one of the highlights of which was the reading aloud of the first two acts of *Blues for Mister Charlie*, with "Mama" taking the role of Mother Henry and other members of the family filling the other parts. Baldwin was so impressed with his mother's performance that he seriously approached David for his opinion as to the possibility of her playing the role on Broadway.

In mid-August Baldwin flew to Paris to elicit expatriate support for the March on Washington that was being organized for August 28 by King and other civil rights leaders. He led a meeting on the seventeenth at the Living Room, a Champs-Elysées jazz club. Present were such celebrities as Memphis Jim, Mabel Mercer, Hazel Scott, and Art Simmons. On the eighteenth, Baldwin preached at the American Church and on the twenty-first he led a procession of Americans to the embassy in Paris with a petition backing the march. The group returned to the church for another talk by Baldwin and freedom songs. On the twenty-sixth he flew home to be a part of the Washington march himself.

He returned to a movement in turmoil. King's nonviolent faction was being challenged by younger militants, who also resented the influence of white liberals. John Lewis of SNCC was forced to tone down his speech in order not to alienate the white religious establishment involved in the march. Baldwin argued on the side of the militants. The Kennedys did not support the event, missing an opportunity for a moral statement. Baldwin was particularly horrified at the attempts by Congressman Adam Clayton Powell and NAACP director Roy Wilkins to oust Bayard Rustin, the event's primary organizer, from the activities, on account of his association with Communists. He suspected that the question of Rustin's alleged homosexuality may have had something to do with the move.

Baldwin knew, too, that people were wary of his own reputation as a homosexual, and he was disappointed that he had not been asked to participate in any meaningful way. Still, the march was like nothing that had ever happened before, and like everyone else there, Baldwin was moved by King's speech and by the sheer size of the crowd. In a way, the demonstration seemed to fulfil his own dream of one nation of blacks and whites who did not know they were black or white, and it was exciting to be with old friends like Harry Belafonte, Marlon Brando, and Sidney Poitier.

But on September 15 King's dream of "little" black and white children walking together "hand in hand" exploded when four black girls were killed and several others injured as they attended Sunday School in Birmingham. Mobs murdered still other blacks in Birmingham that afternoon. Baldwin's anger was that of a Jeremiah: "We are all responsible for Birmingham," he announced at a press conference—the Kennedys, the white liberals, even those blacks who put too much store by nonviolence.

The Evers murder and this attack on children in a church he had visited earlier in the year gave the struggle a special immediacy. *Blues for Mister Charlie* was writing itself. He knew now that he would dedicate it to Evers and the Birmingham children. He left for Selma, Alabama, with his brother David to work with SNCC leader James Forman on the voter registration drive that was in progress there. This was Baldwin's most direct participation in the street work of the movement in the South. He delivered a rousing "Freedom Day" speech at a local church, was tagged by FBI men, and harassed by Sheriff "Big Jim" Clark's police. He was at once terrified, humiliated, and angry. Attempting to enter the Selma courthouse, he sought a confrontation with Clark, only to be removed by the sheriff's minions. A few weeks later, in Vancouver, Canada, where, at the University of British Columbia he was awarded his first honorary degree, he said, "The country still thinks I'm a watermelon-eating darkie."

After the March on Washington, Baldwin retired to the apartment of Actors Studio director Lee Strasberg and worked desperately to finish *Blues for Mister Charlie*. But the somewhat austere life-style there and Strasberg's anxiety over his guest's working habits were irritating, and Baldwin soon made his way to the apartment of old Paris friend Tom Michaelis, who had moved from Paris to the East Village.

Baldwin made the apartment into a real-life Giovanni's room, with Jimmy playing the role of Giovanni and the rest of us (I went several times for dinner during the weeks Baldwin was there) Jacques or David. He flourished in his role. This was no place to come for mere comfort or for the whitewashing of social or sexual issues. Baldwin's conversation—it was nearly always *his* conversation—was challenging and uncompromising. It evaded nothing, paid no dues to convention, and in some ways demanded everything. Jimmy at this stage in his life was at once frightening and mesmerizing. The fire he had predicted was burning, and it was spreading North. In June three thousand black students had boycotted Boston schools in protest against de facto segregation. Two hundred fifty thousand students did the same thing in Chicago in October, and all through the summer civil rights groups had demonstrated against union segregation in Harlem. In his anger at what was happening to the nation and his demand of support, Baldwin was absolutely convincing. Anyone who cared about what was happening was duty-bound to make some sort of contribution to the cause. He asked me if I could help out in his new home and office, which Gloria and Lucien were preparing in a large apartment on West End Avenue, and I agreed.

During October he finally finished *Blues for Mister Charlie* and then threw himself into the movement with a vengeance. He held press conferences, initiated a Christmas boycott in honor of the Birmingham children, and gave speeches such as one for Harlem teachers entitled "The Role of the Negro in the Culture and Life of the United States." Baldwin's voice had become more strident; he was living the events of *Blues*; he was becoming the character of the murdered Richard. On October 18 he led an evening of protest against the atrocities of racism to which he held the white race accountable. The white race would soon "pay some dues" of its own.

The first day of my three-and-a-half-year stint as a Baldwin "secretary" was November 22, 1963. As Gloria and I, sitting on the floor, waded through papers in the still unfurnished West End Avenue office, Jimmy called from downtown. "Turn on the radio," he said, "Kennedy's been shot." This was the second in the series of assassinations that was to preoccupy Baldwin for the rest of his life. Martin Luther King, Jr., received a phone call soon after the first Kennedy assassination. The caller said, "If we can get one as big as him, we can get you next." The tide had changed. The false hope of Camelot had become the reality of the fire next time. This assassination was "only the beginning," Jimmy told us over the phone that day, and he was to be proven right. His public reaction was the unsentimental one of an angry witness. The president, he charged, had been woefully weak in his support of civil rights, but at least he had listened. But such murders were more or less inevitable. They were the product of a nation devoured by an inner sickness. A nation that could murder a Medgar Evers and the Birmingham children and not seem to care was in deep trouble. Everyone was in trouble— "not just the Negroes, but every living soul." As Malcolm X put it, the chickens were coming home to roost.

In December, Baldwin took his second trip to Africa—this time with Poitier, Belafonte, and Thurgood Marshall—to help celebrate the independence of Kenya from Great Britain, the eleventh black "colony" to achieve freedom since Baldwin's first trip to the South in 1957. In 1964 he would present his stage-parable of the African-American's own quest for freedom, a quest still very much in progress.

CHAPTER 23

Blues for Mister Charlie

My mama says I'm reckless,
My daddy says I'm wild.
—Bessie Smith,
"Reckless Blues"

When Elia Kazan, in 1958, had suggested to Baldwin that he write a play based on the 1955 Emmett Till murder, both men had assumed that any such play would be directed by Kazan and produced by the Actors Studio. But by the time Baldwin was well into the play, Kazan had left the Studio and moved to the Lincoln Center Repertory Theater. Kazan still expected that the Baldwin play, when it was ready, would be submitted to him. But Baldwin, now very much more in the public eye than he had been during the *Sweet Bird of Youth* days, listened more than he had earlier to his lingering political doubts about Kazan, and he resented the lack of any black presence on the board or directorship of Lincoln Center.

Just as important, perhaps, were his attachments to the Actors Studio. There were the old Marlon Brando, Tennessee Williams, Geraldine Page, and Engin Cezzar connections; *Giovanni's Room* had been staged in a Studio workshop, and most of all, Rip Torn was a persuasive Studio advocate.

Baldwin remained friendly with Kazan over the years, later discussing a dramatic version of *Another Country* with him and even writing a letter to his son Nicholas's draft board supporting his plea of conscientious objection during the Vietnam War. But the pull of Torn and the Studio were stronger than any influence Kazan could bring to bear.

Baldwin and Torn spent a great deal of time together before and during the actual *Blues* production. There were extensive discussions over the play and Torn's role in it. By any standards, but especially for a Method actor, this role was difficult. Torn was to play the white lead in the play, that of the racist murderer of the black lead. He was a reconstructed southerner for whom such a part involved, necessarily, a painful descent into cultural memory. To add to the problem, Baldwin, whose more radical voice was represented by the murdered black man in the play, fell in love with Torn and became trapped in an impossible emotional situation in which he found himself trying to convince a southern actor whom he loved of the true motives behind the actions of the racist that actor was portraying. The emotional pitfalls were everywhere and as the play moved towards production, Baldwin would go so far as to try to fire Torn at one point and to threaten to leap out of his West End apartment window at another.

From the very beginning of the production process, he clashed with the directorship of the Studio as well. He fought continually with Lee Strasberg, with Cheryl Crawford, the producer assigned to the project, and even with the ANTA Theater's general manager, Arthur Waxman, who complained about what he considered the play's excessive length. Baldwin had never felt comfortable with Strasberg or with his concept of Method acting: "It has *nothing* to do with *acting*." In addition, he deeply resented Strasberg's vacillation over whether to do *Blues* once the decision not to go to Lincoln Center had been made. He disliked Cheryl Crawford even more. She wanted to "clean up" the language of the play, and she advocated a workshop production in preparation for a smoother, more palatable Broadway presentation. Many people at the Studio suggested an "uptown" experimental theater as a more appropriate location for *Blues*. In any case, they said, the low prices Baldwin was insisting on would make a long run impossible. Even Frank Corsaro, the director appointed by the Studio and a man Baldwin liked, complained of the antiwhite feeling generated by the script.

Jerome Smith, the freedom rider who had been so central to the Robert Kennedy meeting, and brother David urged Baldwin not to give in to the pressure, and except for some toning down of the language, he did not. This was to be no ordinary, evasive, or comfortable Broadway play, he told his primarily white and liberal sponsors. A mixed audience—black and white—and the fact of their division would be crucial to its success. In order to attract whites, the play had to be on Broadway. And black people could come to Broadway only if the ticket prices were low. As for the play's length and abrasiveness, it was appropriate to the work's purpose. This was a blues song *for* the white man (Mister Charlie), one that, given the history of the past 350 years, would necessarily be harsh. And a few hours was nothing compared to the time black people had spent waiting for Mister Charlie to recognize them.

On May 10, 1963, Baldwin had delivered a speech in which he suggested that the much discussed "Negro problem" had better be recognized for what it was, a "white problem." The days of black patience, of black humility under attack, were over. And in January 1964, in the *Playboy* essay "The Uses of the Blues," he wrote that the blues were about the "disasters that can be summed up, under the arbitrary heading, 'the facts of life.' " In *Blues for Mister Charlie* Baldwin insisted that his audience face those facts.

His growing lack of confidence in the Actors Studio led to an unusually active participation by the playwright in the production of the play. Pushing the organization's commitment to its limit, Baldwin insisted that Corsaro be fired. His anger partly had to do with the treatment of David, whom he wanted to have a role and whom Corsaro and Strasberg did not wish to include in the cast. Eventually, after much argument, the Studio capitulated; David was given the role of Lorenzo, a student based on Jerome Smith, and Corsaro was replaced by Burgess Meredith, with whom Baldwin got along surprisingly well, perhaps because Meredith took him seriously as a theater person and did not take part in the white liberal versus black militant clash that both Baldwin and the Studio people had allowed the production process to become.

Baldwin was nearly always present during rehearsals, and the scenes that occurred as a result are now fixed in Broadway legend. The most famous involved his arrival at the theater in a towering rage, to which he gave added metaphorical value by climbing an electrician's ladder and haranguing Strasberg, Crawford, Waxman, Torn, and the production staff in general. He accused Strasberg of, among other things, incompetence "to the point of sabotage."

The turmoil of the rehearsals was complicated by a personal drama as well. Lucien was carrying on a relatively open relationship with Diana Sands, the actress for whom Baldwin said he had specifically written the part of the black female lead, Juanita. The relationship so depressed Baldwin that he threatened to fire Lucien as his business manager. He went so far in one horrendous scene as to warn the great love of his life that his remaining in the States depended on his generosity: "I hold the whip this time, baby," he cried, even as he hated himself for saying it.

Too much of Baldwin's time was spent in a bar called Junior's near the theater, where he went to vent his anger and to seek solace. Some of the entourage that joined him at the bar and later at Tout Va Bien for dinner were more parasites than friends and only compounded what was already an extremely stressful situation, both emotionally and financially. It was only the presence of two trustworthy and fairly constant companions, Jerome Smith and Robert Cordier, that kept the hangers-on at least partially at bay during the *Blues* days. Baldwin had insisted that Smith and Cordier be put on the production payroll. Cordier, experienced in film and theater, was called music coordinator, but was, in fact, Baldwin's personal consultant on theater matters. Smith's involvement in the civil rights movement in the South made him a qualified consultant on the material treated in the play. Baldwin had other faithful advisors and support people as well. Frankie Downbeat Brown was a frequent companion and counselor on music for *Blues*. Ted Kupferman, Baldwin's lawyer at the time, and Robert Lantz, his new agent, worked hard to make sense of Baldwin's finances. Frank Karefa-Smart and Tom Michaelis were also trusted advisors. Back at the apartment on West End Avenue, Gloria managed his immediate business affairs, and I handled some correspondence and sorted through his papers for his agent and lawyer.

In addition to his mistrust of the Studio and his "betrayal" by Lucien, and his frustration over Rip Torn, it was intense nervousness about the play itself that caused Baldwin's unreasonableness, his excesses, and near-breakdown during the *Blues* production. Terrified by the thought of opening night, he worried that as a writer he had not succeeded in conveying his vision, one that was intricately tied to his southern experience and his reaction to the death of Medgar Evers. The murder of Evers and the bombing of the Birmingham children had affected him with an emotional force that had changed his life:

> Something entered into me which I cannot describe, but it was then that I resolved that nothing under heaven would prevent me from getting this play done. We are walking in terrible darkness here, and this is one man's attempt to bear witness to the reality and the power of light.

Baldwin wanted his audience to experience that darkness, to bear witness to that reality with him: "I want you to be sitting on the edge of your chair waiting for nurses to carry you out." The sisters in white nursing uniforms, those witnesses in the pentecostal churches of his childhood, form the basis of this image. Baldwin saw the theater as a new church for his Word. The stage would be a new pulpit for the bringing of his gospel to the nation. On the set itself "the pulpit is downstage, at an angle, so that the minister is simultaneously addressing the congregation and the audience," and the stage is split into "Whitetown" and "Blacktown." The gap between the two serves also as the aisle of the black church and that of the segregated courtroom. This basic framework is always visible to the audience, which never loses sight of the break between black and white. Everything that occurs in "Plaguetown, U.S.A."—where the "raging plague has the power to destroy every human relationship"—takes place against that background; the plague of Plaguetown is, after all, division.

The play was to be a process—almost a ritual act, like the great Athenian tragedies—in which the audience, black and white, would explore the anguish of their situation, would begin to see the reality of their condition, and would go home with insight where there had been blindness. Tragedy and the blues were related. In "The Uses of the Blues" Baldwin had discussed the cathartic nature of the art of the blues as an expression of anguish that somehow results in joy, not joy in the sense of happiness, but joy in the sense of an expansion of feeling, the release that comes with facing reality.

The play opens with the murder of Richard. Like so many of Baldwin's friends and fictional creations, Richard is a talented man who had been overcome by the agonies of racial oppression. In a booklet called "The Blues People," which Baldwin wrote to help his actors with the development of their characterizations, he described Richard as a black man who could "forgive" the white race only when and if he could "forgive himself." He returns home to the South angry, deprived of self-respect, bent on suicidal provocation as the antidote to his self-loathing. He is a walking representation of the effects of racism, the perfect victim for a society determined to seek a scapegoat for its own inadequacies. He offers himself up to his murderer, Lyle Britten, by taunting him with the sexual fears that in Baldwin's view lie at the base of white racism. Richard's murder, then, is a given; there is no question of suspense on that score. It takes place at the beginning of the play, close to the audience on a built-out portion of the stage in semidarkness, this arrangement itself being a metaphor for the secret inner life of our social being. The "white problem" is revealed in the reaction of Plaguetown to the scapegoat act, and the motivation for the act is established in a series of flashbacks that form the main body of the drama. In a sense, each of the characters gives voice to an aspect of—sings a stanza of—the blues parable.

After the murder we move to the black church, where the Reverend Meridian Henry's nonviolent approach is being challenged by younger, less patient forces represented by the student Lorenzo and his friends. Meridian has put a part of his trust in the assistance of white liberals, represented by the newspaper editor, Parnell James. For Lorenzo, "when a white man's . . . *good* it is because he wants *you* to be good." He has little faith in the jury system as practiced in Plaguetown and is not impressed by Parnell's joyful announcement that Lyle has been arrested.

Based on the storekeeper murderer in the case Medgar Evers had been working on when Baldwin accompanied him into the backcountry of Mississippi, Lyle is depicted in his home as an ordinary individual with genuine tenderness for his wife and child. But we learn quickly that he is so thoroughly infected with the plague of racism as to make it impossible for him to recognize the humanity of the "niggers" who are boycotting his store while he rapes their women ("poon-tang" has more to do with violence and resentment than with love and sex) and murders their men to assert a masculinity that the cowardice of racism belies. Yet, when we see Lyle and Parnell together as old friends in Whitetown, juxtaposed with the events across the gulf in Blacktown and the friendly but patronizing attitude of Parnell there, we see what Baldwin had discerned from William Faulkner's remarks on race relations in Oxford, Mississippi—the fact that liberal Whitetown and bigoted Whitetown are much closer to each other than either could be to Blacktown. "Parnell, you're my buddy," says Lyle when Parnell comes to tell him about his imminent arrest. "You know more about me than anybody else in the world. . . . You—you ain't going to turn against me are you?" "No," answers Parnell. "No, I'll never turn against you. I'm just trying to make you think."

The sense of desperation is solidified in the play when we turn in a series of flashbacks to Richard and his relationship with his family and with Juanita, the young woman who loves him and with whom he acts out his personal agony, sexually. Richard's reaction to his father's civil rights activities is disdainful. As far as he is concerned, says Baldwin, touching on a painful autobiographical note in "The Blues People," "his father has betrayed him." By not recognizing the fact that his wife, Richard's mother, has been murdered by white people, Meridian has allowed himself to be spiritually castrated and has robbed his son of his self-respect. And he has done so behind a mask of Christianity that has simply served the needs of white people to keep blacks "in their place."

When a man has lost self-respect, even love is not a solution. Juanita's offer of herself cannot save Richard because, as Baldwin has told us so often, you can't love someone else if you can't love yourself. Juanita will have to turn her love for Richard into a sorrow song after his death, to turn the failure of her hopes into a blues mode, which the likes of Parnell cannot understand. Parnell's confession of love for Juanita and her reaction to it—"How can you not know all of the things you do not know?"—are reminiscent of the conflict between Ida and Vivaldo in *Another Country.*

Juanita's song takes concrete form in a long climactic soliloquy where she recalls the anguish of Richard's lovemaking, proclaims her anger at the God who has deprived her of her lover, and cries out: "I hope I'm pregnant. . . . One more illegitimate black baby—that's right, you jive mothers! . . . A man." Her hope is to the audience a warning of a new militancy.

Another aspect of the Baldwin blues song is contained in the character of Meridian Henry, who has lost a son but still dreams of the possibility of supplanting hatred with love. "My heart is heavier tonight than it has ever been before," he says at the beginning of his sermon in act 2. And as he proceeds he outlines the inner struggle that Baldwin himself was engaged in. "What hope is there for a people who deny their deeds and disown their kinsmen . . . in the name of purity and love, in the name of Jesus Christ?" he—and his author—ask. What applies to individuals applies to societies. If a group of people so loathes itself, how can it learn to love another group? Yet "I will not abandon . . . this strange land that is my home."

Meridian Henry's solution before the trial of his son's murderer is the one Martin Luther King, Jr., had preached at the March on Washington and the one Baldwin had preached in most of his work to this point: "Teach us to trust the great gift of life and learn to love one another and dare to walk the earth like men. Amen." But at the very end of the play, after Lyle's acquittal, he is not so sure, as he reveals the presence of Richard's gun beneath the Bible—"Like the pilgrims of old," he chants. The blacks in the New York audiences always cheered this line.

The only hope held out for the reconciliation of the races—a highly conditional one—is contained in the last lines of the play, when the white liberal, Parnell, who had once walked in apparent solidarity with his black friends but who has revealed his deeper commitment to his whiteness at the trial, asks Juanita if he can join the black march to protest the acquittal. "Well," Juanita answers, "we can walk in the same direction."

Blues for Mister Charlie opened on April 23 to an audience of highly appreciative blacks and sometimes angry and often shocked whites. In essence, Baldwin had achieved the kind of audience and audience/player dialogue he had aimed for. The reviews generally praised the acting in the play—especially that of Diana Sands as Juanita, Al Freeman, Jr., as Richard, Rip Torn as Lyle, Pat Hingle as Parnell, and Percy Rodriguez as Meridian. About the play itself, the reviews were mixed and, for the most part, defensive. Baldwin had touched raw nerves. Some reviewers, such as the one for *The Village Voice*, were offended by Richard's brashness and Baldwin's harping on the myths of black and white sexuality. Many whites seemed to feel that Baldwin was somehow turning against them, that he was ungrateful for the white liberal's contributions to the struggle. "Blues for Mr. Baldwin," read one headline. Only Howard Taubman in the *Times* seemed able to overcome this defensiveness: "James Baldwin has written a play with fires of fury in its belly, tears of anguish in its eyes and a roar of protest in its throat." The play was a blues song "for the white man's moral crisis as much as for the Negro's frustration and agony." When Meridian Henry spoke, it was with the "wrath of the prophet."

Opening night represented the fulfilment of a dream that dated back to the early days of *The Amen Corner*. A Baldwin play had finally been produced on Broadway. Furthermore, the audience had greeted the playwright enthusiastically at the curtain call, and he had been joined at the performance by Mary Painter. There was no one with whom he would rather have shared this moment. Mary was one of the chief witnesses of Baldwin's journey from the early Paris days. That she was there gave his life to that point a kind of completeness.

One month after its opening the Actors Studio gave a week's notice of the play's closing. The problem was not so much that the audiences were too small; it was that the low prices, as Baldwin had been warned, did not produce sufficient income to cover the production costs. Still, he felt betrayed by the Studio, and with the help of three white southerners, author Mary Lee Settle and the Reverend and Mrs. Sidney Lanier, he rallied the moral support of friends like Marlon Brando, Lorraine Hansberry, Sidney Poitier, Lena Horne,

Richard Avedon, Harry Belafonte, Sammy Davis, Jr., and June Shagaloff, all of whom signed a petition in the New York papers. The play must be saved, they said, and it was rescued with the direct financial help of two sisters, Ann Rockefeller Pierson and Mary Rockefeller Strawbridge, daughters of the American Dream. For Baldwin, a child of Harlem, the Rockefeller rescue contained a certain irony.

The play was finally closed on August 29 on the insistence of Cheryl Crawford. From her point of view, the reasons were purely financial. Baldwin considered her motives to be vindictive. He was in Istanbul at the time and threatened to (but finally did not) sue the Studio and Crawford. He never forgave them, however, for what he considered their acts of betrayal.

In April of 1965 his anger surfaced publicly in London, where a rather shoddy production of *Blues*, reworked to eliminate the flashback method in favor of a straight chronological development, was taken by the Studio, along with its production of *Three Sisters*. *Blues*, and especially the Studio's production of it, received generally negative reviews, and Strasberg held a press conference in which he, in effect, washed his and the Studio's hands of the play and blamed Baldwin for its failure. For real Actors Studio artistry the critics would have to wait for *Three Sisters*, he said. In response, Baldwin scribbled off a press statement in which he acknowledged the "battle" between himself and the Studio, mentioning Cheryl Crawford and Lee Strasberg in particular. True, he said, Crawford and Strasberg were not responsible for *Blues*, they had done nothing at all to assist in its production. The Actors Studio could not decide whether it was committed to "commerce or to art, and, therefore, totally misunderstands both."

When the production of *Three Sisters* was booed by the opening-night audience and universally condemned by the critics, Baldwin felt somewhat vindicated. But he was to take up his attack on the Studio indirectly in a new novel, *Tell Me How Long the Train's Been Gone*, about which he had been thinking for some time but which would not be finished until the middle of 1967.

During the post–Rockefeller donation run of *Blues for Mister Charlie*, producer Arthur Baron compiled a television program called *My Childhood* which compared and contrasted the childhoods of James Baldwin and one of the country's leading white liberals, Senator Hubert Humphrey. It first aired on June 1, 1964, and was well received by reviewers and audiences. The program contained a classic contrast between the white-oriented American Dream so perfectly illustrated in the nurturing, small-town, midwestern life described by Humphrey and the black American nightmare childhood described by Baldwin. Where Humphrey found a loving father and hope, Baldwin found a stepfather destroyed by despair. If both men could lay claim to the "rags to riches" myth, Baldwin's claim was backed by more agony and by the all too evident failure of the "dream" to reach "my people"; his voice was, understandably, more strident and less grateful than that of the man who would soon become vice president.

It was at about the time of the interviews for the Baron film that Baldwin was given a hard time by the government when he applied for a new passport. He decided to use his connection with Humphrey to circumvent the problem, and after a conversation in Washington with the senator in which Humphrey told him the State Department faulted him for being too critical of America, he received the passport.

Early in June, once again accompanied by Gloria, Baldwin left for Europe. The play was still running then, and he felt he could do no more about the attitude of the Actors Studio than he had done. Furthermore, he was deeply distressed by the upcoming Lucien–Diana Sands marriage and wanted to be somewhere else when it took place. He decided to attend a writers' conference in Helsinki. The conference turned out to be uneventful but for a weekend of unwinding at a house party outside of Helsinki, where he was joined by Richard Avedon. One morning at breakfast Baldwin astounded his old classmate by quoting flawlessly from a poem Avedon had written for the *Magpie* in high school.

On June 27, while in Denmark, Baldwin and his sister managed a visit to Elsinore. For the Broadway playwright it was a pilgrimage. He wrote to his brother David noting that at the pond near the castle "invented" by Shakespeare he had taken notice of a family of black swans being "ignored" by a lone white one.

Baldwin ended the Scandinavian trip by visiting Ingmar Bergman, to whom he gave a script of his play. In 1965 Bergman directed a highly accomplished version of *Blues* on a Stockholm stage. Later there were also successful productions in Germany and the USSR. After Scandinavia, Baldwin went on alone to Paris to visit Beauford and then on to Antibes, where he met with David O. Selznick about the possibility of a film of *Blues for Mister Charlie*. The irony of the producer of *Gone With the Wind* doing *Blues for Mister Charlie* was not lost on Baldwin; in fact, he was thrilled by the idea and was greatly disappointed when the negotiations with Selznick later collapsed. He had also talked to Tony Richardson about his producing *Another Country*, going so far as to sign a contract in October and to spend time in Los Angeles working on a script. With Selznick he even suggested a cast: Diana Sands, in spite of the Lucien relationship, would still play Juanita, and Al Freeman, Jr., and David Baldwin would repeat their roles. Marlon Brando would play Lyle, and Spencer Tracy, Parnell.

Ideas for the new novel, *Tell Me How Long the Train's Been Gone*, were also taking shape, and he decided to go back to Istanbul to work on it. While he was there, the Civil Rights Act of 1964 was passed, and while others were pleased with Lyndon Johnson's "We Shall Overcome" for the benefit of Congress, Baldwin felt the president was sentimentalizing and co-opting the message of the downtrodden, and he saw the murder of civil rights workers, including James Chaney, Michael Schwerner, and Andrew Goodman in Mississippi, as a clear sign of a "backlash" that would lead to a great deal more tragedy before anything like freedom would come to black Americans.

He had already seen the backlash in Harlem, where police brutality had taken a new and uglier turn. Frank Stafford, a young black salesman, had been nearly beaten to death by police for having questioned the necessity of their battering two black children on a Harlem street in April. Later, the beginning of what would become known as the "long hot summer" of Harlem race riots had been inaugurated by the police killing of a fifteen-year-old boy, and six Harlem youths were arrested and questionably convicted of murder. Baldwin was to lead a struggle in behalf of "the Harlem Six" and against the police, the "hired enemies" of the black population. One of his strongest essays of the period is a piece in *The Nation* called "A Report from Occupied Territory"—that is, Harlem—about police brutality and the Harlem Six case.

Baldwin had been in New York during the April events in Harlem and again when the bodies of Chaney, Goodman, and Schwerner were discovered in Mississippi. He was there for the celebration of his fortieth birthday, which turned out to be a depressing experience, not only because of what was happening in Harlem and the South but because he knew that in spite of their continuing business relationship, he had lost Lucien as a lover. Inevitably, he took stock of his life and realized that fame and success and his public activities had done little to change the world, and his personal life continued to be a disaster.

Still, there was his writing. In February he had been elected, along with Hannah Arendt, Truman Capote, Leon Edel, Ralph Ellison, John Updike, Bernard Malamud, and Horace Gregory, to the National Institute of Arts and Letters. Beauford Delaney, who wrote him frequently, constantly reminded him that his art must be his primary concern, that an artist's love is best expressed in his work.

In December of 1964 Baldwin attended the opening of a comprehensive exhibition of Beauford's work that he had helped arrange with Darthea Speyer at the Galerie Lambert in Paris. For several months he had worked with a committee he had founded to raise the money for the exhibition and had contributed to it himself. In the covering letter for the committee he called Beauford his "spiritual father," and he wrote an introduction for the exhibition catalogue. In it he speaks of the importance of Beauford to him, of how Beauford forces the viewer to confront reality. And he concludes by bestowing on his mentor a kind of praise that illustrates just how well he had learned from him. Art, he wrote, could only result from love and "no greater lover has ever held a brush." Beauford's life was sad, in some ways tragic, but his art was a blues song that redeemed everything. Baldwin was determined to follow Beauford's lead.

CHAPTER 24

Lucien and the White Problem

You're the nigger, baby.
—James Baldwin

January 1965 began with what to Baldwin was a maddening controversy over the listing of *Another Country* as required reading at Wright Junior College in Chicago. Black and white schoolchildren could be required to read about "Nigger Jim," but the forces that opposed Wright's requirement argued that black and white college students would be irreparably damaged by the language, the sexual mingling of the races, and the homosexuality in *Another Country*. In disgust at this and the general racial climate, Baldwin decided not to return home following Beauford's exhibition but to travel to the south of France to a village not far from where, years before, he had worked on and set much of *Giovanni's Room*, and just as close to the village that in a very few years would become his home.

Upon arrival he had what he described as "a psychosomatic crisis," marked by severe flu symptoms, including a high fever. As he would remind David later in a letter, the night of January 12, when his fever had reached its rather alarming peak, was the night Lorraine Hansberry had died. She was six years younger than Baldwin, and her passing—and perhaps Beauford's lesson about facing reality—brought home to him his own mortality and reminded him that he had not confronted certain "decisions" in his life.

He meant decisions in regard to his writing, his personal affairs, and, most of all, his business relationship with Lucien. Lucien was urging him to form a film company with him and a would-be film producer called Jack Jordan. Jordan had been a black marketeer in Germany after the war and later had worked in Sweden as a jazz singer-pianist before deciding to become an impresario. He was a very smooth talker who first convinced Lucien and then Baldwin that he would be an appropriate business partner.

Many of Baldwin's closest relatives and friends felt that Lucien had overstepped the bounds of his position and was involving his employer in business transactions that would only get him into difficulty. Baldwin himself was wary of Lucien now, and although he liked Jack Jordan well enough, he had little confidence in his abilities as a producer, especially given the fact that Jordan had succeeded in doing nothing with a film option to *Another Country* he had acquired in 1964. Still, he was a potential black producer in an industry woefully lacking in blacks, so there was some incentive to persevere with him if possible.

Recovery from the illness took several weeks, but he was well taken care of, having the use of a house belonging to Harold Robbins, including a resident cook who was "feeding me as though I were a prize hog." During this prolonged period of quiet, Baldwin did not confront the issues that were bothering him, but he did write, reworking most of the short stories that would become a part of a collection he had promised Dial Press.

By mid-February he was well enough to travel to England, where he would debate William F. Buckley, Jr., at Cambridge University, supporting the motion before the Cambridge Union that "the American Dream is at the expense of the American Negro." Baldwin had always been a successful extemporaneous speaker; he had learned his skills in the pentecostal pulpit. But this was one of his greatest speeches, and all of Buckley's wit and reasoning prowess had little effect against what the audience recognized as genuine power. After comparing himself to the prophet Jeremiah, he proceeded in the allotted time to outline with admirable dexterity what it was like to grow up black in America, to realize as a child "that the flag to which you have pledged allegiance . . . has not pledged allegiance to you," to be shocked to discover that "although you are rooting for Gary Cooper" as he kills the Indians, "the Indians are you." To illustrate the payment of the African-American for the American Dream, Baldwin turned to one of his favorite rhetorical themes: "I picked the cotton . . . under someone else's whip for nothing. For nothing." The second "nothing" was an explosion. The Cambridge students were convinced. Most uncharacteristically, they gave him a standing ovation, and in a postdebate vote, Baldwin's position won 544 votes, Buckley's 184.

Three days after the Buckley debate any satisfaction that Baldwin felt was severely undermined. He and his sister Gloria were in London to attend to publishing business and to consider a school for Gloria's two daughters. As Baldwin described the events of the evening of February 21, they were happily enjoying a rare evening together at their hotel restaurant when the headwaiter called Gloria to take a phone message. Reporters were on their way; Malcolm X had been assassinated in New York.

Baldwin's relationship with Malcolm had evolved over the years. In the late fifties he had "very nearly panicked" when he saw Malcolm sitting in the audience when he gave a lecture in New York after his second trip South. And during their early meetings they had disagreed over the question of the separation of the races. In the very early sixties, however, Baldwin had participated with Malcolm and a southern sit-in student in a radio discussion in which Malcolm had suggested to the student, who spoke of fighting for his rights as a citizen, that without rights he was not a citizen. The boy answered that the issue was not that simple, and Malcolm asked, "Why not?" Baldwin was impressed by this kind of directness. Malcolm's message grew, like Baldwin's, out of real anger and resentment, out of a real experience of poverty and personal deprivation. And if *Go Tell It on the Mountain* was written in what Baldwin might have called the "Martin mode," the more recent *Blues for Mister Charlie* was in the "Malcolm mode."

Baldwin found his admiration for and his personal liking of Malcolm easier to justify after the hajj to Mecca, when Malcolm abandoned his belief that all whites were devils, made a certain peace with King, and became in a sense a part of the larger movement for civil rights. In fact, Kenneth Clark, who had interviewed Malcolm, King, and Baldwin separately on various occasions, had arranged for the three men to spend an afternoon together on February 23, 1965. The meeting never took place because Malcolm was gunned down in the Audubon Ballroom in Harlem two days earlier.

When reporters arrived to interview Baldwin on the night of the assassination, they found a man in deep distress. He spoke in rhetorical terms they had difficulty following. The result was a misunderstanding in which Baldwin seemed to be suggesting that a white man had killed Malcolm. But it was a black man, the reporters said, a member of the Black Muslims who resented Malcolm's heretical diversion from Elijah. Baldwin explained himself later: "What I tried to say then . . . is that whatever hand pulled the trigger did not buy the bullet."

He meant that the murder of Malcolm X was a symptom of the failure of white Americans to accept their black brothers and sisters. It was that failure that had created the white racist murderer of Medgar Evers as well as the black racist murderer of Malcolm X. Both were "protest" killings based on ideology that took precedence over human life; both were the by-products of the plague—the "white problem" in America that made it possible for people to see "niggers" where there were people.

Baldwin joined Martin Luther King, Jr., and twenty-five thousand others on March 25 for the great march in support of voter registration from Selma to Montgomery, Alabama. A photograph circulated in the press showed him walking hand in hand with singer Joan Baez. Later that day Viola Liuzzo was murdered as she ferried people back to Selma. The march followed a voter registration drive and demonstrations in Selma, the arrest of King (who had been awarded the Nobel Peace Prize the year before) and seven hundred others, the dispersal by tear gas of a March 7 protest march from Selma, and the beating of several demonstrators in Birmingham.

The plague showed no signs of abating, and although he continued to participate in the movement through speeches and interviews, Baldwin became more and more disillusioned with the dream articulated by King during the March on Washington. The *New York Times* headline for a report of an April interview with Nat Hentoff said it all: "James Baldwin Gets 'Older and Sadder.' " In a New School for Social Research talk with the novelist John O. Killens on the "Negro writer's vision of the United States," he spoke more strongly than ever of the tragedy of the white falsification of history; whites were "prisoners of their own myth-making."

It was later that spring that he reminded whites at Harvard University, "You're the nigger, baby." Once again he was suggesting that the problem was a white problem, and that now, as Malcolm had said, "the chickens would come home to roost." To create the idea of a "nigger" was to make oneself a "nigger" for someone else, to contribute to the great plague that blinded black and white Americans to each other's being. Given what was happening in America, he said, a warfare of sorts was inevitable. The particularly violent insurrections that summer in Watts and in other American cities proved Baldwin right, as had the "riots" in New York the summer before.

After the Harvard speech, during a reception at the home of Florence Cawthorne Ladd (then Shelton), Baldwin illustrated his point about people becoming prisoners of their own mythmaking. A well-known sociologist sat down on a chair directly across from the sofa on which Baldwin was sitting, with his brother David on one side of him and me on the other, and asked him how many "siblings" he had. After a long period of hesitation Baldwin asserted that he had no siblings. The voice was a whisper, but the signals of an explosion were clear in the enlargement of his eyes. Not recognizing the signs, the sociologist assumed a vocabulary gap on Baldwin's part and explained that he had referred to the number of children in the Baldwin family. Baldwin, still in the softest of voices, explained that he knew what "sibling" meant. He did have brothers and sisters, but no *siblings*. Refusing to accept Baldwin's rhetorical distinction, which he seemed to consider an attack on the vocabulary of his discipline, the sociologist became insistent. "Yes, but they are also siblings," he said. "No," Baldwin now shouted, attracting the attention of the whole room, siblings were a category; you could not smell, touch, or love siblings. When the sociologist persisted, Baldwin raised both hands high in the air, and with his by now enormously enlarged eyes holding the sociologist's attention he brought the hands down with tremendous force on my right arm and David's left arm and literally screamed, still without taking his eyes off the sociologist, "These are my brothers; not my siblings, motherfucker!"

It was not long before the Harvard speech that producer Ellis Haizlip met with Baldwin to discuss a European tour of *The Amen Corner*. Haizlip was to become an important black impresario in New York and would for years sponsor African-American talent on a public television show called "Soul." He had recently been involved in an off-Broadway production of *Trumpets of the Lord*, a musical based on the works of James Weldon Johnson. Haizlip did, in fact, produce *The Amen Corner* in collaboration with an Austrian named Rudolph Stoiber. Lloyd Richards directed this version. Some confusion was caused by the arrival of the Frank Silvera Los Angeles production of *Amen* on Broadway in April. Baldwin had attempted to stop that production in favor of the Haizlip-Stoiber effort but in the end had to allow it to take place. It starred Bea Richards as Sister Margaret and Silvera as Luke and was reasonably well received by the critics.

Also during that time, Baldwin was preoccupied with the question of the film company which he had somewhat reluctantly allowed Lucien to form with Jack Jordan. The partners had agreed that *Blues for Mister Charlie* would be their first effort, and Baldwin set to work on the scenario. He discussed with Miles Davis the possibility of his providing a sound track and approached Marlon Brando and Sidney Poitier about the lead roles. Their reactions were positive but conditional.

In the late spring, Baldwin and I went to Fire Island, where he had been offered a house by a friend of Ellis Haizlip. He was being pressured by Dial Press to finish the title story for the collection of short stories, *Going to Meet the Man.* Cherry Grove, like most villages on Fire Island in May, was quiet, and other than a long night of conversation—primarily about Henry James—with poet Frank O'Hara, whom Baldwin had met in New York several years before, and whom we ran into during a walk on the beach, there was no social life. This meant that Jimmy could concentrate exclusively on the short story, which he wrote quickly and more easily, he said, than he had ever written anything.

Going to Meet the Man would come out in December of 1965 and would be dedicated to Beauford Delaney. It contained only two previously unpublished works, the title story and a little piece called "The Man Child," which Baldwin had written and abandoned many years before and which turned up during the sorting of his files in the West End Avenue apartment. He had reworked "The Man Child" during his recent convalescence in the south of France. An improbable tale of veiled homosexuality culminating in a child's murder at the hands of his father's best friend, it is of interest to the Baldwin scholar as the only fiction of his (besides *Giovanni's Room*) that contains no black characters. In fact, the first version of the piece had been written during the same period as *Giovanni.*

The story "Going to Meet the Man" was a fictional articulation of ideas that its author had also treated in his essays; like all of Baldwin's fiction, it can best be seen as a parable, in this case a parable on the relationship between racism and sexuality, in which the white sheriff, from whose point of view the story of a lynching is told, becomes a representative of the long-held Baldwin belief that the race problem—the so-called Negro problem—was really a white problem. The "man" in "Going to Meet the Man" is the white man, as was "Mister Charlie" in *Blues for Mister Charlie*. The black man who is lynched during the sheriff's childhood is, like so many earlier fictional creations of Baldwin's mind, a scapegoat for the facing of the race problem. Hanging on the tree, deprived of his masculinity in a violent ritual of castration rooted in the white man's myth of black sexuality, he provides the white man—represented by the sheriff—with the sexual power he otherwise lacks. Only by remembering the lynching and pretending that the woman under him is a black woman can the sheriff "perform" with his wife: he thought of the lynched and castrated man, "he thought of the knife and grabbed himself and stroked himself," and then he stroked his wife, and, overcome by the myth enacted in the lynching of his memory and perhaps about to be enacted the next day on a civil rights worker, he whispered, "Come on, sugar, I'm going to do you like a nigger, come on, sugar, and love me just like you'd love a nigger."

It is important that Baldwin chose to tell "Going to Meet the Man" from the white sheriff's point of view. In all of his southern trips his novelist's instincts had gravitated to the white minds behind the racism he observed. The effects of racism on the white southerners, he writes in "The American Dream and the American Negro," was "worse" than the effect on their victims, because their souls have been "destroyed." A man like Sheriff Clark, who could use a cattle prod against a woman, is a fellow human being in whom "something awful" has occurred. That horror takes metaphorical form in the fictional sheriff's loveless bed, where "lovemaking" can take place only through a perverted mental transference to a sadistic context.

In June, Baldwin was once again in a debate with William Buckley, Jr., this time on television. The subject was racism, and Baldwin's particular concern was police brutality. In the television format his emotional approach was less effective against Buckley's carefully researched statistics and "facts" than it had been in Cambridge. Still, Baldwin held his own and focused needed attention on the police question. One of the at least indirect effects of the debate was to put pressure on the New York Police Department. Baldwin had been determined since the events involving Frank Stafford and the Harlem Six to do something about police brutality in New York.

On June 8 he attended the opening of the Richards-Haizlip-Stoiber *Amen Corner* in Vienna. It starred Claudia McNeil as a particularly strong Sister Margaret. Baldwin was delighted by the whole production and so was the audience. There were thirty-one curtain calls and critical raves.

The director and the producers were relieved. They had heard the stories about the Broadway production of *Blues* and were surprised to discover that Baldwin was happy to leave all decisions in connection with their production up to them. The reasons for the hands-off policy were clear to everyone who knew Baldwin well; he trusted Lloyd Richards and Ellis Haizlip to be faithful to his intention in ways that he could never trust the Actors Studio.

Productions in the Netherlands, Germany, and Italy were just as successful, and the Paris opening, with Beauford Delaney and Mary Painter present, was the best of all. In each major city Baldwin was greeted and assisted by long-faithful publishers—Rowohlt in Germany, Bruna and Zoon in the Netherlands, Gallimard in France. The highlight of the *Amen* tour was Israel, where the director of the Jerusalem Museum had the lights of the Old City wall turned on and provided the company with a private late-night tour of the museum. There were other great moments during the Israel trip. Baldwin never forgot watching the cast of *Amen* walking on the Mount of Olives, standing on the road to Calvary, and wading into the Jordan River, exploring, in a literal sense, the metaphors of centuries of black spirituals.

He did not stay continuously with the tour. He spent time with Engin and Gülriz in Istanbul, where he worked on what would become *Tell Me How Long the Train's Been Gone* and wrote an introduction for the Dial Press publication of *The Amen Corner*. He also did work on the outline for a modern-day *Othello* musical called *Our Fathers* or *Jonas* that he had planned with actor Brock Peters and songwriter Joe Liebman, who was also an executive at Cartier. And he wrote an introduction for a previously unpublished WPA collection called *The Negro in New York*. He also gave thought to a revival of his old slave novel project, changing its title to *Tomorrow Brought Us Rain* and then *When the Rest of Heaven Was Blue*. It was now to be an epic treatment of a black and a white family traced from the Civil War to World War II. The novel was never completed, but much of what went into its outline emerged eventually as "The House Nigger," the first part of *Tell Me How Long the Train's Been Gone*, and into the later screenplay *The Inheritance*.

But during most of the summer, fall, and early winter of 1965 Baldwin continued to worry about Lucien and the film company. He still had serious doubts about the company and was hoping that by staying away, things might somehow take care of themselves. With luck, Gloria, Lucien, and David would work out any difficulties. To be safe, he called on Tom Michaelis, his lawyer, Ted Kupferman, and his agent, Robert Lantz, for advice as well. Telegrams came from Istanbul with specific directions that were canceled by subsequent telegrams. One telegram to me was signed "Hamlet B.," indicating that Baldwin himself was well aware of his own indecisiveness.

In June, in spite of advice to the contrary from most of the people who worked for him, he arranged for the signing of papers legally authorizing the film company. He was "still willing to trust Lucien with my life." He felt that the lack of confidence in Lucien's handling of his business affairs had more to do with his family's love for him than with anything "Lulu" had done wrong.

Having come to this conclusion, he left for Germany to support the *Amen Corner* performances there. The play needed a State Department subsidy to remain afloat financially, and Baldwin made public demands that the department recognize the national cultural significance of his play. If they could support Helen Hayes and Arthur Miller, they could support Claudia McNeil and James Baldwin, too. The subsidy was paid, and on August 2 the Berlin audience sang "Happy Birthday" to a triumphant playwright.

Meanwhile, it had become clear that financing for the film company was in doubt, and Baldwin suddenly decided that a break with Lucien was necessary. He gave instructions to that effect, only to countermand them when Lucien called him asking for his trust; "sixteen years of my life" were contained in that call, and "I could not . . . ignore it." As for the movie plans themselves, they were to be frozen until he could return to the States. When the extent of the financial mismanagement became even clearer, he once again decided to fire Lucien, to break with Jack Jordan, and to proceed with the movie with other producers.

Jimmy wrote to David, who had been particularly angry over the film-company fiasco. He asked for understanding. He realized the pain he caused his family and friends, but David must try to see that "a gifted man . . . is burdened with his gift." He would continue to make mistakes, but he would never stop working. He asked his brother to trust him and his love.

He explained to me at about the same time why he had taken so long to act. He had felt betrayed by Lucien's marriage to Diana Sands, as he had earlier by the marriage to Suzy. The "black comedy" that had so long been a part of his life had seemed to be beginning all over again. It was precisely because of what he felt about the marriage that he had been unable to act against Lucien. Lucien's material well-being—his "success"—could not be held hostage to his relationship with Baldwin. Now, however, something that he had always preached in his writing—most recently in "Going to Meet the Man"—had become evident. The public man was the same as the private one; the view of reality that determines how one behaves in the bedroom also "dictates one's behavior in the office." His relationship with Lucien had failed because Lucien had thought that by being a financial success he could overcome those private forces which had brought him so much despair and had made it necessary for him to choose marriages with women rather than a lasting relationship with him. If Lucien's personal failure was based on a denial of reality, it was likely that the same blindness would doom the commercial venture to a dishonest end. There was no choice but to end both the personal and the business relationship, if only for Lucien's sake. He could not participate in keeping him "adolescent forever."

Yet, fifteen days later, having heard again from Lucien, Baldwin was wavering in his intentions. His old friend's letter had been "fair"; it was hard to let go. "The days are dark"; there did not seem to be any way out of the dilemma.

They were made darker by the situation at home. The Voting Rights Bill was followed by the six-day explosion in the Watts section of Los Angeles, in which 34 people were killed, 1,032 injured, and 3,952 arrested. His old friend James Farmer was about to resign as director of CORE, to be succeeded by the more radical Floyd McKissick.

Baldwin did return in the late fall for ten days that were "among the most terrible I've ever known." It was then that he confronted the Lucien question directly. At an emotional meeting in the West End apartment he fired his friend. But he was deeply moved by Lucien's sense that he had been betrayed. They were to see each other with some regularity over the years and would even attempt a business collaboration again. But their love affair, such as it was, was definitively over.

CHAPTER 25

Searching for a New Life

"Live all you can; it's a mistake not to."
—Lambert Strether,
in Henry James's *The Ambassadors*

In a state of some despair over the breakup with Lucien, Baldwin decided to return to Istanbul. He made arrangements to move from the large West End Avenue apartment to a smaller one in a building on Seventy-first Street which he had bought to provide a home for his mother. He would simplify his life in the States in the interest of finances and, for the moment, would consider Istanbul his second home. Sometime before, he had also begun the process of buying an apartment in Paris.

Before he left, Baldwin asked me to take particular care of a framed photograph that had been sent to him in New York while he was in Istanbul in early September. The photograph was of the famous John Singer Sargent portrait of Henry James—painted for his seventieth birthday—and had been autographed for a James nephew by James and Sargent. It had been sent to Baldwin by a great-nephew, Michael James, who had read and been impressed by an article by Baldwin called "The White Man's Guilt" in the August 1965 issue of *Ebony*.

In the *Ebony* article Baldwin had sounded particularly strident. Whites, he said, had built a society of wealth on the backs of a black underclass, whose humanity they had refused to recognize. The white race was hopelessly imprisoned in its own myths about blacks. He ended the essay with an extended reference to Henry James's novel *The Ambassadors*, reminding his reader that Lambert Strether, the first "ambassador" in question and the hero of the novel, has been sent to "rescue" a young American heir from the "fleshpots" of Paris so that he can come home to take over the family factory. But the ambassador is himself seduced, by the "less utilitarian way of life" there, and finally counsels the heir not to return home, suggesting that he remain where he is, in the relationship he has formed with a Parisian woman. Strether urges the young man to "trust life" and allow it to "teach you, in joy or sorrow, all you need to know." For Baldwin, like all those who have lived the blues, this message was clearly understandable, but it is not understood by the young heir or the people he represents, because they are "barricaded inside their history." Indeed, "they remain trapped in that factory to which the son returns" and which, "at an unbelievable human expense, produces unnameable objects."

Michael James had written to Baldwin praising the essay and asking about his interest in his great-uncle. As Baldwin was away, I answered the letter, confirming his admiration for James and mentioning an essay on *The Ambassadors* that he had begun a few years earlier. A response arrived with the autographed photograph of the Sargent portrait. I had told Michael James that Baldwin would write him on his return, but James requested that he not do so. The photograph, he suggested, was, in spirit, really from his great-uncle: "Let this be a curious note across fifty years." He reminded me of the "old man's plea" through his character Lambert Strether that one's obligation in life was to "live all you can," a plea Baldwin had responded to so effectively in the *Ebony* piece.

Baldwin was deeply touched by the photograph and the Michael James letters, and the photograph was eventually placed over his writing desk in the new apartment. He worked on the *Ambassadors* essay from time to time over the next years but never quite finished it. He first called it "The Self as Journey" and later "The Self as a Voyage."

In a formal interview with him in 1986, published in *The Henry James Review*, I asked Baldwin to elaborate on his fascination with James and to talk about the *Ambassadors* essay in particular. He spoke first about the importance to him of James's style and technique. It was something about point of view, something about discipline, that had originally attracted him, he said. But later what drew him most to "the Master" was the realization that they shared a central theme, that of "the failure of Americans to see through to the reality of others." It was this failure that lay at the base of the "white man's guilt" in the current racial struggles in America, and it was this failure that was implicit in the "innocence" from which Lambert Strether—like all Americans—had to free himself if he was to achieve the voyage to selfhood. The essay on *The Ambassadors* was, he said, to have been an exploration of this theme. James was "the only American writer . . . who seemed to have some sense of what was later to be called the American Dilemma . . . some sense of the American . . . personality." Americans "have a tremendous sincerity . . . they are certainly sincere about what they call the 'negro problem' and about the Indians; they're sincere, in fact, about everything. And they understand nothing."

The Baldwin essay on James begins with a discussion of Strether's arrival in Europe and his sense of escape, his sense of having been, before he left America, "one of the weariest of men." By the time he meets Chad Newsome, the heir, and Madame de Vionnet, the wonderful woman with whom Chad is involved, Strether, as Baldwin points out, has begun to live, begun to lose his "innocence" and to discover "freedom."

Was it to redefine freedom and innocence that he had come to France? I asked in the interview. "Certainly," he answered. And he pointed out that by "freedom" he meant "the end of innocence; the end of innocence means you've finally entered the picture. And it means that you'll accept the consequences, too."

In a brief exchange about a connection between *Giovanni's Room* and *The Ambassadors* Baldwin said his novel was "about what happens to you if you don't tell the truth to yourself . . . about the failure of innocence," and that James's novel was "about Strether's struggle with that problem."

In the *Ambassadors* essay Baldwin discusses James's use of manners at some length, commenting on the fact that James demonstrates how disaster arises when we confuse manners with truth. Talking in the interview about Strether's gradual realization of this confusion, Baldwin pointed out that the hero of *The Ambassadors* discovered that "to live," to open oneself to life, "costs something." I suggested that Strether, by returning to America, by denying himself Paris, was somehow paying the price for the American heir's denial of Paris in favor of likely success in business, in favor of the pursuit of the American Dream, and that Baldwin might be paying the same price by not simply embracing fully the life he loved in Europe. Baldwin's answer spoke to the whole question of his connection with America, in spite of the FBI, in spite of State Department harassment, in spite of racial injustice:

> In principle I could stay here and never go back to Harlem and New York City again. I think that's what I'd like to do, in a way. But I can't do it. I can't do it because if I were to avoid the journey back to America I'd be avoiding everything—the people who have produced me (both black and white), the central reality of my life. And once you do that I don't know what you can write about or what you can write out of. To avoid the journey back is to avoid the Self, to avoid "life." . . . I've always felt that I had no real choice about the journey. In a way I learned about it in the streets. If you're frightened of something in the streets you walk towards it. Turn your back and they've got you.

During the mid-sixties the civil rights movement was taking some major turns, and Baldwin was anxious to find a place in it. Malcolm X's death had radicalized him. King's new concern for the inner cities of the North was a useful turn, and Baldwin would fully support King's association of the movement with the anti–Vietnam War cause beginning in April of 1966. He had himself met with Bertrand Russell in London in 1965, and he became, for a time, an active advocate of Russell's War Crimes Tribunal. He announced publicly that he considered the "American adventure in Vietnam a desperate and despicable folly." That a preponderance of blacks were doing the fighting was particularly indigestible considering what was being done to their relatives at home.

In spite of his agreement with King and the majority of white liberals on the subject of Vietnam, Baldwin, like many other black intellectuals, was frustrated with the civil rights movement itself. Something new was needed, something that would speak to the disillusionment he and others felt about the commitment of white liberals and of blacks who allowed themselves to be dominated by whites in the movement. He had long been associated with CORE and had a good relationship with its director, James Farmer. The same was even more true of his relationship with SNCC, led by James Forman. These had been the more activist groups in the movement in the early sixties. He also was friendly and cooperative with Roy Wilkins and the NAACP and Whitney Young of the National Urban League, although he found them too conservative. By the mid-sixties Baldwin felt that even CORE and SNCC and their leadership needed radicalization.

When Stokely Carmichael and Floyd McKissick became directors of SNCC and CORE, respectively, Baldwin was fully supportive of their efforts, in spite of the doubts of many of his friends, black and white. His support would continue even when Carmichael became involved with the Black Panthers. After James Meredith was shot in the leg during his one-man march through Mississippi in June of 1966 and King and Carmichael continued the march for him, Baldwin spoke out in support of the idea of Black Power. It was an idea that was in accord with "an honored (!) canon of Western thought: the self-determination of peoples."

Baldwin was concerned about "deserting" the rights movement when he left for Istanbul late in 1965, but his family and friends knew that, given his emotional situation, it would be best for him to make his contribution for the moment through his writing. Intellectually, if not emotionally, he agreed, and he felt strongly that his writing should not be confined to essays, plays, and fiction. He was especially determined to break the barrier that seemed to stand in the way of his making films.

Before he left New York he discussed a film project with Marlon Brando, James Forman, and Stokely Carmichael. Brando was to play a bigoted white sheriff to Carmichael's black radical. The group brought up the film possibility with Gordon Parks, who, with Sidney Poitier, was the only black name with any influence in Hollywood at the time. Baldwin also approached Warren Beatty about doing a movie on an interracial romance. And he was still anxious to pursue a *Blues* film option. He had made tentative arrangements with a producer named Bob Terry, and with Burgess Meredith, whom he now wanted as his director, to begin shooting in Tennessee in the spring. As he had not shared his arrangements with any of the people who were employed by him, and as the money was not there, this *Blues* plan, like the ones before it, would fail. Still, just after Christmas of 1965, having all too recently undergone the emotional strain of facing the Lucien problem, he announced his intention of returning to New York in mid-January to begin working on the scenario, the casting, and locations.

The idea of uprooting himself was not appealing, and he had found that a period of living alone, although difficult, had made possible a great deal of work on the new novel, *Tell Me How Long the Train's Been Gone*, and had been therapeutic in that it had given him time to allow the Lucien breakup to settle in his mind. He wrote to me that he needed a "positive anchor" in his life. He wondered why he had held on so long to the hope that his relationship with Lucien would provide that anchor. There was certainly little happiness in the relationship. Still, it had driven him to "face" certain things about himself and it had "forced a lot of work out of me."

In a January 2 letter Baldwin asked that I consider returning to Istanbul with him. He said he knew living with him would be difficult, and he hoped he was not asking too much. He had some sense of what he had already "cost" me. He knew he had become increasingly "possessed" and withdrawn, but this was because he had an immense amount of work to do and little time in which to do it. And in any case, the fact that he was inward-looking did not mean he was not concerned with others.

In fact, he said, he was determined to avoid the kind of renunciation of the personal that was the fate of Henry James's heroes. Perhaps this was why he had had so much trouble finishing the James essay. It was not a crime to need another person. The crime lay in the unforgivable "lie" that people do not need each other. There was a terrible price to be paid for that lie. Therefore, he wrote, he was announcing that he needed me in his "arms" as well as in his office.

What was for me an unexpected and, at the time, upsetting declaration of an element that had never before entered our relationship—the element contained in the reference to his needing me in his arms—was followed by an accurate description of what life with James Baldwin would be like and of the personality he presented to the people who surrounded him. I would be coping with an obsessional and demanding man who was a mixture of "ruthlessness" and "helplessness," who was at once highly elusive and available to all. There would, of course, be the usual stream of people, all of whom would hate me for attempting to block the path to the man they wanted to see, a man whose charm lay in the fact that he was in "nobody's box" and "nobody knew [his] name."

The letter ended with a statement of long-term plans. He hoped to write some literary criticism—on Faulkner, James, Proust, Joyce, Dostoevsky, and Balzac, among others. He wanted to become an "honorable old man" who would be missed when he died. The "job requirements" were daunting. But his call was also irresistible. During the next few months, in correspondence and in person, we were able without much difficulty to work out the nature of our relationship. Baldwin's loneliness and desperation following the breakup with Lucien had led him to assume that we would become lovers. In fact, the success of our working relationship probably depended on our not being involved in that way.

By late January, Baldwin had decided he would not be deterred from pursuing the film plans. He said he was well aware that the people who worked for him disapproved, but that he had resolved to give Lucien a second chance through the film. Whether or not Lucien had "betrayed" him, he could not rest with the possibility that he might have betrayed Lucien in return. In short, he recognized Lucien's involvement with the new producer, Bob Terry, and was determined to work with him again. In spite of everything that had happened, he could not rid himself of the spectre of his old lover.

In my letters to him in December and January I had naively suggested that he forget about Lucien and the movie and concentrate on his novel. He answered angrily. He could not possibly write a novel under the emotional pressure of the Lucien situation and the "frightening confusion" that resulted from it. His writing career was at a crucial point and he was in real need of support on the part of his friends, not protection.

If this was a cry for help, it was also a cry for understanding and for freedom from the interference of those who could not understand what it was to be possessed by a mission. It was easy enough, he said, to blame all of his problems on his own "difficult temperament," but it was more important that it be understood that he was "on a journey" and that he—not his friends and business associates—was "paying" for that journey, one that he realized all too well might end in "disaster." What it came down to was the fact that he would have to pursue his path in his own way and that he could not and would not allow himself to be "protected."

Baldwin left Istanbul early in February, stopped in Rome to visit the film director Franco Rossi and eventually arrived in New York to face a hectic schedule dominated by meetings concerning the *Blues* production company. It quickly became evident that the company was not dependable, and once again Baldwin withdrew his support.

During the process of changing the film plans, he managed to avoid another direct confrontation with Lucien. He worried that if he saw him he might again be drawn into the old personal and business connections, especially since there were rumors that Lucien was destitute and that his marriage with Diana Sands was not going well. Then, one night at Tout Va Bien, Baldwin and Lucien met inadvertently. Lucien took a resigned attitude and mentioned the failed movie company only once. Jimmy was surprised at his own composure. He was relieved that he had seen Lucien, that he had been able to avoid painful subjects, and that he had come through the meeting emotionally intact.

On February 26 Baldwin saw Joseph Losey's film *King and Country* with Dirk Bogarde and Tom Courtenay. He had met Losey in London and had liked him a great deal. Now he was so moved by the film that he went back several times. Bogarde's performance impressed him, as it did all the critics, and later they would become friends in Saint-Paul-de-Vence. But it was Losey's subtle and intelligent directing of a highly charged and emotional situation—desertion during World War I and the ambiguous relationship between the "guilty" enlisted man and the officer appointed as his lawyer—that moved him most. He was determined now that Losey should direct *Blues for Mister Charlie* and any other Baldwin work he wanted to direct.

On March 12 Baldwin and I took the night flight to London, where we were to spend ten days before going on to Paris and then Istanbul. This was the beginning of a fourteen-month period during which, with the exception of a few weeks, I was to be more or less constantly with him.

Through the grapevine several people quickly learned that Baldwin was in London. Among the first and most frequent callers was a young man named Richard, whom Baldwin had met the year before, and who would become a fixture in his entourage for the next two years. There was also the wayward son of a peer. In fact, almost immediately the suite at the Carlton Towers became a stage for the reenactment of Baldwin's highly charged and quixotic quest for an emotional base. The confusion in the hotel room was reinforced by the equally charged quest for professional fulfilment in the film world.

One afternoon we were taken to Pinewood Studios, where Marlon Brando was working under the direction of Charlie Chaplin in Chaplin's last film, *The Countess from Hong Kong*. Even though he was by 1966 well used to the famous, encountering Chaplin was a highlight of Baldwin's life. The older man had been one of his heroes ever since he could remember and now he was watching him work with Brando, one of his oldest friends.

During a break Chaplin freed himself for some conversation. It became quickly apparent that he was a genuine admirer of Baldwin's works. The discussion was about Chaplin's films and Baldwin's essays and then about stage as opposed to film acting and Method acting as opposed to what they both called "real" acting. Chaplin was scornful of the Stanislavsky approach. It was especially disastrous on the screen, as acting in short "takes" precluded "living the role." An actor had to act, had to accept the discipline of "pretending." Brando was having trouble in a romantic scene with Sophia Loren in *Countess*, Chaplin said, because he was not getting along with her and he was unwilling or unable to pretend. There was anger in Chaplin's criticism, anger because the scene in question was holding up the production schedule. He went on to say that Brando would be fine if only he would not take himself so seriously: "Marlon's a comedian who won't let himself be one." Later Brando was just as critical of Chaplin, suggesting that his ego caused dissension on the set.

The primary purpose for the London stop had been discussions of the *Blues* film. With this in mind, Baldwin arranged contacts with various movie and theater people who happened to be in town. There was a dinner at Brando's at which Tennessee Williams was also a guest, and meetings with John Huston, Peter O'Toole, Terry Thomas, and Ava Gardner, among others. We also spent an evening with Diana Sands. The meeting was an emotional one because of the relationships both had had with Lucien, but there was an essential affinity that quickly overcame any bad feelings, and joined by some other friends, Jimmy and Diana spent an evening on the town dancing and reminiscing and making film plans.

Most important, there were two long sessions at Losey's home in which the director suggested that Baldwin work on scripts based on his novels and in which he criticized the scenario for *Blues*. He noted the excessive length of the script, comparing it with more efficient work done for him by Harold Pinter. Baldwin's approach would leave the director with little artistic space of his own. He suggested that Baldwin was confusing the stage with the screen, that he had a great deal to learn about the highly specialized art of scenario writing, if, indeed, he felt he wanted to write for films at all. Baldwin expressed a general abhorrence for the idea of having someone else write a script based on his work and announced his intention of redoing *Blues* in light of Losey's criticism.

During the next nine months he and Losey would correspond about *Blues* and other possibilities. Losey liked Baldwin and wanted to work with him. He had "more confidence in your witchcraft than in other religions," he said to Baldwin in a letter. Baldwin wrote to him saying that Anthony Quinn had suggested that he write a movie based on the life of Jelly Roll Morton. The Morton film interested him; in fact, he had been approached years before by Alan Lomax, the curator of the "folklore" archives at the Library of Congress, to do such a film. Losey thought the subject was "fascinating," but he was drawn more to the idea of a film on Billie Holiday. Later Losey would try to generate interest in a film of *Another Country,* suggesting Robert De Niro for Vivaldo and Richard Pryor for Rufus.

In Paris on March 23, we stayed at the Hôtel Pont Royal, not far from the old Grand Hôtel du Bac, where Baldwin had been arrested in 1949. Beauford Delaney was out of town and so was Bernard Hassell, but Bernard's friend Richard Olney came by and so did James Jones, and before long we were exploring Baldwin's old haunts in Saint-Germain. On the twenty-fourth we barely made the night train to Venice, and the next day we boarded the *Ege* for Istanbul. The passage through the Aegean was extremely rough, and when we arrived in Istanbul, Baldwin could barely stand. But Seraglio Point and the great domes and minarets of Saint Sophia and the Blue Mosque made for a spectacular welcome. Perhaps a year in Istanbul would provide the refuge he so desperately needed. He wrote to David that the sea was rough, "as it always is for the lonely long-distance swimmer."

CHAPTER 26

Istanbul

> Seek the peace of the city whither I have caused you to be carried away.
>
> —Jeremiah 29:7

Beginning with his 1961 visit, Baldwin spent some eight years off and on in Istanbul. A local reporter once asked him what attracted him to Turkey, and his response was essentially the same one he gave everyone who asked him that question. He was in Istanbul because he was "left alone" and could work better there. The fact that Turkey was a Moslem country had nothing to do with it, "except, perhaps, that it's a relief to deal with people who, whatever they are pretending, are not pretending to be Christians." As for becoming a permanent expatriate, that was not his intention; his "ties" with his country were "too deep . . . and my concern is too great."

There was, of course, more to the Istanbul attachment than the need to escape. Engin Cezzar was there, and over the years he had proved an especially trustworthy friend. And there was something strangely familiar to him about the city. The streets teemed with life. Istanbul, he said, reminded him of Harlem.

Baldwin settled down to work on *Tell Me How Long the Train's Been Gone*. There were also strolls through the old book market near the Grand Bazaar, afternoons with a samovar in a favorite teahouse along the Bosphorus, late afternoon trips up the steep cobblestoned street to the Park Hotel for drinks, evenings with Engin and Gülriz, Yasar Kemal, or friends from Robert College. But for the most part Baldwin stayed in his apartment and worked.

Early in April we decided to have a party to repay Istanbul friends for their hospitality and kindness. The party itself was a great success, bringing together a cross section of Istanbul society that included fishermen, bartenders, newspaper editors, diplomats, professors, and people in the arts. But while saying good-bye to the last guests in front of the apartment building, Jimmy caught his foot between two cobblestones, fell, and broke his ankle.

Engin suggested a period of recuperation in Erdek, a fishing village on the Sea of Marmara where Jimmy and I and a mutual friend, Hilary Sumner-Boyd, stayed in a small hotel. We settled into a routine of writing and reading during the day and meeting on Jimmy's balcony for drinks at five, followed by dinner in the hotel restaurant. Occasionally we were taken by a local taxi driver on outings to sights in the area.

Baldwin had always wanted to see Troy and was delighted to discover that we could drive there from Erdek in a few hours. The image that remains from that outing is one of Jimmy in his cast standing in a field of red poppies looking out at the ruins of the city and beyond to the great plain where Homer's heroes had once fought. That day he became as melancholy as I had ever seen him. He was not a sentimentalist, but he did tend to give rhetorical or metaphorical value to moments of personal importance. James Baldwin the child on the hill in Harlem had been in his own mind a symbol. The same was true of James Baldwin on the Trojan mound. He had come a long way. He had won great battles as a writer, and he was still fighting. But the society he had hoped to change remained hopelessly at war with itself; an essential evil still plagued his nation and the world, and a personal wound marred his life.

He had written to Kay Boyle a few weeks earlier giving full vent to his unhappiness. It had been necessary, he said, for him to ask himself what he was going to do with his future now that the "central love affair" of his life was over. He was in emotional trouble, but he was prepared to continue doing "battle with the devil." How monotonous the devil and evil were in "their ghastly splendor."

Tell Me How Long the Train's Been Gone would reflect Baldwin's situation by focusing on a public man's mid-life struggle with himself, his career, and the evil that beleaguers him. By the end of May he would finish the first book of *Train.* His frustrations—as well as his ideals—were also at the source of desperate private acts that to everyone around him demonstrated a lack of common sense. But to Baldwin common sense was worthless if it meant avoiding the possibility of love, the willingness to break down old barriers. Even in his most bizarre sexual escapades he saw himself symbolically, from outside of himself. His actions were de facto statements to the effect that safety was the enemy, that fulfilment could come only through risk taking, and that these truths applied to personal encounters as well as to larger social issues. "To escape death and love," he often said, was "to be dead already."

One incident in Erdek soon after the Troy visit can serve as an example of the kind of situation in which Jimmy sometimes found himself in his love-war against "the devil." This was one of those rare "real-life" incidents which, even as they unfold, display the characteristics of fiction. It was an updated version of Thomas Mann's *Mario and the Magician*, complete with portentous setting and a plot and characters that seemed to be selectively arranged around the archetype of the sacrificial victim.

The village of Erdek sits at the end of a peninsula on the southwest shore of the Sea of Marmara. In spite of its seaside location it was seldom visited by Americans and Europeans in the mid-sixties. The occasional foreign sunbathers were sure to be made uncomfortable by the stares of the men and boys who seemed to lurk in the maize and poppy fields bordering the beach just outside of town. These were the gazes of people unused to the sight of bare flesh. A Turkish woman once told me she had never seen her husband naked until she laid him out to be buried. He, of course, had never seen her naked either. In our days in Erdek only the schoolboys stripped down to shorts to swim or to do melancholy line dances and gymnastics in a copse of trees outside of town on the Youth and Sport holiday. The copse is not far from a deeper woods where there is an ancient fountain with water that was said to have mysterious curative powers, especially over "female complaints."

The "downtown" resembled many other Anatolian villages of the time. It was essentially divided into two parts, roughly paralleling the division in the larger Turkish homes between the *selamlik*, or public rooms, and the *harem*, or family quarters. The *selamlik* was the main street along the water, where there was a tea garden, a newspaper stand, a coffeehouse, the businessmen's club, a bank, and three or four restaurants attached to small concrete-block hotels painted in somewhat garish greens or pinks to be "modern." These hotels and restaurants were for *yabanciler*—foreigners—but not so much for Americans or Europeans as for city people from Istanbul or perhaps Bursa. There was also a movie theater on a side street just off the quay. The public bath, the *hammam*, was there, too.

The main street was primarily a male enclave until the evening, when women and men would appear for the primary communal entertainment, the public promenade, or *gezi*, along the quay. The pace was incredibly slow, the men tending to walk together, hands clasped behind their backs, fondling prayer or worry beads called *tespis*. The women's arms were linked, like their soft voices, in a kind of domestic conspiracy, as they followed their men up and down the street. Children darted about randomly in what appeared to be happy amazement at so grand a street and such fine parents. The whole village came out for the promenade, seeming to celebrate, as they walked back and forth from one end of the quay to the other, a sense of ownership and satisfaction.

To the west of the main street was a labyrinth of short narrow streets and wood and stucco buildings. Women hung bed sheets and blankets from the windows for their daily airing, and in the basements men sold the necessities—bread, kebabs, rope, dusty pots and pans, tires, henna, kerosene, charcoal, spices. The experience of these streets—the *harem* of the village—was a mixture of seductive and repellent smells, the chatter of women leaning out of windows, the shouts of men selling yogurt and vegetables carried on the backs of sometimes braying donkeys, the regular calls to prayer of the muezzin from the mosque minaret, and the sound of shop mechanics hammering on dead metal.

By the time the magician came to town Jimmy and our friend Hilary and I were well known to the villagers. A fisherman named Mehmet had become a protector, dropping by regularly to see that "Arap Jimmy"—literally "Arab Jimmy," a term roughly equivalent to "Black Jimmy"—was doing well and enjoying the village. We had all seen the posters advertising "Morgan," the magician-hypnotist, who was to perform on a given night at the movie theater. The whole town would be there and we were urged to go, too.

We laughed at Morgan's apparent confusion of Merlin with Morgan le Fey. That is, our friend Hilary and I laughed; Jimmy did not. He suggested that the magician might have reasons for his sexually ambiguous stage name. We began to take Morgan more seriously. During the day we heard reports that he had been seen eating a glass in the teahouse. The villagers were wary of "dark magic," and tension was rising as the time for the performance approached. Fifteen minutes after Jimmy had casually told the boy from the news kiosk that he would like to meet "this Morgan," the boy was cautiously leading the magician up the stairs to Jimmy's room. He was followed to the space below the room's balcony by a large number of the other villagers, out for the evening promenade. When Jimmy, the magician, the fisherman, and I all came out onto the balcony, the situation resembled, in effect, a stage play.

It all happened rather quickly. Morgan seemed to challenge Jimmy with his arrogance and apparent malevolence; he referred to the villagers as the "shit on the street below us" and boasted of his power over them. He had heard that Jimmy had the "magic of words"; he had the "magic of the mind." The villagers, hearing this conversation, became angry and threatening. Morgan laughed, and offered to display his powers by putting me "under enchantment." By now Mehmet the fisherman was urging us to ask the magician to leave; Morgan was obviously a "devil" and was not to be trusted. Still, we agreed to let him try to "enchant" me, and before long, watching his eyes as he mumbled something over me, I began to lose consciousness of my surroundings. Now Mehmet, who had become both frightened and angry, shoved the magician away and out the door.

The performance in the movie theater began predictably with a series of rabbit-out-of-the-hat tricks but turned ugly when Morgan hypnotized a man from the audience and, assisted by a scantily dressed woman and a surly man, stuck sharp objects into his hand, drawing blood and causing great pain to the victim when he was suddenly awakened. There were other hypnotic "tricks" that compromised villagers in various ways, usually though sexual innuendoes, and the mood of the audience was not friendly by the time the curtain closed on the entertainment.

Late that evening Jimmy and I were having a drink on his balcony when the magician once again made an appearance. Morgan looked hard at me and suggested that I leave. Suddenly becoming extremely tired, I went off to my room without arguing, in spite of the fact that Jimmy presumably needed a translator and maybe some protection. It seemed to be impossible for me to resist the magician's suggestion.

The next morning I went as usual to wake up Jimmy for breakfast and found him on his bed, his face badly beaten. He explained haltingly; it was difficult for him to talk. Morgan had made overtures to which Jimmy, in spite of a strong reluctance, had responded, and they had gone down the street to his hotel. As Jimmy had just had his cast removed, he was able to walk without a crutch, but with difficulty. In his host's room, he had been invited to get into bed, which he did while the magician was occupied in what Jimmy thought was the bathroom. Once in bed, he was set upon by the magician and his male assistant, who castigated him as a "nigger queer" and, after beating him, left the room. Jimmy managed to put on some clothes and to crawl back up the deserted street to our hotel. There he tried without success to shake me out of sleep and finally gave up and went to his own room, where I found him in the morning.

After I asked the hotelkeeper to call a doctor, it was not long before the whole town found out that something bad had happened to Jimmy, and soon Mehmet and several cohorts arrived to question us. For obvious reasons Jimmy did not want an issue to be made of the incident, but the men left saying that something would have to be done to punish Morgan, that his powers were evil.

When, later in the day, I met Mehmet on the quay and asked him about Morgan, he said, with an air of some mystery, that the magician had gone and would not be back. We left for Istanbul the next day, as Jimmy required more medical attention.

Coincidentally, Baldwin had been confronted by another apparently racially motivated beating a few days before the magician incident when I showed him a letter from my sister, who had written to say she had been attacked by a group of black youths in a San Francisco parking lot. Concerned about the effects of the incident on her, Jimmy wrote cautioning her not to compound the damage by allowing herself to become mentally a victim of the racism that made such attacks so much a part of the American scene. He also wrote to Kay Boyle asking her to visit my sister, who must not be drawn by what had happened to her into believing that such events are attributable to the color of the perpetrators. To believe that would be to isolate herself in a state of "aridity" which would make it impossible for her to love or to develop as a human being. She must not be absorbed by the horror that had undone so many. She must find a way, he said, to understand the meaning of the attack on her, to hate the evil in it even as she avoided the pitfall of hating the attacker. There was still a great deal of the former preacher in Baldwin and in his power to speak to personal pain and to soothe.

In Istanbul he got back to work on *Train* and did a narration for a review called *Black New World* undertaken by his *Amen Corner* producers, Ellis Haizlip and Rudolph Stoiber. And once again, in the face of ominous news of the racial situation in America, he began to feel guilty about having physically removed himself from the struggle.

What he could gather of a power struggle at SNCC was confusing. He liked John Lewis and James Forman, but he liked Stokely Carmichael, too. He was wary, however, of what he feared was a turn towards separatism and an ideology centered on a misguided idea of

Black Power. To David he wrote that he would resist getting caught up in "some mystical black bullshit." That was how the "nightmare" had begun in the first place.

He thought it might be best to finish the novel quickly and then return to help organize concrete acts—demonstrations, boycotts, strikes—to reduce the establishment's economic power. He was not willing to embrace communism or any other ideology, but he argued that the economic system of the West would have to be modified—either from within or from without. The American capitalist system in particular had undermined American morality. It was responsible, for example, for the war in Vietnam. Blacks in Vietnam were, in effect, the victims of American economic interests, and American blacks needed new leaders who would understand these underlying matters. The fact that the Johnson administration had placed a few token "niggers in the window" to suggest that racism was no more was a "disgrace" that young blacks would never accept. Baldwin remembered something his freedom rider friend, Jerome Smith, had said to Bobby Kennedy in the famous New York meeting: "When I pull the trigger, kiss it good-bye." Time was running out, as the unrest in American ghettoes was indicating. The dire predictions of the Kennedy meeting were coming true.

In early June I returned to New York with the part of *Train* that was finished. Jimmy remained in Istanbul where he continued to work on the novel. He also spent several days entertaining two friends of his mother's to whom she had given his address in Istanbul. A letter to me about their visit was a mixture of humor, compassion, and some anger. "Mama's . . . white ladies" had appeared, he said, and life was permanently altered by the fact. He had spent several days shepherding them around the city dealing with their "relentless love," their "bravura," and their need for approval, and it had exhausted him.

Under normal circumstances he might have been more sympathetic, but he was finding the work on *Train* hard going, primarily because it was more autobiographical than he had realized, involving a painful self-examination. In another letter to me he said he felt that something long buried within him was stirring and that confronting it would require great patience and courage. He was becoming aware of "how deeply and bitterly" he had been "hurt," almost from the day of his birth. This realization made him more "attentive" than he had ever been before. And he needed some special human support for the journey that he sensed was before him. So it was that Jimmy instructed me to bring two friends of his to Istanbul with me on my way back from New York. I was to collect Richard from London and Beauford Delaney from Paris.

I had met Richard when Jimmy and I had been in England earlier in the year, but I had never met Beauford. Jimmy had, of course, referred to him often, but I wanted more information. What was he like, I asked. "You'll find out," he answered. When I insisted he said, "He's a cross between Brer Rabbit and St. Francis"; that was all I needed to know. It was clear that my "mission" was to be a test of some sort.

In London, Richard informed me that he would drive himself to Istanbul in an old Rolls he had bought with the travel money Jimmy had sent him. Richard embodied the romantic side of the sixties. He loved everything and everyone, from the perspective of what seemed a constant trance that had nothing to do with alcohol and only a little to do with marijuana. He was the Baldwin waif par excellence. He had no money, no prospects, no parents; there had been a Russian-Armenian father who had moved to France and a mother who was perhaps English. In any case, there was an English passport with a photo of an angelic child of six whom the British passport officials refused to recognize as the present Richard. I know this because soon after Richard rammed his Rolls—unlicensed—into another car in London, he joined me on the ferry to Calais. He was allowed to leave, but the passport was marked "Void." I wondered how we would get through the French, Bulgarian, and Yugoslavian borders (twice in each case) with a cross between Brer Rabbit and St. Francis, and a wild-eyed nineteen-year-old poet in rags carrying a voided British passport with the picture of a six-year-old.

The French, at least, did not seem to mind the passport. We arrived in Paris, and Richard promptly disappeared to visit a cousin. I made my way to find Delaney in the fourteenth arrondissement. The building reminded me of Zola's *Assommoir*. I found my way through a passageway into the central courtyard where an ancient woman pointed to a corner entryway when I asked for M. Delaney. The climb to the right floor seemed endless, the corridors were dark and sour-smelling. I knocked on the door on which there was a note, "Welcome David" (Jimmy had written ahead at least). At a faint "Come in" I opened the door onto a vision of the saint in his hermitage. The room was completely draped in white sheets, and the painter was himself dressed in white. The resulting image was of a disembodied black face—very round, very soft—floating in all that whiteness, highlighted by the rays of the sun that came through the little garret window. It was a face with a smile that was at once the saddest and the most inviting I had ever seen.

My memory of those first few days with Beauford is somewhat vague. I remember his opening cans of tuna from time to time. But most of all, I remember lying on a narrow cot with my head practically touching Beauford's head, which rested on another cot that was placed in a line with mine. We stayed on those cots for three days while Beauford and I got to know each other. The conversation was about everything: where I came from, where Beauford came from, Jimmy, the light in Paris, art, Beauford's friends in Paris, his childhood, his attempted suicide in Greece, the relative merits of various kinds of canned tuna. We talked and slept; there was no difference between day and night in Beauford's world. Since our positions precluded sight of each other, he was for those three days a voice from the darkness or a voice from the light. It was a voice that was satin soft with a melody of its own; it ranged into the corners even of the most difficult and painful places. On the morning of the fourth day Beauford said, "Shall we drive to Jimmy now?"

We found Richard at a café in the quarter where he had told me his cousin lived, and he appeared to be waiting for us, completely unsurprised by our arrival at that precise moment. It seemed to me that Beauford and Richard both thought of the drive from Paris to Istanbul as something roughly comparable to the one between Paris and Versailles. There was no question of significant baggage or preparation. Certainly there was no money or any apparent worry on that account. Again I had the distinct sense that this was all a kind of test.

I sent Jimmy a postcard from the café reminding him that I was on my way to Istanbul from Paris with a "carload of poetry." Dark poetry. The trip was nightmarish. There were the borders, difficult in every case because of Richard's passport, Beauford's "spacy" appearance, and the unlikeliness of someone like me driving the other two. Twice the car was stripped by customs officials, and at each border Beauford became more wary. He lost track of time and began to ask where Jimmy was, when we would "find" him. He sat very close to me in the front while in the back Richard crooned mystically over the beauty of things—not fields or ancient castles, but the odd dead animal or discarded shoe along the road. Beauford began to hear the voices, and knowing about the Greek suicide experience, I was frightened.

"Did you hear what they said?" he asked one afternoon, motioning softly over his shoulder at the Yugoslavian car that had just passed us going in the opposite direction on an open highway. "Beauford, they were passing us with the windows closed going at least sixty miles an hour; you couldn't have heard anything."

"Maybe you didn't hear them, but I did."

"OK, what did they say?"

"They said, look at that old black faggot driving with those two white boys."

"Those people were Yugoslavian, Beauford."

"I don't care what they were; that's what they said, and I'm getting out."

I managed to grasp his arm and to stop the car before he could do just that. The saint had given way to Brer Rabbit. Only the trickster could hope to cope with the returned voices. For two days and two nights Beauford pretended to be fine and took every opportunity of getting away.

One night found us at a small hotel in a quiet Moslem village in southern Yugoslavia. Exhausted by a long day's drive, we went to bed right after dinner, the three of us on cots in a large room we shared with other transit travelers. I woke up later to find Beauford's cot empty. The noise of a crowd from outside drew me to a window, and there was Beauford at the foot of a statue of Marshal Tito haranguing the village men. Brer Rabbit had become an Old Testament prophet warning the by now all too real and angry voices of their imminent fall. With some difficulty I brought Beauford back to the room and into my cot. I was frightened by the voices now, too, and from then on for several nights—including our first nights in Istanbul, where we finally arrived on July 7—Beauford and I hung on to each other to keep the voices away.

Even at the time, as I mentally looked at the picture we made together in each other's arms, I began to understand the nature of the test—really, the lesson—Jimmy had prepared for me. I understood that through Beauford I had learned something terrifying about the hidden inner pain that is the most terrible result of racism—a pain that no mere law can relieve. I had also learned a great deal about the anguish that motivated James Baldwin.

During the stay in Istanbul, after he had regained his equilibrium, Beauford once again was St. Francis. He bestowed a kind of peace on the usual turmoil of the Baldwin scene. In fact, he became somewhat of a cult figure during his few months in Istanbul. People who dropped in at Jimmy's little house on the Bosphorus, where he had moved for the summer, usually stayed on into the night to watch and listen to and learn from the man Henry Miller compared to the Buddha and called "amazing and invariable," as "breathing slowly, evenly, gently, deliberately, [he] sets in motion the universal brotherhood of man, the white sisterhood of doves and angels, and the great serpentine constellation of birds, beasts and flowers, all caracoling towards the sun in color, peace and harmony." Beauford returned to Paris at the end of the summer, but not before painting portraits of Richard, Jimmy, and me and becoming a legend in a city built on legends.

During the summer, until the stream of visitors at the Bosphorus house became overwhelming, Jimmy concentrated on *Train* and became increasingly anxious about the racial situation at home. The James Meredith shooting brought back the immediate pain of the attacks on Malcolm X and Medgar Evers. What had happened at CORE and SNCC was still unclear, and so was Martin Luther King's role in triggering the riots in Chicago, where he was stoned during an August 6 demonstration. Then there were the usual summer race riots.

Gloria wrote supporting Jimmy's idea of a lecture tour after he finished the novel. Jimmy himself wrote to *Playboy* suggesting a piece called "The Hallelujah Chorus" on Ray Charles; this would only be realized in a different form a few years later. Interviewers began appearing, including a *Newsweek* reporter who asked about his opinions on Black Power and the Vietnam War. Black Power was obviously positive for black people as long as it did not become too ideological a concept. His position on the war was made clear by his signing of several petitions condemning it and by his association with the War Crimes Tribunal.

Another matter that concerned Baldwin was the element of anti-Semitism that seemed to be creeping into the formerly radical press. In early July he received a letter from Harry Fleischman of the American Jewish Committee complaining about anti-Semitic editorial policies in the *Liberator*, an African-American journal of which Baldwin was an advisory board member. Baldwin had not seen the magazine in some time but was horrified by what Fleischman described and by what he actually read when he received a copy from Gloria. In his answer to Fleischman he reminded him of what he had said for so many years in essays and speeches about "the excesses . . . to which the Negro demoralization could lead." He was ashamed of the *Liberator* but also of America and of American intellectuals for having lacked the courage to do more about the conditions that lay behind the demoralization.

Baldwin, along with Ossie Davis and others, wrote open letters to the *Liberator* denouncing anti-Semitism, which the editor, Daniel Watts, refused to print. And though Baldwin's name was removed from the masthead, as he demanded, Watts criticized him in the letters page of the August issue for "running downtown to the man selling Black."

The essence of Baldwin's *Liberator* open letter was published early in 1967 by *Freedomways* and became the basis for the *New York Times Magazine* article "Negroes Are Anti-Semitic Because They're Anti-White," which can be read as a later commentary on issues touched on in his 1948 article "The Harlem Ghetto." Black anti-Semitism exists, says Baldwin, because the Jew, who, like the black, has suffered at the hands of white Christians, has become "an American white man . . . in effect, a Christian." The white men confronted in the ghetto have mostly been Jews—Jewish landlords, Jewish grocers, Jewish butchers, Jewish pharmacists. And when now liberal Jews point to their own history of suffering and suggest that the African-American must be patient and "wait," they betray the community of sufferers everywhere; they speak as white Americans rather than as Jews who share the African-American desire for a "promised land." Baldwin continued his attempt to understand and explain anti-Semitism among blacks in a *Playboy* interview with Budd Schulberg. Resentment of Jews, he said there, stemmed from the fact that European Jews arrived in America and found opportunity, while African-Americans, who arrived first, still have "no place to go."

In September, after Beauford and Richard had left, Jimmy and I moved into a house on a promontory overlooking the Bosphorus in Rumeli Hisar, a few miles from downtown Istanbul. The house had once been a library belonging to the nineteenth-century intellectual Ahmet Vefik Pasha. It was a red wooden and stucco structure situated in a grove of trees next to the fifteenth-century fortress of Fatih Mehmet, the conqueror of Constantinople. A central room with a decorated vaulted ceiling and a marble fireplace was surrounded by a glassed-in gallery offering views of the Bosphorus and the hills of Asia across the straits. This house, known by everyone as "the Pasha's Library," became our home until the summer of 1967.

Life at the library was quiet and regular at first. Jimmy had been given a very small and contentious white dog, which he named Andromache (Andy for short), who made an unpleasant practice of biting feet under the dining room table. Andy later "brought in" a bedraggled and very black stray puppy whom we appropriately named Flea.

The daily routine was simple. Jimmy got up at noon and ate a substantial meal. He then worked until six or so, when visitors began to arrive. Drinks and dinner followed and then long nights of talking, which usually included Jimmy's reading aloud segments of *Tell Me How Long the Train's Been Gone* or parts of other projects temporarily abandoned or planned: *The 121st Day of Sodom*, a takeoff on Sade's *120 Days of Sodom*, was to be a "drawing room nightmare of six adventurers" in the south of France that much later would take a new form as his last work, *The Welcome Table*. He still talked of his modern *Othello* musical, about "two Negro men and a Greek girl in Greece," and he joked about a musical that would star Odetta on roller skates. More than anything else, we discussed events in America, the state of the movement, the riots in the cities. The discussions were frequently heated and there was shouting and sometimes there were tears.

The participants in these informal nighttime seminars were representative of Baldwin's wide range of interests. There were students from Robert College, American teachers, a young Greco-Turkish lover of Jimmy's, Turkish actors and writers, the woman I later married, the man my sister later married, the singer Bertice Redding and her entourage, Ann Bruno, an American journalist who was writing a piece on Jimmy's life in Istanbul, Yasar and Tilda Kemal, who had named their black cat "Jimmy," much to Jimmy's amusement. A frequent visitor was Sedat Pakay, a Robert College student who would later make a documentary on Baldwin and whom Baldwin accompanied to the American consulate to sign a document committing himself to serve as Sedat's sponsor when he went off to the Yale Drama School in 1968.

And there were visitors from the States and elsewhere. The latter included Olga Carlisle on her way to the Soviet Union to write about the poet—her grandfather—Leonid Andreev, Alex Haley heading for Africa to research *Roots*, Marlon Brando on a mission which was unclear, the novelist Geoffrey Wolff and his wife, Priscilla, back for a visit to the place where Geoffrey had done his first teaching.

My parents visited for several weeks. My Episcopal priest father and Jimmy—in part, I think, to avoid arguments on other matters—often entertained the evening gathering with gospel songs; Jimmy loved to sing and my father both sang and played the piano.

The household ran relatively smoothly. Our daytime cook did

have to be replaced after her afternoon escapades with village men were discovered by their wives, who stoned her one day as she tried to get into the front gate. The house grounds were surrounded by a high wall that usually ensured privacy.

On his way to New York for a brief business trip in December, Baldwin stopped in London to bail a young friend out of difficulty involving a mysterious case of a stolen bust of Hitler. In New York he was questioned by the Immigration Service about Lucien's whereabouts and by the FBI about Jack Jordan. He had several meetings with various people—particularly Jerome Robbins and Sidney Poitier about various film projects. He changed lawyers—from Ted Kupferman to Sidney Davis—and generally made the holiday rounds, visiting family and friends. There were meetings with Philip Roth, Truman Capote, Stokely Carmichael, and James Forman, and several Harlem outings, usually with David and sometimes with my brother Nick, with whom he had been close for several years. He planned to return to Istanbul after spending the New Year's holiday with Beauford and Mary in Paris.

Fearing that Jimmy was losing touch with reality in his complicated personal and business relationships, I had suggested that the anarchic aspect of his life was interfering with his writing, and I had been so insensitive as to accuse him of paranoia in his insistence that his brother and my brother were in danger in America. The letter in which he responded was the most instructive I ever received from him. He declared that although I might be right about the anarchy, I must understand that disorder was in a sense a necessary aspect of his life as a writer. He could not afford to be tamed. The writer's job was to confront life in all its complications. As for the paranoia, they "*are* trying to kill me. Every day and every hour." While he was writing this letter, he pointed out to me, Odette, his father's daughter by his first marriage, was sitting with his mother, telling her—the way Beauford told his friends—about the people who were after her. And his mother had had to face the insanity of her husband. Perhaps paranoia was too easy a word. If he had tantrums and seemed overdramatic to me, there were good reasons for his behavior that I could probably not but must try to understand. A person who had almost been killed would carry his experience with him always. He suggested that I remember Dostoevsky. I had witnessed the magician incident, so I knew what near-killing he was referring to and I understood the larger metaphorical meaning of that near-killing. I never accused Jimmy of anarchy or of paranoia again.

Early in January, accompanied by David, he arrived in Istanbul. One of his first concerns upon his return was the War Crimes Tribunal. He wrote to Bertrand Russell pointing out the need for American intellectuals to see the war in the context of the racial war raging in America. He suggested, in his own name and Stokely Carmichael's, that the tribunal invite James Forman, Fannie Lou Hamer, or Rosa Parks, the catalyst for the Montgomery bus boycott, to participate in its deliberations. There was, after all, a sense in America of a connection between racism there and the Vietnam War. What Americans were doing in Asia in the name of democracy they had done for generations to their black compatriots: "The children they are bombing have always been their own." He went on to emphasize his support of the tribunal. He promised to attend at least some of the tribunal sessions. Other commitments were to make his presence impossible, but his name was included in the list of tribunal members.

By May he had decided that he needed to distance himself somewhat from the Russell project, which he felt did not sufficiently recognize the connection between Vietnam and American racism and which had become too ideological. Furthermore, he was not interested in participating in what he feared was becoming European-based American-bashing. In an open letter to the press in May he pointed out the irony "in the spectacle of Europeans condemning America for a war which America inherited from Europe." He was not interested in criticizing his own country from the perspective of Europe; "Europeans should be holding international tribunals to consider the crimes of the white government in South Africa or of the French government in Algeria." None of this was to support in any way the war in Vietnam. It was a racist war, and Americans had no right to "liberate" Southeast Asians if they could not liberate their own people. A future for America and the West depended on there being a future for black people in America and the rest of the world.

From December on, Baldwin dedicated himself almost exclusively to finishing *Tell Me How Long the Train's Been Gone*. Early in May he wrote to Gloria, who was expecting a baby, "My baby is born, and I hope yours is, too." On May 13 Jimmy and David left, and a few weeks later David returned to help close down the house. I stayed behind, was married that summer, and would continue working at Robert College for another two years. Jimmy did not get back to Istanbul until 1969. Early in 1968 I received a copy of *Train* from him. It had been dedicated to David Baldwin, Engin Cezzar, and me.

CHAPTER 27

Tell Me How Long the Train's Been Gone

> Never seen the like since I been born,
> The people keep a-coming, and the train's done gone.
> —old song

Tell Me How Long the Train's Been Gone is a first-person narrative about Leo Proudhammer, a celebrated black actor who uses a period of convalescence after a major heart attack to examine his life before entering into a sometime relationship with a black "revolutionary." It is Baldwin's most self-conscious novel, the story of his mid-life "night journey." He reminded an interviewer from the *Los Angeles Times* that Henry James had long ago talked about the problems of "surviving success" in America. His novel was "about" that, about the fact that success "destroys your public life and private life. . . . You become famous because you're lonely . . . and *more* lonely when you're famous." He was "famous . . . lonely . . . and furious."

As an act of self-examination, the birth of *Train* was painful. When Baldwin sent the manuscript to his editor—Ed Doctorow at the time—he showed little or no interest in participating in the editing of his book. The new baby gave him no pleasure; it was a book he *had* to write, not one he wanted to write; it was the therapy he needed to break through the psychological crisis that had begun with the breakup with Lucien, had expressed itself physiologically in what he spoke of as his psychosomatic illness in France in 1965, and had undermined his vocation and threatened his very life. In fact, the vocation and the life seemed to be in conflict. As Proudhammer sees it, he had paid a terrible price for fame and prophecy. His "pride" had become his "affliction": "The actor could no longer be distinguished from his role." And when a reporter asks him how it feels to "mean so much to so many people," he answers, "It makes me know that I did not make myself—I do not belong to me."

Leo Proudhammer *is* James Baldwin, complete with large eyes, "pigeon toes," and "jiggling behind." Successful and true to his vocation, Leo is nevertheless tortured by an overwhelming sense of loneliness that has something to do with the loss of his brother, Caleb, to prison and then to the church and with his sexual and racial isolation in the world of his craft. The young Baldwin had been born again on Mother Horn's threshing floor, but he had discovered the unreality of that birth. The bosom of the Lord was not the human affection for which he had spent so much of his energy seeking. And success as a writer and spokesman had not brought him that comfort either. When Leo Proudhammer muses on the essential dilemmas of his life, dilemmas centered in his "tyrannical" defense against a sense of inferiority and, paradoxically, of personal power, his voice and situation are always James Baldwin's. He knows that to "people who imagine themselves to be, as they put it, in their 'right' minds," he was "insane," and that his "absolutely single-minded and terrified ruthlessness" was in conflict with his "vulnerability," his "paradoxical and very real helplessness," his "need to . . . weep long and loud, to be held in human arms, almost any human arms, to hide my face in any human breast, to . . . let it out, to be brought into the world, and, out of human affection, to be born again."

The flashbacks that make up the bulk of the book concern a profound relationship between Proudhammer and his brother and his association with a theater group directed by Saul San Marquand, whose primary producer is a woman named Rags Roland and whose philosophy of theater is based on Stanislavsky's "Method" approach to acting. The narrator-hero, Leo Proudhammer, is bisexual. He has had a long friendship—once sexual—with a white actress called Barbara, but he prefers Black Christopher, on whom he pins his personal hopes and, less confidently, his hopes for his people.

Saul San Marquand, Rags Roland, and their company, the Actors' Means Workshop, are clearly recognizable as Lee Strasberg, Cheryl Crawford, and the Actors Studio. The *Blues for Mister Charlie* experience had been a bad one, and Baldwin, somewhat uncharacteristically, does not resist the urge for revenge in his treatment of Saul and Rags, who are depicted as arrogant, pedantic hypocrites—representatives of the white liberal establishment with which Proudhammer, his ethnic brothers, and those few whites such as his friend Barbara (a reconstructed southerner like Rip Torn of *Blues* days), and Konstantine Rafaeleto (based on Baldwin's old friend Elia Kazan), must cope in their quest for survival.

The most moving sections of *Train* revolve around the brother relationship. The love between the young Leo and Caleb, like that between the brothers in so many Baldwin works, represents an ideal. The emotional center of the novel is the moment in Leo's childhood when Caleb's frustration with the hatred in the world around him and Leo's own need to be touched are concretely expressed in a sexual event between them that stands as the Baldwin model for perfection—love between two people who can accept, trust, and depend on each other totally.

The depiction of the young Leo's relationship with Caleb owes a great deal to Baldwin's dependence on his brother David and also to his memory of times with his older stepbrother, Sam. The Proudhammer family as a whole has autobiographical as well as larger symbolic significance. More idealized than real, it is the cohesive black family, a sociological power base that will take more complex form later, in *If Beale Street Could Talk* and *Just Above My Head*. It grew out of Baldwin's disillusionment with earlier hopes for interracial unity and with a personal longing for acceptance associated with the failure of his relationship with his stepfather and the deep affection and sense of responsibility he felt for his mother, his brothers and sisters, and their children.

At times, Baldwin seems to broadcast the autobiographical nature of the novel with no attempt at fictionalization: Medgar Evers is remembered—"a very beautiful man whom I had known and loved, a black man shot down within hearing of his wife and children." When Leo receives a get-well card "from Marlon" after his heart attack, we have no doubts as to who that is. The incident in which the man helps little Leo home when he is lost on the subway happened to young Jimmy, exactly as described. The Jewish landlord so hated by the Proudhammers is the same Mr. Rabinowitz whom Baldwin remembered as a bane of his own family's existence. The section of Harlem in which the Proudhammer boys had grown up is a mirror of Baldwin's childhood neighborhood. When Mr. Proudhammer says, objecting to little Leo's interest in movies, "He ain't going to get his mind messed up—not by going to the movies"—and when he says, "You don't know the Jew like I know him," he takes the exact words of the Reverend David Baldwin as remembered by his stepson.

But for all its autobiographical elements, *Train* is still a parable.

Giovanni's Room and *Another Country* were stories that grew naturally out of concerns Baldwin was articulating in the fifties and early sixties in his speeches and essays. *Tell Me How Long the Train's Been Gone,* too, especially in the "Black Christopher" section, is clearly related to the social issues he was addressing in the years of its composition. Everything that the novel's hero, Leo Proudhammer, is and does has metaphorical—even allegorical—significance. He is at once the representative black artist and the black American in general. His heart attack is a metaphor for crises in the hearts of both groups.

Through Leo's struggle, Baldwin addresses the conflict within his own mind and within the minds of so many others in the mid-sixties between two basic approaches to the racial question that continued to be at the center of his life as a public figure. This was a conflict between his long-preached prophecy of love and Black Christopher's call to arms against a known enemy. Baldwin had already addressed the question in *Blues for Mister Charlie* and in his most recent public comments, but it was time now to go further.

Leo's heart attack marks in a sense the end of the old Baldwin hero. Part 3 of the novel is the story of the reemergence or resurrection—from the threshing floor of middle life—of that hero, "healed" by Black Christopher, the new, born-again "Christ-bearer" of revolution. Christopher, like the Richards in *Mountain* and *Blues,* Rufus in *Country,* Sonny in "Sonny's Blues," and Arthur in *Just Above My Head,* is a familiar combination of several young men in Baldwin's life, from Eugene Worth in the early days to the SNCC and CORE students and leaders like Stokely Carmichael and other Black Power advocates who were significant presences in Baldwin's later life. He is also an aspect of Baldwin himself.

Years earlier Caleb had taught his brother both something about love and something about the "white problem." "Are white people—*people*? People like us?" Leo had asked. And Caleb had answered that it seemed as if "*they* don't think they are." "You're only white as long as you think I'm black," Baldwin had said to countless white audiences since the fifties. In Black Christopher, Leo finds a later Caleb, one who teaches the same political lesson more powerfully, as Caleb himself withdraws into a life in the church. Through Christopher, Leo hopes to discover the means of translating the fire of prophecy into the fire of love between two human beings, thus fulfilling Caleb's promise as a bearer of love born of rage. Perhaps, Proudhammer/Baldwin hoped, Black Christopher would make possible a breaking of the terrible silence. Perhaps through Christopher the union between vocation and personal need so long sought by Leo and his author could finally be realized.

Perhaps, but probably not. Proudhammer/Baldwin had "conquered the city" contemplated by John Grimes/Baldwin all those years ago in Central Park, but ironically, "the city was stricken with the plague," one that would not end during his lifetime. The result was that "all that I most treasured, wine, talk, laughter . . . the touch of a lover . . . and the mighty joy of a good day's work, would have to be stolen, each moment lived as though it were the last," in the face of "the storm that was rising to engulf us all."

These words describe, in fact, what became Baldwin's "philosophy" of personal life for the rest of his days. He was to fall in love often, but never again would he expect the impossible, which had beckoned him in the early days with Lucien. Until the plague could be overcome, the possibility experienced fictionally in Caleb's arms could only be a dream. Leo Proudhammer loves Black Christopher because he is Black Christopher—the "cat" he wished he could be, but he understands the limitations of their relationship. "All I want is for you to live," he says to Christopher, and Christopher answers, "Alone? . . . Walking over the bodies of the dead?" Until the plague was lifted, joy had to be taken in moments wherever it could be found; the primary concern must be the plague itself.

For Black Christopher the plague meant the necessity of guns, not a life of isolated loving. For Proudhammer that was understandable, but not possible: "I went away to Europe, alone. Then, I came back. I . . . did the movie." Proudhammer's role was not Black Christopher's, and James Baldwin's was not Stokely Carmichael's. But Proudhammer and Baldwin saw where the future lay and understood what motivated their younger compatriots.

The reviews of *Tell Me How Long the Train's Been Gone* were not good. Mario Puzo in the *Times Book Review* criticized it as "one-dimensional" and found fault with its "polemical rather than narrative tone." Stuart Hall in the *New Statesman* thought it erratic, but, like other British reviewers, seemed to understand better than American critics what the author was attempting. The book was a "meditation by a middle-aged black revolutionary on a revolution he has witnessed—but cannot, finally, share." The connection and the "distance" between Leo and Christopher were "crucial."

The most profound review was that of John Thompson in *Commentary*. Although much of the material of *Train* was "the material . . . of our present great social crisis," he said, the work was not a "protest novel," as many suggested, because Baldwin was primarily concerned with the inner human questions, with "what moves his people." Thompson also pointed to the fact that the book was "a deeply personal statement of how Baldwin recognizes that he has driven himself to the dreadful eminence of being representative." While it was true that the ending was "more convincing as personal allegory than as the resolution of a complicated fiction," *Tell Me How Long the Train's Been Gone* was in its own way "a masterpiece by one of the best living writers in America."

Baldwin had always had doubts about *Train* and in later years he felt that it was not successful, but in 1967 he was primarily relieved that it was out and that he could move on, like Leo, to other matters. The last lines of the book had been revised in San Francisco, and it was California that would provide the base for the next installment of Baldwin's struggle to make peace between the demands of his vocation and those of his body and his emotions.

CHAPTER 28

One Day, When I Was Lost

It is a time for martyrs now.
—Malcolm X

From Istanbul, Baldwin had traveled to London, where he had suffered the humiliation of being held up by immigration authorities for several hours while he tried to explain that he was not there as a subversive ally of Lord Russell but to see his publisher. He made his way to Paris, where he stayed until early July, trying unsuccessfully to solve the problems surrounding his badly managed attempt to buy an apartment there. He seemed at a loss as to where to go or what to do. Only David was fully dependable, but Baldwin realized he must not lean on his brother too much. He did write to say that he loved him "more than I love anybody in this . . . terrifying world."

The Hôtel Pont Royal, where he was staying, was expensive, and Paris was not proving to be a productive workplace. Furthermore, he had a phone run-in with Lucien over the Paris apartment fiasco, and this had made him "depressed and reckless." He wrote to David in June telling him it was unlikely that he and Lucien would ever see each other again. He must have wondered how many times in his life he would have to come to this conclusion. He decided, as he often had in the past when under emotional stress, that he had to get away. He considered returning to Istanbul, where he knew both David and I would be by August at the latest. But he realized even as he pondered these matters that his Istanbul days were over—at least for the time being. He had to return home.

On a recent trip to New York he had met with Alex Haley and Elia Kazan about the possibility of doing a play based on Haley's *Autobiography of Malcolm X*, and he had made promises in connection with that project which involved an early return to the States. Also, the "race riots" that were shattering the ghettoes of the great cities were a signal. There was work to be done, as there had been ten years earlier, in 1957, when he had returned home to go South. He sensed that this would be a more difficult journey than the southern one, and he decided to hold off as long as he could, at least until he had a clearer idea of exactly what his role in the States should be.

In 1967 Baldwin looked homeward at a nation in discord. The flower children and hippies had once seemed to give life to the doctrine of love and freedom that he had preached for so long; but now, in light of the worsening social situation—marked by race riots, assassinations, and incarcerations of new and old friends—they struck him as a terribly middle-class and primarily white parody of his message. These were the children of the liberals to whom he had preached and with whom he had marched in the late fifties and early sixties, and all around their celebrations in the wake of their parents' talk of equality lay a wasteland of social failure. To make matters worse, as Baldwin grew more disillusioned with the old approach to America's problems and more radical in his views, he nevertheless found himself criticized as irrelevant by the very young men to whom he so much wanted to give support.

Their criticism was somehow echoed by his personal life. He was growing older, and the youths he met in his continuing quest for love, who could only see him in the context of the glittering world into which his fame had locked him, seemed increasingly removed from his inner life. Furthermore, like his nation, increasingly torn between apparent prosperity and the moral bankruptcy deriving from racism and the Vietnam War, Baldwin felt that he was on the edge of an emotional and political abyss.

For the moment it seemed best to concentrate on several writing assignments he had taken on. He suggested to Beauford and to Bernard Hassell that they go with him to Cannes. They agreed, and once there, Baldwin divided his time between a piece on W. E. B. Du Bois that was never finished, on an article called "A Praying Time," never published, about William Styron and *The Confessions of Nat Turner*, and on the beginnings of the Malcolm play. He also began writing down notes for what he thought at the time would be the first part of a long autobiography, which he was already calling *No Name in the Street.*

But he had difficulty keeping his mind on work. The last fight with Lucien still hurt, and he had come away from it confirmed in the belief that he would never find emotional stability in a relationship. He had, in fact, become so desperate that in Paris he had revived an old connection with "Pierre" (the name has been changed here to protect his privacy), a man with whom he had had a brief affair during his 1962 trip to Africa. He had promised to return to Pierre after the Cannes trip to set up an apartment with him. He had been tempted as well by a recent letter from another former lover in London. In a journal entry he wondered about what seemed his frantic quest for a new lover and admitted that he had been irritated by the London lover's immaturity—his self-centeredness and lack of consideration, his youth. All of these feelings were confirmed later in the year, when, during one of Baldwin's stays in London, the young man in question arrived at his hotel and presented him with a pet white rabbit, the pelletlike droppings of which became a source of irritation to Baldwin—and to the hotel staff.

Yet in the same journal he speaks of the attractions of a young North African he had met recently on the beach. "Jean" (his name has been changed here to protect his privacy) was nineteen or twenty; Baldwin was forty-three. Lucien, too, had been a teenager when Baldwin had met him eighteen years before, and in a sense Jean presented a way to bury Lucien even as the earlier ecstasy was revived. Perhaps Jean could be what Lucien could not be. Baldwin preferred to believe so, and in a very short time he had "hired" him to be his chauffeur and live-in companion in spite of the fact that he had, for the moment, neither car nor home. The affair would be stormy and erratic. Jean's youth made it impossible for him to cope with the contradictions of the situation, let alone with the complexities of Baldwin's life. He became alternately possessive, jealous, and demanding of his "freedom" to have heterosexual relationships. But in spite of all, he attained a certain degree of maturity, and remained a sometime companion for the next three years and a friend even after they separated.

For Baldwin a problem with this as with many of his love relationships was complicated by the fact that he had difficulty putting together his need for a fully supportive equal in love with his sense of responsibility as a father figure, financial sponsor, and teacher for a much younger individual. He could accept one-night stands, but a puritanical streak made it necessary, when it came to any kind of extended relationship, to deny the merely carnal. Sex would simply be the natural physical expression of a symbiotic relationship between

With Martin Luther King, Jr., 1968

With David Leeming and Rosemary and Peter Shiras, Istanbul, 1967

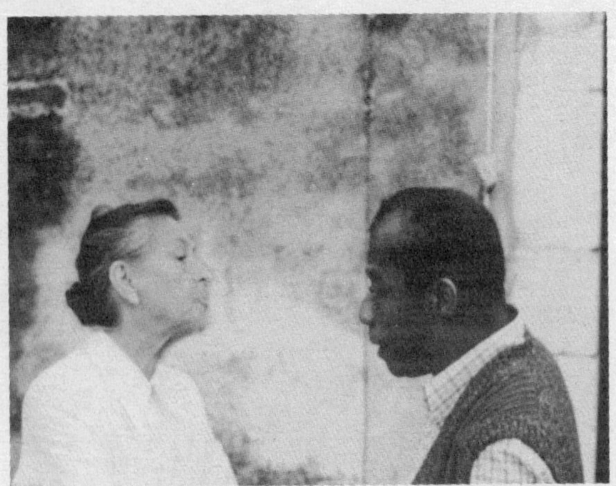

With Mlle Faure, Saint-Paul-de-Vence in the 1970s

Mary Painter

Teaching at
Bowling Green, 1978

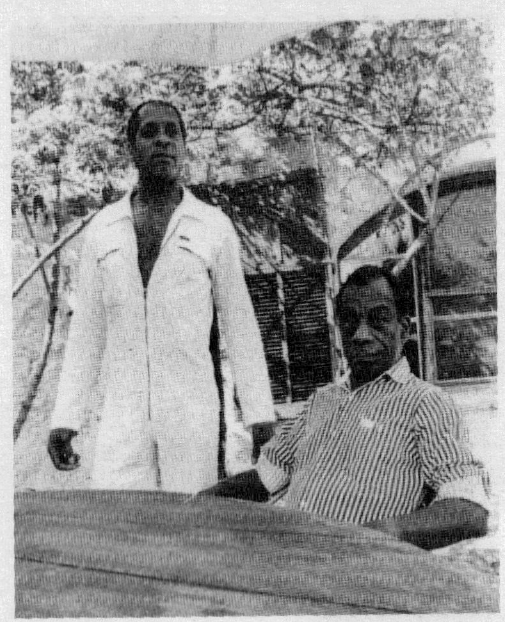

With Bernard Hassell at the outdoor "welcome table" in Saint-Paul-de-Vence in the 1970s

With Beauford Delaney at St. Anne's Hospital in Paris, 1978

With David Baldwin, London, 1981

With Bill Belli, c. 1983

With his mother and Maya Angelou at Baldwin's sixtieth birthday party in Amherst, 1984

With his mother and Sam Floyd at Baldwin's sixtieth birthday party

On the *Amen Corner* set, London, 1986

The final bed, Saint-Paul-de-Vence, 1987

The welcome table, Saint-Paul-de-Vence, 1987

artist-teacher and apprentice and a model for the more general love that could exist between people ordinarily separated by seemingly insuperable boundaries.

The lengths to which Baldwin went with Jean were typical. He had picked up a street boy, but almost immediately he insisted on formalizing the relationship on somewhat paternalistic grounds, by meeting the boy's family. At the same time, he felt all the nervousness of a young man confronting his would-be fiancée's parents for the first time. He washed his white shirt and noted that hanging on the hotel balcony, it reminded him of someone about to be crucified. In this case the family was Jean's grandmother, who had raised him in the absence of his very young mother, who appeared only occasionally in her son's life, including, as it turned out, the day of Baldwin's visit. The meeting went well, Baldwin playing the role of prospective employer, going so far as to discuss hours and wages. To his mind he was committing himself to something more serious, a "marriage" with a much younger individual. He sensed that if the grandmother and mother did not understand this, they "trusted" him, and he decided that whatever happened he "could not fail" them or "this boy."

Jean, like many of Baldwin's waiflike lovers, was representative of the Baldwin idea of "the children" to be saved. The young lovers formed a multicolored, multinational congregation that for Baldwin was literally and metaphorically his "flock."

Given his feelings for Jean, it was necessary to return to Paris to terminate the relationship with Pierre. During a Normandy coast weekend that culminated in a terrifying drive back to the city in Pierre's car, Baldwin and Bernard, who had gone along on the trip as "protection," both sensed that Pierre was purposely endangering all their lives. Jimmy had found his would-be life's companion's conduct depressing. Pierre talked continually of their growing old and made fun of Jimmy's appearance on the beach and ineptness in the water. In Pierre, Baldwin saw a mid-life desperation that came too close to his own inner state. He was reminded of Aschenbach confronting the old dandy on the ship in *Death in Venice*. With great relief he returned to Cannes, where he was met by "my child." He would stay through his own birthday, working during the day and seeing Jean in the evening after the boy got out of work.

In mid-August, having made arrangements for Jean to join him in London later, Baldwin left for the States. On the twenty-fourth he delivered a speech calling for a black economic boycott to support the still imprisoned Harlem Six and then retired for a week in the country with Alex Haley and Elia Kazan to work on the Malcolm project. They already had the support of Betty Shabazz, and Baldwin had spoken as well to Malcolm's sister, Ella Collins.

An attempt to talk with Elijah Muhammad had been unproductive. The Honorable Elijah had simply refused to see him, but Baldwin did not feel this need be an impediment to the play as long as potentially libelous remarks about the Muslims were avoided. By early September he already had a title, *One Day, When I Was Lost*, and a fairly detailed outline, including some radical adjustments to the original story that were intended to divert the potential Muslim lawsuits. A character called Luther would be substituted for Malcolm's brother, Reginald, and would serve as a "superior" who would carry messages from the Honorable Elijah—renamed the Honorable Messenger—to Brother Malcolm. Baldwin wanted his brother David to play this role. The messenger himself would not appear in the play. But the plans fell apart when, in 1968, producer Marvin Worth bought the rights to do the Haley *Autobiography* for Columbia Pictures.

When Baldwin was offered the position as scriptwriter for the Malcolm film, he was faced with a difficult dilemma. He was already deeply involved with the Malcolm story, and the project would provide him with a way of becoming directly involved in the liberation movement in its more radical form. But he doubted Hollywood's motives and was wary of being tainted by them. He wondered, given the fear with which white Americans regarded anything to do with Black Muslims or Black Power, whether the movie industry could allow an honest depiction of Malcolm and his life. Most of his family and other advisors urged him to refuse the offer. But after several days of "soul-searching," he agreed to do a screenplay based on the outline he had already drawn up for Kazan. It was a question of not betraying what he saw as Malcolm's trust, Malcolm's belief in him. He was also succumbing to his persistent dream of writing for the screen. Later he would wish he had resisted.

In late October Baldwin flew to London to spend time with David and Paula, who had established a "hiding place" for him in Chelsea. He arrived full of determination, planning to return to Hollywood in February. Meanwhile, he could breathe for a spell and relax. The London months were good for him, restoring, among other things, his good humor. I had sent him a photograph of our two dogs, who had remained with me in Turkey. In the picture the black dog, Flea, is playfully mauling the white Andromache. Baldwin's answering note ends with a postscript: "Racism in reverse."

Jean arrived, and Paris friend Bill Belli was in town. There were many other friends in London as well, most notably the West Indian director Horace Ove and Raleigh Trevelyan. And though Baldwin was always somewhat uncomfortable with English restraint and with what he considered English hypocrisy on the subject of race, he enjoyed London as a city much more than he had on his first visits there.

But good times were to be short-lived. Early in 1968 two black "revolutionaries" for whom Baldwin felt particular responsibility were in trouble. The first was Tony Maynard, who had once worked for him in New York and who was now in a Hamburg jail about to be extradited to the United States for an alleged murder. The second was Stokely Carmichael, whom he had long admired as a freedom fighter and leader of SNCC, who was soon to become "prime minister" of the Black Panthers and who had had his passport confiscated by the State Department as a punishment for his pro-Cuban, anti–Vietnam War activities. Baldwin's immediate reaction to the Carmichael case was to write a public defense.

This was Baldwin's "J'Accuse," a powerful indictment of his nation. The *Times* of London and *The New York Times* chose not to print it, but the *Guardian* and other papers did. For Baldwin, Carmichael was the political incarnation of Black Christopher in *Train* and Lorenzo in *Blues*. He was the awakening of the figure Jerome Smith had envisioned at the famous New York meeting when he had warned Bobby Kennedy, "with terrible tears in his voice," of impending violence. Like all black Americans, Carmichael was obsessed with "Black Power" only because white America practiced "White Power" against him. If Carmichael and the Panthers were guilty of insurrection, what was George Wallace guilty of when he flew the Confederate flag from the Alabama statehouse? And if Carmichael was a terrorist, what was a government that withheld passports to get its way? The fact that Baldwin might disagree with some of Carmichael's views (or Malcolm's) was "absolutely irrelevant." What was relevant was the fact that Carmichael was a young man who was, in effect, announcing to people of Baldwin's generation that he was unwilling to put up with what they had put up with, unwilling to be "corralled into some of the awful choices I've been forced to make: *and he is perfectly right.*"

Baldwin had written the Carmichael piece on January 2, 1968, while attempting to do something about Tony Maynard, whose case was a more difficult one than Carmichael's because he was an unknown. To save him Baldwin would have to work privately as well as publicly. The mainline black organizations were not likely to get involved with the case of a "street hustler" with a police record. To make matters worse, Baldwin knew that Maynard's anger was such that he was quite capable of violence. No doubt he had in mind the notorious occasion of Richard Wright's successful freeing of a prisoner who repeated his crime soon after he was released. Maynard and he had some time ago had a falling-out over Baldwin's resistance to violence, and in several instances, because of his anger, Maynard had placed Baldwin in difficult social situations. But his rage, and his need to react in accordance with it, was "understandable." When Baldwin visited him in jail in Hamburg, Maynard opened their conversation by saying, "Upon my soul, I didn't do it." Baldwin's answer was just as clear: "Upon my soul," he said, "we'll get you out."

So began a depressing process lasting several years, during which Baldwin did what he could to free Maynard. He made sure his friend had legal representation in Germany and later in New York, and he pleaded his case with New York City and New York State politicians and police. He even attempted to acquire a book contract to write the Maynard story, with the idea of sharing the proceeds with Maynard to get him established if he was finally released. The book, for which only notes and an outline exist, was to have been called *Upon My Soul.* The idea for it would lead to *If Beale Street Could Talk.*

In fact, the case against Tony Maynard was a weak one, a fairly blatant example of "they all look alike" identification and police resentment of a high-profile black man downtown who was a "troublemaker" and who liked white women. Maynard was a type for whom even—perhaps especially—the white liberal establishment would have little sympathy, because he gave none of the reassurance of the "successful" black. In a "To Whom It May Concern" letter Baldwin noted that Maynard was "vulnerable . . . helpless and . . . black." The case was plainly one of "political persecution."

Having done what he could for the moment, Baldwin flew to the States on February 12, Lincoln's birthday, as he reminded David in a letter written on the thirteenth, after his arrival in Beverly Hills. He seemed to be cast in the role of emancipator himself. The slaves, as Malcolm would have said, were still in chains. From the unlikely locale of Beverly Hills, Baldwin hoped to help the Black Christophers of the world to achieve the freedom to live. Somehow, he felt, Malcolm would help if he could free Malcolm's voice in Hollywood, the Mecca of the American Dream. But Hollywood was not ready to become an accomplice in the resurrection of Malcolm X in the American soul.

Baldwin's arrival in Hollywood did cause a stir, however. Columbia put him up at the Beverly Hills Hotel—not far, as he pointed out to David with some obvious pride, from "Marlon" and "Sammy [Davis, Jr.]." Almost immediately he was besieged by visitors who had heard that James Baldwin had arrived to do a scenario on "our brother Malcolm." He suggested to David that the Beverly Hills Hotel was a changed place. There were Black Muslims, Black Panthers, entertainers, and just plain "brothers and sisters" anxious to become a part of a Baldwin entourage. There were also close friends. Brock Peters took Baldwin on extensive tours of the area, and another actor friend, David Moses, invited him frequently to his home. Baldwin loved David, his wife, Sharon, and their three boys (whose godfather he was), and their home became his refuge in Los Angeles. He hated barbershops, and since David cut his children's hair, Baldwin got into the habit of having him cut his as well on a regular basis. Later in 1968, he paid to have Moses's parents flown from the Midwest to meet their grandchildren for the first time.

Never able to say no, he agreed to several talks in high schools and churches in Watts and elsewhere, and before long he found himself at a benefit party for Operation Bootstrap at Eddie Albert's home. He was amazed by the scene there, but the Columbia Pictures people were even more amazed by the unusual presence—for Hollywood—of so many exotically coiffed and robed African-Americans. As for Eddie Albert, he gave the impression of having stumbled upon a "tribal rite" in darkest Africa.

A few days later Stokely Carmichael came to town and Baldwin made a point of appearing with him in public. *Variety* wrote a "reassuring" article suggesting that Baldwin did not agree with Stokely or his methods—Baldwin was, after all, now a part of Hollywood. In fact, he had long thought of himself as a Carmichael ally and was relieved to find that on the day after the appearance of the *Variety* piece, the

Los Angeles *Free Press* carried his "defense" of Carmichael on its front page.

Carmichael and H. Rap Brown, who had recently assumed leadership of SNCC, and the three leaders of the Black Panther party, Huey Newton, Eldridge Cleaver, and Bobby Seale, were, as far as Baldwin was concerned, the future of the civil rights movement. When everything that could be said about nonviolence and the love of one's neighbor had been said, nothing mattered if the black man's integrity was denied him. The oppression, the economic problems, the riots, the deaths of young black men continued unabated. Hope seemed to lie more in the thousands who attended the July Black Power conference in Newark and in the Panthers than in the old nonviolent black-white liberal coalition. Baldwin admired the radicals; he saw them as part of the larger "project" of which the old civil rights movement had been only a stage.

Baldwin had known Carmichael and the other SNCC leaders for some time. He had made his first contact with the Panthers in October 1967 in San Francisco after a depressing summer of over seventy-five major riots in American cities. Through Kay Boyle and his friends Reggie and Helen Major, he had been brought together with Huey Newton at the apartment of his Village days employer, Connie Williams. He met Eldridge Cleaver in 1967 as well.

There was an understandable strain between Baldwin and Cleaver. Cleaver had already written his article "Notes on a Native Son" (collected later in the best seller *Soul on Ice*). The piece chastised the older writer for his homosexuality and for his supposed rejection of his blackness. Still, Baldwin found himself "impressed" by Cleaver and later, in *No Name in the Street,* would go to great lengths to justify the minister of education's point of view: "He was being a zealous watchman" protecting the movement from a man he thought of as a "badly twisted and fragile reed, of too much use to the Establishment to be trusted by blacks." He did complain of the difficulties caused him by Cleaver's attack and suggested that he had spent a great deal of time in the late sixties trying to "undo the damage."

Huey Newton was a different matter. Baldwin felt at ease with him: "He is old-fashioned . . . in that he treats everyone with respect, especially his elders." He and Baldwin promised to maintain contact after the meeting at Connie's. And even after Newton's arrest a few days later and his subsequent imprisonment, Baldwin would do just that, arranging to visit Newton in prison and to correspond with him there. Later, when Newton was finally released, Baldwin visited with him whenever he was in the Bay Area. He went with him on several occasions to the Huey Newton School in Oakland and worked with him and Angela Davis and other activists on various local projects. The two men also developed a real friendship and enjoyed spending time together; there were lunches and dinners at Huey's house and at places like the Soul Food Kitchen in Oakland. Often they were joined by mutual friends—most notably Reggie Major and authors Cecil Brown and David Henderson. Had he lived to see it, he would have been as badly shaken by Huey's murder as he had been by those of Evers, Malcolm, and King.

In February of 1968 Baldwin would be asked by the Panthers to host a birthday party/fund-raising rally for Newton in Oakland. This he did, and during the 1967–69 period he would make several such appearances, including one arranged for Oakland by Bobby Seale, the third member of the Panther leadership, whom Baldwin had met through Marlon Brando.

Baldwin did experience personal discomfort with aspects of the Panther approach, and sometimes he found his association with them embarrassing. The worst of his Panther experiences occurred at a 1968 Los Angeles gathering in honor of Malcolm X's birthday, at which he was to be the main speaker. He took several people with him, including David Moses and producer Marvin Worth. Bringing David, who was black, was fine, but by bringing a white man, who was also a Jew, to a meeting guarded and sponsored by the Panthers, Baldwin was already signifying his determination to be independent of Panther ideology. He was well aware that he was "onstage" in such public appearances. In fact, as he and Moses and Worth were about to pass through the line of gun-toting bodyguards at the entrance of the meeting hall, he turned to his friends and, with a broad smile, gave them the director's command: "Take your places."

On this occasion he found himself caught in a performance for which he had not rehearsed. A Panther guard, who continually patrolled back and forth on the stage behind the participants, had what was said later to have been an epileptic fit and began firing his gun. Another guard, on the balcony, misunderstanding his comrade's motives, returned the fire, endangering the audience, including a young child of Malcolm X, and the speakers, Baldwin and Malcolm's widow among them. The people on the stage dove under tables, except for Baldwin, who ran to the edge of the platform screaming for Malcolm's child and David Moses to get down on the floor.

After this event Baldwin did little in the way of appearances specifically for the Panthers, but in numerous speeches he continued his verbal support of what he considered their righteous anger, and he kept working for Huey Newton's release and later for Bobby Seale's. In 1978 he would even write a foreword to Seale's autobiography.

Baldwin was never a believer in ideology, and he had no sympathy for the Panthers' Marxist argument. What he did believe was that the economic system of the West had no room for the people whose lives were marred by poverty and oppression. If "a form of socialism" was necessary, so be it. Socialism for Baldwin did not mean Marxism necessarily; it meant social change and state responsibility. The Panthers were the logical extension of the position Malcolm had reached at the time of his death. If the state failed to recognize its responsibilities, the oppressed would have to arrange their own lives, their own economics.

There was, as well, a more personal, subliminal aspect to Baldwin's attraction to the Panthers. In *Tell Me How Long the Train's Been Gone* he had been able to embody his sexual and political interests in one individual, Black Christopher. In real life the young radicals, no matter how harsh or even cruel in their remarks about him, were political embodiments of a need that took more personal form in certain of Baldwin's young and angry black lovers of the late years, a need to be a part of something young, something that could carry him beyond the lethargy that came with disillusionment and the failure to change the world in *his* time. It seems fair to say, too, that by supporting the "revolutionaries," he was pledging his allegiance to Malcolm and preparing himself for the experience of reworking the *Autobiography*.

Baldwin was aware of the complex relationship between his public and private roles and of the importance of keeping the boundaries between them clear. He wrote to David that he had to protect himself as a public, even "historical," figure from his private self. And he began in some sense almost to identify with Malcolm—taking up his voice in his treatment of the *Autobiography*: there was, he said, "a whole lot on my shoulders" in the absence of those fighters for freedom who were dead or in jail. He was at once sad and full of anticipation.

On March 16, 1968, Martin Luther King, Jr., arrived in Los Angeles, accompanied by Andrew Young, on a mission to raise money for the Southern Christian Leadership Conference and a Poor People's Campaign in Washington. Feeling his familiar discomfort around King, Baldwin was quite nervous when he was asked to introduce him at the Los Angeles meeting. He followed Marlon Brando, who spoke of the confusion which marked the post–March on Washington period, with an eloquent statement on the American betrayal of brotherhood both at home and abroad. The nation was as callous in its treatment of the peasant in Detroit as it was in its treatment of the peasant in Saigon, and this was not only a great crime but a great miscalculation, as America had a great deal to learn from those it mistreated.

When Baldwin described this occasion in *No Name in the Street*, he emphasized his affection for King but pointed out that "Martin and I had never got to know each other well, circumstances, if not temperament, made that impossible." By this time he was well into his association with the Black Panthers, and King's concerns seemed less important in Los Angeles than they had seemed in Montgomery and Selma. Rightly or wrongly, he sensed a note of skepticism in King's response to him and a new "dubiousness" in his reaction to the Malcolm project, and this inevitably revived the old comparison between "Martin and Malcolm" in his mind.

Because of his work on the film Baldwin had by now closely identified with Malcolm and thought of him as a soul mate. As early as their meeting on the 1961 radio program with Eric Goldman, they had joined forces in a verbal attack on the conservative George Schuyler of the *Pittsburgh Courier*, to whose "middle-class Negro" attitudes they had had similar reactions (Baldwin's mother and brother David had once worked at a party in New York at which Schuyler's daughter, Philippa, had played piano). The Baldwin-Malcolm alliance that was forged in the early sixties was built on an understanding that they were clearly "coming from the same place," a place from which King, a college-educated member of the southern black bourgeoisie, just as clearly, like Schuyler, did not come. Baldwin and Malcolm shared a temperament and an anger that was based in self-education and the deprivation of the northern ghettoes.

Furthermore, Malcolm respected Baldwin's independence and shared his suspicion of the motives of those white liberals who had surrounded King in the early civil rights days. He knew that at early pre–March on Washington meetings with June Shagaloff, Clarence Jones, Bayard Rustin, and others, Baldwin had advocated radical civil disobedience to accompany the march and that he had been overruled by those unwilling to offend the white liberals.

Malcolm wholly sympathized with Baldwin's disappointment at being denied a public voice during the march itself: "They wouldn't let him talk because they couldn't make him go by the script," he had said. He appreciated Baldwin's having the courage to confront the white liberal adulation of King as a collective self-defense ploy. Americans were in favor of the nonviolent movement only "if it seems as if I'm going to get violent," Baldwin had said to Kenneth Clark, and Malcolm agreed. Malcolm had made his feelings and his doubts, even about his own movement, clear to Baldwin and, while chiding him for his "integrationism," had encouraged him with genuine friendship.

Yet when King spoke in Los Angeles, Baldwin was greatly impressed, as always, by his presence and his determination. He felt that King's attitudes had become much closer to those of Malcolm in the post-Mecca period, that, especially with Malcolm dead, he was still the overall leader of the movement, and he was always willing to work with him. Less than a month before the Los Angeles meeting, for example, he had appeared with King in a Carnegie Hall celebration of W. E. B. Du Bois in New York, bringing some of his Malcolm-inspired message with him. Baldwin said a few words there in praise of Du Bois and continued by reading aloud his defense of Stokely Carmichael.

In mid-March, Baldwin spent time in New York making brief television appearances and working on the Maynard case. He also appeared with Betty Shabazz before a House of Representatives subcommittee in support of a bill for the establishment of a commission on "Negro History and Culture." The subcommittee chairman referred to Baldwin as "the very distinguished playwright," and in the record Betty Shabazz's name was spelled "Shadazz," but Baldwin did get a full hearing and was able to make the point that by whitewashing American history, the white establishment had effectively worked to deny the black American a sense of identity.

While in New York he also saw Alex Haley and Frank Dandridge and discussed President Johnson's Civil Disorders Bill on television with representatives of the World Council of Churches. He accused the churchmen of failing to live up to the spirit of their faith and of therefore being responsible for much of the evil in the world. They had lacked the courage to "chase the money-changers out of the Temple." The ex-preacher seemed to take genuine pleasure in preaching to the church he had left, and in so doing he pointed to the heart of his hatred of the white liberal establishment. The church bemoaned its own guilt, its own racism, but would not see its role in perpetuating the economic system that lay behind the social disorder.

Baldwin returned to California, this time to a house that had been rented for him in Palm Springs, where the studio hoped he could get more work done. He renewed an acquaintance with Billy Dee Williams, a young African-American actor whom he had first seen on the stage in New York. He had fallen in love with Williams in 1965 and had taken him with his brothers, David and Lover, on a trip to Paris and London. Williams was decidedly heterosexual, and the relationship did not materialize as Baldwin had hoped it would. But his yearnings lingered on, and his interest in and respect for Williams remained strong and genuine on other grounds. Williams had for some time been his leading candidate to play Black Christopher in his life; now he became his choice for the Malcolm X role in his film. Their relationship, if not sexual, was warm and playfully physical. Billy Dee would pick up Jimmy and carry him around the house like a child and there was a great deal of bear-hugging affection. This gave Baldwin pleasure even as he suffered increasingly in the knowledge that the relationship could not go further.

As for the question of the starring role in the film, this became the center of Baldwin's fight with Columbia Pictures, which had other actors—James Earl Jones or Sidney Poitier or even, it was rumored, Charlton Heston darkened up a bit—in mind for Malcolm. In this fight with Columbia over Williams, Baldwin was saying, in effect, that he had to have a Malcolm he could love. This was not the goal of Columbia Pictures.

The battle lines between Columbia and its scriptwriter had been fairly clearly drawn for some time. Columbia wanted a tempered story, a sanitized Malcolm, but Baldwin was determined not to let the studio interfere with his work. He listened regularly to Aretha Franklin, as he had listened to Bessie Smith in the *Mountain* days. He told David he wanted to write the way Aretha sounded. He wanted to capture the combination of the "heart-breaking" and the "peaceful" that was in the Malcolm story and in Aretha's music. His goal was to reveal Malcolm to the world, and he felt he was succeeding: "I'm really creating Malcolm," he wrote. The pain and deprivation of his own childhood were coming to his aid. With luck he would "change this town" and, by extension, America itself.

On April 4, 1968, having spent most of the day being interviewed about his problems with Columbia Pictures, Baldwin was sitting by the Palm Springs swimming pool with Billy Dee Williams having a drink and listening to an Aretha Franklin record when David Moses called to say that Martin Luther King had been shot. Baldwin dropped the phone and wept. Several days later, after federal troops had put down "riots" all over the country, he made his way, still dazed, to Atlanta for the funeral. He was dressed in the suit he had bought for the Carnegie Hall appearance with King a few weeks earlier and would give away to his old church friend Arthur Moore a few weeks later rather than wear it again.

At first the large crowd kept him from entering the church, but someone recognized him and helped him across the police lines. In the church he saw the compatriots of a more hopeful time: Sammy Davis, James Brown, Eartha Kitt, Marlon Brando, Harry Belafonte, Sidney Poitier—he and the last three had done a Voice of America show for Edward R. Murrow during the March on Washington and had listened to King's "I Have a Dream" speech on television from the studio. Bobby Kennedy was there, too, and memories of the New York confrontation came back. But most of all, he remembered the feeling of hope and exhilaration that accompanied the end of the great speech: "We . . . could see our inheritance." Now, with Medgar, Malcolm, and Martin all dead, it seemed that Malcolm had been right about the march. In one sense it *had* been a "sellout," but King had provided something in his time and his place that Malcolm had begun to see at the end of his time and which King's death forced Baldwin to reexamine now.

On April 6 the Panther House in Oakland had been raided. Several people had been killed, and a protest was arranged. Marlon Brando asked Baldwin to go, but he was emotionally unable to do so. On the twelfth he wrote to Engin Cezzar. He would struggle against "despair," even in the face of the murders of Evers, Malcolm, and now King. At this point it was impossible to do anything else but "pray to those gods who are not Western . . . not Christian." His nation had lost three prophets. This left him with a great deal more responsibility, not only to the militant revolutionary, Malcolm, but to the nonviolent revolutionary, Martin. His work took on a new importance in that context. He wrote to one correspondent that the work he was doing was "an act of love and an act of faith." Through it he hoped to save his country from its own injustice.

But the struggle with Columbia Pictures went from bad to worse.

At one point Baldwin received a memo that said he had to "avoid giving any political implications to Malcolm's trip to Mecca." In an interview for *Cinema* he signaled his anger and his determination. He was, he said, "the custodian of a legend," one which white America found it convenient to alter to fit its own beliefs and fears about Malcolm. He would tell the true story, and he would tell it "my way or not at all." America must not be allowed to avoid what Malcolm had said and done.

Columbia did not appreciate Baldwin's outburst, and even Brock Peters suggested that with a lower-key approach he might get more of his own way. Eventually the studio insisted on hiring a scriptwriter to assist Baldwin, and with the support of his brother Lover, Jean (who came from France), and Billy Dee Williams, he continued working. Although he liked the scriptwriter, Arnold Perl, well enough—he had met him earlier in New York and had even suggested his name to the studio—he resented what he saw as an intrusion. The Malcolm story, after all, was his story; it could not be Arnold Perl's. "This story is my confession," he said, and "it turns out to be Medgar's and Martin's—it's the story of any black cat in this curious place and time."

The film, then, was to be a historical statement. The burning of the Littles' house and the murder of Malcolm's father would be juxtaposed with the burning of Malcolm's house and his murder in the Audubon Ballroom. In *One Day, When I Was Lost,* we follow Malcolm on his journey from burning house and murdered father to burning house and murdered self. The one day is today, yesterday, and every day. Nothing has changed in four hundred years of history. Baldwin would rearrange the chronology to open America's eyes to the parallels and the history that Malcolm saw. He would reveal Malcolm as a previously unrecognized "tragic hero" of American history—of the American soul. Eight years later, in *The Devil Finds Work,* Baldwin would accuse Hollywood of attempting to make substantial changes in his script that indicated a failure to understand the portrait he was painting.

In mid-May, King's poor followers began to set up Resurrection City, a sixteen-acre compound near the spot in Washington where their leader had preached his "dream." On June 5 Robert Kennedy was shot. It seemed to be a predictable anticlimax; the liberal dream, like Martin's, had become a nightmare. On June 24 Resurrection City was closed down and its residents forcibly ejected.

Baldwin traveled around the country promoting *Train* and giving interviews in which, in the face of more ghetto riots, he accused the white race of economically "looting" the ghettoes and the black race long before the rioting had been contemplated. He announced his agreement with the militant position of Black Christopher at the end of his novel and suggested—Malcolm style—a form of separatism: "I want to control my own schools, because you have poisoned my children and you have poisoned your own children's minds." In "A Letter to Americans" he warned of a growing loss of patience among African-Americans. He traveled to Sweden and challenged the church directly again in an address to the World Council of Churches, suggesting that it was guilty of having forgotten the meaning of the words "Insofar as you have done it unto the least of these, you have done it unto me." In one interview he suggested for a hypothetical course in black history Du Bois's *The Souls of Black Folk*, all of Du Bois and John Hope Franklin, Lerone Bennett, Sterling Brown, E. Franklin Frazier, Langston Hughes, and Frederick Douglass. When asked what book he would recommend to a "Black Power militant," he suggested Henry James's *The Princess Casamassima*, and for Lyndon Johnson he recommended *Don Quixote* and, more seriously, Richard Wright's *Black Boy*. Northern liberals should read Dostoevsky's *The Possessed* and the southern redneck should try *Crime and Punishment*.

In early January he was once again in Hollywood, making a last attempt to retrieve his vision of Malcolm for the screen. But the prognosis was not good. The studio had become as adamant in its point of view as he was in his. Producer Marvin Worth and others felt Baldwin had not produced a viable screenplay and that he was interfering in matters beyond the writer's rightful domain. The first treatment he composed was a manuscript of more than two hundred pages that read more like a novel than a screenplay. Furthermore, his presence was disruptive, his working habits deplorable, and his life-style expensive. Baldwin saw things differently. As he told one interviewer, he had spent sixteen months in Hollywood speaking Hindustani to people who spoke a language he could not understand.

There were friends who helped—Sedat Pakay, the young Turkish filmmaker-photographer, who visited for several weeks and assisted in entertaining a somewhat restless Jean. There were happy moments. Jean added a playful Mediterranean note to the household. Simone Signoret came by occasionally and so did the Greek actress

Irene Papas, who, one day at lunch, looked at Sedat and said, "Look at those eyes; four hundred years of oppression in them," causing a great deal of nervous laughter. Most of all, Baldwin found support in David Moses and in Billy Dee Williams. But as he became increasingly frustrated with the studio, he made impossible demands on these friends, especially Williams, who was a more or less constant fixture in the house. At the low point, just before he finally abandoned the project, angered over the time wasted in Hollywood, depressed by the assassinations and by the imprisonment of Tony Maynard and so many others, exhausted by the pace of his life, frustrated by his relationship with Williams, and upset after a particularly bitter fight with Jean, he took an overdose of sleeping pills, as he had done years before in Paris. Once again he was discovered in time and rushed to the hospital to have his stomach pumped. But he realized now just how much of a failure the Hollywood venture had been.

He had recently written the draft of what was to be an essay on the problems involved with being a black artist in a white world. A version of it would appear in *The New York Times* as "The Price May Be Too High." The catalyst for this essay was his situation in Hollywood, where, it seemed to Baldwin, the commercially driven system made it impossible for "black and white artists"—all of whom were seen primarily as "properties"—"to work together, to learn from each other."

The price, he had decided, for his involvement in the Malcolm project had proven to be too high. In March he wrote to a friend asking him to "imagine" being told by cigar-smoking Hollywood moguls "how a black man lived and died!"

Baldwin left Hollywood. Columbia thought of doing a docudrama using the Baldwin-Perl script (it is this script that is the basis for the Spike Lee film on Malcolm), but then sold the property to Warner Brothers, for whom Perl and others, still under Marvin Worth, created the documentary that eventually was screened and soon buried by Warner Brothers, presumably because it was thought to be inflammatory. Baldwin never saw the documentary, and when he decided to publish *One Day, When I Was Lost*, he went back to his own version as it had stood before Perl's alterations.

Discouraged by what seemed to be a terrible defeat, Baldwin traveled to New York for the Maynard trial—which ended in a hung jury and, in the second trial, in a conviction that was overturned several years later—and then went back to Europe. He stopped in London and then in Paris to pick up Beauford and in Cannes to collect Jean, who had returned there a few weeks earlier. After a brief stopover in Greece, primarily to please Beauford, whose only other trip there had been such a disaster, the unlikely trio made its way back to Istanbul, as far away from Hollywood as it seemed possible to get.

CHAPTER 29

No Name in the Street

His remembrance shall perish from the earth, and he shall have no name in the street.

—Job 18:17

Jimmy, Jean, and Beauford settled into a quiet apartment in Bebek, a section of Istanbul on the European shore of the Bosphorus, not far, as Baldwin was fond of saying, from where Voltaire's Candide and his motley entourage had cultivated their garden. But in spite of the defeat in Hollywood, Baldwin was not ready for retirement from the world. He wanted to get *One Day, When I Was Lost* finished and published to forestall any unauthorized use by Hollywood of his work. Simultaneously, he was reworking *No Name in the Street*, which for a while he had called *No Name in the Streets* because he saw the book as a comment on what he considered the racist American "police state," a state aptly and ironically represented by an act before Congress called the Safe Streets Act. He fully expected that this act and others like it would be used to suppress justifiable black anger rather than to improve life in the cities. He also worked on a novel he had started earlier called *If Beale Street Could Talk*, made some notes for *A Trembling Soul*, which would merge several years later with *The Inheritance*, and found time to do a short foreword to his friend Louise Meriwether's *Daddy Was a Number Runner*. He talked about writing a play based on the Gospels, called *Brother Joe*, and later *The Life and Times of the Great Sir Shine*. It was always to star David Baldwin and, at various points during its inception, Diana Sands, Gloria Foster, Abbey Lincoln, Al Freeman, Jr., Richard Pryor, David Moses, and Rosalind Cash. Ralph Waite was to play "the Roman soldier, father of . . . Pontius Pilate."

But his apparent energy could not hide the fact that Baldwin was still suffering emotionally from the Hollywood fiasco and from the increasing criticism he was facing from the young radicals he had tried so hard to cultivate. Even as he was working for the release of Huey Newton and Bobby Seale, he was finally reading Cleaver's *Soul on Ice*, which spoke of his "shameful, fanatical, fawning sycophantic love of the whites." It was not only Cleaver who felt that way. He had gathered from conversations with close friends and remarks made in the media by young blacks that he was seen by many as not only passé but as a "Tom." There had been indications of the negative trend as early as 1963, when LeRoi Jones, now Amiri Baraka, whose plays *Dutchman* and *The Slave* he so admired, announced in "Brief Reflections on Two Hot-Shots" that Baldwin was so antiblack that if he were "turned white . . . there would be no more noise from [him]." Later he would be insulted by other such attacks, especially by one attributed to (and later denied by) Ishmael Reed to the effect that he was "a hustler who comes on like Job."

He wrote to David that he was "estranged" from both white and black intellectuals and that he appeared to have "moved beyond the terms" in which the whole discussion of race and America was taking place. The discussion had plenty of "heat" but not much "light." In the criticism leveled against him he sensed "childish jealousy." It was all undermining his morale, and he was "weary" of being passive in the face of it.

The difficulty with personal relationships continued to plague him as well. There had been a seemingly definitive fight with his old friend Bill Weatherby in New York, and there was increased tension with Jean. But although the public and private problems were a burden, he announced to his brother in a long, self-analyzing letter in July that he had no intention of evading what he still saw as his mission. There were three distinct beings within his psyche, he said: a "mad-man" determined to change the world, a "fragile, gifted . . . child" with overly sensitive feelings, and a "superbly paranoiac . . . ridiculous ice-and-fire intelligence" that remembered every wrong that had been done to him and waited with enthusiasm for the ultimate "Reckoning." He proceeded to describe the constant struggle between these beings within himself—the child dancing through life, the intelligence outraged at the nature of things, the madman often blowing the house apart. The child was Baldwin's metaphor for the vulnerability and the longing for the protection of others—lovers, brothers, fathers—that had been such an important factor in his life and had brought him so much personal pain and disappointment. The intelligence was the James Baldwin the world saw through his fiction and especially through his incisive essays and speeches. The madman revealed himself in the sudden explosions for which he was now famous. He asked David to remember that although it was, he realized, sometimes difficult for others to tolerate his unpredictability—his volatility—it was just as difficult for him.

After Beauford left for Paris in July, it certainly became difficult for Jean. He could not understand the older man's strange moods or his absorption in his work. Each was possessive in his own way; one, said Baldwin, was "famous and touchy," one was "touchy and obscure." Jean's way of showing affection was to nag him about his drinking, his smoking, and his socializing. And then, Jean sometimes brought home women, and he often treated Jimmy in an offhand manner. In some ways this had healthy results. Through Jean's reaction—or lack of reaction—to his fame, Baldwin was forced, he told David, to reexamine himself and to come to the realization that a "famous" person "does not exist for most people as a man." In his psychological "house" the intelligence was reeling in the child as both warily watched the madman stir. There were individuals who were not meant to live with other people, he wrote in a journal. He saw himself as never having "belonged" to another, and he thought now that he never would. But "I have my work, or my work has me." By late October, Jean had returned to Cannes, something he did periodically during the long relationship with Baldwin, who wrote to David admitting that he, himself, could be "a very crushing presence," but complaining that trying to work and live with Jean was like "living with a cyclone."

A day came in August when the "mad-man" had to explode if for no other reason than to relieve the pressure that had accumulated since the beginning of the Hollywood experiment. The madness usually required a pretext and a temporary victim, who discovered, only after the explosion, that he or she had been merely a rhetorical device. One evening Baldwin went with Engin and Gülriz, as he often did, to a little outdoor nightclub on the Bosphorus in Yeniköy. There they met up with a young woman named Zeynep Oral, a drama critic who had interviewed Baldwin the day before. The club entertainment that night was provided by a Turkish singer whose repertoire included several blues songs. The group seemed happy with the ambience and with the music, and Zeynep turned to Baldwin and said something complimentary about the music. The result was an outburst over which Baldwin seemed to have no control. The music was terrible, he said. "You are trying to steal my music, my pain." The young woman disagreed, and what followed was probably the worst of the "mad-man's" escapades.

Dishes and glasses were scattered, the music stopped as everyone watched and listened to what became a prolonged harangue against Zeynep Oral in particular and those who would undermine black culture in general. Oral bore the burden of everything that *No Name in the Street* and *One Day, When I Was Lost* would describe. She became the murderers of Medgar, Malcolm, and Martin, the jailers of Tony Maynard and Huey Newton. She became the Hollywood co-opters of Malcolm's life.

The next day she received a bouquet of flowers and a note of apology, and before long she had contracted to work as Baldwin's assistant and translator in his directing of John Herbert's *Fortune and Men's Eyes* for Engin and Gülriz's theater company. Baldwin had agreed to direct the Turkish cast, even though he knew no Turkish, because he had always wanted to direct, because he was interested in the play, because it was a way of repaying his Turkish friends for years of love and hospitality, and because it might take his mind off other things.

Fortune and Men's Eyes "saved my life," he was often to say later. The Hollywood experience had left him doubting his own ability. Here was a chance, albeit in a smaller arena, to prove to himself and others that he knew something about the dramatic arts. It gave him a chance to work in such a way as to make a play *his* play. He could do in the theater in Istanbul what he had hoped to do in New York with *Blues* and in Hollywood with *One Day*; he could make the play an act of love. He had told David Moses that he hoped someday they would be able to "make love" as director and actor. As a director he felt he must use his own sensitivity, his own vulnerability, his own willingness to take the risk of opening himself—the risk of loving—to bring out the truth in each of his players and create a working ensemble. Baldwin wanted what he called full "confession" between director and actor and audience.

As Engin Cezzar put it, Baldwin "directed from inside," from the perspective of individual motivation and personal pain. He spent hours with the cast, headed by Engin, which quickly became "my cast," revealing to them through his translator the nature of his and society's pain as expressed by the characters they were playing, five young men confronting themselves in the context of prison, homosexuality, and each other. The process was intense, and unlike anything anyone in the cast had ever experienced in the theater. Some said it was more like psychoanalysis than directing. One of the actors—himself a homosexual who had never made his sexual preference public—was having particular trouble playing the homosexual scenes, but Baldwin understood his problem and was able to ease him away from self-consciousness to a position from which he could not only channel his own dilemma into the character he was playing but change his own life. Another actor, who had difficulty accepting the idea of homosexuality at all and who at first felt uncomfortable around Baldwin, found that after working with him he could play his role with genuine feeling, because he thought of his director "almost as if he were a lover."

This was Baldwin's kind of play, a perfect metaphor for the tragedy he had spent thirty years combating. It was a play about prisoners and about the prisons we make of our minds. For him it spoke to the imprisonment of Huey Newton, Bobby Seale, Tony Maynard, and all of those people—black and white—trapped in the myths of gender, race, and class. In the program notes to *Fortune* he compares the play to Chekhov's *The Cherry Orchard*. Seeing the cutting down of the trees at the end of Chekhov's play as "the destruction of human possibility doomed by human folly," he suggests that "the boys in *Fortune and Men's Eyes* are, like those trees, cut down, and, in this case, before our very eyes." He had long since given up believing in conventional "moral categories," he told his brother. In *Fortune* he was furthering a "vision" of freedom "by which I have always been possessed."

Journalist Charles Adelsen had come to town to see the play and to do a piece on Baldwin in Istanbul for *Ebony*. He described the prison bars that took the place of a stage curtain for *Fortune*—a device that effectively separated the audience from the players, emphasizing the punishment of outcasts by a "righteous society." Baldwin told Adelsen that he saw his production as a "twentieth century morality play," a play that protested the corruption of "the children."

In spite of an attempt by the local government to close it down on the grounds of obscenity—Baldwin's name prevented them from doing so—*Fortune* ran for several months after rave reviews. Baldwin's directing was especially praised, as was the background music, provided by Don Cherry, whom Baldwin had been surprised to find in Istanbul and had "hired" during the early stages of rehearsals. The African-American presence in the Istanbul theater was prolonged when, during the next season, Engin and Gülriz persuaded Bernard Hassell to direct *Hair* for their company.

Baldwin was ecstatic about *Fortune*'s success, and so was the cast. On December 23 they had an elaborate party for him, which they called the "Baldwin Christmas." They presented their director with a replica of the kind of medal given by Ottoman sultans to honor great deeds. The recipient of such a medal became a "pasha." "In other words, baby," as he wrote to David, in English he was now "*Sir* James Baldwin."

Because of the success of the play, he was no longer "left alone" in Istanbul. He had too many friends and too many people petitioning him for help with their particular causes, many of which had to do with a highly ideological and volatile Turkish political situation, which was a mystery to him. To make matters worse, the USIA/USIS, which had approached him about a lecture tour, had announced that he was "unsuitable for use," and he began to become suspicious of several of his American friends in Istanbul, many of whom—including one African-American—worked for the USIS. He had developed what seemed to be genuine friendships with these people, even going so far as to instruct his family to allow the mother of one USIS employee to stay in his office/apartment in New York during her visit there. When Jimmy and David and I had shared the Rumeli Hisar house in 1966–67, we had often joked about the possibility that one USIS woman had "bugged" the grand piano she had asked us to store for her in our living room. We joked, too, about the probability that many of our friends were, in fact, spies sent to watch Jimmy. As I had been approached to work for American intelligence in Istanbul in 1958, we had little doubt as to the validity of our suspicions, but we all decided that we liked the friends in question well enough to take the risk. Still, Baldwin remembered the rumors of CIA involvement in Richard Wright's death, and this was an age of assassinations. Our jokes seem less funny now, in light of the FBI files on Baldwin that have been revealed since the Freedom of Information Act.

Baldwin left Istanbul at the end of the year and returned home to pursue the Maynard case and to see if he could help with Bobby Seale's problems in Chicago, where two Panthers, Fred Hampton and Mark Clark, had recently been killed—in their beds—during a police raid. In an interview he spoke out against the price paid by black Americans for the Vietnam War: "We are all Viet Cong!" he said. A brief visit to Hollywood did nothing to change his opinion about working with Columbia Pictures on the Malcolm script. Still hopeful of finding a producer for his version of the story, he made unsuccessful overtures to both Ingmar Bergman and Costa-Gavras, the director of Z.

A bright spot during these days was the manuscript of Maya Angelou's *I Know Why the Caged Bird Sings*, which Baldwin was reading for her publisher. The book made him want to "gather tribes together . . . and *celebrate* . . . the triumph of [the] human spirit." Back in Istanbul in February, he once again felt he should be in America. He wrote home about the possibility of his returning to do a lecture tour to raise money for the defense of Panthers in jail. Like it or not, his "demons" and the "Lord" were calling him, "keeping me awake at night." In Istanbul he was becoming "impossible." He could think of nothing but "my people!" Late one night he wrote out a new "Pledge of Allegiance" to "my brothers, of whatever color . . . everywhere."

To David Moses he complained of the difficulty he was having finishing *No Name in the Street.* He was called to be a witness. He was pregnant by the "Mighty Mother Fucker" and there was nothing he could do but push the book out, however painful the process might be. He was caught "in the hands of the living God."

In May, following a long bout with hepatitis, he allowed Sedat Pakay, who had just made a film on Walker Evans, to shoot a short black and white film on him. *James Baldwin from Another Place* is a brief but insightful work which follows Baldwin around his favorite Istanbul haunts: the old book market in the courtyard of the Beyazit Mosque, the streets near the Yeni Mosque, the Asian shore of the Bosphorus, a teahouse on the European shore. As we watch him mingle with people on the streets and in the squares, he talks about how being away from America helps him to see it better, how he resents the interest that people—especially Americans—have in his sex life: "Americans are paranoiac on the question of homosexuality. . . . I've loved a few men and a few women . . . love comes in very strange packages . . . the trick is to say yes to life." The Pakay film would be screened in New York in 1973.

By early summer Baldwin was genuinely worried about his health. In London he was told that the hepatitis had damaged his liver and that he ought to give up drinking. For a while Jean joined him, and the couple stayed some time in Neuilly, reenacting the painful pattern into which their relationship had fallen almost from the beginning: "You have your journey now, and I have mine," Jimmy wrote in a poem to Jean.

Depression and health problems continued to plague Baldwin

during the summer. In August he returned home, having agreed to a taped discussion with anthropologist Margaret Mead that would be published as *A Rap on Race.* Mead had decided she must make an extended comment on racism and that a conversation with a leading black intellectual—preferably James Baldwin—would be a logical format for such a statement. The idea appealed to Baldwin as well. With Evers, Malcolm, and King gone, "I'm the last witness . . . that's my responsibility. I write it all down," he had recently said. It was in this context that he saw himself representing African-Americans in the conversation with Mead as well as in the writing of *No Name in the Street.* After reading a segment of *No Name,* Raleigh Trevelyan wrote that the "voice of doom" in it reminded him of "one of the Old Testament prophets." *No Name* was to be the sequel to *The Fire Next Time,* and *A Rap on Race* could help the prophetic process along.

Mead and Baldwin met to get acquainted on August 25 in New York, and on the twenty-sixth and twenty-seventh they recorded some seven hours of conversation. Very quickly a feeling of rapport and trust seemed to develop between them, and most of the discussion was unforced and natural, with each having sufficient respect for the other to listen as well as to talk. Parts of the exchange, however, were sharp, marked by a gap between Baldwin's tendency to speak rhetorically and Mead's less flamboyant and more historical approach. It was a classic confrontation between a white, nonracist scientist looking for answers and a black rhetorician bent on revealing pain and a larger "truth" than facts can provide. Baldwin worried later that by having appeared to be "reckless" and "violent" in the conversation, he might somehow have damaged the overall cause. For example, he did not disavow all violence, and declared himself against the state of Israel as a cynical Western creation that did "a great injustice . . . to the Arabs." He rejected Mead's "long-range, historical" point of view because, as he would write later to David, history was all very well, but "me and mine are being murdered . . . in time."

In the course of the conversation Mead talked about her experiences as an observer in New York, New Guinea, and elsewhere. Racism, she said, was universal. Baldwin traced the effects of racism on his own life from early childhood, agreed about its universality, but announced his unwillingness to accept it. His job was to redeem his society.

When *A Rap on Race* was published the next year, the reviews were mixed. Anatole Broyard in *The New York Times* found Baldwin's rhetoric sometimes irritating but the book "rich . . . in perspectives." Richard Ellmann, also in the *Times*, found it a bore. But a book by James Baldwin and Margaret Mead was bound to become a best seller anyway.

On September 1 Baldwin was horrified by a French newspaper's front-page picture of a dozen naked Black Panthers being "searched" by Philadelphia police for weapons. In a London television interview a few days later his anger exploded rhetorically. He was, he said, "the 'gook,' . . . the . . . Viet Cong . . . the nigger, who is the key to America." The United States had consistently mistreated its black people. And "if you can do that to your [blood relatives] . . . you can do it to anyone at all . . . because, as far as America's concerned, most of the rest of the world are niggers."

A month later Baldwin was asked to be the main speaker at a meeting organized by the Radical Actions Projects Group in support of Angela Davis, George Jackson, and the Soledad Brothers. Jean Genet, a friend of Baldwin's from the early Paris days, was another speaker. Baldwin admired Jackson and Davis, not for their Marxist ideology, but for their willingness to risk everything in defiance. Many Panthers, including Jackson's brother, Jonathan, had already paid the full price for that defiance, and George Jackson would himself soon die in a prison shoot-out with guards, leading Baldwin to accuse the authorities of murder and to predict revenge. In keeping with his preoccupation with imprisonment, he had expressed interest in doing a film based on *Soledad Brother*, Jackson's letters from prison, and when he saw the picture of Davis as a prisoner on the cover of *Newsweek*, he would write an impassioned public "Dear Sister" letter in her defense and would make other public appearances in her behalf in England and Germany. Davis, like Jackson, Newton, Seale, Brown, and Carmichael, was a vibrant symbol of "the enormous revolution in black consciousness," a revolution that "means the beginning of the end of America" and the evolution of "a new people, an unprecedented nation." It was time to take an unambiguous stand, to "render impassable with our bodies the corridor to the gas chamber. For if they take you in the morning, they will be coming for us that night."

The Angela Davis and Soledad appearances caused Baldwin difficulty with the French authorities, and for the first time in his long association with his adopted country, it seemed possible that he would be refused residence papers. Public statements in support of Yasar Kemal, who had been imprisoned in Turkey for his work in connection with the Marxist Turkish Workers party, perhaps added to the difficulty. But with the help of influential French friends, the problem was overcome, and later, with the freeing of Newton, Seale, Erica Huggins, Davis, Maynard, and Kemal, Baldwin would feel that it had all been worthwhile.

He spent most of the early fall living in Neuilly, working on *No Name* and mulling over a plan for a film company that he and Joseph Losey had discussed in London. He gave several interviews, and a talk at a ceremony in honor of Beauford Delaney at the American cultural center. He also hired a new agent, Tria French, a black expatriate who would play an important part in his life during the next few years.

In mid-October, Baldwin had a physical and mental relapse and had to spend time in the American Hospital. Mary Painter persuaded him to move to Saint-Paul-de-Vence, near Nice, where she and her husband, George, had stayed for a vacation. From the Hameau, a quiet hotel on the route de la Colle just below the walls of the medieval village, Jimmy wrote to David that once again he was taking stock of both his personal and public lives. There were failures enough in both, but he knew that he still had a "journey" to "accomplish."

The journey was still stalled on the final draft of *No Name*. And *If Beale Street Could Talk* was progressing slowly. Still, he was working, and but for the occasional trip to Paris to see Beauford and Mary, to Cannes to see Jean, and to New York to make publishing and legal arrangements—he named David the executor of a new will he drew up—he remained in the Hameau until March 1971.

At that time, urged on by Simone Signoret, he inquired about the "For Rent" sign on the old property just across the street from the hotel. The place belonged to Jeanne Faure, who lived in a part of the house with her brother, had written a history of Saint-Paul-de-Vence, and had a particular aversion to blacks, whom she associated with those who, from her point of view, had exiled her from Algeria, the land of her birth. But with the recommendations of Signoret, Yves Montand, and the owners of the famous restaurant-hotel, the Colombe d'Or, where Baldwin was a highly favored and regular customer, she agreed to rent the ground-floor garden apartment.

Later Mlle Faure would come to admire and respect her tenant, and he her. When her brother died she would ask Baldwin to do her the singular honor of walking in the funeral procession with her.

And when she eventually moved up to the village proper, she sold him the property.

The "spread," as Baldwin liked to call it, consisted of a large, old Provençal farmhouse and a garage-gatehouse on ten acres of somewhat unkempt but beautiful land with views of the village above and the sea in the distance. The large green gate on the route de la Colle opened onto a long, cobblestone path that led to the house and through a tunnel-like passageway to a lower level and back garden-apartment that Baldwin rented during his first year (it had once been the studio of the painter Georges Braque). Outside of the kitchen, on the upper level, was a large table under a straw canopy on a platform surrounded by wildflowers and scythed grass. Wonderful but simple lunches—*pot-au-feu, boeuf en daube,* and the like—were served there with a great deal of local red wine and fresh bread by Valerie Sordello, a woman hired to clean and cook, who became a member of the family and was with Baldwin to the end. In the spring of 1971, after a successful run of *Hair* in Istanbul, Bernard Hassell moved into the gatehouse and began a new career as general overseer of the establishment. At about the same time, at David's urging, Baldwin finally turned in the manuscripts of *One Day, When I Was Lost* and *No Name in the Street. No Name* is one of Baldwin's most original works. Like the Malcolm scenario, it dispenses with strict chronology in order to suggest parallels and significant connections that might otherwise be missed—between the stonewalling of Malcolm X and the Baldwin screenplay and the "burial" of Tony Maynard in the Tombs and Attica, between the murders of "Malcolm, Medgar, and Martin," the persecution of the Panthers, and the systematic denial of the real American history in the "teaching" of "the children." Like *One Day, When I Was Lost, No Name in the Street* is constructed as a rite of passage through the hell that lies beneath American hypocrisy. It is an autobiographically based search for identity that reveals the moral failure of white Americans, who are as blind in 1969 to the curse that undermines the nation as they had been in the days when Baldwin first realized that his humanity was somehow invisible to them. Baldwin dedicated *No Name* to his mother, to his surrogate father, Beauford Delaney, and to Rudy Lombard and Jerome Smith—two of the many Black Christophers. In so doing he pointed to a model black "family" that would be developed in the novels of the seventies.

Baldwin and his ever-changing entourage became a part of the

Saint-Paul scene. They could be seen at the little bar of the Colombe d'Or or across the square, where Yves Montand and others played boule at the Café de la Place. If people at first were suspicious of the newcomer with a reputation for an unorthodox life-style, they came in a very short time to love him as one of their own. Without having planned to do so, he had made a place for himself that he would consider home for the rest of his life.

In early December 1971 Baldwin traveled in connection with publicity for *A Rap on Race* to New York, where he appeared on "Soul," Ellis Haizlip's television program on the black arts. Also on the program was the young black poet Nikki Giovanni, whose "new generation" attitudes towards race and gender helped him to understand that generation more fully than he had before. *A Dialogue*, the transcript of the Baldwin-Giovanni conversation, was published by Lippincott in 1973 and made an interesting companion volume to the "rap" with the much older and more established Margaret Mead.

Signing contracts with Lippincott for the Mead and Giovanni books caused a row with Dial Press. Baldwin had long been dissatisfied with Dial and was attempting to force the issue. When he made still another agreement with Lippincott for a novel, to be called *No Papers for Mohammed*, a new Dial editor, Richard Marek, traveled to Saint-Paul to argue his house's case. As it turned out, Baldwin liked Marek, and agreed eventually to stay with Dial, which he did through *Just Above My Head*.

No Papers was based on Baldwin's own recent scare with the French immigration authorities and on the case of an Arab friend whom he had hired as a gardener and who had been deported to Algeria. The novel never got written, but the advance provided a down payment on the Saint-Paul house and money for the long-dreamed-of car, a Mercedes. Baldwin even went so far as to take driving lessons, but after a potentially disastrous although minor wreck, he hired a young chauffeur who later absconded with the car.

The Mercedes was to figure centrally in a 1973 incident recorded by Nicholas Delbanco in his *Running in Place*. Delbanco, who had met Jimmy in Istanbul and spent time in the seventies living in the south of France, captures the sense of the Baldwin "court," complete with endless lunches and a "hierarchy" of lovers, friends, relatives, and sycophants who "answered the phone and door . . . sorted the mail," and made up parts of a sometimes large and expensive traveling entourage. Delbanco remembers one day in particular when he and his wife asked the Baldwin household to lunch. The people next door had invited the remnants of two ancient royal families, the Hapsburgs and the Hohenzollerns, who drove up in "an ancient gray Renault . . . followed, funereally, by a Deux Chevaux," out of which struggled several elderly people in dark suits carrying canes. Almost immediately after the royalty, the Baldwin Mercedes, piloted by the white chauffeur, arrived to the accompaniment of "the trumpeting bravura of the horn" and emptied itself of a company of seven or eight wearing "boaters and foulards" and boots that "gleamed." This was a new royalty, led by Jimmy, who embraced his hosts while the prime minister, Bernard, "emerged twirling his scarf and waist-sash of pink silk."

By early 1972 work on *If Beale Street Could Talk* had started going well. Jimmy complained to David that he could no longer write as fast as he once could, but he was relieved to be composing fiction again. He went to Paris to attend an exhibition of black painters, and he "kidnapped" his favorite of these painters, Beauford Delaney, and took him back to Saint-Paul for the holidays, along with Tria French, her two children, and her secretary, a black American in his twenties, who became a friend/secretary to Baldwin until French "fired" him for leaving his employer alone during a bout of sickness.

Other regulars at Saint-Paul in the early seventies were Cecil Brown, the author of *The Life and Loves of Mr. JiveAss Nigger*, whom Baldwin had met in Paris, and their mutual friend, Nidra Pollier, an American expatriate writer who remained close to Baldwin for several years. Baldwin was especially fond of Brown. He enjoyed showing him his old Parisian haunts, and he helped him meet people who could be of use to him—Carlos Fuentes, James and Gloria Jones, William Styron, among others. At first he was simply grateful that Cecil seemed to like being with him. He had become so used to the criticism of the younger black writers that during his first meeting with Brown he surprised him by saying, "I thought you would hate me."

Brown would become, in fact, his closest friend among the younger black male writers. He loved chauffeuring Baldwin around in the Mercedes, and when Bernard complained that he sometimes took the car at night and stayed out late, Jimmy assumed the conciliatory parent's role, reminding Bernard that Cecil was "young" and needed to find a little excitement. One day, when Cecil was sitting on the bed in his room, depressed over the recent breakup with a woman friend, Baldwin came in, sat next to him on the bed, put his arm around him, and asked, "Is this the first time your heart's been broken, baby?" He wanted to give to Cecil what Beauford had given him—a father's care and support.

When *No Name in the Street* was published in the spring of 1972, the reviews were generally positive if not enthusiastic. Mel Watkins in *The New York Times* recognized in it the old Baldwin ability to convey the national anguish and to see that anguish through his personal tragedy, and both *The Nation* and *Saturday Review*, while upset by Baldwin's new militancy and critical of his tendency to "skim," recognized the essential power of the work.

Baldwin was hurt by some of the reviews. White Americans were complaining of his "ingratitude," and the black militants appeared to assume that he was playing up to them so as to be welcomed "home." "Have you ever known me to kiss ass?" he asked his brother. He was trapped, he said, between the "white fantasy" and the "black fantasy."

Following a pattern established long before, Baldwin dropped work on his major project, *Beale Street*, and suddenly turned his attention to a new screenplay, *The Inheritance*. In this he was in part inspired by the recent success of Jack Jordan as a producer of a film called *Georgia, Georgia*, with a script by Maya Angelou and starring Diana Sands. If Jordan could do it for Maya, why not for him? Within a very few weeks, through the mediation of Lucien, with whom he had reestablished friendly platonic contact, he had once again set up a film company with Jordan in association with Lucien. He worked on *The Inheritance* with sufficient determination to complete it by August.

Originally entitled *In the Cross, a Trembling Soul: The Inheritance*, the screenplay sets up, by means of Baldwin's trademark flashbacks, a parallel between the early 1930s and the early 1970s, between Nazi Germany and racist America. The story concerns a black American dancer (to be played by Diana Sands) who flies to Berlin to confront her white German father, who has long ago returned to Germany and accepted the horrors of Naziism. The father's sister was to be played by Simone Signoret. The film was to be directed by Baldwin himself.

The connections between Baldwin's life and *The Inheritance* are tenuous, but they are present. With the heroine of the work, Brigid Bryant, Baldwin creates one of a series of central or "main" female characters, including Tish in *Beale Street* and Edith in the posthumous work, *The Welcome Table*. It is not insignificant that Brigid is illegitimate, that she has been brought up by a black stepfather (to be played by David Baldwin), that she is loved by a young black man (to be played by David Moses), and that she travels to Europe to retrieve her birthright—her inheritance.

The fate of *The Inheritance* was that of all of Baldwin's film projects. He had difficulty working with producers, and in this case he was right to remove himself from the Jack Jordan–Lucien Happersberger partnership just before the project could get started. The money Jordan claimed to have did not exist and the company quickly went bankrupt. The penultimate blow came with the death of Diana Sands of cancer.

The final act occurred in Saint-Paul in March 1973, only a few days after Baldwin had informed Jordan in Paris that he would under no circumstances consider continuing a professional relationship with him. Lucien called to say that he and Jordan were in Nice and wanted to pay a visit. Bernard and Baldwin took them to the Colombe d'Or, where a public argument took place, with Baldwin chastising Lucien for using him financially in spite of their having "once meant so much to each other." He begged him to come back, to leave "this dreadful person" who was such a bad influence on him, and then he literally drove Jordan from the restaurant with verbal abuse. Jimmy realized later that the explosion was the result of long years of repressed pain over Lucien, who left Saint-Paul with Jordan.

During the next few years Baldwin searched for a new production team, but Hollywood was wary, and people who admired him, like Joseph Losey, were more interested in filming versions of Baldwin's novels. Losey, in fact, approached him at the Cannes Film Festival of 1972, suggesting that they consider *Another Country* again; and when *Beale Street* appeared, Losey wrote saying how much he would like to film it. Unfortunately, scheduling problems and then Losey's death would preclude a collaboration that both men had looked forward to for many years.

Richard Long, the African-American scholar he had met through Owen Dodson in the early *Amen Corner* days, had called in September 1972 from Paris to say that Beauford had had a breakdown, and Baldwin and Bernard asked that he bring the painter to Saint-Paul. During three weeks with his friends Beauford regained some lucidity, but it was clear that he would never again recover fully. His admirers were determined to arrange a retrospective one-man show for him in Paris. In fact, there would be a major exhibition in March 1973 at a Left Bank gallery opened by Darthea Speyer, a longtime Delaney promoter. James Jones, Henry Miller, Georgia O'Keeffe, and Baldwin all wrote tributes in the catalogue.

Beauford's problems accelerated after the exhibit. The voices were whispering again, and an old hernia problem was aggravated by a fall in the studio. Gloria Jones called Baldwin and Bernard Hassell in early April, and Bernard went up to Paris and brought Beauford to a clinic in the south for an operation. The hospital stay turned into a Brer Rabbit tragicomedy. Beauford disliked the surgeon, who had hurt him during the preliminary examination. He locked the door to his room to keep out the nurses who told him he had to be shaved: "I will not expose myself before a woman," he proclaimed in outrage. A locksmith had to be called and a male orderly did the shaving. On the day the operation was scheduled, Beauford broke his prescribed fast by stealing a tray from an unattended food cart in the hallway and eating a huge breakfast. The operation was rescheduled for the next day, but when the nurses came to get him he was not in his room. He had gone to Cagnes for coffee and a croissant. On the way he had taken a jar of thermometers from the nurses' station and passed them out as gifts to each person he met as he left the hospital. Bernard was called to retrieve him, and this time the staff took his clothes and hid them. In spite of his hospital tricks, or more likely because of them, the staff came to love Beauford, and after his recovery from the operation he presented everyone—everyone but the hated surgeon—with sketches he had done during his convalescence. In the weeks in Saint-Paul after the operation Beauford was rarely totally lucid, but he received a great deal of gentle care from Jimmy and Bernard.

Beauford's deterioration was difficult for Jimmy to face, and to make matters worse, Tria French had a cerebral hemorrhage and died in the American Hospital. April found Baldwin and Bernard in Saint-Paul with no money, since the income that came by way of Tria's agency was held up by probate, and with temporary responsibility for the care of Beauford and of Tria's children. Some relief arrived late in May, when Darthea Speyer sent Fr 1,500 owed to Beauford from his exhibition. This covered a part of the hospital bill. To Baldwin she commented, "It is wonderful the way you have looked after [Beauford]."

Back in Paris in the fall, Beauford fell apart completely. The painter's friend and sometime caretaker, Charley Boggs, wrote to Baldwin that "his memory-banks are practically depleted." The old man claimed he was "surrounded by those bad people." There was little anyone could do. He would disappear for days at a time, running from the voices, forgetting who he was or where he lived. Twice he turned up in hospitals. Twice his friends released him and took him home.

Between trips to Paris to see Beauford and work on *Beale Street*, Baldwin found solace in a renewed friendship with Yoran Cazac, an artist he had met through Delaney in earlier Paris days. The friendship was close and productive, resulting in *Little Man, Little Man: A Story of Childhood*, a children's book written by Baldwin and illustrated by Cazac. But Yoran was not a solution to Baldwin's need for a full and lasting relationship. He was committed to his marriage and his children and spent most of his time at his home in Italy. When Baldwin went to Italy to stand as godfather to Yoran's third child on Easter Sunday, he must have been reminded of another friend, another marriage, and another baptism of another godchild in Switzerland in 1952. He was to dedicate *If Beale Street Could Talk* to Yoran, as he had dedicated *Giovanni's Room* to Lucien.

It was in June of this difficult year that a tape-recorded plea for money from Eldridge Cleaver arrived from a hideout in France by way of an emissary. Baldwin felt "ashamed" for Cleaver, whom he felt had become "not much more than a hustler"; he might even be "an agent." Already having had some difficulty himself with the French authorities, Baldwin was wary of being drawn into a web of international intrigue by someone who had treated him the way Cleaver had. He sent some money, but not the $10,000 requested.

Beale Street was almost done, but Baldwin had made a commitment with producer George Wein of the Newport Jazz Festival in New York to write, direct, and narrate "The Hallelujah Chorus—The Life and Times of Ray Charles" on July 1 at Carnegie Hall. He went to Los Angeles in mid-June and spent ten days there getting to know the man who had always been one of his favorite musicians. During those days he was "very nervous," trying to accustom himself to his subject's blindness. For the most part he "hung around a lot, watching him playing and talking." His idea for the performance was "to reflect what Ray's music expresses and what it comes out of." He remembered his wartime job in New Jersey and watching black laborers sing as they worked, and he thought of black musicians as laborers representing African-Americans in general. Music—particularly jazz and the blues—was "one of the keys to black survival," a subject he hoped one day to pursue in depth.

Featured in the performance along with Charles, his band, and Cicely Tyson were David Baldwin and David Moses, who read a segment of "Sonny's Blues." The group had only one day to rehearse together and they were all understandably nervous, but the overall effect was moving.

The truth of the blues, the truth of Ray Charles, spoke to Baldwin's own recent history with prisoners, a history that had been given new life by letters he was beginning to receive from an old lover from *Blues for Mister Charlie* days, who was now in prison near Boston. Baldwin wrote to him, and his friend wrote back thanking him for "the warmth I felt from your open compassion and understanding." Soon another, much younger lover, a Frenchman, would also be imprisoned, and after several months Baldwin was able to get him released. But the Frenchman was one of the rare lucky ones. So many were being ruined "in silence," Baldwin wrote to David Moses. It was not possible to break down the prison walls, but "we can begin to break the silence."

In New York he had talked to Toni Morrison, then an editor at Random House, about signing a contract there: "I dig Toni, and I trust her," he wrote to David. In the end the Random House negotiations would come to nothing, but for the moment Baldwin seemed unconcerned. Pleased to be back in France in time for his birthday, he settled down to the last pages of *Beale Street*, and a long essay, "Letter from a Citizen of Carthage, to a Friend Lately Removed to Pompeii" that would later spawn *The Devil Finds Work*. He began work, as well, on still more film projects. Cecil Brown had agreed to write a new screenplay of *Blues* and a French-American company wanted to do *Giovanni's Room*.

Soon after his birthday Baldwin received a phone call from a young African-American graduate of Yale who was a correspondent for *Time* during his vacations from graduate studies at Cambridge University. This was Henry Louis Gates, Jr., who wanted to interview him in connection with a story on "black expatriates." Gates hoped to see Josephine Baker in Monte Carlo as well, and she agreed, as long as he promised to bring James Baldwin with him. Baldwin suggested that he escort Baker to Saint-Paul for dinner instead, and he did just that. Without realizing it, Gates had become an important catalyst for Baldwin's last work, *The Welcome Table*, a play completed in rough form the year the author died. Among the potential "characters" collected around Baldwin's "welcome table" that night in August of 1973 were Baldwin himself, Josephine Baker, Mlle Faure, Gates and his wife, Sharon, Bernard Hassell, and Cecil Brown, who was staying with Baldwin at the time.

Time refused to print Gates's story because Baldwin and Baker were "passé." It was a great mistake, since Gates had been instrumental in organizing a very special historical moment. The conversation seemed to reflect an awareness of that fact. Both Baldwin and Baker looked back over their careers, both spoke with sadness of their having had to expatriate themselves. "America was the promised land," said Baker. "I just want to give them my spirit; they've lost the path. . . . They said I was a Communist because I dared love." And Baldwin said of his self-imposed exile, "I realized that the truth of American history . . . is what happened to black people."

Early in September, Baldwin did an interview show with Dick Cavett that publicized the plight of black prisoners in America and made the connections between their plight and American racism. The reaction of prisoners was enthusiastic. Baldwin received so many letters from them that he determined to arrange a Christmas version of "The Hallelujah Chorus" that would include Lena Horne, Nina Simone, and others and would tour American prisons. He was not able to carry out this plan, though he tried for several months to raise the necessary money and interest.

But the Cavett show was in effect an advertisement for the novel that would serve as the parable for the prison question that had preoccupied Baldwin from the beginning of the Tony Maynard and Huey Newton cases through the *Fortune and Men's Eyes*, Bobby Seale, George Jackson, Angela Davis, and "Hallelujah Chorus" periods.

On October 12, 1973, Baldwin finished *If Beale Street Could Talk*, his first novel since *Tell Me How Long the Train's Been Gone* had been completed in 1967. He wrote to David announcing that it was "the strangest novel I've ever written." After sending Bernard to New York with the manuscript, he spent a few days taking stock of the past and the future. In an October letter to his primary confidant he outlined an almost apocalyptic vision. The "blood" was "on the wind." Western civilization was in deep trouble. His mission was to work towards a new way. He realized, he said, that he must sound like the "witness as prophet." That was probably the result of his religious upbringing. But his mission was centered in his being above all a "lover" and the idea that lovers recognize the need of human beings for "each other."

As he approached the year of his fiftieth birthday, Baldwin looked back at the achievements of the recent years: *No Name*, *A Rap on Race*, the Malcolm X scenario, *The Inheritance*, the Nikki Giovanni dialogue, most of the children's book with Yoran, and his fourth novel. He was enjoying visits with Yoran in Paris and Saint-Paul, Beauford was in "remission" for the moment, Mary Painter and her husband, George, had moved from Paris to a small village nearby, he had begun trying to straighten out his finances—he had hired an accountant in Paris and Philippe Bebon, in whom he finally had an efficient secretary-manager—and Bernard was coping with the running of the house with the help of Valerie. Finally, he spoke of formalizing his arrangements in a new will and asked David and Gloria to visit him in December to go over his affairs.

In early December he took a vacation with Yoran to L'Ile-de-Ré and came close to the old sense of security he had had with Lucien in the Swiss mountain village. In fact, the end of 1973 found him "happier than I ever thought I could be, happier than I have ever been in my life."

In March 1974 Baldwin returned to the States, where he was honored at the Cathedral of St. John the Divine with its centennial medal in recognition of "the artist as prophet." Earlier recipients of the medal were Tennessee Williams and Martha Graham. There were short speeches by friends and members of the Baldwin family—including his mother. The Old Testament text for the day was the story from Samuel of David's slaying of Goliath and the Philistines. A stamp was put on that text when the very small man who had been born some fifty years ago just up the street in Harlem stood in the high pulpit so different from the one from which he had preached his last sermon in 1942 and, in the course of a rousing condemnation of his nation's betrayal, referred to Richard Nixon as a "motherfucker." "The artist and poet," he reminded his congregation, "is disruptive of the peace. . . . It's time to think about the Messiah in a new way . . . time to learn to love each other. The love of God means responsibility to each other."

I had brought to the service an old friend who had visited Jimmy and David and me in Istanbul in 1966. During the visit my friend had mentioned an unpublished novel of his called *Still Bravely Screaming*, and Jimmy had loved the title. Freddy and I were making our way to the east end of the cathedral, where Baldwin was sitting near the high altar in the bishop's throne being interviewed by the press. My friend was saying that he was sure Baldwin would not remember who he was when Jimmy looked down over the crowd and shouted, "Still bravely screaming, baby." At about the same time the old and very conservative subdean of the cathedral, unhappy about the general tone of the whole service, was heard to say to the new dean, "No one ever before has said 'motherfucker' from the pulpit of St. John the Divine." "It's about time someone did," answered the dean.

CHAPTER 30

If Beale Street Could Talk

> . . . the blind man on the corner who sings the Beale Street Blues.
>
> —W. C. Handy

Prisons and prisoners were a significant part of Baldwin's personal experience. They also served him as a dominant metaphor. Prisoners were those who were deprived of their birthright in the unfeeling and unseeing prison that was racism in America. And they were in another way the homosexual in his prison and the artist in his. Baldwin himself was therefore a prisoner, and so, in a sense, were all Americans. In one of his last essays, "Notes on the House of Bondage," Baldwin would speak of the black man's bondage evident in the streets of Harlem and the shantytowns of the South and of the inevitable and related emotional imprisonment of whites. Racism could destroy the oppressed but the price for the oppressor was the loss of his "sense" of morality and of "reality." The effect of racism "is that white Americans have been one another's jailers for generations, and the attempt at individual maturity is the loneliest and rarest of the American endeavors."

If Beale Street Could Talk is Baldwin's prison parable, a fictionalization of his prison concerns during the 1968–73 period, and the natural illustration and culmination of his long meditation on psychological, emotional, and intellectual imprisonment. It is another Baldwin blues song that transforms tragedy into a celebration of community or union. As he said, "it's partly about the price that we all have to pay and the ways in which we help each other to survive." Beale Street in Memphis is synonymous with the blues. The story told by Baldwin's heroine, Tish Rivers, is a version of the story—a very old story—that Beale Street could tell if it would.

The novel is a love story involving the twenty-one-year-old Tish and her boyfriend, Fonny, a sculptor. Fonny has been imprisoned for a rape he did not commit. He is in jail because of the animosity of a white policeman that has much to do with the sexual anxiety of white males in the presence of black males. The "legal" basis of his conviction is a contrived police lineup that plays directly into the witness's "they all look alike" attitude.

While Fonny is in jail Tish realizes that she is pregnant. Her family and Fonny's father are fully supportive and work tirelessly to raise bail money to free Fonny. Tish's mother travels to Puerto Rico to try to bring back the woman who has falsely accused him. The only other witness to Fonny's alibi is a former convict, Daniel, who is picked up by the police and held incommunicado. After a great deal of sacrifice and the suicide of Fonny's father, whose churchgoing wife and daughters are frivolous and hypocritical—perversions of the Beale Street ideal of community—the bail is raised and Fonny returns home, and the baby is born.

The characters and their situation in *Beale Street* are idealized. The Riverses represent community, the only possibility of survival in a hostile white world that cannot see humanity in blackness. They point the way out of the bondage of racism and the bondage of the "safe" life. Never the sweet-talking willing victims exuding humility—the kind of "black folk" whites might prefer—they are angry, determined, hard-talking blues people who recognize the "motherfucker" for what he is and, through the power of their love for each other, are able to overcome his power to oppress. Like Faulkner's Dilsey and her people, they "endure," but they do so actively, by fighting back from the fortress of their self-respect and their love for each other. Oppression draws people together, creates strong ties. The Riverses are "Black Power," "Black Is Beautiful" people. They speak and act out of Beale Street's long and terrible history and they know who they are. They will not wait for the "promised land" across the river; they will not be patient. They articulate the old prophet's cry of "Let my people go"—to which they add James Baldwin's cry: "now."

In his early essays on Richard Wright, Baldwin had suggested that *Native Son* was marred by the fact that "a necessary dimension has been cut away" from it, "this dimension being the relationship that Negroes bear to one another, that depth of involvement and unspoken recognition of shared experience which creates a way of life." Bigger Thomas reflects the "the isolation of the Negro within his own group" and a belief "that in Negro life there exists no tradition, no field of manners, no possibility of ritual or intercourse." The Riverses, like the Proudhammers of *Train* and later the Montanas of *Just Above My Head*, are Baldwin's answer in this period of his career to the deficiency in the protest novel, his attempt to "make this tradition articulate. . . . For a tradition expresses . . . nothing more than the long and painful experience of a people; it comes out of the battle waged to maintain their integrity or . . . out of their struggle to survive."

Everything the Riverses do or say is done or said in that context. The baby in Tish's womb is a prisoner yearning to be free as surely as her lover is a man in bondage longing to become himself through his love and his art. Tish says, "I understand that the growth of the baby is connected with his determination to be free. So I don't care if I get as big as two houses. The baby wants out. Fonny wants out. And we are going to make it: in time." Her words echo Juanita's "I hope I'm pregnant" speech in *Blues for Mister Charlie*.

She also speaks to her author's personal longing for love. When Tish cries for Fonny and longs for his freedom, she is the Baldwin voice expressing his life's search for a lover free of the bondage of society's taboos, a lover whose presence could allow him to give birth not only to his art—Baldwin always spoke of his novels in terms of pregnancy and birth—but to a self free of the need to be a prophet, a spokesman free of the need to be anything other than a human being.

The Riverses are representative of Baldwin's private hopes and of the hope of all those strangers in the "house of bondage," all those forgotten and invisible people whose names nobody knows. Theirs is a community of knowledge achieved in a history of repression—knowledge that Ida told Vivaldo he would have to gain if they were to remain together, knowledge that, in this blues song of survival, keeps Fonny alive where other Baldwin heroes had died. And theirs is a community of language derived from that history. If the "black English" of *Beale Street* is foreign and offensive to the white reader, it tends not to be to the black reader. The author of *Notes of a Native Son* had spoken in the voice of Henry James and the King James Bible in order to reach out to his white brethren and perhaps to convert them. Now Baldwin says to his white readers, even more clearly than he had in *Blues for Mister Charlie* or *Tell Me How Long the Train's Been Gone*, "Follow me if you will into my blues world, but don't expect me to hold your hand once you're there."

Beale Street remained on the best seller list for seven weeks.

The reactions of reviewers were predictably varied, to some extent dependent on race or attitudes towards race. With the exception of Anatole Broyard in *The New York Times*, who disliked the book to the point of derision, denouncing it as badly written white-bashing, reviewers were enthusiastic. Rosalind Davis in *New York Age* wrote: "James Baldwin knows it all: how blacks live, love, and struggle; as they relish the good times and endure the bad times that constitute their lives. If Beale Street could talk, it would tell you James Baldwin has got it all together." Revish Windham in the *New York Amsterdam News* suggested that Baldwin had "created a story with characters who live the picture of bitter-sweetness. They react in a kind of sadness whose only equal is the blues." Martha Duffy in *Time* magazine, on the other hand, found the novel "too sentimental and predictable by half."

The most thorough reviews were those by John McCluskey in *Black World* and by Joyce Carol Oates on the front page of *The New York Times Book Review*. Oates found the book to be "timeless" and "economically, almost poetically constructed." She saw its likeness to parable, too, suggesting that it "may certainly be read as a kind of allegory" which stresses "the provisional, tentative nature of our lives." She especially admired Baldwin's treatment of narration through Tish's "absolutely natural" voice: "We come to know her from the inside out." McCluskey stresses the blues aspect of *Beale Street* and in that context finds it "his most convincing novel. . . . Tish and Fonny's blues force us back into ourselves at the same time they open us up for those impulses aggressive and tough, impulses as ancient and grand as rivers."

Baldwin decided to return to the States for a publicity tour. Gloria urged him not to come: he had done the "book beat" and the "TV trail *ad infinitum*." She thought he should stay in Saint-Paul in the interest of his health, his finances, and his and everyone else's sanity. Furthermore, there was the question of his safety. There were people who clearly disapproved of him, and others, after all, had been eliminated by the "house of bondage."

His first impulse was to write a telegram in which he pointed out that there was "no hiding place down here." He was not about to deny his mission. But not wishing to sound "combative," he did not send the cable. After his initial irritation he realized that his sister was simply interested in his welfare, and he valued his family's love above all else. Still, he was determined to return to New York, and he wrote to David explaining why in a voice that speaks with the authority of Beale Street. He could not afford to worry about his "safety," he said. The publication of *Beale Street* could provide a forum for his continuing message, which was that he did not "belong" to himself but to "you," and that the "horror" of his life was the "price you pay" for that fact. His work was something he had to do for the generations who would come later—"Yes, amazing grace"—and being public and speaking out as a witness was an important part of that work.

Baldwin arrived in New York on May 23 and began what would be an extensive and exhausting tour. The nation was once again in turmoil. This time it was Watergate, and by August, Baldwin's prime Philistine had fallen. In an interview in the *Washington Post* he spoke with some disdain of Nixon and Watergate as indications of the falseness of the American myths of "success" and integrity. How could black people be surprised by Watergate, he asked. It was "just one more rather sordid scandal in a rather predictable history."

Back in Saint-Paul he found a letter from still another of the imprisoned. An actor friend whom he had seen in New York a few weeks before, whose constant struggle to find work had driven him to the brink, wrote him from the mental ward of Bellevue. He had been incarcerated there after having been picked up for praying and preaching in connection with a new "religion" he had founded called the "Love Chapel of 69." He had been wearing a dress at the time. It seemed somehow an ironical comment on Baldwin's gospel of love and a sad commentary on the state of the "children."

The fiftieth-birthday party on August 2, 1974, was an occasion long talked about in Saint-Paul-de-Vence. More lights than ever were strung in the little orange grove, the food and wine "never stopped." There were the celebrities, and most important, there was the family: Gloria and Frank, Paula, and David and his friend Carole. But the good times soon turned sour.

The summer was marred by a fight with and the firing of Bernard Hassell. Philippe Bebon remained, but without Bernard the Saint-Paul establishment fell into a state of semichaos. The hangers-on seemed to arrive in droves and simply overwhelmed Baldwin. They encouraged him in his most destructive tendencies, alcoholism, and unproductive "scenes." As was often the case, David Baldwin sensed from letters that something was wrong and he returned to Saint-Paul in early September, emptied the house, and accompanied his brother on a *Beale Street* tour of Germany.

Baldwin had not spent much time in Germany since a speaking

engagement there in 1972 with Chester Himes under the auspices of the American Armed Services Radio Network. During a brief stop in Paris for some research on an *Esquire* article on black films, which turned into *The Devil Finds Work*, he was informed that the USIS had withdrawn promised support for the German trip. The American cultural centers would be, in fact, unavailable for his lectures. With the help of his German publishers he undertook a tour anyway and spoke out against the American "Reich" even as he chastised those in Germany who seemed to have forgotten the history of their own Third Reich. The end result of the tour was an enthusiastic reception for *Beale Street* in Germany.

After Germany the brothers returned to New York for the Christmas holidays. It was a season capped by a New Year's Eve celebration at Mikell's on Ninety-seventh and Columbus, where David had been working as the bartender for some time. Mikell's, run by "Mike" Mikell and his wife, Pat, had been, from the early seventies, Baldwin's social "headquarters" in New York. If he was in town he could often be found there, happy and comfortable in the knowledge that this was David's world and that he could be "David's brother" there, could meet people *through* his brother. Old friends turned up often, too; Sam Floyd was a habitué, as were Maya Angelou, Quincy Troupe, Verta Mae Grosvenor, and Louise Meriwether, to mention only a few of Baldwin's "favorite people." He liked to sit at the far end of the bar near the jazz musicians, where he often discussed the music critically with Pat Mikell; he had definite likes and dislikes in jazz; he liked Art Blakely and was mesmerized by Wynton Marsalis during his first "gig" at Mikell's. Sissy Houston was a favorite with her gospel beat. But he caused something close to a scene in his anger over one group, several very large women in see-through dresses, whose musical integrity he doubted and whose costumes offended the puritanism that perhaps had its source in the pulpit of his childhood.

On a trip to California he touched base with friends, put out feelers to gauge the movie prospects for *Beale Street*, and attempted to revive the "Hallelujah Chorus" idea. *Beale Street* itself continued to be a real-life story; Tony Maynard was finally released from jail and reunited with his sister, Valerie—the real-life version of Tish's supportive sister, Ernestine.

Out of prison, however, Maynard did not live up to Baldwin's hopes for his future. He was no Fonny. Instead, he appeared to be broken, uncommunicative, and uninterested, not only in the *Beale Street* connection, but in the book about his prison experience that

Baldwin hoped to write with him. He was not sympathetic to Baldwin's idea that all "accomplices" in systems tainted by prejudice are prisoners. Baldwin, for his part, complained that Maynard was in need of "confession," not a confession of crime, but of "heart-break, isolation, pride, and despair." He wanted Maynard "to confess *himself*, as all of us must . . . to live." His old friend was a victim, Baldwin felt, a prisoner within himself. The prison was one Baldwin found he could not "break." Maynard reminded him, in fact, of his stepfather, who had gone insane and ended his life "in silence." If Beale Street could only talk, so much could be told, so much could be learned. But in this case it would not talk. Tony Maynard had been hurt too badly; he chose withdrawal rather than the liberating blues.

On February 25 the Honorable Elijah Muhammad died, marking the end of an era and causing Baldwin to think back over the last years, from the visit to Elijah that led to *The Fire Next Time*, to his later association with Malcolm X, and with the whole question of prisons and prisoners that had culminated in *Beale Street.* An interviewer for *Penthouse* asked him if he had any hope for the future of his nation. He answered that he was "a lover and therefore an optimist . . . the trick is to love somebody. . . . If you love one person, you see everybody else differently." These might well have been the words of Tish Rivers after Fonny came home and her baby was born.

CHAPTER 31

The Devil Finds Work

> Many a time have they afflicted me from my youth: yet they have not prevailed against me.
>
> —Psalms 129:2

In a letter to David Moses early in 1974, before the publication of *Beale Street*, Baldwin discounted what people were calling his long literary silence and proclaimed that "this devil" could still "find work." Soon after the new novel he had turned to his book on the movies and had decided to call it *The Devil Finds Work*. And in March 1975 he wrote to his brother that he was "circling around" *Just Above My Head*. There were some final revisions to be done on *Little Man*, and he and Yoran went to London to try to work with their publisher on that. But there was melancholia, too; once *Little Man* was done he would see much less of his friend. And the idea of being fifty was taking its emotional toll. "Pray for the Old Warrior . . . weary, but not downcast," he wrote to David.

Little Man, Little Man was a minor work, hardly noticed when it appeared in 1976, but for Baldwin it held great significance. It was a celebration. The final stages of its writing coincided with the birth of sister Paula's baby and another baby for sister Gloria; "That's what it's all about," he told David. It was also a tribute to Josephine Baker, the world's most famous protector of "the children," who had died on April 10, 1975. Finally, *Little Man* gave voice to Baldwin's own concern for the children. It was a picture of New York, of the world, from the perspective of a child based on his seven-year-old nephew, T.J., and more generally those "who are black, poor, and less than four feet high." The language of *Little Man* was "black English," and Baldwin's respect for it was a natural outgrowth of his concern with the whole question of black self-esteem.

As Baldwin was turning to the final stages of his career, the last chapter of Beauford Delaney's life was beginning in Paris. In April 1975 friends of Beauford found his apartment unlocked with no sign of him. They informed Baldwin, who, before the American consul in Nice, declared himself financially responsible for Beauford and then went to Paris to try to find him. With the help of Bernard Hassell, with whom he now reconciled, he rented an apartment in his own name and moved Beauford's paintings there for safekeeping. Soon the painter was picked up by the police as a vagrant and was placed in St. Anne's Hospital for the insane. It was clear that he was in no condition to survive on his own. Baldwin would travel to New York in December in an attempt, eventually successful, to find Beauford's brother, Joseph—also a painter—who approved of all the steps already taken and authorized him to act as the Delaney family's representative in affairs relating to Beauford.

In July a group of Paris artists accused Baldwin of stealing the Delaney paintings and having Beauford locked up in St. Anne's. The group even succeeded in getting him released briefly, before his illness made it necessary that he be returned to the hospital. Baldwin was outraged and hurt by the accusations. "I think of Beauford as my father," he said in an interview at the time, and in a press statement he argued that anyone who knew him or Beauford or their relationship would know how impossible it would have been for him to steal his friend's paintings or to "abandon" him. As far as he was concerned, Beauford Delaney was "one of the greatest men" he had ever known. His had been a "mighty life."

Beauford recognized only a few people during the last years; Baldwin was always one of them. When Jimmy and Bernard visited him, he seemed to gain some clarity of mind and to enjoy walking with them on the hospital grounds smoking the Gitanes they always brought. He had grown a long white beard and become in appearance (as in reality) the archetype of the teacher and father in James Baldwin's life.

Since the late 1950s Baldwin had witnessed Beauford's mental deterioration and was able to see in it the price of a struggle that was also his stepfather's and, ultimately, his own. He always said that Beauford had helped him to understand his stepfather's pain. He wrote to David after one of his hospital visits, crediting Beauford with having saved him as a child, and having made his survival possible. Watching the disintegration of a man and an artist who more than anyone else had understood his own passage, he was "discovering (in fear and trembling) the truth about . . . *Just Above My Head.*"

The pain of Beauford's slipping away was alleviated in part by a long visit in the summer by his nephew Daniel, David's three-year-old son. Daniel was accompanied by his mother, Carole Weinstein, and he succeeded in turning what, with Beauford's deterioration and the problems with a new novel, could have been a depressing summer, into something original and revitalizing. Jimmy wrote to David saying he wished he could "keep the laughing Daniel . . . but honor is a tyrant." He loved doing avuncular things, taking the boy to the aquarium in Monte Carlo, showing him off at the bar of the Colombe d'Or, where, according to a letter to David from his brother, entitled "Intercepted Memo: Classified," he talked happily with the parrots, the owners, and the guests. He was even spotted teaching an English couple how to play dice and watching television with Simone Signoret. Much of the time was spent "with his Uncle's Arab gardener" and speaking "a kind of creole" with Valerie. After Daniel left, Baldwin told his Saint-Paul friends that the child had made him feel alive again.

On July 29 he finished *The Devil Finds Work* and not long afterwards sent it off to Richard Marek at Dial Press. He dedicated the book to Paula for her birthday, to friend John Latham, and to "brother" David Moses. *Devil* is, in effect, a continuation of a long autobiographical essay, which he had begun with several pieces in *Notes of a Native Son* and in *Nobody Knows My Name*, followed by *The Fire Next Time* and *No Name in the Street.* The de facto autobiography would conclude with several late essays, "Every Good-bye Ain't Gone," "Dark Days," and "Here Be Dragons," all collected in *The Price of the Ticket.*

In *The Devil Finds Work* Baldwin uses movies as catalysts for an extensive discussion of the American psyche, his own life, and the sociopolitical climate in America. The book is in one sense a fifty-year-old's evaluative reminiscence. It touches on several important themes and subjects that had been treated less fully elsewhere. Baldwin pays extensive tribute to Orilla Miller, the teacher who had introduced him to serious theater and cinema as well as to serious politics. He revisits his Harlem childhood and his early reading. *Uncle Tom's Cabin* and *A Tale of Two Cities*, and the 1936 film version of the Dickens work clearly had "something to tell me. It was this particular child's way of circling around the question of what it meant to be a nigger." Sylvia Sidney and Henry Fonda in *You Only Live Once* was Bill Miller's compensation for the fact that no one resembling the Scottsboro Boys, "nor anyone resembling my father" had yet "made an appearance on the American cinema scene."

The voice speaking in the pages of *The Devil Finds Work* is that of a celebrity/elder statesman who dares to carry his work as a witness into the heart of popular culture. It is his cleansing of the temple. John Wayne was the white race making the world "safe" for itself by stomping out the Indians. The real devil in *The Exorcist* is "we" Americans. "The mindless and hysterical banality of the evil presented" in it "is the most terrifying thing about the film." The little girl is not the devil, we are.

Baldwin reaches even to the sacrosanct classics of the "temple" and the politically correct films of the post–civil rights period. The cleansing instrument is his language, his irony, his wit. D. W. Griffith's *Birth of a Nation* was "really an elaborate justification of mass murder." *In the Heat of the Night*, with Sidney Poitier and Rod Steiger, "helplessly conveys—without confronting—the anguish of people trapped in a legend. . . . The people of *In the Heat of the Night* can be considered moving and pathetic only if one has the luxury of the assurance that one will never be at their mercy." *Lady Sings the Blues*, a film "related to the black American experience in about the same way, and to the same extent that Princess Grace Kelly is related to the Irish potato famine," is one that Baldwin turns to to illustrate the reasons for his having failed to make the Malcolm film he wanted to make. The script he would have had to write would have been like the one in the Holiday film, "as empty as a banana peel, and as treacherous."

Christopher Lehmann-Haupt in *The New York Times* found the book dated but nevertheless worthy of respect for its honesty. Mary Blume in the *International Herald Tribune* admired it for its "power," its "rage," and its "overwhelming compassion." The most thorough review was Donald Bogle's in *Freedomways*. He welcomed the author's "keen intelligence and piercing insights" and found the work "one of the most literate *good reads* of the year"—the return of "a terrifyingly unpredictable, fiercely aggressive and ambitious writer . . . a fiendishly complicated and often misunderstood man." In *The Devil Finds Work* Baldwin, "the man and the legend, comes alive and takes on a new shape" of celebrity witness. "And it is a sheer pleasure to know he's still around." If Bogle had any criticism of the book, it was that it "leaves us hungry" for more.

Baldwin fully intended to give more. He told Mary Blume that the book "demanded a certain confession of myself," a confession of his loneliness as a celebrity left behind by assassinated comrades, a confession of compassion and hope even as he was being criticized for being passé, a confession of his fascination with the American fantasy, epitomized by Hollywood, even as he condemned it. It was "a rehearsal for something I'll deal with later." That something, *Just Above My Head*, would be the major work of his later years.

With the publications of *The Devil Finds Work* and *Little Man, Little Man*, Baldwin paused, as he had done several times at pivotal stages in his career, and took a long look at what it meant to be an artist, a black artist, and a celebrity. Perhaps Tony Maynard could not "confess," but he could. In a 1975 Los Angeles interview with Maya Angelou, he suggested that "a writer can never be a success," that once he thinks he is, he is finished, left with nothing to do. All art is flawed, making it necessary for the artist to forge ahead. Time was passing by, and Baldwin sensed he might not have much time. *Just Above My Head* was proving to be his most difficult writing experience. It was, he was discovering, more about his inner world than anything he had ever written.

On October 2 he got together with Yves Montand and Harry Belafonte at the Colombe d'Or. It was a meeting of icons, and Baldwin sensed the attention they commanded in the courtyard of the hotel. The conversation turned to the fact that all three men were in their fifties, that time was growing short. It was a question now of using what time was left to make sense of what one had done. At fifty it seemed necessary to look back, he wrote David on October 3. When he had written *Another Country*, *Mountain*, "Stranger in the Village," and *Giovanni's Room* he had done so at great personal cost, but survival had seemed to depend on what he wrote. The characters he had created had somehow taken some of the weight off him. Now, however, there were segments of his past work that he considered badly written, even "pompous." There were times when he examined that work and wondered if he had any idea as to who he was.

He looked back at his long quest for love, too. He had never been able to resolve the old struggle within himself between the witness-prophet and the lonely man longing to be cradled and protected in love. He could understand now—too late—how his "helpless ruthlessness" had frightened Lucien away, not only emotionally, but sexually; how could anyone feel contentment "in the arms of a tornado"? Yet, he did not regret having searched so hard for love. It was better to love, even badly, than to choose the emptiness of "safety." All of this, he said to David, was material for *Just Above My Head*.

In mid-October, Baldwin was in the States for a bicentennial symposium with Toni Morrison, Coretta King, Norman Cousins, Archibald Cox, Arthur Schlesinger, and others on "the nature of a humane society." His contribution was a talk called "In Search of a Basis for Mutual Understanding and Racial Harmony." Much of what he said was related to the thoughts revealed in the October 3 letter to David. Conflict in life is inevitable, he said, and can itself be productive; there is, for example, "no love without conflict." For mutual harmony to exist—in the personal or larger social context—people must give up their "dreams" of "safety" and "power." Only by this "surrender," this "re-creation of oneself," can we hope to preserve love or, for that matter, life. And racial harmony, like personal harmony, would come only when there were "no more wretched."

Near the end of his speech Baldwin, who at this stage in his career was routinely dismissed by whites as a "bitter" man, turned to the question of his relation to white people and revealed clearly that he had "kept the faith" that had come to him on the way to his father's burial, a faith he had first articulated in "Notes of a Native Son." There was more than ample reason for him to "hate white people," but "due to mysteries of temperament, luck, and my private history and my sense that hatred is always, in the depths, self-hatred," he did not.

Baldwin spent Christmas and a good part of the first half of 1976 in the States. He gave talks, spent time with his family and friends at home, at El Faro—made somewhat famous by his having mentioned it several times in *Beale Street*—and especially at Mikell's. He wrote Guggenheim recommendations for Nicholas Delbanco and Louise Meriwether and a publisher's blurb for Ishmael Reed's *Flight to Canada* (Reed, he wrote, had successfully "dissected" the "American myths"). He also wrote a flattering review of Alex Haley's *Roots*, visited Riker's Island, where he was interviewed by a group of women inmates, wrote a bicentennial speech celebrating the NAACP, and did a book tour to publicize *The Devil Finds Work.*

In July, Baldwin was at the Relais Bisson in Paris. The main purpose of the Paris visit was to check on Beauford at St. Anne's Hospital, and he had brought with him an eighteen-year-old French-speaking West Indian named "Bill" (the name has been changed here to protect his privacy). Once again he had placed himself in a situation in which the roles of lover and father surrogate and protector were confused. He was well aware of the confusion and frequently tried to extricate himself. When a young female African-American writer he had met in 1975 in New York arrived in Paris, he seemed almost to throw her at Bill as a means of keeping him happy. His own relationship with the boy was doomed from the beginning and caused some of the worst emotional pain Baldwin ever suffered. It would dominate his life during 1976 and 1977.

Like Jean before him, Bill did not understand or approve of his friend's life-style. He became easily jealous of visitors, even of David's son, Daniel, and his mother, Carole, who returned to Saint-Paul for Jimmy's birthday. He clashed with Philippe Bebon and with Mlle Faure. He was less difficult with friends who did not in any way threaten his central position in the Baldwin household. Nina Simone visited often during the 1976–77 period, and Bill enjoyed watching these two "stars" dancing, shouting, and laughing, as they often did late into the night. And he warmed to Beauford when he went with Jimmy to visit him in Paris on several occasions. These happy moments were, however, rare.

In his frustration, Bill became violent, and there were times when it was necessary to send him away to Paris to visit his mother. But Baldwin always called him back. When Philippe left in despair over what he considered his employer's self-destructiveness, Bernard returned to try to bring some order to the household, but terrible scenes still occurred. On one occasion an outbreak of Bill's led to the direct intervention not only of Bernard but of Mlle Faure, two policemen, and a doctor.

At least twice Baldwin left his lover for the States. In October of 1976, for example, he went on what did not seem to be pressing business, and in the spring of 1977 he went to deliver a lecture at Bowling Green State University that would lead to his "second career" as a teacher in the late seventies and early eighties. He also saw Kay Boyle, who was about to be operated on for cancer. During an earlier operation she had worn Baldwin's ring for good luck, and she had written to say that she wished she had it on now. He had cabled in reply, "The ring is on your finger."

Although personal problems interfered with and significantly slowed his writing of *Just Above My Head*, they did not put a stop to it, and he did manage to work on various political projects. Late in January, for instance, he wrote an open letter in *The New York Times* to the new president, Jimmy Carter. Baldwin saw a certain hope for America in a southerner who appointed as his United Nations ambassador Andrew Young, a former associate of Martin Luther King and a man Baldwin admired and liked. In the letter he took a familiar position in support of the imprisoned, this time the Wilmington Ten, a group questionably convicted in 1972 of firebombing a grocery store during a race riot, and the Charlotte Three, three black men being held on "preposterous" charges of arson. These were cases in which blacks were clear victims of racist southern law enforcement authorities and juries, and Baldwin called on the new president to take appropriate action. He ended his letter pointing out that Carter was "in my lifetime . . . the only President to whom I would have written."

In May, Baldwin joined Mary McCarthy and Stephen Spender at the International Book Fair in Nice, where, led by his dramatic argument, they succeeded in convincing a French-dominated jury to give the Nice Literary Prize to Edmund Wilson. Baldwin had known McCarthy since 1947, through William Phillips of the *Partisan Review*, and had met Spender in the early fifties in Paris and again in the *Encounter* offices in London in the 1960s, where Spender, then the *Encounter* editor, had introduced him to Wole Soyinka. He had long admired Wilson, whom he had met at the Institute of Arts and Letters.

He gave an interview to Robert Coles for the cover of the July 31 issue of *The New York Times Book Review*, entitled "James Baldwin Back Home." Baldwin's comments to Coles are important for what they reveal about his thinking in connection with *Just Above My Head*, specifically about his evolving use of black English. In Harlem, he told Coles, he had grown up as an outsider. His language had reflected that status. From his teachers he had learned "standard English." In his own world—the streets, the church—he had learned the language of "jazz, spirituals, the blues; the language of testifying and signifying; and the language of cool black cats, street kids, holding on to life by their fingernails while they heard their parents screaming up to God in heaven, asking him what's going on." The new novel would explore his people's questioning, their anguish, their language. In this sense, as Baldwin often said, *Just Above My Head* was a continuation of the "history" begun in *Go Tell It on the Mountain* and the blues song begun in "Sonny's Blues." The blues, of course, spoke to both personal and communal concerns.

Between February and October of 1977 Baldwin complained of the pain that dominated his life at the time. He wrote to me that it had to do with the "despair that accrues in time." He spoke of the new novel, characteristically, as a baby he had "carried" for a particularly long time, one that had caused him more difficulty than anything else he had written: "Talk about shitting bricks!"

As the relationship with Bill deteriorated even further, Baldwin made a series of journal entries suggesting that he was in a trap, that Bill had become a "respectable . . . patriarch" who "disapproves of me." Once again a lover had awakened to the reality of his situation, realized he could not accept it, and like so many before and after him, he was making Baldwin pay for the mistake. As for Baldwin, he found himself, like Sonny in "Sonny's Blues" and Sonny's descendant, Arthur, the musician-hero of *Just Above My Head,* isolated and lonely in the face of Bill's disapproval. The failure of this relationship was the reason he could describe 1977 in his journal as "a dreadful year." He hoped the coming year would "be merciful." The Bill affair would, in fact, fade away in 1978.

Lucien visited in February, and strangely enough, this seemed to help. One day Baldwin spent the morning signing autographs for an anniversary edition of *Go Tell It on the Mountain* for the Franklin Library. Mlle Faure and Bernard were helping him pack the autographed sheets in boxes, and Lucien stood by for moral support. This was oddly appropriate, since the book had been written twenty-six years earlier in Lucien's chalet.

He had agreed to teach for two months at Bowling Green in the spring of 1978 and a month at Berkeley the next year. These were his first long-term commitments in the States since the Malcolm X project some ten years earlier. The return was celebrated with a "homecoming tribute" at City College in New York on March 17. It was a gala event with spirituals, readings from Baldwin's works, tributes by Wilfred Cartey and Ellis Haizlip, a presentation to Baldwin of the Martin Luther King Memorial Medal for his "lifelong dedication to humanitarian ideals," and an address by the guest of honor called "The Artist in an Alien Culture."

In his speech Baldwin took issue with the title itself. An artist's job, he said, was to redefine culture. In a sense, there was no such thing as an artist in an alien culture "because it's the culture that produces him. . . . I was born in the crucible of the American republic," he reminded his audience, and the republic was stuck with him; he defined it as much as the "white man" did.

In a column on the April 5 op-ed page of *The New York Times,* he built on the City College remarks, noting, in his role as "disturber of the peace," that "the news from all the northern cities is . . . grim; the state of the Union is catastrophic." The problem was the refusal of Americans to understand that "theirs is not a white country."

On May 12 he participated as a guest speaker with Julian Bond in a forum at Hunter College protesting a Broadway play about Paul Robeson. Baldwin had met Robeson when the latter had come home in the 1960s and had attended a public sixty-fifth birthday celebration in his honor when many black leaders had not, fearing that they might be tainted by his political notoriety. Robeson had died in 1976, and Baldwin was one of several prominent African-Americans anxious to protect the singer's integrity, which they felt was being undermined by a moneymaking, whitewashing theatrical venture. This was what Hollywood had wanted to do with Baldwin's Malcolm project. "The popular culture," he reminded his audience, was trying to make Robeson "irrelevant" by removing those aspects of his work and personality that were a threat to the myth of "white America." America wanted a "chocolate John Wayne" and should not be allowed to have him.

Also in May, Baldwin had begun his teaching at Bowling Green. The person most responsible for introducing him to the university was Ernest Champion, a Sri Lankan who taught in the Ethnic Studies Department. Baldwin was not accustomed to daily routines, and it was difficult for him to keep to an academic schedule when he was also leaving frequently to fulfil other commitments, such as the Robeson forum in New York. Champion spent a great deal of time waiting in airports or doing substitute teaching for him. He was assisted by Robert Early in the creative writing program, Bob Perry, the head of Ethnic Studies, and Perry's wife, LaRuth, with whom Baldwin formed a warm friendship.

The Bowling Green experience was not limited to the 1978 residency. Baldwin was so successful as a teacher that he was invited to come back for the fall 1979 semester and again for the fall of 1981. But there were especially difficult moments for his Bowling Green sponsors. He was several weeks late for his third appointment there, and once he was "kidnapped" by a group from Wayne State University in Detroit, who wanted him to do for that institution what he was doing for Bowling Green. It took a supreme effort on the part of Champion and others to get him back. The stories of Baldwin escapades at Bowling Green and later at the University of Massachusetts are now legends on both campuses, but no one who taught with him or was taught by him ever suggests that it would have been better had he not taken up teaching.

In graduate and undergraduate courses in contemporary literature and creative writing, he used his own works, several Faulkner novels, Roth's *Goodbye, Columbus*, and even *Uncle Tom's Cabin*, but the classes quickly became forums for larger questions of identity. What did it mean to be "white" or to think one was "white" or "black"?

When he walked into his first class at Bowling Green and asked, "What shall we talk about?" and a white student stood up and inquired in apparent innocence, "Why does the white man hate the nigger?" Baldwin sensed what he later described as the student's "terrifying innocence" and threw the question back at the class: "Why do *you* think the white man hates the 'nigger'?" The discussion that followed, as Ernest Champion said later to Baldwin, was like *Blues for Mister Charlie* come to life, with Blacktown and Whitetown squaring off, but with Baldwin there to constantly urge the "children" to "be better than you are," to "attempt the impossible." They must see that to recognize one's true identity as an American, and ultimately as a human being, was to recognize the history—however painful—of the black-white experience, with all its fantasies and attendant myths. To dehumanize another was to dehumanize oneself, he taught: You must free yourselves from the common captivity, from the "house of bondage" in all its forms—racial, sexual, ideological.

Describing that first class later in an *Esquire* article called "Dark Days," Baldwin suggested that the students were not really talking about race; "they were talking of their desire to know one another, their need to know one another; each was trying to enter the experience of the other." To him education meant the courage to ask questions, to confront the dominant priorities, and to challenge them. The student, the teacher, and the poet were at their best when they were disturbers of the peace, when they threatened any given society's sense of safety.

Baldwin's sense of responsibility to the "children" extended beyond the classroom. He kept groups of students—and faculty members and their wives and children—up all night exhorting them to choose "honor over safety." Walking across campus with some students one day, he stopped to listen to an itinerant fundamentalist preacher who spoke of the uncleanness of the body and the danger of ideas. Baldwin confronted him directly and with such vehemence that the preacher was literally driven from the field. A band of followers—disciples, black and white, male and female—formed over the weeks. There was a nun from Toledo who took him to the local Catholic church, where he made a convert of the priest. There were sons and daughters of white Ohio farms and black city slums. There was a young unmarried graduate student who a year after Baldwin's Bowling Green stay wrote for advice about an unwanted pregnancy.

A few days later came a call from France. "You are to carry and keep that baby," he ordered, and she did.

That same graduate student (now married with several children), a professor who teaches James Baldwin's books, remembers many poignant moments with her mentor. Once she was driving him home late at night: "He is half asleep, holding my hand on the stick shift. I see a state trooper and slow to the speed limit. The trooper does not notice and I drive on. I look over at Jimmy. His eyes are still closed. But he is smiling. Loud." That same night they talked about death. A particularly close friend had recently died, having warned no one of how sick he was: "It was his decision, Jimmy says, not to burden his friends with that awful knowledge. The conversation makes me nervous. I try to defuse it with a protest. Promise me, I say, promise you would not keep something like that from me. What if there were important things left unsaid? They're not, he says. They're not unsaid at all. He smiles, takes my hand from the shift, but he does not promise. Stop biting your lip, baby, he says."

After the two months at Bowling Green in 1978, Baldwin threw himself into the New York scene. On June 25 he appeared on WABC-TV on a show called "Like It Is." In July he chatted with Jerzy Kosinski and his old adversary Norman Mailer at the American Civil Liberties Union Convocation.

But he was not finishing *Just Above My Head*, and that fact preyed on his mind. When his new agent, Jay Acton, suggested that he spend the summer at his house on Cape Cod, where he could work without interruption, Baldwin accepted, leaving the Cape only occasionally for special events. Finally, at 5 a.m. on February 6, 1979, now back in Saint-Paul, he wrote to his brother David announcing the completion of *Just Above My Head*. He was not completely happy with it, he said. It had turned out to be a "lyric" compared to the "mighty song" he had planned. Perhaps he had not been equal to that song, but deep down he thought this was his best book.

On March 26 news that he had been half expecting hit him hard. Beauford Delaney had died at St. Anne's Hospital in Paris. For several days Baldwin was too ill to do anything. He had accepted a position at Berkeley for one month beginning April 9, and he was unable to make himself go until a week of the contracted time had elapsed. For that week he stayed mostly to himself, with the pain "bottled up inside."

The Berkeley appointment was fortunate. The combination of Beauford's death and the postpartum letdown that was always a part of Baldwin's novel-writing experience might well have brought about one of his major depressions. Instead, received as a literary and political "lion," he was kept so busy that there was no time for depression. Erskine Peters of the Afro-American Studies Department, his official host for the Berkeley stay, said later that it took several hours after his arrival for Baldwin to "wind down" before they could go anywhere. He needed to talk about Beauford, to face the fact of his death. But then began some twenty days of nonstop activity. On the first night there was a party—lasting until 5:30 a.m.—at the Church by the Side of the Road in Oakland, and that set the tone for Baldwin's "disturbance of the academic peace" at Berkeley. The official activities began with a reception, complete with jazz combo, the press, members of the university community, and a large representation of the Bay Area black community—including Ishmael Reed, Angela Davis, Cecil Brown, and Huey Newton. Baldwin himself arrived late—it is said that he was at least an hour late to every appointment during his Berkeley stay. The *San Francisco Examiner* carried a story called "The Lion in Berkeley," in which Baldwin's appearance was described in some detail. He was "dressed in black." A tan scarf was "thrown rakishly around his neck," and he was "carrying a single long-stemmed red rose." He looked "like a black Oscar Wilde." He was greeted by cheers. During the following days Baldwin attended classes, led question-and-answer sessions, including a large public forum on the Berkeley campus, and visited several local schools. The students reacted enthusiastically.

The culmination of the Berkeley appointment was a public address, "On Language, Race, and the Black Writer." In that speech Baldwin described how, when he had first gone to France in 1948, knowing very little French, he had withdrawn into himself somewhat and really "heard, for the first time, the beat" of the black English with which he had grown up. This was important, because a black writer knows that the English taught in the schools is "white English," geared to white assumptions—"black as sin," a Desdemona who is a "pearl . . . richer than all [Othello's] tribe"—whereas the language of his heritage is one that has grown orally out of an experience that has little to do with formal education in a "standard" language and much more to do with signifying and testifying in words that, because of circumstances, happen to be mostly English. Baldwin described himself, for example, as "a witness to and a survivor of the latest slave rebellion," the "so-called civil rights movement"—itself a sentimental white term for a reality the white world preferred not to recognize.

It was in truth a rebellion by a people "freed" to enter a society that would then lock them in ghettoes and "enslave" them economically. It had taken him a while; he had "paid his dues" in the language of the oppressor, but now he would write according to the "beat of the language of the people who . . . produced" him.

Baldwin would continue pursuing the subject of black English during the next few months in connection with the publication of *Just Above My Head*, which was in great part a celebration of that language. He would lecture on the subject at the Institute of Contemporary Arts in London and he would write about it in *The New York Times* in July 1979 in an op-ed piece called "If Black English Isn't a Language, Then Tell Me, What Is?"

Baldwin's point in the *Times* piece is that "people evolve a language in order to describe and thus control their circumstances, or in order not to be submerged by a reality they cannot articulate." Language, he said, is "a political instrument . . . the most crucial key to identity." Black English is the code language of African-Americans, spawned in the fields and in part in the black church from the only available common language by people who came from several linguistic traditions. It developed out of "brutal necessity" and is as legitimate as any language.

From Berkeley, Baldwin moved on to other University of California campuses for appearances: April 27 at Santa Barbara, May 3 at UCLA, May 4 at San Diego. And there was a speech at the booksellers' convention in Los Angeles at the end of May, where he was honored along with Thomas A. Dorsey, a man he greatly admired as the composer of the gospel song "Precious Lord."

There was time for relaxation in California as well. At the booksellers' convention he got together with Stan Weir, his old friend from the Calypso days, and his wife, Mary. He spent time in Berkeley with Claire Burch, the wife of his old school friend Brad, with whom he had attempted to found a literary magazine in the 1940s. Claire had moved to Berkeley, and she made a documentary film of Baldwin's stay there. He had lunch in the Berkeley Hills with Cecil Brown, Huey Newton, and Angela Davis, and spent a wonderful day with Cecil and several other "brothers" just "running" in Los Angeles in Cecil's new red Fiat sports car. Days like that were important to Baldwin. The talk—the easy, free, and clever use of the signifying language, the reveling in the "beat"—was a means of releasing tension.

One of the most memorable moments was a "picnic" with Maya

Angelou. It began in Malibu and ended in Sonoma and took some thirty hours. There was roast chicken, bread, and champagne in crystal glasses and a long stop in a rough bar in Carmel, where Baldwin and Angelou were recognized by the bartender, who brought out copies of their books to be autographed after several games of Ping-Pong and darts.

Baldwin returned to France for the summer in a particularly happy state of mind. Through Jay Acton he had met a new friend, "Joe" (the name has been changed here to protect his privacy), a black American in his twenties who would be with him off and on for several years, and he looked forward to a relatively peaceful summer in Saint-Paul before returning to the States in September for the semester at Bowling Green and a book tour for *Just Above My Head.*

During the summer he wrote two short pieces, "An Open Letter to the Born Again," in support of Andrew Young, who had resigned from his United Nations ambassadorship under fire because he had met with Palestinian leaders, and an article on black music called "Of the Sorrow Songs: The Cross of Redemption" for *The Edinburgh Review.* The latter had been solicited by an editor of the review, James Campbell, who would later visit Baldwin in Saint-Paul and would write a Baldwin biography. It is an interesting article because it is really a continuation of the black English subject. Black music had begun "on the auction block." Black music "is our witness, and our ally," he wrote. "The *beat* is the confession which recognizes, changes, and conquers time. . . . Then, history becomes a garment we can wear and share, and not a cloak in which to hide; and time becomes a friend." History was King Oliver, Ma Rainey, Bessie Smith, Miles Davis, Billie Holiday, Nina Simone, and so many others who made "of . . . captivity a song."

This was an appropriate article to appear before *Just Above My Head,* which was published in the fall and was Baldwin's final great parable of the "beat" and the "history," his ultimate sorrow song. The devil had found more work than the world had given him credit for during these past six years. He was ready now for the final push.

CHAPTER 32

Just Above My Head

Just above my head
I hear music in the air.
—old song

Sometime in the mid-1970s, in Saint-Paul-de-Vence, David Baldwin had a vivid dream in which he was sitting with his brother on a porch watching a group of friends walking down a nearby road. In the dream he and Jimmy knew all about the lives of these people. "Shall we tell them?" David asked. "No," Jimmy said. "They'll find out." At lunch David described the dream, and Jimmy seemed surprised. He too had had a strange dream, in which the ceiling of his bedroom had moved menacingly down "just above my head." He told David he thought their dreams must have something to do with each other; the people in David's were looking for an author, crowding into his head, demanding to tell their story. It was time for another novel, not *No Papers for Mohammed* as he had planned, but one that would take its title from Jimmy's dream and the old gospel song.

Just Above My head would be his last novel, the longest and most ambitious. It would take the characters some five years to tell their story. The novel would serve as an extended metaphor through which Baldwin could once again examine his own life and career as an artist and witness.

The plot of *Just Above My Head* is divided into six parts. Book 1 introduces Hall Montana as the chronicler of the life of his brother Arthur, who has just died on the floor of a rest room in a London pub. Hall is a family man with middle-class aspirations, whereas his brother is a singer-witness who has carried his music to the secular world and paid the ultimate price of making one's self the vehicle for a people's pain.

In the course of the novel Hall will take the dark journey up the road into his brother's seemingly disreputable, irresponsible, and tortured life in order to place his own experience as a black American in proper perspective. The "good life" cannot be lived if the price paid for it is not recognized; it can only come down on one's head. As the ceiling descends towards Arthur's head in death and his blood spills, his sacrifice becomes clear to Hall, and he knows, as James Baldwin had always known, that he had no choice but to tell his story. Hall begins by answering his son's question about his uncle Arthur's being a homosexual—he was a homosexual but never a "faggot"—and then proceeds through flashbacks to answer his own questions about his brother, gradually discovering in his life and work a pattern of witness and prophecy.

Hall, who has children, has fought in the Korean War and is his brother's manager, has his source in David Baldwin, but he also mirrors the Baldwin driven to tell the story of his "nation." His voice often becomes identical with Baldwin's, preaching the familiar gospel: "What do I care, if you are white? *Be* white: I do not have to prove my color. I wouldn't be compelled to see *your* color, if you were not so anxious to prove it."

Arthur, the celebrity and homosexual, is, of course, an embodiment of his author, too. There are any number of direct connections, from the youthful affair with a Harlem "gangster" to the lonely search for love and the sense that his art is a vehicle for witness that cannot be denied. Baldwin's middle name was Arthur, and in a letter to David Moses he described his novel as a story of a singer who "knew who I was." He noticed the "interesting slip" and mentioned to Moses that he had intended to say "who *he* was."

Book 1 also introduces Julia Miller, who, as we learn in Book 2, has moved by way of incest, the streets, and Africa to a position as strong family center. Julia's childhood preaching and her abuse at the hands of her father are directly and metaphorically related to Baldwin's own childhood. And Julia's brother, Jimmy, whose name suggests a connection with Jimmy Baldwin, is also in some ways a reflection of David Baldwin. Both David and the fictional Jimmy were sent away in childhood to live for a while with southern relatives, for example. As in dreams—and this is a novel that grew from two dreams—the characters and situations simultaneously reflect the world around the dreamer and the world within him.

Early in the novel a contrast is established between Julia's parents and the Montana family. A similar contrast had existed in *If Beale Street Could Talk.* In both cases Baldwin's intention was to comment on an aspect of African-American experience. The Millers, like Fonny's family, are rendered dysfunctional by their pretensions, their adherence to a hypocritical religion, and ultimately, by their depression. The Montanas, like Tish's family, are "Black Pride," blues people who through their African-American identity have achieved genuine strength in the face of the harsh realities of their life.

Book 3 takes up the theme of the artist as lover that we first saw illustrated in the characters of Ida and Eric in *Another Country*. Baldwin, in a 1973 interview in *The Black Scholar*, had made the connection between the "roles" of the artist and the lover: "If I love you I have to make you conscious of the things you don't see." Billie Holiday and Nina Simone were at once poets and lovers because they "gave you back your experience . . . and you recognized it for the first time because [they] were in and out of it . . . and made it possible for you to bear it."

The teenage Arthur and his friends Peanut, Crunch, and Red have formed a gospel quartet like David Baldwin's quartet, described in his brother's early essay "Journey to Atlanta." During a southern tour, also reminiscent of that essay, Arthur and Crunch become lovers. Later Crunch will become involved with Julia, and still later Arthur will help Julia through her difficulty with her father before becoming the lover of Julia's younger brother, Jimmy. As in *Another Country*, Baldwin celebrates here, almost allegorically, the ability to overcome the barriers of gender in the interest of genuine love between individuals, and his belief in love as the basis for the artist's "song." Baldwin once told Jewell Handy Gresham that "the only reason to try to become a writer is not to tell the world how *I've* suffered . . . but it's an act of 'I love you.' "

Book 4, "The Stepchild," is a parable of the artist's loneliness, suggested by such earlier Baldwin titles as "Stranger in the Village," *Nobody Knows My Name, No Name in the Street*, and "The Artist in an Alien Culture." There is much that is autobiographical in this section. Arthur's relationship with Jimmy, who reminds us of any number of Baldwin's young lovers, will eventually be ruined by the demands of Arthur's creative life. Like Baldwin, Arthur settles for a while in Paris, where, echoing his author, he speaks of being "invisible and free" and visits many of the old Baldwin haunts—the Brasserie Lipp, the Café Flore—and has a significant French love affair, which ends when other commitments interfere.

Back in New York, there are familiar Baldwin restaurants in Hall's life as well—the Red Rooster and the Russian Tea Room, for example—and after his return from Korea Hall finds himself living for a while, like Baldwin himself, on West End Avenue. Meanwhile, Julia, like Gloria, spends time in Africa. Peanut, Crunch, and Red suffer the fates of so many of Baldwin's own friends. Crunch goes mad, Peanut is, in effect, lynched in the South, and Red becomes a junkie. All are victims, like Eugene Worth and Tony Maynard, of a society cursed by its racism and consequent inability to accept love as a basis for life.

Book 5, "The Gates of Hell," tells of Arthur and Jimmy's fight and separation and of Hall's brotherly attempt to save Arthur by becoming his manager. It also brings Hall and Julia together at the Russian Tea Room, where, through the kind of full "confession" between people that Baldwin so often preached, they speak as a chorus to the tragedies they have witnessed in their lives and make of those tragedies the lyrics of a sorrow song that can celebrate their communion with each other.

Book 6 takes us to the "stepchild's" death in London after the lover's quarrel with Jimmy and finally to Hall's dream, that dream of David's which had been the catalyst for the novel. Once again the people—now recognizable as the characters whose lives we have just shared—are walking up the road, and this time Arthur asks whether they should be told "what's up the road." And it is Hall, the narrator-storyteller, the witness, who says, "No, they'll find out what's up the road, ain't nothing up the road but us, man."

Here Baldwin once again made clear his rejection of the protest novel and reaffirmed the commitment to celebrate the "shared" black "experience which creates a way of life." It is the journey up the road that counts, not so much an illusory goal at the end: "Ain't nothing up the road but us, man"—the life lived and the life witnessed. Through witnessing, Baldwin seems to say, we are redeemed, and the victims—the Eugenes, the Rufuses, the Medgars and Malcolms and Martins, the Beaufords—are resurrected through a new sense of African-American community.

Like *Giovanni's Room, If Beale Street Could Talk, Tell Me How Long the Train's Been Gone*, and several of Baldwin's short stories, *Just Above My Head* is told from a first-person perspective. Hall Montana is clearly related to the wary narrator of "Sonny's Blues," and Arthur's death dance with his art reminds us of Sonny's struggle as well as of Leo Proudhammer's, the difference being that whereas Sonny and Leo survive, Arthur does not.

Baldwin himself recognized the connection with the earlier

works. He spoke of it in an interview with Wolfgang Binder in 1980: "The central situation" in *Just Above My Head* and in "Sonny's Blues" and even in *Tell Me How Long the Train's Been Gone* was the relationship between two brothers, he said. And in a letter to David he explains that *Just Above My Head* revolves around one man's attempt to understand his brother—an attempt by one side of human experience to make its peace with another. In "Sonny's Blues" the main character's brother is ashamed of him until he can comprehend Sonny's "journey," which then can be related to his own journey. In *Just Above My Head* Hall must learn to face Arthur's inner world—and his "love"—in such a way as to be able to see Arthur in himself. The people Jimmy Baldwin had loved in his life, he reminds *his* brother, were all reflections in some way of him. "Life" was based on "recognitions," and this was what *Just Above My Head* was about.

No one has identified Baldwin's purpose in *Just Above My Head* better than his friend Eleanor Traylor in her essay "I Hear Music in the Air: James Baldwin's *Just Above My Head*." Traylor notes that the story starts on the note of death but "celebrates a life," that it is at once "a blues moan and a gospel shout." She reminds us that the story told here is a retelling and development of all of the earlier Baldwin novels and stories, that we have met Arthur in earlier Baldwin heroes, "blues boys" who "must become blues men." Theirs is "the perilous journey of love" which must be made if one is to experience "the glorious in human life." Those who "risk" the journey discover both "the depths of sorrow" and "the ecstasy of joy." Those who "betray" or refuse it court "madness . . . death . . . misery."

In "Sonny's Blues" Baldwin had written:

> For, while the tale of how we suffer, and how we are delighted, and how we may triumph is never new, it always must be heard. There isn't any other tale to tell, it's the only light we've got in all this darkness.

It is this tale that Luke tells David in *The Amen Corner*, that, in a sense, Giovanni tries to teach David in his room, that Ida urges on Vivaldo in *Another Country*, that Sonny's music tells his brother. It is the tale Arthur provides for Hall, and it is the tale Baldwin tells us, even as he, with Luke, Giovanni, Ida, Sonny, and Arthur, asks us whether we can afford to hear it.

As we trace our ways through the histories of each of the characters in the novel, then, we follow the history of a people's struggle for their birthright. Hall, Jimmy, and especially Julia and Arthur are all, like John, Elizabeth, Florence, and Gabriel in *Go Tell It on the Mountain*, making their individual dark journeys on the historical threshing floor. Their problems, their longings, their music, their language all pick up the "beat" of that history, that communal experience. Arthur's music, his anguish and his death, Julia's childhood, her African revelation, and her rise to womanhood are all notes in the larger blues song.

As Baldwin himself said to Wolfgang Binder, Arthur dies relatively early in his "journey, and all the rest are left with his legacy" and "an enormous question: . . . What is history, what has it made of us, and where is a witness to this journey?" In *Just Above My Head* Baldwin, through Hall, is literally his own witness and, metaphorically, his people's.

The critics did not receive the new Baldwin novel with enthusiasm, though they did recognize the immensity of the attempt. Whitney Balliett in *The New Yorker* complained that it lacked density of texture, that we are told that "the streets [of Harlem] are full, but there never seems to be anyone there," that we are told about Arthur's genius, but we never see or hear it. Nevertheless, Baldwin's "great and peculiar power is to re-create the maddening halfway house that the black man finds himself in in late-twentieth-century America. Baldwin is a prophet, a master of exhortation. Only weariness makes his voice crack." Stanley Crouch in *The Village Voice* chided the author for a tendency to resort to clichés and tired ideas. He especially resented what he saw as his attempt to glorify homosexuality. Crouch did find greatness in certain of the book's moments, as, for example, in the description of Julia's incestuous father, Joel, where "Baldwin's language moves from the Bible to the blues with actual eloquence," or in the confrontation between Hall and a white salesman in an expensive store, where "animosity and suspicion are as charged as the best of Pinter or Thelonius Monk." In *The New York Times Book Review* John Romano appreciated Baldwin's passion—especially in his treatment of sexuality and friendship—but complained of his lack of concreteness: "hundreds of faces . . . but hardly a place in any detail."

What the critics for the most part missed about this novel was its relation to Baldwin's earlier work, as the culmination of a long continuous tale based in his own life and related to the themes he treated in his essays. Critics looked to Baldwin for realist fiction. What Baldwin gave them was parable in the form of confession. The characters, the places, the situations in his novels do not satisfy the general audience's desire to see Harlem or the political reader's desire for corroboration of opinions; rather, they represent aspects of their author's philosophy and provide insight into the struggle behind and the price paid for the social and individual making of the sorrow song.

Near the end of *Just Above My Head* Arthur's lover, tapping into the "beat" of brotherhood and communion that Baldwin sought to convey, and thus speaking for his author, says:

> The song does not belong to the singer. The singer is found by the song. Ain't no singer, anywhere, ever *made up* a song—that is not possible. He *hears* something. I really believe, at the bottom of *my* balls, baby, that something hears *him*, something says, come here! and jumps on him just exactly like you jump on a piano or a sax or a violin or a drum and you make it sing the song you hear: and you love it, and you take care of it, better than you take care of yourself, can you dig it? but you don't have no mercy on it. You can't have mercy! That sound you hear, that sound you try to pitch with the *utmost* precision—and did you hear me? Wow!—is the sound of millions and millions and, who knows, now, listening, where life is, where is death?

Baldwin was still obsessed by a mission that knew no boundaries.

CHAPTER 33

The Evidence of Things Not Seen: Remember This House

> Faith is the substance of things hoped for, the evidence of things not seen.
> —St. Paul, Hebrews 11:1

In 1979 Baldwin had arranged with *The New Yorker* to write an article on the South revisited. He wanted to call it *Remember This House,* and for the rest of his life that title remained in his mind. The *New Yorker* article would never be written, and a Maysles Brothers film project with the same title was cut short by Baldwin's death. In any case, by then McGraw Hill had paid Baldwin the largest advance he ever received for still another *Remember This House,* a book on the civil rights movement and the assassinated leaders "Medgar, Malcolm, and Martin," as seen through the eyes of their children's generation. Baldwin would never finish that book.

Remember This House was also the first working title for a project that was, in fact, completed. In the late seventies he had become friendly at Mikell's with an Englishman named Dick Fontaine, who had suggested making a film that would bring the Baldwin essays, novels, plays, and short stories together into a single work. At first Baldwin was fascinated by the idea, but when, in the summer of 1979, he read the script that Fontaine brought to Saint-Paul-de-Vence, he reacted with anger. From his point of view, the piece was a kind of collage that did not do justice to any of his works. *Tomorrow Brought Us Rain,* as it was now called, was no longer James Baldwin, it was James Baldwin distorted by an Englishman who could not possibly understand him. "I am *not* going to let you define me," he shouted during a confrontation. What he would do was allow Fontaine and his African-American wife, Pat Hartley, and their cameras to follow him as he took a 1980 trip South, ostensibly to research the article planned for *The New Yorker*. His plan was to revisit places and people who had been important to him in the fifties and sixties, to explore the condition of "civil rights" all these years after the great events of the movement. If the filmmakers could find a film in that trip he would be happy to cooperate with them.

I Heard It Through the Grapevine, as it was eventually called, was presented in 1982 on prime-time television in England, at the Film Forum in New York, on public television, and at a private screening party at Mikell's attended by members of the Baldwin family, Toni Morrison, Ossie Davis, Ruby Dee, and many other friends. The film was reasonably well received, but it lacked the coherence Fontaine had worked towards in his original script. It consisted of fragmentary "takes" of Baldwin listening to and talking to a variety of people involved in civil rights. It did have a certain cinéma vérité spontaneity.

The trip itself, as opposed to the film, began in Gainesville, Florida, where Baldwin had gone to participate in the annual meeting of the African Literature Association with the Nigerian writer Chinua Achebe. Baldwin's participation in the conference had been arranged by Ernest Champion from Bowling Green University. Hearing of the event, Fontaine and Hartley arrived with the idea of including it in their film.

Baldwin and Achebe had long admired each other's work. Their meeting was momentous for both men: "When at last I met Jimmy in person in the jungles of Florida in 1980," wrote Achebe, "I actually greeted him with 'Mr. Baldwin, I presume!' " For Baldwin, Achebe's remark was not only humorous but significant. Following his tendency to attach symbolic and rhetorical importance to situations, he saw the meeting as representative of the reunion between black America and Africa in the face of white oppression. In his opening statements to the conference, he said of "my brother whom I met yesterday—whom I have not seen in four hundred years"—that "it was never intended that we should meet."

The conference featured a dialogue between Achebe and Baldwin on the black aesthetic. Achebe emphasized the social purpose of art "in the service of man." Baldwin took up Achebe's point that the Earth Goddess of African mythology was goddess of both art and morality, suggesting that whether the people accept him or not, the artist is produced by his people, because they need him. The black American artist is here to reveal that the black American has forged an identity of his own in spite of a dominant race who "thought they could define you." Something of the reason for Baldwin's anger at Fontaine's original script is contained in these remarks and something of the reason for his insistence in the seventies and eighties on the importance of "black English."

During his opening statement a heckler somehow broke into the microphone transmission from the stage. The interference served as a living reminder of the presence of racism in the "new South" and presented Baldwin with an opportunity to remind the heckler and everyone he represented that the "doctrine of white supremacy on which this country is based has had its hour and is finished." An emerging African-American aesthetic was to be built on that knowledge, a knowledge centered in black self-affirmation and a refusal to be "contained" or "defined" in white terms. As he would say in a speech called "A World I Never Made," delivered at several universities and the Library of Congress during the eighties, "the person who has defined the other, and marked him for death, has not so much defined the other as defined himself."

From Gainesville, accompanied by the film crew and his new friend, Joe, Baldwin moved around the southern landscape in April and May, beginning with Washington, D.C., where he talked with Sterling Brown and with John Lewis, the onetime SNCC leader. In Atlanta he visited the monument to Martin Luther King—a monument "as absolutely irrelevant as the Lincoln Memorial." Making monuments was "one of the ways the Western world has learned . . . to outwit history [and] time—to make a life and a death irrelevant. . . . There's nothing one can do with a monument." Monuments belonged to the "white aesthetic," were the sculptural equivalent of "white English." He saw the Reverend Fred Shuttlesworth, the Birmingham leader he had met on earlier southern trips. In Selma he talked with Amelia Boynton, who had led the voter registration struggle there. He spoke with James Meredith in Jackson, Mississippi, and with Charles Evers, Medgar's brother, in Fayette. In Louisiana he met with former freedom riders, including his old friend Jerome Smith. With Jerome he went to Bunkie, where his stepfather had been born and where he confronted a picture of the Reverend David Baldwin's light-skinned but otherwise look-alike brother: "It's strange to see your father in whiteface." Once again he found fuel for his argument that blackness and whiteness are delusions. The truth contained in his "white" uncle's face was there for all to see: "We are all of us kinfolk."

Late in the Fontaine-Hartley film, Baldwin is shown in the North, visiting Amiri Baraka, strolling with him through the still ruined stretches of Newark affected by the "rebellion" of the sixties and talking to young people. Baraka had been one of those who had once found Baldwin no longer relevant, but by the early eighties the two writers were once again friendly. Over the years, Baldwin's point of view had moved closer to Baraka's concerning the unlikelihood of the white world's changing its ways. The film ends with Baldwin discussing his journey with his brother David. It is not a hopeful discussion, and the film is anything but optimistic. It conveys Baldwin's prevailing sense at the time that the moment of opportunity had passed.

The same general pessimism is reflected in a 1980 interview entitled "James Baldwin Finds the New South Is a Myth" and in two essays of the same year, "Dark Days" and "Notes on the House of Bondage." In the absence of a genuine "white" desire for brotherhood, "we have come to the end of a language"—the language of "equality," "Manifest Destiny," and the "American Dream"—"and are now about the business of forging a new one." He would elaborate on this theme in a later interview with Julius Lester, when he suggested that to say a "new language" was needed was the same as saying a "new morality" was needed. It was time to redefine morality in the area of race, of sex, of identity. It was necessary to reconsider the meaning of "love in a consumer society."

In July, Baldwin was back in Saint-Paul, but without the domestic satisfaction he had hoped he would find there with Joe. It was yet another problematic relationship that sometimes verged on violence. The scenes were often bizarre: Joe sleeping with a female secretary hired to do paperwork for Baldwin, Lucien visiting and "stealing" the secretary away from Joe, fights with Mary Painter, who visited frequently from her nearby village and who, urged on by too much alcohol and by Bernard's worrying over the general situation, challenged Jimmy and made everything worse. Joe was especially offensive to white guests, one of whom described him as acting like a "white caricature of a Black Panther." When, one evening, as he was, according to the same guest, uttering a "hissing vituperation," he fell over into the brush only to return "scowling" to deliver an even more violent harangue.

As always, however, Baldwin managed to make use of the turmoil around him. In July, after a particularly unpleasant argument involving himself, Bernard, Mary, Lucien, and Joe, he wrote a long letter to David announcing that he had begun a play called *Inventory*. The play, he said, had been "triggered" by a letter about his confusing personal life that he had begun writing to David and then discarded. He suggested that it might perhaps better be called *Investments*, because he had been forced to concern himself since his return to France with the failed personal "investments" of several old friends who were close associates or frequent houseguests. In looking back at his own "investments" and those of others, he recognized the danger of "allowing" himself to "become empty enough to commit" the "crime" of "nostalgia."

Inventory, or *Investments*, would become *The Welcome Table*, which he would not, as it turned out, concentrate on just yet; the play would involve the kind of self-examination he was not quite ready to attempt. He tried to work on *No Papers for Mohammed*, for which he had only the beginnings of a first chapter, but it seemed to go nowhere. He had also promised his publishers a book of uncollected essays, introduced by a new essay to be called "The Price of the Ticket" or "Notes from the Belly of the Whale." Later this would become a collection of mostly already collected essays, of which the new title essay would, in fact, be "The Price of the Ticket." There were many ideas, many projects, even a novel based on the life of Beauford Delaney called *A Higher Place*, but for the moment nothing seemed to catch on.

It was almost with relief, then, that he accepted an invitation in the spring of 1981 to travel to Atlanta to do an article on the spate of child murders that had been taking place there since 1979. The idea for the piece came from Walter Lowe, Jr., an African-American on the staff of *Playboy*. Lowe had wanted to go to Atlanta to do the writing himself, but his superiors at the magazine suggested that a known writer such as Baldwin could draw more attention.

Baldwin spent several weeks in Atlanta, accompanied by Joe and Bernard and Lowe. On his first night there he made a surprise appearance on the steps of city hall, where a group of students was protesting the failure of the authorities to put an end to the murders. The students recognized him, and he urged them on in a short impromptu speech. Within a week he had established contacts with Andrew Young, Coretta Scott King, and others, who welcomed him and filled him in on events in the city from their particular perspectives.

After a week it became clear that none of the theories circulating through Atlanta was sufficiently believable to warrant Baldwin's support. He decided that his mission must not be to write on who was killing the children but on the larger issues surrounding the killings: the "new South," the peculiar predicament of the city's black administration, the place of black children in Atlanta, the presence of racism in the city. Rather than examine the externals, he would do what he did best; he would investigate the inner life of Atlanta and, by extension, of America. This was not a surprising approach. As Walter Lowe expressed it, all of Baldwin's works suggested that "true horror was never obvious," that "ugliness, *real ugliness*, is of the spirit rather than physical."

The title of the *Playboy* article—and eventually of the book based on it—would be "The Evidence of Things Not Seen." "Faith," said St. Paul, "is the substance of things hoped for, the evidence of things not seen." The "evidence" in Atlanta indicated a failed faith, a national dream that had died.

After returning to France, Baldwin worked several weeks on the article and produced only five pages. Part of the difficulty was the situation with Joe, which went from bad to worse, but the primary problem was that Baldwin felt there was something missing in his story. Then Wayne Williams was arrested in June, and accompanied only by Bernard, Baldwin went back to Atlanta to consider this new development. He was to return several times during the next three years as he became increasingly intrigued by the case.

Before he could turn to the question of *Evidence* as a book, however, he had to finish the commissioned essay for *Playboy*. After missing the deadline for one issue and being prodded by an unpleasant scene with Walter Lowe, who accused him of being "a man who likes to talk a lot and drink a lot, but who hates to write," a writer in whom the "fire" had burnt out, Baldwin produced an article in the December 1981 issue of *Playboy* that won that magazine's 1981 Best Nonfiction Award.

Deeply depressed by the situation with Joe—it got so bad that a temporary separation had been agreed to after the return from the second Atlanta trip—Baldwin put off the *Evidence* book for a while and accepted an invitation from Engin Cezzar to return to Turkey. Engin had visited Saint-Paul several times during 1979 and 1980 to urge his friend's participation as scriptwriter for a film based on a play called *The Sacrifice* (*Kurban*) by the Turkish writer Güngör Dilmen. Baldwin had read a translation of the play and had not liked it. But he thought he saw possibilities in it as a film and once more gave in to his moviemaking obsession. He and Engin called their mutual friend, Costa-Gavras, who agreed to consider the project, and Cezzar went to Paris to discuss the matter with him and then to Hollywood to find a producer.

The early fall of 1981 was an interlude of almost idyllic calm in Baldwin's life. Joined by David, he spent two months with Engin and Gülriz on a farm near Bodrum in southern Turkey, working on the script, which he alternately called *The Swordfish* and *The Sacrifice*. When he left Turkey at the end of October, he had finished the screenplay.

The film was to be the story of two families—one Greek and one Turkish—on the island of Cyprus. It involved an interethnic love affair and had strong political overtones. The original novel was full of clichés and sentimentality, but Baldwin worked hard to make it something viable. However, Costa-Gavras, after reading the script, felt he had not succeeded. And when Engin revised it Baldwin became resentful, much as he had been resentful of Arnold Perl's interference with the Malcolm X script or of Dick Fontaine's attempt to "define" him in his original script for *Grapevine*. He suspected that Costa-Gavras had really rejected his script for reasons having to do with the political situation in Greece. In fact, the Greek director, like Joseph Losey before him, felt that Baldwin was not a screenwriter, that his very long and detailed script left little room for a director's art. The project collapsed, and Engin and Jimmy, sadly, never saw each other again.

The semester at Bowling Green was marred by the return of Joe, who, among other things, interfered with Baldwin's classes and announced to the press that he was his lover. Baldwin had always avoided publicity in his relationships, and he began to suspect that Joe was attempting somehow to lock him into a situation that was not necessarily healthy for either of them. He had generally avoided taking a public stance on issues involving the "gay movement." Sexuality was a private matter, and he resisted the idea of being called "gay." To be "gay" was to be defined—imprisoned—in still another way. Besides, he felt, words like "gay" and "queer" belittled the reality of love. He was not a "queer" or a "gay" man; he simply loved individuals, many of whom were men.

Yet in 1982 he lent his support to Black and White Men Together/New York and spoke on the topic "Race, Racism and the Gay Community" at the group's June 5 meeting. "One has to reject, in toto, the implication that one is abnormal," he announced to his audience. "That is a sociological and societal delusion that has no truth at all. I'm no more abnormal than General Douglas MacArthur." Gays were merely the "latest example" of America's apparent need to repress difference in the name of morality. Gays were, like blacks, like American Indians, one more group of prisoners in a society that was not aware that it was itself an emotional and spiritual prison.

Imprisonment continued to be an important leitmotif in Baldwin's thinking. In 1982 and 1983 he wrote articles in support of prisoners for journals with which his old friend Marc Crawford, who was actively involved in exposing the abuses of the prison system, was associated. In two short articles, "A Letter to Prisoners" and "This Far and No Further," he proposed that artists and prisoners have much in common, that both are inconveniences to the state, that both are "free" in a way that a society which boasts of its freedom, even as it incarcerates huge percentages of its poor, cannot be. The state, Baldwin suggested, uses prisoners to create the illusion of safety in a society committed to economic gain for itself. Prisons do not rehabilitate; they deny the possibility of mutual responsibility, which is the backbone of any authentic society. In these articles Baldwin was gradually working his thoughts towards the larger questions in the book that would be *The Evidence of Things Not Seen.*

Cecil Brown visited Saint-Paul during the summer of 1982 and said the house was like a writers' colony. Baldwin was busy on *Remember This House, The Welcome Table,* and *Evidence,* and he had set writing tasks for Joe and a new friend named Skip, both of whom had creative aspirations. Only Bernard seemed to have been exempted. Baldwin was also turning more and more frequently to the composition of poems, which he spoke of somewhat dismissively as "finger exercises." Urged on by David, he was to collect and publish these as *Jimmy's Blues* in London in 1983. He had come upon the title in the mid-seventies, when he wrote a poem called "Imagination" and sent it to his brother, suggesting that "it could be set to music, and called *Jimmy's Blues.*"

Baldwin had written poems since childhood, often in honor of family birthdays or other special occasions. *Jimmy's Blues* contains several such poems. "The Giver" is dedicated to his mother: "I cannot tell how much I owe." There are several poems for David, one for Lena Horne after the Saint-Paul household heard her sing at Monte Carlo, another for Skip. And there is a poem to "baby sister" Paula, one of several birthday advice poems he wrote to her over the years celebrating the "tight-rope lover" or the necessary risks of commitment.

Most of all, as Baldwin told his brother, "poetry is probably my way of experimenting" with language, with "black English" as a vehicle for seeing as well as for saying. This is especially evident in the major poem of the collection, in which the poet takes the voice of the black tall-tale/trickster character, Staggerlee (Stagolee—"the baddest nigger that ever lived"). "Staggerlee Wonders" is a poem that assumes an African-American understanding of reality to which racism makes the oppressor essentially blind: "I . . . wonder," says Staggerlee, "what they think the niggers are doing." In this sense, it is, like most of the poems in the book, a private dialogue with the "brothers and sisters" who can hear; it carries the *Beale Street* and *Just Above My Head* viewpoint one step further. The poet sings his blues to those who share his knowledge, his language. And he reminds white Americans, his "stricken kinsmen," that "the party is over."

Baldwin sent the Staggerlee poem to David, telling him he planned to do a whole series like it. He read it to Cecil Brown, too, and told him he saw him as a Staggerlee model. He even began a Staggerlee novel. As far as the poetry itself was concerned, Jimmy agreed essentially with Countee Cullen, who had suggested to him in junior high days that he was a better prose writer than a poet. Still, poetry provided an emotional release for him, and he genuinely liked some of his more recent attempts. When David reacted enthusiastically to the Staggerlee poem, he decided to go ahead with the publication, first with Michael Joseph in London and two years later with St. Martin's Press, where Richard Marek, his onetime editor at Dial, had become editorial director.

The "writers' colony," pleasant and productive as it might have seemed to outsiders, was fraught with the emotional tension characteristic of the Baldwin entourage and with severe financial problems. What money he had Baldwin was spending on upkeep for the Saint-Paul household, on "allowances" for members of the entourage and even for former lovers, many of whom did not hesitate to write asking for funds. It was becoming increasingly difficult to make the mortgage payments on the house, and losing the property became a distinct possibility.

When, in the winter of 1983, Cecil Brown called from Berlin to let Jimmy know that a German producer wanted to buy the film rights to *Giovanni's Room* Baldwin flew immediately with Bernard to Berlin to negotiate. Brown was amazed not only by the fact that he had a screenplay with him—which Bernard told him had been written "last weekend"—but that he bargained with such expertise and determination. The negotiations were successful. Baldwin got a large sum of money, and he got it in cash. Cecil was reminded of old countryfolk stereotypes as this modern-day Staggerlee handed him his "commission" from a large wad of German marks that he had stored—literally—in a sock.

In January 1983 the entourage shrunk temporarily, and Baldwin, with only Bernard and Valerie in the house, turned his attention exclusively to *The Evidence of Things Not Seen*. On May 4 he wrote to David Moses, using the familiar birth terminology to describe its completion. *Evidence* seemed "to consent to be born. Lord. Nobody knows."

As if he had had a premonition that this would be his last book, he dedicated it to "David Baldwin, the father and the son," arguably, with his mother and Beauford Delaney, the two strongest influences on his life. *Evidence* was an act of remembering as well as an analysis of the present. As a treatise on the inner effects, the unseen results, of racism, it acknowledged a certain truth in the prophecy of David Baldwin the father. The only hope was the brotherhood represented by David Baldwin the son.

Evidence was to the aftermath of the "civil rights" movement what *The Fire Next Time* had been to its heyday. As such, it has not been appreciated by white readers. It is commonplace to hear that Baldwin had lost touch with reality, had spent too much time in France to understand the America of the 1980s. Publishers even refused to publish it. Both Editions Stock in France and Michael Joseph in England brought the book out before Holt, Rinehart and Winston picked up the American rights. For Baldwin it was ironical that not so many years before, Dial Press had refused to let him change publishers.

White people wanted to be told that the "new South," that the existence of black mayors and police chiefs in American cities, the presence of blacks as television anchors, and the emergence of black men and women as "successful" authors, meant that the civil rights movement had worked and that America was on its way "to glory." Baldwin, always the Jeremiah, always the disturber of the peace, let it be known in *Evidence* that they were wrong.

For many years he had told audiences and friends that there had never been a "civil rights" movement; civil rights had, after all, supposedly been outlined in the Constitution. The "civil rights" movement was a wishful, sanitizing, "white English" phrase for what was in fact the beginnings of revolution, of a great "slave rebellion." The 1965 Watts events—and surely Baldwin would have said the same about the 1992 events in Los Angeles—were not "riots" but an insurrection against racism. To say mere "hoodlums" and "thugs" rioted was to accept a racist version of events and to evade the harsh truths behind them. Crime was always crime, and no one liked seeing cities burn and people hurt, but where was the general outcry as blacks hung from trees in the South or had their birthright "looted" by centuries of prejudice and a "market economy" that had made them—literally, in the slave days—a commodity? The American Dream was a dream for those white males willing to trample on others to get ahead. For American blacks as well as for American Indians and for many women it was a nightmare.

In *The Evidence of Things Not Seen* Baldwin held up Atlanta and the situation there as proof of these truths. With sunset each day the city "became a black enclave. The whites flee by way of the bristling system of freeways—known as 'ring around the Congo.' " The South might on the surface be "new," but "there is absolutely nothing new in this city, this state or this nation about dead black male bodies floating, finally, to the surface of the river." White America had found a way to have its cake and eat it, too. It had turned over the inner city to the blacks, given them the vote and even the control of city hall, but had preserved both separatism and real economic power: "It is a concession masking the face of power, which remains white."

The price paid for the ticket to "white supremacy" was high—obviously so for the blacks who suffered in terms of economics and self-esteem and more subtly so for those who, because they could not accept the kinship with their "darker brother," destroyed themselves morally in the delusion that they were "white." Such a delusion—the dream of separation from and essential difference from kinfolk—would lead inevitably to war and even genocide.

The children murdered in Atlanta were perceived as black. If Wayne Williams murdered them, he was a terrifying example of that result of racism which makes it possible for the black man to hate his own flesh. And, whether Williams was guilty or not, his attitude on the stand indicated that he was such a man. Like America itself, he had said no to community—"our endless connection with, and responsibility for, each other." Community, as illustrated in those two parables of community, *If Beale Street Could Talk* and *Just Above My Head*, was the black American's salvation. But Williams—arrogant and aloof, denying his own flesh—was a sad parody of the racist failing, the nightmare of the American delusion to which David had fallen prey in *Giovanni's Room*. Baldwin was highly skeptical of the case against a man he saw as a victim of the American curse—Williams was himself one of the murdered "children."

From the beginning, Baldwin had also been fascinated by Williams on a purely personal level. The eighties for him were years of retrospection and introspection, and he recognized in Williams a shadowlike version of what he might have been. He saw in him a lonely, homosexual, angry man who, like himself, had been denied a father's love, and who loved more than he was loved. To Joe he had written, "A passion suppressed . . . becomes an insupportable torment"; to love and not be loved in return was to be "driven to . . . madness."

Hope for the nation lay in refusing to yield to that madness and in embracing "community," community that could break down the delusions of color or, failing that, community of those who were seen by the majority as the "other." Real "community," he wrote in *Evidence*, as he had said many times during his career, involved risk, the choosing of honor over safety:

> It means doing one's utmost not to hide from the question perpetually in the eyes of one's lovers or one's children. It means accepting that those who love you (and those who do not love you) see you far better than you will ever see yourself. It means accepting the terms of the contract you signed at birth, the master copy of which is in the vaults of Death. These ruthless terms, it seems to me, make love and life and freedom real: whoever fears to die also fears to live. Whoever fears to die also imagines—*must* imagine—that another can die in his place. . . . The dream of safety can reach culmination or climax only in the nightmare orgasm of genocide.

So it was that David chose safety over Giovanni or that the sheriff in "Going to Meet the Man" required the castration of lynched black men to maintain the "safety" of his marriage bed, or that the American Dream had to be at the expense of the murdered "children" of Birmingham, Atlanta, and elsewhere.

Baldwin's last hope was based in the evidence of things not seen but true. At the end of *The Fire Next Time* he had called on "relatively conscious whites and relatively conscious blacks, who must, like lovers, insist on, or create, the consciousness of others" not to "falter in our duty," but to "dare everything" and, in so doing, to "end the racial nightmare, and achieve our country, and change the history of the world." He no longer believed he would "live to see anything resembling this hope come to pass," but as always, it was necessary to "keep the faith."

In September of 1983 Baldwin was in Washington watching rehearsals for a musical version of *The Amen Corner*. The play was directed by Phil Rose and starred Rhetta Hughes as Sister Margaret. It ran for six weeks at Ford's Theater to enthusiastic audiences and then had an abbreviated run in New York. Returning to Washington in 1983 for a new version of a play that had first been produced at Howard University twenty-eight years before was an exercise in nostalgia, and though moved by the musical performances in the play, Baldwin was not sure he approved of all of these productions of his earliest play—there had been still another one in Harlem the year before and there would be several more during the next three years. He was anxious to be recognized for his newer work, especially for his writing on the Atlanta murders.

Also in September, Baldwin began teaching at the Five Colleges in and around Amherst, Massachusetts. The Amherst connection had begun in 1978, when he had been awarded an honorary degree by the University of Massachusetts. At first, Baldwin was to teach full-time. Later, when he found that full-time teaching meant no space for writing, he agreed to work alternate semesters. He began the 1983–84 academic year, accompanied by his sometime companion Skip, on the campus of Hampshire College, but he found that his life-style was more conducive to off-campus living, and at the beginning of the spring semester he moved with Skip, and now Joe, to the home of James Tate, poet and professor at the University of Massachusetts, who was away on sabbatical.

It was a white Afro-American Studies graduate student, Cynthia Packard, who made these arrangements and who became Baldwin's organizer and de facto secretary in Amherst. When Joe and Skip eventually left, he and Packard shared a house in Pelham, an arrangement they maintained until the summer of 1986, after which time bad health prevented Baldwin's return to the Amherst position.

Cynthia Packard was one of the most important women in his life. The time with her was the closest thing to married life Jimmy ever experienced. They shared their problems and concerns, there were regular meals, he brought his students home for classes. And Cyndie was strong enough and sure enough of his love to protect him from the people who were anxious to exploit him in one way or another. Baldwin had certainly never planned to "marry" a white woman half his age in Amherst, Massachusetts, but there he was.

He had, in fact, always been tempted by the idea of married life. Although he knew his sexual inclinations militated against it, he would have liked to "settle down," at this point in his life, with a wife and children. With Cyndie this was at least partly possible. She respected his particular sexual orientation and the few sexually based relationships he developed in Amherst, but they loved each other in something of a romantic way, and he became close to her children. When Jimmy died a letter from Cyndie and a ring she had given him were by his bed. David Baldwin wore the ring to his brother's funeral and later returned it to Cyndie.

At Amherst, Baldwin formed friendships with several of his colleagues, including novelist John Edgar Wideman and especially Michael Thelwell, who had been a student at Howard during the *Amen Corner* days, and Julius Lester, both of whom taught in the Afro-American Studies program. Later he would have a falling-out with Lester over what he considered the latter's hostile attitude in a *New York Times Book Review* interview and Lester's accusation that Baldwin had made anti-Semitic statements in a class (Lester had converted to Judaism). This charge the Afro-American Studies Department so vehemently denied that it produced a pamphlet to support its and Baldwin's case.

An examination of the pamphlet and the opinions of students—African-American, Jewish, and others—indicate clearly that Baldwin's remarks, in answer to a student's question, were taken out of context and that his point was essentially one he had made repeatedly for some time, that to the ghetto resident, the Jew as landlord and store owner was the representative white man. Baldwin also never hid the fact that he disapproved of Zionism and of Israel as a political entity. He saw Israel as the representative of Western colonialism and capitalism in the Middle East. But he had removed himself from the masthead of *Liberator* magazine when it printed anti-Semitic articles. And in his class he criticized Jesse Jackson's use of the term "Hymietown" even as he pointed out the possibility that people were using that slip as a golden opportunity to set blacks and Jews against each other.

During five semesters between the fall of 1983 and the spring of 1986 Baldwin taught a variety of courses, including one on the history of the civil rights movement. He also ran writers' workshops and lectured on expatriate writers—among them Henry James, Richard Wright, Ernest Hemingway, and himself—and on the "Afro-American cultural experience," which treated such old Baldwin concerns as *Uncle Tom's Cabin* and *A Tale of Two Cities*, as well as such subjects as the black church, Malcolm and Muhammad, Black Power, and "women's liberation and the black community." The last issue was somewhat new to him, though he had suggested before what he emphasized now as the unique, almost matriarchal situation of black women forced to be family heads as they were faced by the reality of white society's systematic attempt to castrate their men psychologically and economically.

Baldwin enjoyed the experience at Amherst even though, as Cynthia Packard suggested, teaching at 11 a.m. for him was like teaching in the middle of the night for most people. He was sometimes late for classes, but he was, according to his students, always prepared, and he never missed office hours. In fact, what he liked best was the contact with students. He made a point of getting to know as many of "the children"—male and female—as possible, often taking them out "on the town" and showing a genuine concern for their personal as well as their academic lives. Sometimes he surprised them with nonacademic lessons. One night he was with a group in a pool hall when a very drunk man he had never seen before asked for his autograph and then vomited on him before falling to the floor. Baldwin helped him up and, with a few of the students, took him to the hotel where the man was staying, put him to bed, and left.

Baldwin was no academic recluse. There were parties at Cyndie's where friends from New York met his new Amherst acquaintances, trips to Atlanta for last-minute work on *Evidence*, a long promotion tour for *Evidence*, frequent visits to New York, one to a Gordon Parks exhibit at the New York Public Library, where he only somewhat facetiously told a friend he hoped to do a new *Gone With the Wind* from Mammy's perspective. He traveled to Bern, Switzerland, to speak at a conference on South Africa, to the Block Island and Massachusetts homes of Bosley Bratman Wilder, his old friend from the early Paris days, to my home in Connecticut, and to California to visit friends, including Bill Miller.

While he was in Los Angeles in February of 1985, he spoke out on the subject of recent shootings in the South Central area: "It's no different today than it was twenty-five years ago," he said. "This kind of killing is going on in the ghettoes, the projects, and all across poor urban America," and the economic system based on racism and greed was the cause. He was still possessed by his mission. During the question period after a SUNY Stony Brook lecture in February, he said, "You see, I don't belong to myself." And to Julius Lester he said, "I am a witness. In the church in which I was raised you were supposed to bear witness to the truth."

He was present at a gala party celebrating the 120th anniversary of *The Nation*, where he met, among many old friends, Jesse Jackson. Jackson was in the midst of a presidential campaign, of which Baldwin only mildly approved, because he resented the assumption that black Americans could be counted on to vote in a herd and that one man should presume to represent them in general. He admired Jackson's courage and perseverance, but once again he felt he was being "defined," and in any case, he had little faith in the political system and never voted.

One of the highlights of the period was his sixtieth-birthday party in Saint-Paul. Members of the family were there with Cecil Brown, Yves Montand, Simone Signoret, and many others. Visitors continued to pass through during the eighties. Bobby Short was often present. Miles Davis stopped by whenever he was in Nice. Toni Morrison, Bill Cosby, Maya Angelou, and Nina Simone were guests, and so was a new friend, Ann Beattie. Baldwin enjoyed entertaining and, with the help of Bernard and Valerie, did it well. There were several lovers in the late years: a young African-American in whom Baldwin thought he saw real writing talent, another whose ashes, after his death from AIDS, were scattered in the garden.

The Amherst years were not unproductive as far as his writing was concerned. Not only did he finish *Evidence* and the collected essays *The Price of the Ticket*, he wrote a retrospective introduction to a 1984 reprint of *Notes of a Native Son*, and a piece for *Essence*, "On Being White and Other Lies," stressing his old point that by considering themselves "white," white people were depriving themselves of a viable identity. He answered a *New Statesman* invitation to speak out on South Africa by writing an open letter to Bishop Desmond Tutu stating his belief that the so-called civilized world's "present social and economic arrangements cannot serve the world's needs" and that since "racism is the cornerstone and principal justification of these arrangements," the freedom of black people was the only hope for the future. Real freedom for "white" people could come only when the oppressed were free.

Baldwin kept himself so busy that in the early fall of 1984 he was hospitalized in Boston for heart problems brought on by exhaustion related to work and to a general life-style his body could no longer sustain. But on September 22 his official sixtieth-birthday party was celebrated with a formal dinner and series of receptions at the University of Massachusetts. Sam Floyd, who would not live long after, presented a moving personal tribute, as did Maya Angelou. Lerone Bennett spoke, and Gloria's youngest daughter presented a dance offering.

In January 1985 a longtime dream was realized as one of his novels was made into a film. *Go Tell It on the Mountain*, starring Paul Winfield, James Bond III, Olivia Cole, and Rosalind Cash, was aired on the Public Broadcasting System as an American Playhouse presentation. Baldwin was thrilled. "I still see myself there," he wrote of the character of John and his situation. "I was John once, in some way, and the actor who plays John is very accurate." The film, directed by Stan Lathan and produced by Robert Geller, received high ratings and seemed to promise more films of Baldwin works. It turned out to be the only one in his lifetime.

June 1986 marked the end of Baldwin's teaching career. His health had begun to deteriorate badly. He tried to "burn away" what he thought was some sort of sore throat with excessive doses of straight whiskey. This aggravated the problem and brought about a severe case of depression. He complained of having no strength to do anything, yet he spent whole nights entertaining hangers-on at restaurants and bars all over New York. At times he became alternately antagonistic and tearful. One night in New York he returned home in a particularly sorry state and fought with Bernard, who had come to take him back to France and was trying to put him to bed. After a struggle he allowed himself to be undressed as he sobbed and murmured repeatedly, "You don't understand, you don't understand, I'm just so lonely."

He seemed to revive when he left New York. He was buoyed by the presentation to him of the French Legion of Honor by President François Mitterrand on June 19. He had always promised his cook,

Valerie, a trip to Paris, where she had never been, so he took her and Mlle Faure, who would die later in the year, to the ceremony. David and Lucien were also there, and he was pleased to discover that another friend, Leonard Bernstein, would receive the Legion of Honor at the same time.

In October he completed an article for *Playboy* called "To Crush the Serpent," still another retrospective piece on religion and sexuality. It was his last published work, but for a short piece on the Saint-Paul house for *Architectural Digest* and Leonard Baskin's special illustrated posthumous edition, *Gypsies and Other Poems*. "To Crush the Serpent" is a final version of the Baldwin gospel, a prophet's cry for sanity. He had once been converted to a religion in which salvation was initiated by the fear of eternal damnation. Now he knew that salvation could not be based on fear. Real salvation "connects, so that one sees oneself in others and others in oneself," and it clears the way to "that which is greater than oneself." The simplistic salvation preached by ideologues and fundamentalists was delusory and dangerous: "Complexity is our only safety and love is the only key to our maturity. And love is where you find it."

Also in October, Baldwin and his brother David joined Yasar Kemal, Peter Ustinov, Arthur Miller, and others on a trip to the Soviet Union for a conference of "intellectuals" dedicated to a consideration of the world's future. On the shores of Issyk-Kul ("the pearl of Kirghizia," as the lake, surrounded by the beautiful Tien Shan Mountains, is called) the group talked of bringing a "new cultural thinking" into the realm of world politics, of ushering in the "Century of the Planet." Addressing the group in Moscow, Mikhail Gorbachev asked the delegates—according to Baldwin's own notes—to consider that they were living in a moment which "demands" a reexamination of "history as though for the first time." It was necessary to break old habits of thought and action, to address the question of saving the earth. Baldwin was impressed by Gorbachev but, as always, concerned himself more with the inner man than the public figure. He thought he saw the kind of man he liked, one who could put past suffering to good use in the present and future.

His primary official duty during the Soviet conference was to deliver a speech on racism and its terrible effect on the oppressor as well as the oppressed. This he did, but with some difficulty, as he was feeling poorly. What turned out to be the real highlight of the trip for him occurred during an informal evening party near the lake in Kirghizia, when he and Yasar Kemal traded songs. Baldwin sang

"Precious Lord" and some blues songs and Yasar answered with some Turkish folk tunes. Then Baldwin asked Yasar if he remembered a Turkish song they had sung in the sixties in Istanbul. He did, and somehow Jimmy did, too. They sang together again, embraced, and the next day said good-bye for the last time.

Once again back in Saint-Paul, Baldwin turned to various projects. The Beauford novel had now combined somehow with *No Papers for Mohammed* to become *Any Bootlegger Can*. But most of all, he tried to work on *Remember This House*. It was proving an almost impossible task, and he realized he did not have the strength to do the necessary research. Before he died he managed to complete thirty or forty pages. The first section would take its name from *A Tale of Two Cities*. The second part would be about Medgar Evers, Malcolm X, and Martin Luther King; it would be called "Somewhere Around the Throne." A final section would be suggested by the remark by Jesus in the New Testament to the effect that he needed to attend to "my Father's business." On the manuscript's title page he writes "remember" as "re/member" suggesting the goal of the book as the witness's attempt to put a broken "house" together again. He had left "my father's house" years ago, when he left Harlem for Paris. His life and his nation's life had been a "tale of two cities" determined to remain separate. He was returning now to proclaim the urgency of remembering the "house" of the fallen heroes and to give them their due. As to his own life and what others might or might not expect of him, his only answer would be that he, like the prophet of that church to which he had once belonged, and, in fact, like all prophets, was "about my father's business." "As for me and my house," Baldwin's father had preached, "we will serve the Lord." Baldwin, in his own way, was doing just that.

He made several starts on the book. The first was an autobiographical record beginning with his own flight in 1948 from the "mad-house" that was his nation. The second was a sketch of first meetings with Medgar, Malcolm, and Martin, which took up the question of the relationship between the three martyrs, one which personality and different priorities had made somewhat distant. But circumstances of the movement had linked them together in Baldwin's experience and made *Remember This House* for him a responsibility. He had no choice but to present a "valid testimony"; he was called upon to be a "witness."

The process would involve his sorting out his relationships with the three men. With Medgar this was easy. He liked him, even loved him, and admired him deeply. At first he had found Malcolm aloof, but later they would discover each other's value. As for Martin, the shared experience in the Christian pulpit formed at once a connection and a reason for wariness. Malcolm revealed the black "rage" to America, and Martin, through nonviolence, revealed white America's "spiritual poverty."

Baldwin then turned to a history of the black protest from the early days of the NAACP to CORE and SNCC, but he quickly drifted towards the question of the duality represented by the approaches of Malcolm and King. One was aggressive, the other nonviolent, but one could not say one was good and one was bad. This conclusion sparked a third attempt at the beginning of *Remember This House*, an offshoot entitled "Upon His Shoulder."

Here Baldwin turned to a favorite subject, innocence and knowledge. Taking the Tree of Knowledge as his metaphor, he reminds us that originally the tree in the garden had contained both good and evil and suggests that the cause of human pain was not the fruit of the tree but the way we think of and react to the tree. It was the eating of the fruit of the knowledge of good and evil, after all, that brought about the end of "innocence," which in turn led to the possibility of "responsibility."

"Upon His Shoulder" is a final statement of one of Baldwin's major themes. One day it will certainly be published, along with another offshoot of *Remember This House*, an essay on de facto genocide, called "Show Me the Way," which suggests that black America no longer expects anything of white America: "Black people have managed to survive White sympathy."

In the fall of 1986 a version of *The Amen Corner* opened in London. It was acted by a British–West Indian rather than by an American cast. The play ran for several months to packed houses and received enthusiastic reviews. Baldwin spent time in London to consult with director Anton Phillips. The success of the production surprised and pleased him, encouraging him to get back to *The Welcome Table*.

CHAPTER 34

Gathering Around the Welcome Table

> I'm going to sit at the Welcome Table
> I'm going to feast on milk and honey
> One of these days. —old song

At the end of March, when Baldwin arrived back in Saint-Paul-de-Vence from London, Bernard realized that something was terribly wrong. There was none of the usual enthusiasm for new projects, there was no companion, no interest in food or even, oddly enough, drink. Jimmy confided in his old friend that he could barely swallow, but he was so depressed that he refused to see a doctor. Bernard called one anyway, and an appointment was arranged for April 1 at a nearby hospital. The diagnosis was cancer of the esophagus. Laser treatment improved the situation temporarily so that he could swallow and eat and drink. A more radical operation was performed on the twenty-fifth.

Jimmy realized that he might not survive this crisis. He wrote to his old friend Bill Belli on the twentieth, an hour before leaving for the hospital. The letter begins with a memory of films of the forties, the kind that started with George Brent or Robert Young ripping open a letter against a background of crashing waves and Beethoven. The movie letter would be from the heroine—Bette Davis or Joan Crawford—whose voice would be heard announcing her imminent death, which by now had already taken place.

Baldwin assured his friend that he had no intention of dying, but clearly he worried that he might. And he used the letter as a final statement of sorts. He sensed he had been using his public life as a kind of escape from himself and his doubts about the meaning of things. It was frightening to realize that "one knows nothing." Could it be that we are "not equipped" to know? This "icy suspicion" made the question of his surviving the operation "irrelevant." After the operation the doctors told Bernard—but not the patient—that the case was terminal. There would be temporary improvement and then quick deterioration.

By May, Baldwin began to feel much better and talked about his various projects, especially *The Welcome Table*, the title of which seemed to take on new significance in light of his illness and the ever-present reminders of his mortality; it was to be his last work, and he knew it. The play was linked in his mind with Walter Dallas, a black director and teacher trained at the Yale Drama School, whom he had met in 1981 in Baltimore in connection with his Center Stage production of *The Amen Corner*. Baldwin had nothing to do with the production itself, but when he saw it he knew immediately that the director was a man with whom he wanted to work someday. He liked the staging so much that he returned three times with friends and members of his family.

What Dallas had succeeded in doing was to bring out the real essence of the play, the inner trials of Sister Margaret and her son David, the tension, which applied to Baldwin's life, between the sacred and the secular, the struggle to find a way to bear witness. Dallas used the set to emphasize the war between the religious threshing floor upstairs in the church and the secular one downstairs in the apartment, forcing the viewer to see that while safety was upstairs with the "saints," honor was downstairs with personal love, embodied in the dying Luke and the rebellious David.

At the time of the Center Stage production, Baldwin had already begun a tentative writing of *The Welcome Table*. After meeting Dallas he attacked it in earnest, and for the next five years he and his director met whenever they could. By 1986 they had a dramatic reading, with Dallas's students taking the roles. When Baldwin heard this performance, he was sure that the play would succeed, and he and Dallas began looking for a producer, eventually finding one in Marion Shaw, who was hard at work on the project when Baldwin died.

Whereas *The Amen Corner* and *Blues for Mister Charlie* were what Walter Dallas calls "folk drama," *The Welcome Table* is "slice-of-life" theater that depends on Chekhovian innuendoes, on "the subtext, the unspoken," as Baldwin told a friend. What happens on the surface seems to go nowhere, but we sense below the surface a struggle with open wounds. "It's about exiles and alienation," Baldwin said. It "comes out of a need to get away from it [the "horror" of our time], to ventilate, to look at the horror from some other point of view." It was to be, as Dallas saw it, "history happening," a play about love, suffering, and memories. There could be no resolution to "history happening," and the play has no resolution.

The literal point of view was very much Baldwin's Saint-Paul-de-Vence "scene," the biracial, bisexual, confessional milieu that had been so important to his personal life and to his prophecy. In fact, the welcome table in Baldwin's dining room (or the one outside under the arbor), around which life in the household centered, was the source for the play's set design as well as for its central metaphor. One evening, while Dallas was visiting Baldwin at Saint-Paul in January of 1987, the two men sat watching the New Year's fireworks, drawing set designs on napkins, when both noticed that they were working around marks left in the napkins by wet glasses. Both saw the marks as an image of a table and realized that the play had to be anchored by that image. They knew, too, that although the welcome table was Baldwin's table at Saint-Paul where they were sitting, it was rooted metaphorically in the welcome table of the other world, where the weary traveler would find "milk and honey" and in the welcome table/altar of the church that had once been Baldwin's, where the sacrificial victim becomes food for the "children," for the "saints" of the "amen corner" and the "hallelujah chorus." It could serve now as a metaphor for the work in which his "gospel" or prophecy was celebrated and around which the "brothers" and "sisters" of his communion congregated, as they actually had done in the house at Saint-Paul. The welcome table was a place of witness, where exiles could come and lay down their souls.

In light of the source of *The Welcome Table*, it is not surprising that the characters in the play are based on recognizable people close to Baldwin and that he used the play to stand back and look at their lives and his own as well as to consider more universal questions. This semiautobiographical approach to larger issues had been his method since *Go Tell It on the Mountain*.

The Welcome Table takes place in a house in the south of France during a ninetieth-birthday party for Mlle LaFarge, a French exile from Algeria who, like her source, Mlle Faure, for whom Baldwin had thrown a similar party in 1985, is a woman torn between a deep-rooted racism and a desire to accept life, whatever its color. Paralleling the real-life situation of Mlle Faure, she is the former owner of the house now belonging to the play's main character, Edith, with whom, despite their differences in background and outlook, she has a close friendship.

Edith is a famous Creole singer-dancer from New Orleans who shares her house and its provisions with a constantly shifting and interacting entourage of friends, lovers, and observers who use her "table" to face themselves. The source for Edith was Josephine Baker and, of course, James Baldwin, whose initials, he often pointed out, were the same as the singer's.

Other guests and members of the household include Laverne, Edith's assistant and, in one version, "cousin"; Regina, an old friend of Edith's; Peter, a black journalist from America; Terry, a photographer; Daniel, who had once been a Black Panther; and two young white men, Rob and Mark. There is also a maid, Angelina, and a gardener, Mohammed.

Peter has arrived, like his antecedent, Henry Louis Gates, Jr., to interview the great singer. In the play the interview becomes a direct challenge to Edith to face truths about herself that have long been buried in a life of fame and fast living. It becomes a metaphor for self-examination. Biographer James Campbell is right in making a connection between this process and Baldwin's preoccupation with "confession." It was the lack of confession—the failure to risk the necessary lowering of barriers—that had destroyed David in *Giovanni's Room* and which Baldwin had complained of in Tony Maynard. It was confession that he demanded of his lovers and was so often refused. It was confession that Ida had demanded of Vivaldo and confession that saved Tish and Fonny. The refusal to risk the danger of confession was at the base of the great social failure revealed by American racism. Only by letting go, by entrusting one's life to another, could an individual or a society hope to achieve wholeness. The doctrine of confession was a staple at the real-life Baldwin welcome table, as it is in the play.

Daniel, the Black Panther, was inspired by a combination of Cecil Brown, who was visiting Saint-Paul at the time of the Gates interview, and the Panther emissary sent by Eldridge Cleaver to ask Baldwin for money. Peter and Daniel strike up a "confessional" father-son type of relationship that speaks to Baldwin's own preoccupation with that bond. For the play to work, he wrote a friend, that relationship had to be "clear."

Rob is in some respects the typical Baldwin lover. Bisexual, he is Edith's lover as well as Mark's. In this he also resembles Baldwin himself, who was ever nostalgic about past loves and could rarely pass up the opportunity to reconnect with an old lover even if the relationship endangered a new one. For him, as for Rob, the risk of love had to take precedence over the safety of orderly relationships. Baldwin's other feelings on the matter are represented in Edith's desire for just such domestic stability.

Angelina is based on Baldwin's maid, Valerie, and Mohammed the gardener has the same name as Baldwin's own onetime gardener, who had been the catalyst for the unfinished *No Papers for Mohammed.*

Edith's assistant, Laverne, is, Baldwin felt, the most tragic character. She was derived from Bernard Hassell and remains at the end of the play where she had been at the beginning. Confession is beyond her; she has a relationship with her employer that is marked by "ambiguity"—a combination of loyalty and "smoldering envy." Baldwin had complained to his brother many times of what he saw as his own assistant's self-denial and envy. In fact, in the letter in which he told David about beginning *Inventory* (the earlier title of *The Welcome Table*) he had spoken specifically of having had a fight with Bernard in which he accused him of being a victim of envy and an inability to break out of himself.

A somewhat undeveloped character is Regina, Edith's white alcoholic friend, "recently widowed," whose source is Mary Painter, who in the 1980s had lost her own husband and been defeated by alcoholism. Baldwin's letter to David about *Inventory* had indicated a certain impatience with Mary, who was a frequent visitor in the house and a source of some irritation, in spite of the many years of close friendship. Regina is also a shadow figure of sorts, a representation of that "lost" part of James Baldwin, wearing the all too familiar mask of the lonely drinker who has once again lost a love companion. All the characters in the play are, Baldwin said, in one way or another, "displaced." They are all "exiles," and, of course, all are self-portraits; the house itself is a metaphor for Baldwin's mind, for his many selves gathering around and finally attempting to face the welcome table, where everything will have to come together. The eighties, as has been suggested, were years of retrospection for him. This being the case, it is of interest that the main characters in the play are female.

The female within the male had long fascinated Baldwin. He had been interested in his own ability to work through a female persona in the narration of *If Beale Street Could Talk,* and he particularly enjoyed "hanging" out with women who had a certain style, women with whom he could in some sense identify, for the most part black women who could accept him unromantically for what he was without making sexual demands on him. He could love a Cyndie Packard or a Gidske Anderson, a Mary Painter or a Bosley Wilder, even wish he could marry them, but when he was with Maya Angelou, or Bertice Redding, or Verta Mae Grosvenor, or Louise Meriwether, or Paule Marshall, or Eleanor Traylor, he was able to relate with the freedom of a "sister." And Baldwin not only enjoyed female company, there was a part of him that envied their style, their clothes, their gestures. For much of his life Baldwin avoided flamboyant clothes because he believed it was important not to "signify" a particular sexual stereotype. Yet by the 1980s he had long since given in to a love of silk, of the recklessly thrown scarf, the overcoat draped stole-like over the shoulders, the large and exotic ring, bracelet, or neck-piece. Even his movements assumed a more feminine character.

In moments of what might be called wish fulfilment or psychological nostalgia for the lost woman within his manhood, he dreamed of novels he could write about women who would convert the Jimmy Baldwin he still sadly thought of as an ugly little man into someone tall, confident, beautiful, and, to use a favorite word of his, "impeccably" dressed in silks and satins and bold colors. She would still possess the brilliance and even the potential for tragedy of her male source, but she would be irresistible to the Luciens, the Jeans, and the Black Christophers who had made Baldwin so miserably unhappy. In this character James Baldwin would be transformed into a Josephine Baker. He had planned to write a novel whose title he even scribbled on a piece of paper in an airplane somewhere on a trip between Los Angeles and Nice by way of New York, London, and Paris: *The Bloody Life and Stormy Death of a Certain Miss Shelley St. John.*

For some time Baldwin had given a great deal of thought to the idea of gender identity. In the late seventies he had run into an old school and, later, Paris friend in Greenwich Village who had been bisexual but had not "come out." "Jay" (the name has been changed here to protect his privacy) had, in fact, married and had a child but was considering a sex-change operation. Baldwin had reacted angrily to the idea, suggesting it might be better for Jay to face himself as he was, a combination, like everyone, of male and female. The fact that his biological equipment was male or that he preferred sleeping with men need not prevent him from expressing himself fully. Jay, nevertheless, became Jayne in 1979. He wrote to Baldwin admitting to the difficulty in having to cope with his old self on occasion. He wondered whether his having become a woman was simply a means of legitimizing his having relations with men. In a second letter he asked Baldwin for his blessing and suggested that they meet for a meal. Baldwin's answer reveals both generosity of spirit and good humor. He leaped at the rare chance to "unleash the male chauvinistic pig" in himself by suggesting that Jayne was "even more ridiculous" as a female than he had been as a male. He would not confer either approval or disapproval on his friend's operation. He was "not, thank God, God." He could only wish her happiness and agreed to meet her at the Russian Tea Room for lunch.

One of Baldwin's last major essays had been an autobiographical article for *Playboy* called "Freaks and the American Ideal of Manhood," later included as the last piece in *The Price of the Ticket* as "Here Be Dragons." In that essay he wrote, "We . . . are all androgynous . . . born of a woman impregnated by . . . a man . . . each of us, helplessly and forever, contains the other—male in female, female in male, white in black and black in white." In the idea of androgyny, as in *The Welcome Table* itself, Baldwin found still another metaphor to contain his gospel.

With Dallas he discussed many possibilities for the cast of the play, which for a very brief time underwent a title change to *Speak My Name*. Baldwin's favorite cast included Lena Horne or Diahann Carroll as Edith, Ruby Dee as Laverne, Geraldine Page as Regina, Sylvia Sidney as Mlle LaFarge, David Baldwin as Peter, and David Moses as Daniel. He was making revisions until the last week of his life. Dallas did a studio performance of the play in 1989 before David Baldwin, Ruby Dee, and other friends. The reaction of the audience was enthusiastic and a Lincoln Center reading was planned for the early 1990s.

THE LAST STAGE OF James Baldwin's life began in July 1987. After the operation in April, he gradually improved until the summer, when the predicted process of rapid deterioration had started. On July 4 he wrote two important letters, one to Walter Dallas and one to Cyndie Packard. As in the case of the April 20 letter to Bill Belli, these communications served as a means of facing the reality of death and the meaning of his life. He used his correspondence, as Edith had used her interview with Peter in *The Welcome Table*, to confess to himself.

In the letter to Dallas he spoke of his sense of his own life. His "Hopes" had sometimes turned to "ashes" or "poison," but he had no "real regrets." The "awful" thing was the fact that it took so much time "to learn so little."

The letter reminded Dallas of the scene from *The Amen Corner* when Luke, who has come home to die, is speaking to his son, David. The dying Luke says:

> Son, don't try to get away from the things that hurt you. The things that hurt you—sometimes that's all you got. You got to learn to live with those things, use them.

To Cyndie, Baldwin wrote about the "journey" that he was undergoing. As he experienced "the stillness at the center" of the night, he said, he listened to the darkness and felt that "something" was "listening to me."

To himself he wrote something less optimistic, a journal entry which he took the trouble to type on a new typewriter that he had bought for the use of a part-time typist hired during the early summer. He wrote of the "small cell" which was "despair," and of how it could be "the death of love." He worried that he was "mean," even "spiteful," that his liver was "diseased," and wondered what he should do next.

His liver was, in fact, diseased, the cancer having spread there and elsewhere. He had not indicated to anyone—not even his family—that he was as sick as he was. So Bernard wrote David suggesting that he come to Saint-Paul. George and Lover and David all visited, and after a comparatively quiet last birthday party, attended by old friends, David stayed on in Saint-Paul. Lucien came, too. By October, Jimmy could no longer go to the Colombe d'Or, but Yvonne or Pitou, friends from there, would sometimes bring him meals. Quincy Troupe visited in November for a "last interview" and found Baldwin very weak.

By then David had moved him from the "dungeon" downstairs, where he had for many years lived and worked. The room that had once been Mlle Faure's kitchen became the "office," where each day Jimmy said he would go "tomorrow." Mlle Faure's living room, with its ancient faded frescoed walls, Provençal tile floor, and deep fireplace, was turned into the bedroom, where, but for short trips to the table, to which David sometimes carried him, he stayed for the rest of his life.

Jimmy had written me on August 11 referring to his operation but indicating he would get better; he had, after all, never been told that his tumor was malignant. He spoke of being sixty-three, of having lost weight, and of how much he longed for a drink and a cigarette. Convalescence was possible to bear only when one thought about the "alternative—Andy Warhol!" It was humbling to have to accept the fact that one's self-image was a myth.

He would not be able to travel right away, he said. In any case, he thought the rest of his time should be spent working. There was much to be written. We were living during a period of redefinitions, and he wanted to be a part of that process or be witness to any reaction to it: "Chad Newsome deep-throats Ollie North on Nigger Jim's deep river!"

He spoke of *The Welcome Table*, mentioning that he was waiting to hear from Walter Dallas about the most recent revision. Meanwhile, he was anxious to get back to *Remember This House*. As it was not possible for him to travel, would I consider going as his emissary to interview the wives of Evers, Malcolm, and King? His nephew T.J., Gloria's son, who had recently spent a summer vacation in Saint-Paul, could possibly be enlisted to interview their children.

Not realizing how sick he was, I wrote back saying I thought it would be much better for him to do the interviewing even if it meant waiting a year, but that I would come to Saint-Paul to discuss the matter with him. Several months later, just before Thanksgiving, David telephoned to say that I had better come as soon as possible, that Jimmy could not last long.

I arrived in Nice on the morning of the twenty-first and took the bus up to Saint-Paul. As usual, the outer gate was unlocked and so was the door to the house, which appeared to be empty. I knew nothing about the rearrangement of the rooms. When I came to what had been Mlle Faure's living room I found Jimmy in a large bed; he was barely recognizable. He had lost a great deal of weight and had a deathlike, sunken look about him. There was an IV in his arm and some blood on the sheet from the needle.

Jimmy woke up, saw me, smiled weakly, and said, "Hey, baby." We embraced, and I lay down next to him and conveyed greetings from mutual friends. He had asked for a few things from the States, and I opened the package I had brought for him: Aunt Jemima pancake mix, Aunt Jemima syrup, Brer Rabbit molasses, and some jelly beans. There was a spark of the old laughter, and he whispered, "We can't escape our culture." Then the smile faded into a confused, frightened look.

When the doctor arrived a few minutes later, I went to find David and his friend Sophie, who were in Jimmy's old quarters downstairs. We all went upstairs, Valerie arrived to cook, Bernard came in from the gatehouse, and while Jimmy slept we had lunch. David was irritated with Bernard and seemed particularly tired. He had been caring for his brother since August, sitting up most nights with him, and the strain was evident. I suggested that since I was the latest arrival I should handle some of David's "watch." To get a much needed change of scene he took Sophie to a wine bar in Saint-Paul. Bernard and Valerie left as well and I sat with Jimmy, who was awake. When I asked if I could help him in any way, he wondered if I would mind seeing to the correspondence that had piled up since the summer. There were papers that required sorting that David and I could deal with as well; these involved some notes for various novels and the beginnings of *Remember This House*. If David and I could manage these things, the desk would be "clear" enough for him to begin working "in a day or so." He had some things he wanted to do on *The Welcome Table*, and he was anxious for me to read a draft.

Before he drifted off to sleep again—he was heavily medicated for pain—he talked about feeling "demoralized" and "bored." He complained at some length about how thin he was, how embarrassed he was at looking like "skin and bones." Death, he said, did not seem such a terrible idea in the circumstances. We spoke of his accomplishments and his hopes for the new projects.

At dinner David, Bernard, and I undertook what seemed to be a necessary exercise in retrospection. We talked a lot about Istanbul and the *Blues for Mister Charlie* days and the trip South David had taken with Jimmy, about how they had had to share a bed in Selma, how it was near a window and David had slept on the window side so that if anyone fired at the room he rather than Jimmy would be hit. Bernard wanted to speak about the immediate past, especially about Jimmy's operation. David resented his insistence on discussing the medical details of his brother's illness. Jimmy woke up and asked for pancakes, which David made for him right away. He ate, the medication promptly took over again, and he slept.

Sitting with Jimmy on the first night, I read *The Welcome Table*, and when, at about 3 a.m., he woke up we talked about the autobiographical aspects of the play. Then he felt nauseous and I carried him to the commode. My suggestion that it was "Aunt Jemima's revenge" brought miserable laughter. David came in at 5 a.m., and I went to bed.

At 10:30 on the twenty-second, I relieved David and, as Jimmy was awake, suggested a shave, a bath, and a change of pajamas and sheets. The bath was necessarily a sponge bath. The intimacy of the process struck me, and I was taken back to our time in Erdek, the Turkish village to which we had gone in 1966 and where, because of Jimmy's leg cast, I had had to sponge-bathe him every morning in the hotel's *hammam.* When David came back "on duty," we rigged up a more comfortable commode out of a plastic bucket and an antique chair out of which, to Bernard's horror, we cut out the seat and substituted a toilet seat. Jimmy said it wasn't the Hôtel Pont Royal but it was better than an outhouse.

While Jimmy slept David and I sorted some manuscripts for him, and, according to his instructions, I wrote to Howard Dodson at the Schomburg Center in New York agreeing that his "papers" should be deposited there. David and I were to collate the material first. He was anxious that David remove some of the more personal letters, and he did.

At lunchtime Jimmy wanted scrambled eggs but he could eat very little. The rest of us then sat around the table and talked about him and about how different we all were—David, Bernard, and I—and how Jimmy and our love for him made us somehow, in spite of disagreements and different backgrounds, a community. There had always been an unwritten law in Jimmy's households that people greet each other with a kiss on each cheek at the first encounter of the day. This applied to men and women, to the maid, the gardener, the doctor, and even to those who might have had a terrible dispute the night before. Such arguments were commonplace around the welcome table, but the house demanded the recognition of community in the ritual kiss.

Caring for Jimmy in his sickness was a logical extension of this ritual. He was insistent on not going to a hospital or having a nurse. He wanted men to take care of him—not, I was sure, because he disliked or mistrusted women, but because it was important to him that men express the feminine within themselves, that they adopt the kind of tender nurturing usually associated with women. We became "disciples" of his gospel, "gentle" men of the "welcome table." To put it another way, we ritually experienced the "stink of love" in Giovanni's room. Even as he was dying Jimmy insisted on his role as a witness and lived his prophecy.

On the afternoon of the twenty-second he seemed better and for a while sat in a chair. Later we put him to bed and had dinner around the table. Again we felt drawn to retrospection. We talked about Beauford and the Paris days and about Mary Painter, who was so addicted to alcohol that she was only vaguely aware of Jimmy's condition. The bell rang from his room and we took him soup. I gave him his medicine, and he said, "I'll try to walk around tomorrow."

In the middle of the night he asked me to read aloud from his Turkish screenplay, *The Sacrifice*. Since I knew Turkey well and had been several times to Greece and to Cyprus, he wanted my opinion on whether or not he had captured the atmosphere of that part of the world. We discussed that question before he slept again.

On the twenty-third the doctor came and reminded us that his patient must have calmness around him. There had been guests from the village when he arrived, and he was concerned about the number of people in the house at any given time.

On the twenty-fourth, Jimmy said he would get up. He wanted help brushing his teeth, but then decided he would nap before rising, after all, and slept until lunchtime. Mary Painter called, seemed confused, and said she would visit soon if Jimmy could not come to her. It was a ghostly conversation. This was no longer the woman who had "saved" Jimmy's life, the woman he would have married if ever he had married.

David carried Jimmy to the table for lunch. The talk was lively, Jimmy speaking, with more strength than he had shown in weeks, about Nina Simone, who had been telephoning and who appeared to be suffering a breakdown—the "price," he said, of being a black entertainer. The retrospection continued as well; we passed around a copy of a story Jimmy had written in his school days—a story about soldiers called "Peace on Earth"; he read a paragraph aloud, and then David carried him back to bed.

Earlier in the day he had asked for doughnuts. Bernard had found some in the village, and now Jimmy wanted one before going to sleep. He had not eaten much of anything at the table. The doughnuts were not right. He searched a box of chocolates for a certain cream-filled type. He was insistent; "at this point," he said, "why take second best?"

That night Jimmy and I talked about theater. If he could have started all over again, he might have concentrated on being a playwright and maybe an actor; he liked the immediacy of the stage, working with live people and having the audience right there.

Later, as Jimmy slept, the conversation at dinner became tense; David and Bernard were at odds again and there was a disagreement between Sophie and David as well. Meanwhile, behind us, on the television, was a program on the Holocaust. A real-life version of *The Welcome Table* was taking place as Jimmy lay in the other room.

He rang, and we all went in to see him. Ironically, he wanted to discuss the cast of *The Welcome Table*. Lena Horne would play Edith; he was sure of that now. Tomorrow he absolutely had to get back to the play. He wondered how my work on the correspondence was going and was relieved to hear that it was almost done. During the night he wanted to talk about religion. He realized that the church's role in his life had been significant, especially with respect to what he called his "inner vocabulary." As for the larger questions, he did not "believe" in God, but he felt—especially when he was alone—that there was "something out there."

On the twenty-fifth I went up to the village, lit a candle in the church, and bought the makings of a pumpkin pie. Jimmy wanted a "real Thanksgiving dinner" on the twenty-sixth. That day he spoke by telephone for the last time with his mother and Gloria. "I'm glad we did that," he said.

Pat Mikell from Mikell's and Lucien arrived later on the twenty-fifth. Lucien had been there earlier in the month and was back to be present at what we all now referred to as "the end." David carried his brother to the table for the last time that night, but Jimmy had no strength and had to be taken back to bed after fifteen minutes or so. The weather had turned cool, so we built a fire in his bedroom and each of his friends kissed him before he fell asleep.

Jimmy's last Thanksgiving resembled the day depicted in *The Welcome Table* in its high level of personal confrontation and self-examination. In the morning I shaved him and bathed him and read the *Tribune* aloud. Unfortunately, it contained the story of the death of his friend Mayor Harold Washington in Chicago. Jimmy became more melancholy than I had seen him since my arrival. "We were both in our sixties," he said. "There's so little time."

Meanwhile, the disagreements that had begun the night before had broken out again, and all the combatants but Bernard left for the village to work out their problems. Bernard, in the manner of Laverne in the play, retired to his house with "the flu." I had volunteered to cook the Thanksgiving dinner, and by 10:30 p.m. everyone but Jimmy had gathered around the table. The conversation was still welcome-table confessional, with each of the disputants exposing his or her emotional wounds for treatment by the others. Only Bernard held back. Jimmy rang and we took him dinner on a tray. He could not eat, but he sat in the chair and seemed to bring some peace to the group before he had to be returned to bed.

During the night I picked up the book I had been reading the night before and was well into it when I realized Jimmy was watching me.

"What are you reading?" he asked.

"Something from your bookcase, *Pride and Prejudice*," I answered.

"Which part?"

"Chapter Nineteen. Mr. Collins is proposing to Elizabeth." He asked me to read the chapter aloud, and when I had finished he chuckled and then whispered, "so economical, so devastating."

By the twenty-seventh, Jimmy had become much weaker. He slept while the rest of us continued our examination of the past. This was Beauford's day at the welcome table. Bernard told the story of a man attempting to pick up the painter in Cannes and recounted the hospital fiasco. I described the drive to Istanbul with Richard and Beauford. We all knew these stories already; this was a ritual process.

Bill Belli arrived, and Jimmy spent some time in the afternoon talking alone with him. The whole group met in the bedroom in the evening. Jimmy had asked to watch television. Miraculously, one channel was showing a documentary about Bessie Smith with old clips of her singing. Jimmy was moved. These were songs he had listened to on the Swiss mountain with Lucien as he wrote his first novel. Now Lucien was here and Bessie Smith was singing again. The documentary was followed by one of his favorite films, Charlie Chaplin in *The Great Dictator*. Jimmy was fully attentive. It was his last night at the movies; no "stars" could have pleased him more.

That night we had our final real talk. He was still preoccupied with the casting of *The Welcome Table*. Would Lena and Ruby like it? He wanted to get well; he had things to do, and his record was "not bad." We talked about Chaplin, Horne, Bessie Smith, Simone Signoret, and then, after a pause, he said, "Sometimes I can't believe that I'm famous, too." We spoke about my leaving the next day. He asked if he could give me something, and I had him sign a copy of *The Amen Corner* to take home to my wife. With great difficulty he signed the book, "For Pam, with love, Jimmy B."

In the morning we embraced and he and David and I talked of my returning in a few days. He rested quietly on the twenty-eighth and on the twenty-ninth the doctor told David that nothing in Jimmy was functioning, that he would die within hours. He woke up during that evening and asked David whether he could see Simone and other friends passing along the wall. On the thirtieth he slept most of the day but was still lucid when he roused from time to time. The doctor said it was almost over. Lucien had been sitting with Jimmy all day and into the night. The others were talking at the table when Lucien called David, saying he thought it was time. David sat on the bed and took Jimmy's hands, Bernard squeezed water from a napkin onto his lips. Jimmy looked at them and seemed to drift away. David and Lucien both had the sense that they were taking the journey with him as far as they could go. It was after midnight. They all kissed Jimmy. David said, "It's all right, Jimmy; you can cross over now," and Jimmy passed.

David got up, went to the welcome-table room, and put on a record. Sara Jordan Powell's "Amazing Grace" filled the house while people found their own corners in which to begin mourning. The weather had turned cold and rainy. David sat with his brother through the rest of the night. The next morning Jimmy was laid out, and later in the day people from the village came to see him. Mary Painter arrived, and was horrified and confused to find him dead. Even worse, Jean came from Cannes, asked where Jimmy was, and was directed to the bedroom by someone who assumed, wrongly, he knew Jimmy had died. He rushed out in tears.

At about 6 p.m. David told Sophie he was going to Nice to "walk for Jimmy." She asked to go with him. David knew he had to leave the house for a while; the strain of the past months and the reality of Jimmy's death were suddenly overwhelming. He remembered a poem Jimmy had once written for him about his boots standing together outside the door "learning the price of the stormy weather." It was in *Jimmy's Blues*. He put on socks and a shirt of Jimmy's, and a pair of Jimmy's boot-shoes, and since it was still raining, he wore Jimmy's green poncho. The taxi came and drove him and Sophie to the train station in Nice, and for several hours they walked in silence "up, down, across, and under Nice for Jimmy." Late at night a naked man appeared—he was later, according to the television news, arrested—walked directly up to David, and said, *"Bonjour, Monsieur,"* having spoken to no one else on a promenade down the street. David returned the greeting, looked up, and said, "That was for you, too, Jimmy."

The next day the coffin arrived and was taken with great formality by gendarmes and transported to the airport. On December 7 there was an emotional funeral-home viewing in Harlem, Jimmy looking terribly small behind the glass window of the French casket, people constantly filing by to see him for the last time.

The funeral, at New York's Cathedral of St. John the Divine, where in 1974 Baldwin had received the award as a "prophet of the twentieth century," was on David's birthday, December 8. As many have said, it was a "celebration" of Baldwin's life, attended by several thousand people: friends, relatives, lovers, and admirers—leaders of the old civil rights movement, classmates from De Witt Clinton, friends from France and Turkey. The coffin, draped in black, stood at the cathedral crossing in front of the high altar. The procession of the family and the honorary pallbearers, led by Baldwin's grieving mother in a wheelchair, moved down the long aisle to the African drumbeats of the Babatunde Olatunji Ensemble.

The cathedral choir, led by the head chorister, brother Wilmer's son Trevor, sang the psalms. The words of the King James Bible provided a strange contrast to the drums and suggested, like the mix of the congregation, Baldwin's role as a prophet to the *whole* nation, his constant insistence on the blood kinship of American blacks and whites. This was a ceremony conducted in the author's two languages: "black English" and "white English."

The scripture lesson—verses from the prophetic Book of Revelation of St. John the Divine—was read by Gloria's sister-in-law, the Reverend Rena Karefa-Smart. Odetta sang the congregation through the first moments, during which Berdis Baldwin's mournful moaning echoed through the cavernous church, with "Sometimes I Feel Like a Motherless Child," "Glory, Glory, Hallelujah," and "Let Us Break Bread Together." There were moving tributes from Maya Angelou and Toni Morrison, who spoke of Jimmy as a "brother" and as now an "ancestor." There was a jazz salute and then the main eulogy, a stirring speech by Amiri Baraka, who reminded the congregation of Baldwin's righteous anger and of the fact that "he lived his life as witness," that he was "God's black revolutionary mouth."

Perhaps the highlight of the service was Baldwin himself on tape singing "Precious Lord, take my hand, lead me on." This part of the service had been announced in the program, but, nevertheless, it startled the listeners. He seemed to be there, still witnessing, and people were moved.

The pallbearers led the family and the coffin to the great west doors, which opened to give the witness back to his city, and a caravan of cars took him through Harlem, through the world of his childhood, a world that had never been out of his thoughts, into the Bronx, and on to Ardsley-on-Hudson and Ferncliff Cemetery, where, in a quiet ceremony led by Canon Lloyd Casson from the cathedral, he was buried, not in a family plot, but close to Malcolm X and Paul Robeson, other witnesses.

One person stood out at both the funeral and the burial. He was not a family member, yet he seemed to be everywhere and somehow in charge. He had been with the family at the house during the days immediately before the funeral, he led them into the cathedral, he joined the Baldwin brothers as they carried the casket down the long cathedral steps, and appeared almost to stand guard over the grave as the friends and family filed past him after leaving their flowers on the lowered coffin. He wore the overalls of the SNCC freedom rider rather than dark mourning clothes. This was Jerome Smith, who had been dragged from the buses and beaten in Mississippi, who had become in the meeting with Robert Kennedy the embodiment of the prophecy of *The Fire Next Time*, who had stood by his friend as a guardian of the truth during the difficult days of *Blues for Mister Charlie*. No one knew the "price of the ticket" better than Jerome Smith, and nobody had a better right than he to be where he was now, as, in a sense, the first mourner. Berdis Baldwin was there, of course, and David and Gloria and all the brothers and sisters, and Bernard—the people who had nurtured him in childhood, supported him in his work, been with him through joy and depression, nursed him in sickness, and witnessed his passing over. But Jerome, in his "uniform" of the struggle, signified a changing of the guard. James Baldwin did not belong any longer to his close friends, to his lovers, or even to his family, but to the many thousands gone and to the many millions still struggling to be free. These had always been his people. Now, in death, he was to be theirs.

Notes

The sources for quotations are usually indicated in the text itself. Listed below are those sources and others for particular subjects treated in each chapter. Conversations with James Baldwin and David Baldwin can be considered additional sources for virtually all topics but have sometimes been mentioned specifically for emphasis. Many of Baldwin's letters are undated, but often dates can be deduced from the contents. When first names are placed in quotation marks, the last name is unknown or the first name is changed to protect privacy or the named person does not wish the last name to be known.

Chapter 1

3 James Baldwin's (JB) metaphorical use of his life: Horace A. Porter, *Stealing the Fire: The Art and Protest of James Baldwin* (Middletown, 1989), 24; *Notes of a Native Son*, 6; *Go Tell It on the Mountain*, 33.

4–8 The Reverend David Baldwin (stepfather) and family: *No Name in the Street*, 3–9; *Notes*, 87–92; *The Devil Finds Work*, 12–16; *The Fire Next Time*, 18.

8–11 Berdis Baldwin (BB)(mother): *No Name*, 3–6; undated JB letter to BB.

11–12 Harlem in the early days: "Fifth Avenue, Uptown" (in *Nobody Knows My Name*, esp. 55–57); unpublished interview with JB by Christian Bartillat; *The Price of the Ticket*, 560; "The Deathbed Conversion" (notes for "Fifth Avenue").

12 On Baldwin's interest in suicide: Henrietta Miller to Orilla Miller Winfield (OMW), and OMW interview with David Leeming (DL).

12–13 P.S. 24: JB introduction to *The Negro in New York*, by William J. Weatherby and Ottley Roi; Fern Maria Eckman, *The Furious Passage of James Baldwin* (New York, 1965), 43; *Notes*, 4.

Chapter 2

14–20 Orilla ("Bill") Miller (Winfield): *Devil*, 10–39; *Notes*, 91; letter from OMW to Shaun Henderson, 28 Jan. 1988; letter from OMW to JB, 15 May 1963; JB letters to OMW, 1955–86—most undated; DL conversations with Steve Winfield; tape of OMW's memorial service, Ojai, Calif., 1991.

Chapter 3

21–3 Junior high days, influence of Countee Cullen and Bill Porter: Eckman, 46ff.

23–5 Awakening sexuality and the church: *Fire*, 30ff.; "To Crush the Serpent," *Playboy*, Jan. 1987, 66–70; *Price*, 681–83.

26–9 High school days: *Fire*, 48; Karen Thorsen interview with Emile Capouya; DL conversation with Emile Capouya and interview with Leonard Nelson (Baldwin classmates).

Chapter 4

32–6 Beauford Delaney (BD): introduction to *Price*; DL interview with JB on BD, 1986; JB introduction to BD exhibition, Galerie Lambert, Paris, 1964, and in *Beauford Delaney: A Retrospective*, ed. Richard Long, catalogue for Studio Museum in Harlem exhibition of BD's works, 1978; DL conversations with BD, 1966–69; BD autobiographical notes; Henry Miller, "The Amazing and Invariable Beauford DeLaney [*sic*]," in Studio Museum catalogue.

Chapter 5

37–40 The early 1940s: Karen Thorsen interview with Emile Capouya, DL conversation with Capouya; "Notes of a Native Son," part 1; JB undated letters to Daniel Fink, Schomburg Collection.

40–2 Stepfather's death: "Notes of a Native Son."

43–5 The Greenwich Village years: introduction to *Price*; DL interviews with Katherine Shipley, Ruth Robinson Dean, Stan Weir, and Connie Williams; DL conversations with BD; letter from Jimmy Callahan to DL; Stan Weir, "Meetings with James Baldwin," *Against the Current* 18 (Jan.–Feb. 1989); JB journals and notes.

45–6 Sexual experience during Village years: "Freaks and the American Ideal of Manhood," *Playboy*, Jan. 1985 (in *Price* as "Here Be Dragons," esp. 685).

46 Eugene Worth: introduction to *Price*; William Weatherby, *James Baldwin: Artist on Fire* (New York, 1989), 61.

Marlon Brando: JB's notes for an essay on Brando.

47–9 JB's Village "preaching": DL interview with Claire Burch.

49 Early meeting with Richard Wright: *Nobody*, 152–53.

49–51 Early publishing: introduction to *Price*; first published work—on Gorki—*Nation*, 12 Apr. 1947; early review of Lockridge's *Raintree County*, *New Leader*, 10 Apr. 1948; first published essay, "The Harlem Ghetto," *Commentary*, Feb. 1948 (in *Notes*); first published fiction, "Previous Condition," *Commentary*, Oct. 1948 (in *Going to Meet the Man*); Eckman, 112.

51 Harlem and the Jew: *Notes*, 72.

51–2 DB's trip South and the Progressive Party: *Notes*, 73ff.

52–4 *Ignorant Armies* and the evolution of *Crying Holy: Paris Review* interview with Jordan Elgrably, 1984, in *Conversations with James Baldwin*, ed. Fred L. Standley and Louis H. Pratt (Jackson, 1989); Eckman, 110–11.

54 *Unto the Dying Lamb*: JB notes for project.

Chapter 6

56 Moving to Paris: *Price*, 640ff.; "Paris 1958" (unpublished draft).

56–62 The early Paris years: JB, "A Question of Identity" (in *Notes*), "The New

Lost Generation" (in *Price*), "Encounter on the Seine" (in *Notes*); DL conversations or interviews with Themistocles Hoetis, Mary Keen Blumenau, Otto Friedrich, Priscilla Boughton Friedrich, Tom Michaelis, Herbert Gold; Otto Friedrich, "Jimmy," in *The Grave of Alice B. Toklas* (New York, 1989); letter from Tom Maltais to DL; Tom Maltais, "Go Tell It at the Metro Bar" (unpublished); JB's unpublished journals; JB undated letter to BB, Jan. 1949.

62–6 The Wright-Baldwin relationship: JB, "Everybody's Protest Novel" (in *Notes*), "Many Thousands Gone" (in *Notes*), "Alas, Poor Richard" (in *Nobody*); DL conversation with Ellen and Julia Wright; *Conversations*, 202–4, 237.

66 The "blood relationship" between blacks and whites: *Notes*, 42.

The first London trip: JB undated letter to Mary Keen Blumenau, 1949.

Homosexuality and American sexuality: JB, "The Preservation of Innocence," *Zero*, Spring 1949; JB, review of *The Moth, New Leader* 31 (Aug. 1948): 12.

67 "Too Late, Too Late" review: *Commentary*, Jan. 1948.

68 JB and Gidske Anderson: letter from Anderson to Bosley Bratman (Wilder); JB journals; DL interview with Mary Keen Blumenau; letter from Anderson to Mary Keen Blumenau; DL conversations with JB.

JB's brooding: journals; "An American in Paris" (notes for later essays).

69–73 Paris, Dec. 1949, and the bed sheet incident: JB undated letter to BB, Dec. 1949; JB, "Equal in Paris" (in *Notes*).

73 JB's growing reputation: *Commentary*, Mar. 1950, 257.

On JB's disillusionment with Paris: *Price*, 311.

On the singing of "Lover Man": DL interview with Mary Keen Blumenau.

Chapter 7

74–7 Early JB–Lucien Happersberger (LH) relationship: DL interviews and conversations with the principals; DL interview with Mary Painter (MP).

77 JB-MP relationship: DL interviews and conversations with the principals; DL interview with LH.

Johnnie O'Hara poem: in *Janus* 5 (Autumn 1951): 30.

80–2 JB and his family: *Nobody*, 88; JB letter to Wilmer ("Lover") Baldwin, 31 July 1952; JB undated letters to DB, Apr. 53, 13 May 1953.

Chapter 8

84 JB's theories of fiction: *Notes*, 20, 35–36.

84–5 *Mountain* as JB's *Portrait of the Artist* . . .: Porter, 99.

88–9 The "Baldwin Hero": Eleanor Traylor, "I Hear Music in the Air," in *James Baldwin: The Legacy*, ed. Quincy Troupe (New York, 1989), 96.

89 JB on *Mountain*: unpublished notes for the Franklin Library.

Chapter 9

90 JB in Paris, 1953: letter from a friend to Mary Keen; DL conversations and interviews with Themistocles Hoetis, Mary Keen Blumenau, LH, MP,

Bernard Hassell (BH), BD, Richard Gibson, Mrs. Chester Himes, Herb Gentry.

91–2 JB's dream: JB journal, 31 Aug.–1 Sept.; DL conversation with JB.

92–3 BD in Paris: DL conversations or interviews with BD, JB, BH, MP, Richard Olney, LH, Richard Gibson, Herb Gentry; BD's autobiographical notes; JB introduction to 1964 BD exhibition in Paris (Harlem Studio catalogue).

94–5 BD letters to JB: Aug. 1954, Sept. 1954, 22 Oct. 1954.

95–6 JB in Grasse: JB undated letter to BB, c. Dec. 1953.

96 "A Question of Identity," *Partisan Review*, July–Aug. 1954.

Chapter 10

98 JB's 1954 revisit to Mother Horn's church: Karen Thorsen interview with Bill Cole; DL conversation with Bill Cole.

98–9 JB on Gide: "The Male Prison" (in *Nobody*, esp. 132); Eckman, 135.

100–1 JB on writing about "being a Negro": *Notes*, 8.

101 Examples of JB's distancing himself from subject: *Notes*, 27, 64.

Langston Hughes on *Notes: New York Times Book Review*, 28 Feb. 1956.

102 JB's goal in *Notes: Notes*, 9.

JB on Ralph Ellison: *Notes*, 8.

103 JB on American sexuality and the black man: *Notes*, 53.

JB on the bond between blacks and whites: *Notes*, 123.

104 Henry James influence: quotes in *Notes*, 128–29.

104–5 JB on white "civilization" and the black man: *Notes*, 174.

105 Review of *Notes: Commonweal*, 13 Jan. 1956.

Chapter 11

106–7 Owen Dodson and *The Amen Corner*: DL conversation with Owen Dodson (1965); DL interview with Richard Long; DL conversation with James Hatch (Dodson biographer); JB 1984 introduction to new edition of *Notes*.

108 Dilemma of the black woman: JB introduction to *Amen*, xvi.

108–9 Leaving the U.S.: *Amen* introduction, xiii; JB undated letter to BB, 1956.

110 JB on E. Franklin Frazier and Sterling Brown: notes for 1984 introduction to *Notes*, and the introduction itself.

112–13 JB on his despair, hopes, and reasons for returning to Paris, 1955: undated JB letters to DB, summer and Sept. 1955.

Chapter 12

114 Arnold and JB: DL interviews with MP and LH.

115–16 JB's financial and emotional problems, Nov. 1955: JB undated letters to DB and BB, c. Nov. 1955.

116–17 JB's writing plans: JB undated letter to Bill Cole, spring 1956.

117 "The Crusade of Indignation": *Nation*, 7 July 1957 (in *Price*).

JB on *Uncle Tom's Cabin: Price*, 156.

JB on racism and self-identity: *Price*, 157.

117–18 "Faulkner and Desegregation": *Partisan Review*, Winter 1956 (in *Nobody*), as answer to Faulkner remarks in interview in *Reporter*, Mar. 1956.

119 JB's 1956 loss of direction: in "The Black Boy Looks at the White Boy," *Esquire*, May 1961 (in *Nobody*, esp. 175–77).

119–20 JB's suicide attempt: DL interview with MP; DL conversation with JB.

120–1 Paris conference: "Princes and Powers" (in *Nobody*).

Chapter 13

122 JB on connection between characters in various novels: interview by Bartillat, 1974.

125 JB on *Giovanni: Paris Review* interview; Bartillat interview; DL interviews and conversations with JB.

JB on love: DL conversations with JB.

127 JB to Bill Cole on *Giovanni*: Karen Thorsen interview with Cole.

JB on "private life" and "American conduct": *No Name*, 54–55.

JB's longing for relationship: Bartillat interview.

127–8 Specific sources for characters, places, situations in *Giovanni*: DL conversations with JB.

Chapter 14

130–2 JB and Arnold in Corsica: unpublished draft, *The Last Days*; DL conversations with JB.

132–3 JB on work on *Another Country*: JB undated letter to BB, c. Jan. 1957.

133–4 The missing portrait of JB by BD: DL conversations with Jim Hatch, JB, BD, DB.

Chapter 15

135 "Sonny's Blues," *Partisan Review*, Summer 1957 (in *Going*).

135–6 JB sounding like Sonny: *No Name*, 51.

136–7 JB's social life on return to U.S.: DL conversations with Lonie Levister, Gloria Jones; Karen Thorsen interview with William Styron.

137 JB letter to John Williams: draft form, undated.

JB at Dial function: DL interview with James Silberman.

137–8 Information on JB's trip South: DL conversations with JB; JB's notes on trip; *No Name*; "The Hard Kind of Courage," *Harper's*, Oct. 1958 (in *Nobody* as "A Fly in Buttermilk"); "Nobody Knows My Name," *Partisan Review*, Winter 1958 (in *Nobody*).

138 JB and Kenneth Clark: Weatherby, 140; Karen Thorsen interview with Clark.

138–9 JB and Sterling Brown: *Nobody*, 75–76, 88; JB notes on trip South.

139–40 JB on Dorothy Counts: *No Name*, 50.

140 JB on Julian Sheers: JB notes on trip South.

140 JB and the principal: *Nobody*, 84.

141 JB over Georgia: *Nobody*, 87.

140–2 JB on myths of sexuality in South: *No Name*, 61; *Nobody*, 93–94.

142–3 JB and Martin Luther King: "The Dangerous Road before Martin Luther King," *Harper's*, Feb. 1961 (in *Price*); quotes from *Price*, 246–50; JB notes on interviews with King.

143–6 JB and Montgomery and Little Rock: *No Name*, 60ff.

146 America's need of self-examination: *Nobody*, 99.

Tuskegee: JB undated letter to DB, c. fall 1957.

147 JB on commitment: *No Name*, 57–59.

Chapter 16

148 JB, Engin Cezzar (EC), and *Giovanni*: DL interviews and conversations with the principals.

JB on Horatio Street: JB to DB, 14 Dec. 1957.

149 Sources for "Come Out the Wilderness": DL conversation with JB.

150 JB's dreams at MacDowell Colony: JB journals; DL conversations with JB.

150–1 JB on EC's performance: Weatherby, 144.

151 JB in New York in 1957: DL interviews with Lonie Levister and EC.

151–2 JB quote on French vs. American problems: JB undated letter to Gallimard editor.

152 JB and Paris, 1958: JB to DB, 23 July 1958; "Paris 1958."

"The Discovery of What It Means to Be an American": *New York Times Book Review*, 25 Jan. 1959 (in *Nobody*).

153 "This Morning, This Evening . . .": *Atlantic Monthly*, Sept. 1960 (in *Going*).

155 JB on *J.B.* and Kazan: Weatherby, 147.

JB and Tennessee Williams: DL conversations with JB and Williams (1966).

155–6 Poitier article: *Look*, 28 July 1968, and see Weatherby, 150–51.

Chapter 17

157–60 JB and Langston Hughes: Clayton Riley interview with JB, 14 Feb. 1986; letters from LH to JB, 8 Mar. 1948, 7 Mar. 1953 (on "Everybody's Protest Novel," in *Perspectives USA* 2 [Winter 1953]), 25 July 1953; JB letter to LH, 25 Mar. 1953—many of the letters are at Yale; see Chapter 10 for Hughes on *Notes*; "The Negro in American Culture" symposium, *Cross Currents*, Summer 1961, and in *The New Negro*, ed. Mathew H. Ahmann (Notre Dame, Ind., 1961); Hughes telegram to JB on opening night, 15 Apr. 1965; JB's note on Hughes's death, undated draft to Rose Hayes.

160 The Horatio Street scene: DL conversations and interviews with JB, MP, Sam Floyd, EC, Lonie Levister, Lowell Todd; Weatherby, 152ff.; Dan Wakefield, "James Baldwin: Mentor and Friend," *GQ*, Aug. 1968, 217.

161 The bar fight: DL interview with EC; JB letter to "Tom," Apr. 1959.

161–2 JB review of *The Cool World*: 21 June 1959; JB undated letter to Miller's agent, 1959.

162 JB's plans from Fire Island: JB letter to DB, 6 May 1959.

163 "Mass Culture and the Creative Artist": reprinted in *Daedalus* 89 (Spring 1960).

JB from Paris, 1959: JB letter to DB, 21 Aug. 1959.

163–4 "On Catfish Row": *Commentary*, Sept. 1959 (in *Price*); JB letter to DB, 21 Aug. 1959; *Price*, 181.

164–5 JB on friend's breakdown: JB letter to DB, 22 Sept. 1959.

165–6 JB on Ingmar Bergman: "The Precarious Vogue of Ingmar Bergman," *Esquire*, Apr. 1960 (in *Nobody* as "The Northern Protestant").

166 JB's hypothetical film: *Nobody*, 144–45.

166–7 Progress on *Country*: JB letter to DB, 3 Oct. 1959.

167 Life in Paris, 1959: DL conversations with James Jones (1966), Gloria Jones, JB, BH, BD.

The affair with the horseman: DL interviews with MP and LH.

168 JB's despair over LH: JB letters to DB, 3 Oct. 1959, 17 Dec. 1959, 27 Dec. 1959, c. Jan. 1960 (undated).

"Fifth Avenue, Uptown": *Esquire*, July 1960 (in *Nobody*).

JB quoted on effects of racism: *Nobody*, 66.

169 King article: "The Dangerous Road before Martin Luther King" (in *Price*).

Cordier on JB's Thanksgiving party: Eckman, 150–51.

169–71 "This Morning . . ." quotes: *Going*, 170–75.

171 JB on Horatio St. apartment: JB letter to DB, Jan. 1960.

Chapter 18

173–4 JB and Kay Boyle (KB): DL conversations and interviews with the principals; letters from KB to JB, 25 Apr. 1960, 8 Aug. 1969; "Words of a Native Son," radio broadcast, 23 Feb. 1963 (in *Playboy*, Dec. 1964). I am indebted to Charles Blocksen of the Charles Blocksen Collection at Temple University for supplying many items of the JB-KB correspondence.

174 "They Can't Turn Back": *Mademoiselle*, Aug. 1960 (in *Price*).

JB on "Colored Men" sign: journal.

174–5 Tallahassee airport: *Price*, 215.

175–6 JB on sexuality and racism: journal.

176 The students at Tallahassee: *Price*, 227; JB to DB, 25 May 1960.

JB's speech in Tallahassee: journal.

176–7 JB's 1960 interview with King: *Price*, 253.

178 JB and William Belli: DL interview and conversations with the principals.

179 JB on writer's problem: *Nobody*, 125.

179–80 JB and Stan Weir: DL conversations with Weir; Weir, "Meetings."

180 JB and Pelatowskis: DL conversations with Marjorie Pelatowski and Pelatowski friend, Robert Friedman.

JB's reactions to wives of friends: DL interviews with Lonie Levister and William Belli.

180–82 JB and Richard Wright: "The Exile," *Preuves* and *Encounter*, 1961 (in *Nobody*); "The Survival of Richard Wright," *Reporter*, Mar. 1961 (in *Nobody*); *Nobody* quotes, 148–60, 170.

Chapter 19

183 Beat funeral: DL conversation with DB.

183–4 JB and Norman Mailer: DL conversations with JB; Weatherby, 195, 211–12; JB fight article, *Nugget*, Feb. 1963; "The Black Boy Looks at the White Boy," *Esquire*, May 1961 (in *Nobody*); JB on Mailer's contribution, *Nobody*, 190.

184–5 JB and William Styron: Karen Thorsen interview with Styron; Eckman, 161.

185–6 *Nobody Knows My Name*: introduction on facing identity, 11–13.

186 Review of *Nobody: Reporter*, 17 Aug. 1961.

187 "The Angriest Young Man": *Ebony*, Oct. 1961 (JB quote on America as free-world leader, 24).

Terkel interview: *WFMT Perspective*, Dec. 1961.

188 Malcolm and JB radio discussion: 23 Apr. 1961.

188–9 JB and Elijah Muhammad: *Fire*, 71–92.

190 Algren and JB on *Raisin*: DL interview with Marc Crawford.

Airport incident: DL interview with Marc Crawford; *Fire*, 69.

190–1 JB in Paris, 1961: JB letter to DB, 5 Sept. 1961; DL interviews with BH, LH, Belli, Crawford.

191 Paula in Paris: Eckman, 162.

192 BD's trip to Greece: DL conversations with BD (1966–69), letter from Charley Boggs to JB on BD's description of events.

192–3 Israel: "Letters from a Journey," esp. 49–50.

195 JB on Paula in Paris: JB letter to DB, Nov. 1961.

JB on *Country*: JB letter to Mary Painter, Dec. 1961.

"The New Lost Generation": July 1961.

"They Will Wait No More": *Negro Digest*, July 1961.

JB's sense of unease: JB undated letter to DB, c. Dec. 1961.

197 Color as prison: "Letters from a Journey," 52.

JB on black press: JB letter to Bob Mills, Jan. 1961.

198 JB and Katherine Anne Porter: *Letters of KAP*, ed. Isabel Bayley (New York, 1990).

199 JB and Michael Joseph: DL interview and conversations with Raleigh Trevelyan, Susan Watt.

"The Creative Process": in *Creative America*, the National Cultural Center (New York, 1962), and *Saturday Review*, 8 Feb. 1964, 14–15, 58 (in *Price*); *Price*, 315–18.

Chapter 20

200 On *Country*: letter from James Meyers to JB, 29 Feb. 1968; JB response, 10 Mar. 1968.

200–1 JB on love: *Nobody*, 113.

201 JB on his characters: interview with Charles Childs.

JB on *Country: Paris Review* interview in *Conversations*, 243–44; *Price*, 397–401.

Effect of racism on whites: *Nobody*, 114.

204–5 JB on truth and innocence: JB letter to Meyers.

205 The Small's party: DL interview with James Silberman.

205–6 Reviews of *Country: New York Times*, 26 July 1962; *Mid-Century*, Sept. 1962; *New Leader*, 25 June 1962; *New York Times Book Review*, 2 Dec. 1962 (also includes JB's comment on reviews).

CHAPTER 21

207–11 Trip to Africa: DL conversations with JB and Gloria Karefa-Smart (1963–66); JB's notes on trip.

207 JB on being American in Africa: Eckman, 166–67; JB notes.

207–8 JB affected by trip: Eckman, 167.

208–9 Africa and color: Eckman, 167.

209 USIS incident: JB notes.

210 JB on Frank Karefa-Smart: JB notes.

JB in Sierra Leone parliament: JB notes.

JB on "the children": JB notes.

211 JB on writing "Down at the Cross": JB letter to Mary Painter, Dec. 1961.

JB on being of African descent in this world: JB letter to "Dan," Dec. 1961.

"Letter from a Region . . .": *New Yorker*, 17 Nov. 1962, 59–144 (*Fire*).

211–13 "Letter to My Nephew . . .": *Progressive*, Dec. 1962, 19–20 (*Fire*).

The publication of *Fire*: Dial, 1963; DL interview with James Silberman.

214–15 Reviews of *Fire: Guardian*, 17 July 1963; *Observer*, 14 July 1963.

CHAPTER 22

216–21 The 1963 trip South: Eckman 172–73; DL conversations with JB, DB, Sam Floyd.

217 JB on Meredith: *Life*, 24 May 1963, 86A.

217–18 JB and Medgar Evers: Eckman, 173.

218–19 JB's Southern tour speeches: *Life*, 24 May 1963, 81ff.

219–21 King, JB on civil rights, history, change: *Time*, 17 May 63, 22–23.

221–2 Connie Williams's party: DL interview with Connie Williams; Weir, "Meetings . . . ," 38.

222 JB at Wesleyan: DL interview with KB.

222–5 JB and Robert Kennedy: see earlier biographies (Eckman; Weatherby; and James Campbell, *Talking at the Gates: A Life of James Baldwin* [London, 1991)]; DL conversations with JB; JB notes on meeting for *No Name* and for unpublished *Remember This House*. For RFK view see Edwin O. Guthman and Jeffrey Shulman, *Robert Kennedy: In His Own Words* (New York, 1988).

224–5 JB on Lorraine Hansberry: JB notes.

225 Kenneth Clark on RFK meeting: JB interview with Robert Spivak, *New York Herald Tribune*, 2 June 1963.

JB to M. S. Handler on despair: *New York Times*, 3 June 1963.

225 JB and Clark interview: "A Conversation with James Baldwin," *Freedomways* 3 (Summer 1963): 361–68 (in *Conversations*, 38ff.).

225–6 FBI file on JB: no. 100-146553; quoted segment, 29 Mar. 1966.

226–7 Avedon on *Nothing Personal*: Eckman, 200.

227 Paula on family week in Puerto Rico: Eckman, 201.

228–9 JB trip to Selma: DL conversations with JB and DB.

CHAPTER 23

231–5 The *Blues for Mister Charlie* days: DL interviews and conversations with JB, DB, LH, Diana Sands (1966), Al Freeman, Jr. (1965).

233 Speech: "The White Problem," in *100 Years of Emancipation*, ed. R. A. Goldwin (Chicago, 1964), 80–88.

234 JB on Evers and *Blues*: introduction to *Blues*, xv.

234–5 JB on audience and *Blues*: *Life*, 24 May 1963, 90; *Conversations*, 165.

235 "Plaguetown, U.S.A.": *Blues* introduction, xv.

233, 235 "The Uses of the Blues": *Playboy*, Jan. 1964, 131–32, 240–41.

235–6 "The Blues People": Eckman, 228.

238 "Blues for Mr. Baldwin": William Glover interview, *Newark Evening News*, 26 Apr. 1964.

Review of *Blues*: Taubman, *New York Times*, 24 Apr. 1964.

240 JB in Elsinore: JB postcard to DB, 27 June 1964.

241 "A Report from Occupied Territory": *Nation*, 11 July 1966.

242 JB on BD: Harlem Studio Museum catalogue.

CHAPTER 24

243–4 JB on passing of Lorraine Hansberry and his recovery from illness: JB letter to DB, 29 Jan. 1965.

244–5 Buckley debate: version published as "The American Dream and the American Negro" in *Price*.

245 JB on radio program with Malcolm: *No Name*, 95.

245–6 JB on Malcolm murder: *No Name*, 118.

246 Hentoff *Times* interview: 11 Apr. 1965.

248 Reviews of Silvera *Amen: New York Times* and *New York Herald Tribune*, 16 Apr. 1965.

249 JB on Sheriff Clark: *Price*, 405.

251 JB on trusting Lucien: JB letters to DL, June 1965 and July 1965.

JB on State Department: JB letter to DL, July 1965.

JB on being a "gifted man": JB letter to DB, July 1965.

JB on Lucien and film company: JB letters to DL, 31 Aug. 1965 and 15 Sept. 1965.

CHAPTER 25

253–5 JB and Henry James: *Price*, 414; letter from Michael James to DL, 6 Oct.

1965; DL interview with JB on James in *Henry James Review* 8 (Fall 1986): 47–56.

256 JB on Vietnam: *Conversations*, 61.

257 JB on Black Power: *Conversations*, 60.

JB on *Blues* film and Lucien relationship: JB letters to DL, 27 Dec. 1965, 2 Jan. 1966, 25 Jan. 1966.

258–9 JB on relationship with DL: JB letter to DL, 2 Jan. 1966.

259 JB and *his* journey: JB letter to DL, 25 Jan. 1966.

260–2 JB and Joseph Losey: Letters from Losey to JB, 13 June 1966, 13 Mar. 1967.

262 Arriving in Istanbul: JB undated letter to DB, c. Mar. 1966.

Chapter 26

263 JB on Istanbul: *Conversations*, 59; unpublished interview by Ann Bruno.

264 JB and Kay Boyle: JB letters to Kay Boyle, 3 Apr. 1966, 12 May 1966.

268–9 JB and black ideology: JB letter to DB, 31 May 1966.

269 "Mama's white ladies": JB letter to DL, 10 June 1966.

JB's self-examination: JB letter to DL, 10 June 1966.

273 Henry Miller on BD: "The Amazing and Invariable Beauford DeLaney [*sic*]."

273–4 JB and anti-Semitism: JB letter to Fleischman, 12 July 1966, JB open letter to *Liberator*, *Freedomways* 7 (Winter 1967), 75–77; "Negroes Are Anti-Semitic Because They're Anti-White," *New York Times*, 9 Apr. 67 (in *Price*); interview by Budd Schulberg, "Dialog in Black and White," *Playboy*, Dec. 1966 (in *Conversations*).

276 JB on his life-style and paranoia: JB undated letter to DL, Dec. 1966.

277 War Crimes Tribunal: JB letter to Bertrand Russell, 9 Jan. 1967; JB letter to Readers' Forum, *Freedomways* 7 (Summer 1967): 242–44.

Completion of *Train*: JB letter to Gloria, May 1967.

Chapter 27

278 JB on *Train: Los Angeles Times West Magazine*, 7 July 1968, 20.

282–3 Reviews of *Train*: Hall, *New Statesman*, 28 June 1968, esp. 871; Thompson, *Commentary*, 20 May 1968, esp. 80.

Chapter 28

284 JB's love for DB: JB letter to DB, 28 May 1967.

286–7 JB on "Jean": unpublished journals.

287 "Pierre" incident: unpublished diary.

288 JB deciding to do the Malcolm film: *No Name*, 97.

288–9 JB in London, 1968: DL interview with Belli; DL conversations with DB; DL interview with Horace Ove; JB letter to DL, 28 Dec. 1967.

289–90 JB and Stokely Carmichael: "Black Power: James Baldwin in Defence of Stokely Carmichael," *Guardian*, 14 Feb. 1968.

290 JB and Tony Maynard: *No Name*, 100ff.

290–1 JB in Hollywood: DL interviews with Brock Peters, David Moses; *No Name*; JB letter to DB, 26 Feb. 1968.

291 JB meeting with Panthers: *No Name*, 170ff; DL conversations with Connie Williams.

JB on Cleaver: *No Name*, 171; *Conversations*, 251–52.

292–3 JB on Huey Newton: *No Name*, 173; JB letters to KB, 29 June 1969, 22 July 1969; DL interview and conversations with Cecil Brown.

JB on Bobby Seale: JB letter to DB, 22 Sept. 1968. See also "Stagolee," Foreword to Seale's *A Lonely Rage*.

293–4 Panther shooting incident: DL interview with David Moses; DL conversation with Marvin Worth.

294 JB's public vs. private life: JB letter to DB, 25 Sept. 1967.

294–5 King and JB in Los Angeles: tape of 16 Mar. 1968 meeting courtesy of James Cone; *No Name*, 133ff.

295 JB and Malcolm vs. George Schuyler: 23 Apr. 1961.

295–6 JB and Malcolm: James Cone, *Martin and Malcolm and America* (New York, 1991), 117; Kenneth Clark, *King, Malcolm, and Baldwin*, 61.

296 Congressional hearing: H.R. 12962, vol. 91, 40–46.

JB in program with World Council of Churches: JB letter to DB, 10 Mar. 68.

297 JB on screenplay: JB letter to DB, 10 Mar. 1968.

297–8 Death of King: *No Name*, 140, 151ff.; JB letter to EC, 12 Apr. 1968.

298 The suit and Arthur Moore: *No Name*, 11ff., 151ff.

298–9 JB on Malcolm script: JB letter to "Mr. Leonard," 24 Apr. 1968; *Conversations*, 167, 88; "I Can't Blow This Gig," *Cinema* 4 (Summer 1968), 3; *Devil*, 99–103.

299 JB on riots and "looting": "How Can We Get the Black People to Cool It?" *Esquire*, July 1968, 49ff.

300 JB's agreement with Black Christopher: *Chicago Daily News*, 6 July 1968, 8.

JB's impatience with Americans and Christianity: "A Letter to Americans," *Freedomways* 8 (Spring 1968), 112–16; *Afro-America*, 16 July 1968.

World Council of Churches speech: "White Racism or World Community" (in *Price*, 435–42).

JB's hypothetical course: *Book World*, 14 July 1968, 2.

300–1 JB's frustration with Hollywood: DL interviews with Brock Peters, David Moses, Sedat Pakay.

301 Suicide attempt: DL conversations with DB, JB, David Moses.

Emotional cost of Hollywood experience: "The Price May Be Too High," *New York Times*, 2 Feb. 1969; JB letter to "Peter," 7 Mar. 1969.

Chapter 29

303 *Brother Joe*: JB letter to DB, 7 Dec. 1969.

303–4 JB on antagonism of militants: JB letter to DB, 17 Nov. 1969.

304 JB's self-analysis: JB letter to DB, 27 July 1969.

305 JB on "Jean": JB letter to DB, 29 Oct. 1969.

JB and fame: JB letter to DB, 11 Sept. 1969.

305–6 JB and Zeynep Oral: DL interviews with Oral and EC.

307 Adelsen on JB: *Ebony*, Mar. 1970.

308 "Sir James" Baldwin: JB letter to DB, 18 Dec. 1969.

JB "unsuitable": *Newsweek*, 1 Dec. 1969.

On Viet Cong: Interview with Karen Wald, *Nickel Review*, Feb. 1970, 5.

309 JB and Maya Angelou: JB letter to DB, 17 Feb. 1970.

JB's "call" to action: JB letter to DB, 10 Mar. 1970.

JB's new "Pledge of Allegiance": JB letter to David Moses, 10 Mar. 1970.

Pakay film: *James Baldwin from Another Place.*

310 *A Rap on Race*: Lippincott, 1971.

No Name: letter from Raleigh Trevelyan to JB, 18 Aug. 1970.

JB on *A Rap on Race*: JB letter to DB, 7 Dec. 1970.

JB against Zionism: *Rap*, 209.

310–11 Review of *Rap*: Broyard in *New York Times*, 21 May 1971.

311 JB's anger on treatment of Panthers: "James Baldwin Talks to Michael Dean," 9 Sept. 1970.

JB on George Jackson killing: *New York Times*, 25 Aug. 1971.

JB and Angela Davis: "Dear Sister" letter, *Guardian*, 27 Dec. 1970, and *New York Review of Books*, 7 Jan. 1971.

312 Moving to Saint-Paul-de-Vence: JB letter to DB, 7 Dec. 1970.

314 Interviews in early seventies: *Conversations*, 98–141.

314–15 Delbanco incident: *Running in Place*, 160ff.

315 Tria French on "secretary": letter from French to DB, 1 May 1972.

Saint-Paul in the seventies: DL interview and conversations with Cecil Brown, Nidra Pollier, BH, Mary Carter.

316 Reviews of *No Name*: Watkins in *Times*, 28 May 1972; *Nation*, 10 Apr. 1972; *Saturday Review*, 27 May 1972.

JB's reactions: JB letters to DB, 16 June 1972, 24 June 1972.

317 JB and LH argument, 1973: DL conversations with JB, LH, Bernard Hassell; JB letter to DB, 29 Mar. 1973.

Losey on *If Beale Street Could Talk*: letter from Losey to JB, 21 Jan. 1975.

317–18 BD in hospital: DL interview with BH.

318 Darthea Speyer on JB and BD: letter from Speyer to JB, 26 May 1973.

319 JB on Cleaver: JB letter to DB, 1 June 1973.

JB on Ray Charles: *New York Times*, 30 June 1973.

320 JB and prisons: JB letter to David Moses, 24 July 1973.

JB on Toni Morrison: JB letter to DB, 19 July 1973.

320–21 JB, Gates, Josephine Baker: *Conversations*, 260ff.

321 JB finishes *Beale Street*: JB letter to DB, 12 Oct. 1973.

322 Settling affairs and JB's "happiness": JB letter to DB, 9 Nov. 1973.

Chapter 30

323 "House of Bondage": *Nation*, 1 Nov. 1980 (in *Price*, esp. 672–73).

324–5 JB on Wright in *Notes*: *Notes*, 35–36.

326 Reviews of *Beale Street*: Davis in *New York Age*, 25 May 1974; Windham in *Amsterdam News*, 25 May 1974; Duffy in *Time*, 10 June 1974; McCluskey in *Black World*, Dec. 1974; Oates in *New York Times Book Review*, 1ff.

326–7 JB on safety and mission: JB to DB, May 1974.

327 *Washington Post* interview: 21 July 1974.

328 Mikell's: interviews with Pat Mikell, DB, Dick Fontaine.

328–9 JB and Maynard: JB letter to Jay Acton, 7 Mar. 1975, and JB letter to DB, 22 Aug. 1975.

329 *Penthouse* interviewer: quoted in *Amsterdam News*, 3 Aug. 1975.

Chapter 31

330 JB's work plans, 1975: JB letter to DB, 8 Mar. 1975.

Little Man: JB letter to DB, 20 Apr. 1975; *Book News from Michael Joseph*.

331–2 Beauford: JB letter to DB, 20 Apr. 1975; DL interview with JB, 1986; JB letter to DB, 22 Aug. 1975.

332 Nephew Daniel: JB letter to DB, 22 Aug. 1975, 28 Aug. 1975; "Intercepted Memo: Classified," JB undated letter to DB, Aug. 75.

332–3 *Devil*: see esp. 16, 124, 50, 61, 62, 103.

333 Reviews of *Devil*: *Times*, 15 June 1976; *Tribune*, 29 July 1976; *Freedomways* (Summer 1976), esp. 103, 108.

333–4 JB on *Devil*: *Tribune*, 29 July 1976.

334 Angelou interview: "Conversation with a Native Son," PBS, 1975.

JB on writing *Just Above My Head*: JB letter to DB, 3 Oct. 1975.

Belafonte, Montand discussion: JB letter to DB, 3 Oct. 1975.

JB on being in his fifties: JB letter to DB, 3 Oct. 1975.

335 Oct. 1975 symposium: proceedings published by Fortress Press (Philadelphia, 1976); JB talk, 231–40 (esp. 232, 238, 239).

JB on *Roots*: *New York Times Book Review*, 26 Sept. 1976.

JB visit to Riker's Island: *Conversations*, 159–167.

336 JB and friend and life in Saint-Paul: DL interviews and conversations with Valerie Sardello, BH, Philippe Bebon, LH, Calua Dundy; JB letter to Dundy, 30 Mar. 1977.

336–7 "An Open Letter to Mr. [Jimmy] Carter": *New York Times*, 23 Jan. 1977.

337 JB, Spender, Soyinka: Troupe, 47, 17.

Coles interview: *New York Times Book Review*, 31 July 1977, 1, 20–22.

JB to DL on *Head*: 1 Apr. 1977.

338 JB journal entries: 23 Dec. 1977, 10 Feb. 1978.

Writer as "disturber of the peace": *Conversations*, 171.

339–41 Bowling Green: DL interviews and conversations with Ernest Champion, Robert Perry, Robert Early, LaRuth Perry, and several students of JB; JB, "Dark Days," *Esquire*, Oct. 1980; Catherine McLaughlin, "Jimmy: A Memoir," unpublished.

341–3 JB in Berkeley: Claire Burch documentary; DL interviews and conversations with Claire Burch, Cecil Brown, Ishmael Reed, David Major, Barbara Christian, KB; Walter Blum, "The Lion in Berkeley," *San Francisco Examiner*, 10 June 1979; JB, "On Language . . . ," in part in *Los Angeles Times*, op ed, 29 Apr. 1979.

343 JB on black English: *Los Angeles Times* piece above; "If Black English Isn't a Language . . . ," *New York Times*, 29 July 1979 (in *Price*).

343–4 Angelou "picnic": Karen Thorsen interview with Maya Angelou.

344 "Open Letter to the Born Again": *Nation*, 29 Sept. 1979, 263–64.

Black music piece: "Of the Sorrow Songs: The Cross of Redemption," *Edinburgh Review* 47 (Aug. 1979).

Chapter 32

345 Genesis of *Head*: DL conversations with JB and DB; *Head*, 18, 595; JB letter to David Moses, 6 Jan. 1979.

347 JB on artist as lover: *Conversations*, 155, 162.

Arthur and JB and Paris: *Head*, 468.

348 The "shared" black "experience": *Head*, 596–97; *Notes*, 35.

348–9 Connection between *Head* and earlier works: *Conversations*, 141, 205; JB letter to DB, 3 Oct. 1975.

349 Traylor essay: Troupe, 95–106 (esp. 95–97).

Sonny's brother quote: *Going*, 139.

350 JB on Arthur: *Conversations*, 191.

Reviews of *Head*: *New Yorker*, Dec. 1979, 218–21; *Voice*, 28 Oct. 1979, 38, 39; *Times*, 23 Sept. 1979, 3.

Chapter 33

353 *I Heard It Through the Grapevine*: DL interview with Dick Fontaine; DL conversations with JB and DB.

353–4 JB and Achebe: DL conversation with Achebe; DL interviews with Champion and Fontaine; Achebe in Troupe, 215; JB-Achebe conference dialogue in *Conversations*, 210–21.

354–5 JB and the "new South": *Atlanta Journal*, 22 Apr. 1980 (in *Conversations*).

355 JB pessimism: "Dark Days," *Esquire*, Oct. 1980; "House of Bondage," *Nation*, 1 Nov. 1980 (both in *Price*, esp. 675).

JB on language: *Conversations*, 231.

JB in Saint-Paul 1980s: DL interviews with MP, LH, BH, DB, Valerie Sardello, anonymous "friend" of JB, Ann Beattie, and Florence Ladd.

356 Genesis of *The Welcome Table (Investments)*: JB letter to DB, 17 July 1980; JB letter to David Moses, 27 Sept. 1981.

JB's plans: JB letter to Anthea Michael Joseph, 27 Oct. 1980.

357 Genesis of *The Evidence of Things Not Seen*: Walter Lowe in *Emerge* 1 (Oct. 1989): 54–63.

Evidence work: DL discussion with JB during writing; DL interview with Richard Long.

358 Turkish trip: DL interview with EC and conversations with JB and DB.

358 *Sacrifice (Swordfish)*: DL discussion with JB.

359 "A Letter to Prisoners": *Inside/Out* 3 (Summer 1982): 1.

"This Far and No Further": *Time Capsule* 7 (Summer/Fall 1983): 8.

Genesis of *Jimmy's Blues*: JB letter to DB, c. 29 Aug. 1975.

360 Staggerlee: JB letter to DB, 5 Oct. 1982; DL interview with Cecil Brown.

360–1 Berlin incident: DL interview with Cecil Brown.

361–3 *Evidence* quotes: 142, 26, 122, 101–2.

363–4 JB, safety and daring: *Evidence*, 125; *Fire*, 119.

364–6 Amherst: conversations with JB; DL visits to JB at Amherst; DL conversations with DB, Cynthia Packard, Catherine McLaughlin, Bosley Bratman Wilder, several students; Lester interview, *New York Times*, 27 May 1984 (in *Conversations*); Karen Thorsen interviews with Michael Thelwell and Alexa Birdsong.

366 N.Y. Public Library party: DL interview with Marc Crawford.

367 JB on L.A. shootings, 1985: *Los Angeles Times*, 25 Feb. 1985.

JB as witness: *Conversations*, 236.

JB and politics: DL conversations with JB, 1983–86.

New introduction to *Notes*: Beacon, 1984.

"On Being White . . .": *Essence*, Apr. 1984.

Letter to Tutu: *New Statesman*, 23 Aug. 1985, 8.

368 JB on *Mountain* movie: *New York Times*, 10 Jan. 1985.

JB sickness, late eighties: DL interviews and conversations with Lonie Levister, DB, and BH.

369 "To Crush the Serpent": *Playboy*, June 1987, 66ff.

On Saint-Paul house: *Architectural Digest*, Aug. 1987.

369–70 Russian trip: DL conversations with JB, DB, and Yasar Kemal; JB notes on trip.

371 *Amen* in London: DL conversation with Anton Phillips.

Chapter 34

372–3 JB illness: DL interviews with BH and DB.

373–4 *Welcome Table* development: DL interview with Walter Dallas and conversations with JB and DB; JB letter to "Lon," 20 Jan. 1985; JB in *Philadelphia Inquirer*, 2 Dec. 1986, 6E; Campbell, 273; JB letter to DB, July 1980.

378 "Here Be Dragons" quote: *Price*, 690.

379 Troupe interview: Troupe, 19–26, 186–212.

379–86 Last days: DL interviews with DB, BH, and LH; Pat Mikell piece in Troupe.

386 DB's "walk": DL interviews and conversations with DB and Sophie.

Poem to DB: *Jimmy's Blues*, 35.

Chronological Bibliography of Printed Works by James Baldwin

Compiled by David Leeming
and Lisa Gitelman

The titles of Baldwin's books, when indicating reprinted versions of shorter works, have been abbreviated as follows:

Go Tell It on the Mountain as *Go Tell It*
Notes of a Native Son as *Notes*
Nobody Knows My Name: More Notes of a Native Son as *Nobody*
The Fire Next Time as *Fire*
Going to Meet the Man as *Going*
The Price of the Ticket: Collected Non-Fiction, 1948–1985 as *Price*
Conversations with James Baldwin as *Conversations*

In general, excerpts from Baldwin's books and plays have been included in the Bibliography only if they predate or are relative contemporaries of their source.

Works with less specific publication dates (1968 rather than February 1968, for example) generally appear first under their year of publication and are arranged alphabetically.

[1947]

"Maxim Gorki as Artist." *Nation* 164 (12 Apr. 1947): 427–28.
"When the War Hit Brownsville." *New Leader* 30 (17 May 1947): 12.
"Smaller Than Life." *Nation* 165 (19 July 1947): 78–79.
"Without Grisly Gaiety." *New Leader* 30 (20 Sept. 1947): 12.
"History as Nightmare." *New Leader* 30 (25 Oct. 1947): 11, 15.
"Battle Hymn." *New Leader* 30 (29 Nov. 1947): 10.
"Dead Hand of Caldwell." *New Leader* 30 (6 Dec. 1947): 10.

[1948]

"Bright World Darkened." *New Leader* 31 (24 Jan. 1948): 11.

"The Harlem Ghetto." *Commentary* 4 (Feb. 1948): 165–70. Repr. in *Notes* and *Price.*

"Literary Grab-Bag." *New Leader* 31 (28 Feb. 1948): 11.

"Present and Future." *New Leader* 31 (13 Mar. 1948): 11.

"The Image of the Negro." *Commentary* 5 (Apr. 1948): 378–80.

"Lockridge: 'The American Myth.'" *New Leader* 31 (10 Apr. 1948): 10, 14. Repr. in *Price.*

"Change within a Channel." *New Leader* 31 (24 Apr. 1948): 11.

"Modern Rover Boys." *New Leader* 31 (14 Aug. 1948): 12.

"Previous Condition." *Commentary* 6 (Oct. 1948): 334–42. Repr. in *Going.*

"Journey to Atlanta." *New Leader* 31 (9 Oct. 1948): 8–9. Repr. in *Notes* and *Price.*

[1949]

"Too Late, Too Late." *Commentary* 7 (Jan. 1949): 96–99.

"Everybody's Protest Novel." *Zero* 1 (Spring 1949): 54–58, and *Partisan Review* 16 (June 1949): 578–85. Repr. in "Two Protests against Protest," *Perspectives USA* 2 (Winter 1953): 89–100, and in *Notes* and *Price.*

"The Preservation of Innocence." *Zero* 1 (Spring 1949): 14–22.

[1950]

"The Death of the Prophet." *Commentary* 9 (Mar. 1950): 257–61.

"The Negro in Paris." *Reporter* 2 (6 June 1950): 34–6. Repr. as "Encounter on the Seine" in *Notes* and *Price.*

[1951]

"The Outing." *New Story* 2 (Apr. 1951): 52–81. Repr. in *Going.*

"The Negro at Home and Abroad." *Reporter* 5 (27 Nov. 1951): 36–7.

"Many Thousands Gone." *Partisan Review* 18 (Nov.–Dec. 1951): 665–80. Repr. in *Notes* and *Price.*

[1952]

"Roy's Wound." *New World Writing* (New York: New American Library, 1952) 2:109–16. Excerpt from *Go Tell It.*

"Exodus." *American Mercury* 75 (Aug. 1952): 97–103. Excerpt from *Go Tell It.*

[1953]

Go Tell It on the Mountain. New York: Alfred A. Knopf, 1953.

"On an Author." Excerpts from letters. *New York Herald Tribune Book Review* 29 (31 May 1953): 3.

"Stranger in the Village." *Harper's* 207 (Oct. 1953): 42–48. Repr. in *Notes* and *Price.*

[1954]

"The Amen Corner." *Zero* 2 (July 1954): 4–8, 11–13. Act 1 of play by the same title.

"Paris Letter: A Question of Identity." *Partisan Review* 21 (July–Aug. 1954): 402–10. Repr. in *Notes* and *Price* as "A Question of Identity."

"Gide as Husband and Homosexual." *New Leader* 37 (13 Dec. 1954): 18–20. Repr. as "The Male Prison" in *Nobody* and *Price*.

[1955]

"Life Straight in De Eye." *Commentary* 19 (Jan. 1955): 74–77. Repr. as "Carmen Jones: The Dark Is Light Enough" in *Notes* and *Price*.

"Equal in Paris." *Commentary* 19 (Mar. 1955): 251–59. Repr. in *Notes* and *Price*.

"Me and My House." *Harper's* 211 (Nov. 1955): 54–61. Repr. as "Notes of a Native Son" in *Notes* and *Price*.

Notes of a Native Son. Boston: Beacon, 1955.

[1956]

Giovanni's Room. New York: Dial, 1956.

"The Crusade of Indignation." *Nation* 183 (7 July 1956): 18–22. Repr. in *Price*.

"Faulkner and Desegregation." *Partisan Review* 23 (Fall 1956): 568–73. Repr. in *Nobody* and *Price*.

[1957]

"Princes and Powers." *Encounter* 8 (Jan. 1957): 52–60. Repr. in *Nobody* and *Price*.

"Sonny's Blues." *Partisan Review* 24 (Summer 1957): 327–58. Repr. in *Going*.

[1958]

"Come Out the Wilderness." *Mademoiselle* 46 (Mar. 1958): 102ff. Repr. in *Going*.

"The Hard Kind of Courage." *Harper's* 217 (Oct. 1958): 61–65. Repr. as "A Fly in Buttermilk" in *Nobody* and *Price*.

[1959]

"A Word from Writer Directly to Reader." In *Fiction of the Fifties*, 18–19. Ed. Herbert Gold. New York: Doubleday, 1959.

"A Letter from the South: Nobody Knows My Name." *Partisan Review* 26 (Winter 1959): 72–82. Repr. as "Nobody Knows My Name: A Letter from the South" in *Nobody* and *Price*.

"The Discovery of What It Means to Be an American." *New York Times Book Review*, 25 Jan. 1959. Repr. in *Nobody*.

"Sermons and Blues." *New York Times Book Review*, 29 Mar. 1959, 6.

"Mass Culture and the Creative Artist: Some Personal Notes." Paper presented at a symposium sponsored by the Tamiment Institute and *Daedalus*, June 1959. In *Culture for the Millions? Mass Media in Modern Society*, 120–23 (discussed 176–87). Ed. Norman Jacobs. Princeton: Van Nostrand, 1959. Appeared also in *Daedalus* 89 (1960): 373–76.

"On Catfish Row: *Porgy and Bess* in the Movies." *Commentary* 28 (Sept. 1959): 246–48. Repr. in *Price*.

[1960]

"In Search of a Majority." Address delivered at Kalamazoo College, Feb. 1960. Repr. in *Nobody* and *Price*.

"Any Day Now." *Partisan Review* 27 (Spring 1960): 282–94. Excerpt from *Another Country*.

"The Precarious Vogue of Ingmar Bergman." *Esquire* 53 (Apr. 1960): 128–29, 132. Repr. as "The Northern Protestant" in *Nobody* and *Price*.

"Fifth Avenue, Uptown: A Letter from Harlem." *Esquire* 54 (July 1960): 70–76. Repr. in *Nobody* and *Price*.

"They Can't Turn Back." *Mademoiselle* 51 (Aug. 1960): 324–26ff. Repr. in *Price*.

"This Morning, This Evening, So Soon." *Atlantic Monthly* 206 (Sept. 1960): 34–52. Repr. in *Going*.

"The Role of the Writer in America." Address delivered at the third annual *Esquire* magazine symposium, San Fransisco State College, 22 Oct. 1960. Repr. as "Notes for a Hypothetical Novel" in *Nobody* and *Price*.

[1961]

The New Negro. Symposium including James Baldwin. Ed. Mathew H. Ahmann. Notre Dame, Ind.: Fides, 1961.

"The Dangerous Road before Martin Luther King." *Harper's* 222 (Feb. 1961): 33–42. Repr. in *Price*; Repr. as "The High Road to Destiny" in *Martin Luther King, Jr.: A Profile*. Ed. C. Eric Lincoln. New York: Hill and Wang, 1970.

"Richard Wright, tel que je l'ai connu." Trans. Marie-Ange and Michel Manoll. *Preuves* 11 (Feb. 1961): 42–45. English version: "Richard Wright," *Encounter* 16 (Apr. 1961): 58–60. Repr. as "The Exile" in *Nobody* and *Price*.

Letter to the Editor in "Among the Recent Letters to the Editor." *New York Times Book Review* (26 Feb. 1961): 52.

"A Negro Assays the Negro Mood." *New York Times Magazine*, 12 Mar. 1961. Repr. as "East River, Downtown: Postscript to a Letter from Harlem" in *Nobody* and *Price*.

"The Survival of Richard Wright." *Reporter* 24 (16 Mar. 1961): 52–55. Repr. as "Eight Men" in *Nobody* and *Price*.

Nobody Knows My Name: More Notes of a Native Son. New York: Dial, 1961.

"The Black Muslims in America." Radio discussion with Eric Goldman, George Schuyler, C. Lincoln, Malcolm X, and James Baldwin. 23 Apr. 1961.

"Is *Raisin in the Sun* a Lemon in the Dark?" *Tone*, Apr. 1961.

"James Baldwin on the Negro Actor." *Urbanite*, Apr. 1961.

"The Black Boy Looks at the White Boy." *Esquire* 55 (May 1961): 102ff. Repr. in *Nobody* and *Price*.

Nationalism, Colonialism and the United States One Minute to Twelve: A Forum. Liberation Committee for Africa, first-anniversary celebration, 2 June 1961. New York: Photo-Offset Press, 1961.

"The New Lost Generation." *Esquire* 56 (July 1961): 113–15. Repr. in *Price*.

"They Will Wait No More." *Negro Digest* 10 (July 1961): 77–82.

"Almanac." Program on WFMT, Chicago, including an interview by Studs Terkel, taped 15 July 1961 (aired 29 Dec. 1961). Repr. in *Conversations*.

[1962]

Another Country. New York: Dial, 1962.

"Easy Rider." *The Dial: An Annual of Fiction* (New York: Dial, 1962): 3–26. Excerpt from *Another Country*.

Foreword to *Freedom Ride;* by Jim Peck. New York: Simon and Schuster, 1962.

"As Much Truth as One Can Bear." *New York Times Book Review*, 14 Jan. 1962, 1, 38.

"Geraldine Page: Bird of Light." *Show* 2 (Feb. 1962): 78–79.

"T.V. and Radio: An Interview with James Baldwin." Robert Lewis Shayon. *Saturday Review* 45 (24 Feb. 1962): 35.

"The Negro's Role in American Culture; Symposium." *Negro Digest* 11 (Mar. 1962): 80–98. Originally "The Negro in American Culture," a discussion with Lorraine Hansberry, Langston Hughes, Alfred Kazin, and Emile Capouya, moderated by Nat Hentoff, on Pacifica Radio, WBAI, New York, 1961.

"Color." *Esquire* 58 (Dec. 1962): 225–52. Repr. in *Price*.

"The Creative Process." In *Creative America*, 17–21. The National Cultural Center. New York: Ridge Press, 1962. See also "The Creative Dilemma: 'The War of an Artist with His Society Is a Lover's War,' " *Saturday Review* 47 (8 Feb. 1964): 14–15, 58. Repr. in *Price*.

"Letter from a Region in My Mind." *New Yorker* 38 (17 Nov. 1962): 59–144. Repr. as "Down at the Cross" in *Fire*.

"A Letter to My Nephew." *Progressive* 26 (Dec. 1962): 19–20. Repr. as "My Dungeon Shook" in *Fire*.

"What's the Reason Why: A Symposium by Best Selling Authors." *New York Times Book Review*, 2 Dec. 1962, 3.

"The Image: Three Views—Ben Shahn, Darius Milhaud and James Baldwin Debate the Real Meaning of a Fashionable Term." Symposium at Hofstra Univ. moderated by Malcolm Preston, May 1961. *Opera News* 27 (8 Dec. 1962): 9–12. Repr. in *Conversations*.

[1963]

"An Interview with a Negro Intellectual." In *The Negro Protest: Talks with James Baldwin, Malcolm X, Martin Luther King*, 1–14, 49. Ed. Kenneth B. Clark. Boston: Beacon, 1963.

"Envoi." *A Quarter Century of Unamericana 1938–63; A Tragico-Comical Memorabilia of HUAC*. Ed. Charlotte Pomerantz. New York: Marzani and Munsell, 1963.

The Fire Next Time. New York: Dial, 1963. Repr. in *Price*.

"The Fight: Patterson vs. Liston." *Nugget*, Feb. 1963. Repr. in *Antaeus* 62 (Spring 1989): 150–61.

"The Artist's Struggle for Integrity." Partial transcript of a talk delivered in New York City, taped by WBAI. *Liberation* 8 (Mar. 1963): 9–11.

"Liberalism and the Negro: A Round-Table Discussion." With Nathan Glazer, Sidney Hook, and Gunnar Myrdal. *Commentary* 37 (Mar. 1963): 25–42.

"New York and Negroes and Bobby—Both Shocked." Interview with Kenneth Clark by Sue Solet. *New York Herald Tribune*, 5 Apr. 1963, 1, 31.

"Disturber of the Peace: James Baldwin." Interview by Eve Auchincloss and Nancy Lynch (later Lynch Handy). *Mademoiselle*, May 1963. Repr. in *Black, White and*

Gray; Twenty-one Points of View on the Race Question. Ed. Bradford Daniel. New York: Sheed and Ward, 1964. Also repr. in *Conversations.*

"Letters from a Journey." *Harper's* 226 (May 1963): 48–52.

Untitled inset to cover story "The Negro's Push for Equality," which presents excerpts from writings and lectures. *Time* 81 (17 May 1963): 26–27.

"The Negro Writer in America: A Symposium." *Negro Digest* 12 (June 1963): 54–65.

" 'It's Terrifying,' James Baldwin: The Price of Fame." Interview by Nat Hentoff. *New York Herald Tribune Books,* 16 June 1963. Repr. in *Conversations.*

"A Conversation with James Baldwin." Interview by Kenneth B. Clark, taped by WGBH-TV, 24 May 1963. *Freedomways* 3 (Summer 1963): 361–68. Repr. in *Conversations.*

"There's a Bill Due That Has to Be Paid." *Life,* 24 May 1963, 81–84.

" 'Pour libérer les blancs . . .' (propos recueillis par François Bondy)." *Preuves* 13 (Oct. 1963): 3–17. For English original see *Transition* (1964).

"We Can Change the Country." *Liberation* 8 (Oct. 1963): 7–8.

"A Talk to Teachers." Originally a speech entitled "The Negro Child—His Self-Image," delivered in New York City, 16 Oct. 1963. *Saturday Review* 46 (21 Dec. 1963): 42–4 Repr. in *Price.*

[1964]

Blues for Mister Charlie. New York: Dial, 1964.

"Color and American Civilization." In *Freedom Now!,* 3–9. Ed. Alan F. Westin. New York: Basic, 1964.

"A Talk to Harlem Teachers." Adaptation of a speech delivered in 1963. In *Harlem, U.S.A.* Ed., John Henrik Clarke. Berlin: Seven Seas, 1964. Rev. ed. New York: Collier, 1971.

"The White Problem." Speech delivered 10 May 1963, and adapted for print. In *100 Years of Emancipation,* 80–88. Ed. Robert A. Goldwin. Chicago: Rand McNally, 1964.

"A Prayer and Sermon." Excerpt from *Blues for Mister Charlie* used as an editorial. *Show* 4 (Jan. 1964): 14.

"The Uses of the Blues." *Playboy* 11 (Jan. 1964): 131–32, 240–41.

"James Baldwin: A *New York Post* Portrait." Interview by Fern Marja Eckman. *New York Post,* 13, 15, 16, 17, 19 Jan. 1964, 21, 35, 25, 39, 24 respectively.

"An Interview by François Bondy." *Transition* (Uganda) 3 (Jan.–Feb. 1964): 13–19. Publications of French and German translations predate this. See *Preuves* (1963) and *Der Monat.*

" 'This Nettle, Danger.' " *Show* 4 (Feb. 1964): 78–79.

"Blues for Mr. Baldwin." Report of interview by William Glover. *Newark Evening News,* 26 Apr. 1964.

"A Conversation with James Baldwin." Portions of an interview on the Barry Gray show, WMCA. *New York Post,* 3 May 1964, 23.

"What Price Freedom?" Speech delivered in Washington, D.C., Nov. 1963. *Freedomways* 4 (Spring 1964): 191–95.

"Playwright at Work." Interview by Walter Wager. *Playbill,* July 1964.

"Four A.M." With photographs by Richard Avedon. *Show* 4 (Oct. 1964): 35–8. Excerpt from *Nothing Personal.*

Nothing Personal. Photographs by Richard Avedon and text by James Baldwin. New York: Atheneum, 1964. Text repr. in *Price.*

"Words of a Native Son." *Playboy* 11 (Dec. 1964): 131–32, 240–41. Repr. in *Price.*

[1965]

Going to Meet the Man. New York: Dial, 1965.

"On the Painter Beauford Delaney." *Transition* 4:18 (1965): 45.

Preface to *Olé*, by Harold Norse (1965). Repr. in *Memoirs of a Bastard Angel: A Fifty-Year Literary and Erotic Odyssey*, by Harold Norse. New York: William Morrow, 1989.

"The American Dream and the American Negro." *New York Times Magazine*, 7 Mar. 1965. Originally a talk given Feb. 1965. Repr. in *Price.*

"James Baldwin Gets 'Older and Sadder.' " Report of interview by Nat Hentoff. *New York Times*, 11 Apr. 1965.

"What Kind of Men Cry?" With Harry Belafonte, Sidney Poitier, et al. *Ebony* 20 (June 1965): 47.

"Race, Hate, Sex, and Colour: A Conversation with James Baldwin and Colin MacInnes." James Mossman. Originally recorded by the BBC. *Encounter* 25 (July 1965): 55–60. Repr. in *Conversations.*

"The White Man's Guilt." *Ebony* 20 (Aug. 1965): 47–48. Repr. in *Price.*

Introduction to *The Negro in New York*, by William J. Weatherby and Ottley Roi. New York: Oceana Publications, 1965.

"Going to Meet the Man." *Status* 1 (Oct. 1965): 47–49, 69–72. Repr. from *Going.*

[1966]

"The Man Child." *Playboy* 13 (Jan. 1966): 101ff. Repr. from *Going.*

"James Baldwin in Conversation." *Arts in Society* (Univ. of Wisconsin) 3 (Summer 1966): 550–57.

"A Report from Occupied Territory." *Nation* (11 July 1966). Repr. in *Price.*

"Theatre: The Negro In and Out." *Negro Digest* 15 (Oct. 1966): 37–44.

"Dialog in Black and White." Budd Schulberg. *Playboy* 13 (Dec. 1966): 133ff.

[1967]

"Anti-Semitism and Black Power." Letter to "Readers' Forum," *Freedomways* 7 (Winter 1967): 75–77.

"Tell Me How Long the Train's Been Gone." *McCall's* 94 (Feb. 1967): 118–19, 154ff. Excerpt from 1968 novel by the same title.

"James Baldwin Breaks His Silence." Interview by the Turkish magazine *Cep Dergisi.* English version in *Atlas* 13 (Mar. 1967): 47–49. Repr. in *Conversations.*

"God's Country." *New York Review of Books* 8 (23 Mar. 1967): 20.

"Negroes Are Anti-Semitic Because They're Anti-White." *New York Times Magazine*, 9 Apr. 1967. Repr. in *Price.*

"The War Crimes Tribunal." Letter to "Readers' Forum." *Freedomways* 7 (Summer 1967): 242–44.

[1968]

The Amen Corner. New York: Dial, 1968.

Tell Me How Long the Train's Been Gone. New York: Dial, 1968.

"Sidney Poitier." *Look*, 23 Jan. 1968, 50–58.

"Why a Stokely?" *St. Petersburg Times*, 3 Mar. 1968, 1D.

"Statement of James Baldwin, Accompanied by Mrs. Betty Shadazz [sic]." Hearing before the Select Subcommittee on Labor. House Committee on Education and Labor, 18 Mar. 1968, "To Establish a National Commission on Negro History and Culture," H.R. 12962. 90th Cong., 2d sess., vol. 91, 40–46. Repr. as "The Nigger We Invent," *Integrated Education* 7 (Mar.–Apr. 1969): 15–23.

"A Letter to Americans." *Freedomways* 8 (Spring 1968): 112–16.

"I Can't Blow This Gig." Interview by G. Nagata. *Cinema* (Beverly Hills) 4 (Summer 1968): 2–3.

"How Can We Get the Black People to Cool It?" *Esquire* 70 (July 1968): 49–53.

"Baldwin Excoriates Church for Hypocritical Stance." *Afro-American* (16 July 1968).

"White Racism or World Community?" Address to the World Council of Churches, Uppsala, Sweden, summer of 1968. *Ecumenical Review* 20 (Oct. 1968): 371–76. Repr. as part of "Our Divided Society: A Challenge to Religious Education." *Religious Education* 64 (Sept.–Oct. 1969): 342–46, and in *Price*.

[1969]

"From Dreams of Love to Dreams of Terror." In *Natural Enemies? Youth and the Clash of Generations*. Ed. Alexander Klein. Philadelphia: Lippincott, 1969. (Original edition published by the Los Angeles Free Press, 1968.)

"The Price May Be Too High." *New York Times*, 2 Feb. 1969.

"Sweet Lorraine." *Esquire* (Nov. 1969). Repr. in *Price*.

"Writer Foresees Collision Course." Report of interview by Nick Ludington. *Washington Post*, 14 Dec. 1969, E8.

[1970]

"Are We on the Edge of Civil War?" Interview. In *The Americans*, by David Frost, 145–50. New York: Stein and Day, 1970. Repr. in *Conversations*.

Foreword to *Daddy Was a Number Runner*, by Louise Meriwether. Englewood Cliffs, N.J.: Prentice-Hall, 1970.

" 'We Are All Viet Cong!': An Interview with James Baldwin." Karen Wald. *Nickel Review* 4 (Feb. 1970): 5.

"Conversation: Ida Lewis and James Baldwin." *Essence* 16 (Oct. 1970): 23–27. Repr. in *Conversations*.

"Dear Sister." *Manchester Guardian Weekly*, 27 Dec. 1970, 31.

"James Baldwin Interviewed." John Hall. *Transatlantic Review* 37–38 (Autumn–Winter 1970–71): 5–14. Repr. in *Conversations*.

[1971]

"An Open Letter to My Sister, Miss Angela Davis." *New York Review of Books*, 7 Jan. 1971.

"*A Rap on Race*: Mead and Baldwin." Excerpt from *A Rap on Race. McCall's* 98 (June 1971): 84–85, 142ff.

A Rap on Race. With Margaret Mead. Philadelphia: Lippincott, 1971.

"Of Angela Davis and 'the Jewish Housewife Headed for Dachau': An Exchange—James Baldwin and Shloma Katz." *Midstream* 17 (June–July 1971): 3–7.

"Soul." Television program first shown in the United States on WNET-TV (Dec. 1971). Transcript used for *A Dialogue.*

[1972]

No Name in the Street. New York: Dial, 1972. Repr. in *Price.*

One Day, When I Was Lost: A Scenario Based on "The Autobiography of Malcolm X." New York: Dial, 1972.

"James Baldwin." Interview by John Hall. *Transition* 41 (1972): 21–24.

"For James Baldwin, a Rap on Baldwin." Report of interview by George Goodman, Jr. *New York Times,* 26 June 1972, 38.

"It's Hard to Be James Baldwin." Interview by Herbert R. Lottman. *Intellectual Digest* 2 (July 1972): 67–68. Repr. in *Conversations.*

"Let Me Finish, Let Me Finish . . ." Television conversation with James Baldwin and Peregrine Worsthorne, moderated by Bryan Magee, BBC broadcast. *Encounter* 39 (Sept. 1972): 27–30.

"Exclusive Interview with James Baldwin." Joe Walker. *Muhammad Speaks* 11–12 (8, 15, 29 Sept., 6 Oct. 1972). Repr. in *Conversations.*

[1973]

"Compressions: L'homme et la machine." In *Cesar: Compressions d'or,* by Cesar Baldaccini, 9–16. Paris: Hachette, 1973.

A Dialogue. With Nikki Giovanni. Philadelphia: Lippincott, 1973.

"*The Black Scholar* Interviews James Baldwin." *Black Scholar* 5 (Dec. 1973–Jan. 1974): 33–42. Repr. in *Conversations.*

[1974]

"Beale Street Blues." *Encore* 3 (May 1974): 61–63. Excerpt from *If Beale Street Could Talk.*

If Beale Street Could Talk. New York: Dial, 1974.

"James Baldwin, the Renowned Black American Novelist, Talks to Godwin Matatu." *Africa: International Business, Economic and Political Monthly* 37 (1974): 68–69.

"Book and Author: James Baldwin." Report of interview by Jerry Tallmer. *New York Post,* 8 June 1974.

"U.S. System Can't Last, Writer Says." Report of interview by Chris Conkling. *New Orleans Times-Picayune,* 30 June 1974, sec. 8, p. 4.

"The Black Situation Now: An Interview with James Baldwin." *Washington Post,* 21 July 1974, C1, C4.

"James Baldwin Claims a 'First.'" Report of interview by Milt Freudenheim. *New Orleans Times-Picayune,* 13 Oct. 1974, sec. 2, p. 15.

[1976]

The Devil Finds Work. New York: Dial, 1976. Repr. in *Price.*

Little Man, Little Man: A Story of Childhood. Illustrated by Yoran Cazac. New York: Dial, 1976.

"In Search of a Basis for Mutual Understanding and Racial Harmony." In *The Nature of a Humane Society*, 231–40. Symposium proceedings edited by H. Ober Hess. Philadelphia: Fortress, 1976.

"*Roots*: The Saga of an American Family." *Unique* 1 (1976): 31–32.

"A Challenge to Bicentennial Candidates." Op ed, *Los Angeles Times*, 1 Feb. 1976. Repr. as "Looking for the Bicentennial Man," *San Francisco Chronicle*, 15 Feb. 1976.

"Growing Up With the Movies." *American Film* 1 (May 1976): 8–18. Modified excerpt from *The Devil Finds Work.*

"James Baldwin: God Bless the Child." Report of interview by Dorothy Gilliam. *Washington Post*, 2 May 1976, G8.

"James Baldwin Comes Home." Interview by Jewell Handy Gresham. *Essence* 7 (June 1976): 54ff. Repr. in *Conversations.*

"James Baldwin: 'We're Much Stronger than White People.'" Interview by Sid Cassese. *Newsday*, 1 Aug. 1976.

"Baldwin Still Finds It at the Movies." Report of interview by Mary Blume. *Los Angeles Times*, 21 Aug. 1976, part 2, p. 7.

"How One Black Man Came to Be an American." Review of *Roots*, by Alex Haley. *New York Times Book Review*, 26 Sept. 1976, 1–2. Repr. as "A Review of *Roots*" in *Price.*

[1977]

"An Open Letter to Mr. Carter." Op ed, *New York Times*, 23 Jan. 1977. Repr. in *Price.*

"James Baldwin Back Home." Report of interview by Robert Coles. *New York Times Book Review*, 31 July 1977, 1, 20–22.

"Last of the Great Masters." *New York Times Book Review*, 16 Oct. 1977, 9.

"Every Good-bye Ain't Gone." *New York*, 19 Dec. 1977. Repr. in *Price.*

[1978]

"The Artist Has Always Been a Disturber of the Peace." Interview by Yvonne Neverson. *Africa: International Business, Economic and Political Magazine* 80 (Apr. 1978): 109–10. Excerpted in *Conversations.*

"'The News from All the Northern Cities Is, to Understate It, Grim; the State of the Union Is Catastrophic.'" Op ed, *New York Times*, 5 Apr. 1978.

"Have Mercy." *Penthouse* 9 (July 1978): 121ff. Excerpt from *Just Above My Head.*

"Stagolee." Foreword to Bobby Seale's *A Lonely Rage: The Autobiography of Bobby Seale.* New York: Times Books, 1978.

[1979]

"James Baldwin: Looking Towards the Eighties." Interview by Kalamu ya Salaam. *Black Collegian* 10 (1979): 104ff. Repr. in *Conversations.*

Just Above My Head. New York: Dial, 1979.

"*Lorraine Hansberry* at the Summit." *Freedomways* 19 (1979): 269–72.

"James Baldwin: The Fire Still Burns." Report of interview by Hollie I. West. *Washington Post*, 8 Apr. 1979 F1.

"James Baldwin: No Gain for Race Relations." Interview by Hollie I. West. *Miami Herald*, 16 Apr. 1979, D1, D3. Repr. in *Conversations*.

"On Language, Race, and the Black Writer." Op ed, *Los Angeles Times*, 29 Apr. 1979, part 5, p. 1.

"If Black English Isn't a Language, Then Tell Me, What Is?" Op ed, *New York Times*, 29 July 1979. Repr. in *Price*.

"Of the Sorrow Songs: The Cross of Redemption." *Edinburgh Review* 47 (Aug. 1979).

"James Baldwin Writing and Talking." Interview by M. Watkins. *New York Times Book Review*, 23 Sept. 1979, 3, 36–37.

"An Open Letter to the Born Again." *Nation* 229 (29 Sept. 1979): 263–64. Repr. in *Price*.

[1980]

"James Baldwin Finds New South Is a Myth." Comments reported by Leonard Ray Teel. *Atlanta Journal*, 22 Apr. 1980, B1–2. Repr. in *Conversations*.

"Dark Days." *Esquire* (Oct. 1980). Repr. in *Price*.

"James Baldwin, an Interview." Wolfgang Binder. *Revista/Review interamericana* 10 (Fall 1980): 326–41. Repr. in *Conversations*.

"Notes on the House of Bondage." *Nation* 231 (1 Nov. 1980): 425ff. Repr. in *Price*.

[1981]

"In Dialogue to Define Aesthetics: James Baldwin and Chinua Achebe." D. R. Tsuruta. *Black Scholar* 12:72–9 (Mar.–Apr. 1981). Repr. in *Conversations*.

"Achebe and Baldwin in C.B. Land—10–4 Good Buddy!" Dialogue at the African Literature Association meeting, Gainesville, Fla., Mar. 1980. *Pacific Coast Africanist Association. Occasional Paper* 3 (Apr. 1981): 7–9.

"Black English: A Dishonest Argument." In *Black English and the Education of Black Children and Youth: Proceedings of the Invitational Symposium on the King Decision*. Ed. Geneva Smitherman. Detroit: Harlo, 1981. The symposium was held at the Center for Black Studies, Wayne State Univ., 21–23 Feb. 1980.

"The Evidence of Things Not Seen." *Playboy* 28 (Dec. 1981): 140ff. Adapted portion of book by the same title.

[1983]

Jimmy's Blues: Selected Poems. London: Michael Joseph, 1983. American ed. New York: St. Martin's, 1985.

[1984]

Introduction to the New Edition. *Notes of a Native Son*. Boston: Beacon, 1984.

"Blacks and Jews." Lecture delivered at Univ. of Massachusetts–Amherst, 28 Feb. 1984. *Black Scholar* 19 (Nov.–Dec. 1988): 3–15.

"The Art of Fiction LXXVIII: James Baldwin." Interview with Jordan Elgraby and George Plimpton. *Paris Review* 26 (Spring 1984): 48–82. Repr. in *Conversations*.

"On Being White and Other Lies." *Essence* 14 (April 1984): 90–92.

"James Baldwin—Reflections of a Maverick." Interview by Julius Lester. *New York Times Book Review*, 27 May 1984. Repr. in *Conversations*.

" 'Go the Way Your Blood Beats.' " Interview by Richard Goldstein. *Village Voice* 29 (26 June 1984): 13ff.

"A través del fuego: Entrevista con James Baldwin." *Quimera: Revista de literatura* 41 (Sept. 1984): 22–29.

"Revolutionary Hope: A Conversation Between James Baldwin and Audre Lorde." *Essence* 15 (Dec. 1984): 72ff.

[1985]

The Evidence of Things Not Seen. New York: Holt, Rinehart and Winston, 1985.

The Price of the Ticket: Collected Non-Fiction, 1948–1985. New York: St. Martin's, 1985.

"Freaks and the American Ideal of Manhood." *Playboy* (Jan. 1985). Repr. as "Here Be Dragons" in *Price*.

"Go Tell It on the Mountain: Belatedly, the Fear Turned to Love for His Father." *TV Guide* 32 (12 Jan. 1985): 26–29.

"Blues for Mr. Baldwin." Report of conversation by Angela Cobbina. *Concord Weekly*, 28 Jan. 1985, 31ff. Repr. in *Conversations*.

"An Interview with Josephine Baker and James Baldwin." Henry Louis Gates, Jr. *Southern Review* 21 (Summer 1985): 594–602. Repr. in *Conversations*.

"The Fire This Time." *New Statesman* 110 (23 Aug. 1985): 8–9. Partially repr. as "Whites' Freedom Depends on Blacks,' " *Los Angeles Times*, 21 Jan. 1986, part 2, p. 5.

"Removing Barriers; To James Baldwin, the Goal Is 'To Sail Through Life on at Least One Smooth Tide of Unity.' " Report of interview by George Hadley-Garcia. *New York Native*, 14–20 Oct. 1985, 28.

[1986]

"An Interview with James Baldwin." David C. Estes. *New Orleans Review* 13 (Fall 1986): 59–64. Repr. in *Conversations*.

"An Interview with James Baldwin on Henry James." David Adams Leeming. *Henry James Review* 8 (Fall 1986): 47–56.

[1987]

Perspectives; Angles on African Art. James Baldwin et al. Interview with Michael John Weber. New York: Center for African Art, 1987.

"When a Pariah Becomes a Celebrity: An Interview with James Baldwin." Clayton O. Holloway. *Xavier Review* 7 (1987): 1–10.

"To Crush the Serpent." *Playboy* 34 (June 1987): 66ff.

"Architectural Digest Visits: James Baldwin." Photographs by Daniel H. Minassian and text by James Baldwin. *Architectural Digest*, August 1987.

"Going to Meet the Man: An Interview with James Baldwin." James A. Baggett. *New York Native*, 21 Dec. 1987, 20–23.

[1988]

"Last Testament: An Interview with James Baldwin." Quincy Troupe. *Village Voice*, 12 Jan. 1988, 36. Repr. in *Conversations*.

"The Last Interview." Quincy Troupe. In "James Baldwin, 1924–1987: A Tribute." *Essence* 18 (Mar. 1988): 53, 114ff. Repr. in *Conversations*.

"Blacks and Jews." Lecture delivered at Univ. of Massachusetts–Amherst, 28 Feb. 1984. *Black Scholar* 19 (Nov.–Dec. 1988): 3–15.

[1989]

Conversations with James Baldwin. Ed. Fred L. Standley and Louis H. Pratt. Jackson: University Press of Mississippi, 1989.

Gypsies and Other Poems. Edition limited to 325 copies. Leeds, Mass.: Gehenna Press/ Eremite Press, 1989.

Index

Permissions Acknowledgements

Grateful acknowledgment is made to the following for permission to reprint previously published and unpublished material:

Beacon Press: Excerpts from "Notes of a Native Son," "Equal in Paris," "A Question of Identity," "Many Thousands Gone," and "A Stranger in the Village" from *Notes of a Native Son* by James Baldwin, copyright © 1955, copyright renewed 1983 by James Baldwin. Reprinted by permission.

Estate of Beauford Delaney: Excerpt from unpublished autobiographical notes by Beauford Delaney. Reprinted by permission McCampbell & Young on behalf of the Estate of Beauford Delaney.

Doubleday: Excerpts from *The Devil Finds Work* by James Baldwin; excerpts from *Giovanni's Room* by James Baldwin; excerpts from "Sonny's Blues" and "This Morning, This Evening, So Soon" from *Going to Meet the Man* by James Baldwin. Reprinted by permission of Doubleday, a division of Bantam Doubleday Dell Publishing Group, Inc.

Doubleday: Excerpts from *No Name in the Street* by James Baldwin, copyright © 1972 by James Baldwin. Reprinted by permission of Doubleday, a division of Bantam Doubleday Dell Publishing Group, Inc.

Grove/Atlantic Monthly Press and *The Estate of Katherine Anne Porter*: Excerpt from April 2, 1963, letter from Katherine Anne Porter to Glenway Wescott from *Letters of Katherine Anne Porter* by Isabel Bayley, editor, copyright © 1990 by Isabel Bayley. Reprinted by permission of Grove/Atlantic Monthly Press and Barbara Thompson Davis, Trustee for The Estate of Katherine Anne Porter.

The Johns Hopkins University Press: Excerpt from David Leeming interview with James Baldwin on Henry James (*Henry James Review*, Vol. VIII, No. 1, 1986). Reprinted by permission.

Langston Hughes Estate and *Yale University*: Excerpts from letters of March 1959, and May 4, 1961, from Langston Hughes to James Baldwin. James Weldon Johnson collection, Yale Collection of American Literature, Beinecke Rare

Book and Manuscript Library, Yale University. Reprinted by permission of Arnold Rampersad on behalf of the Langston Hughes Estate and Yale University.

Catherine McLaughlin: Excerpt from unpublished work "Jimmy: A Memoir" by Catherine McLaughlin. Reprinted by permission of the author.

Thomas Maltais: Excerpts from *Go Tell It on the Metro Bar* by Thomas Maltais. Reprinted by permission of the author.

New Directions Publishing Corporation: Excerpts from "Outcast" from *Remember to Remember* by Henry Miller, copyright ©1947 by New Directions Publishing Corporation. Reprinted by permission.

The Paris Review: Excerpts from "The Art of Fiction LXXVIII: James Baldwin," Jordan Elgrably and George Plimpton interview with James Baldwin (*The Paris Review*, 26, Spring 1984). Reprinted by permission.

Orilla Miller Winfield Estate: Photograph and excerpts from May 15, 1963, letter from Orilla Miller Winfield to James Baldwin, and June 28, 1988, letter from Orilla Miller Winfield to Shaun Henderson. Reprinted by permission of Steve Winfield on behalf of the Orilla Miller Winfield Estate.

Excerpts from *Nobody Knows My Name* by James Baldwin (Vintage Books, 1993), copyright © 1954, 1956, 1958, 1959, 1960, 1961 by James Baldwin, copyright renewed 1988, 1989 by Gloria Baldwin Karefa-Smart; excerpts from *The Fire Next Time* by James Baldwin (Vintage Books, 1993), copyright © 1962, 1963 by James Baldwin, copyright renewed 1990, 1991 by Gloria Baldwin Karefa-Smart; excerpts from the essay "The Dangerous Road Before Martin Luther King" from *The Price of the Ticket: Collected Non-Fiction 1948–1985* by James Baldwin (St. Martin's Press, 1985). Reprinted by permission.

READ MORE IN PENGUIN

In every corner of the world, on every subject under the sun, Penguin represents quality and variety – the very best in publishing today.

For complete information about books available from Penguin – including Puffins, Penguin Classics and Arkana – and how to order them, write to us at the appropriate address below. Please note that for copyright reasons the selection of books varies from country to country.

In the United Kingdom: Please write to *Dept. JC, Penguin Books Ltd, FREEPOST, West Drayton, Middlesex UB7 OBR.*

If you have any difficulty in obtaining a title, please send your order with the correct money, plus ten per cent for postage and packaging, to *PO Box No. 11, West Drayton, Middlesex UB7 OBR*

In the United States: Please write to *Consumer Sales, Penguin USA, P.O. Box 999, Dept. 17109, Bergenfield, New Jersey 07621-0120.* VISA and MasterCard holders call 1-800-253-6476 to order all Penguin titles

In Canada: Please write to *Penguin Books Canada Ltd, 10 Alcorn Avenue, Suite 300, Toronto, Ontario M4V 3B2*

In Australia: Please write to *Penguin Books Australia Ltd, P.O. Box 257, Ringwood, Victoria 3134*

In New Zealand: Please write to *Penguin Books (NZ) Ltd, Private Bag 102902, North Shore Mail Centre, Auckland 10*

In India: Please write to *Penguin Books India Pvt Ltd, 706 Eros Apartments, 56 Nehru Place, New Delhi 110 019*

In the Netherlands: Please write to *Penguin Books Netherlands bv, Postbus 3507, NL-1001 AH Amsterdam*

In Germany: Please write to *Penguin Books Deutschland GmbH, Metzlerstrasse 26, 60594 Frankfurt am Main*

In Spain: Please write to *Penguin Books S. A., Bravo Murillo 19, 1º B, 28015 Madrid*

In Italy: Please write to *Penguin Italia s.r.l., Via Felice Casati 20, I–20124 Milano*

In France: Please write to *Penguin France S. A., 17 rue Lejeune, F–31000 Toulouse*

In Japan: Please write to *Penguin Books Japan, Ishikiribashi Building, 2–5–4, Suido, Bunkyo-ku, Tokyo 112*

In Greece: Please write to *Penguin Hellas Ltd, Dimocritou 3, GR–106 71 Athens*

In South Africa: Please write to *Longman Penguin Southern Africa (Pty) Ltd, Private Bag X08, Bertsham 2013*

READ MORE IN PENGUIN

BIOGRAPHY AND AUTOBIOGRAPHY

Freedom from Fear Aung San Suu Kyi

This collection of writings gives a voice to Aung San Suu Kyi, human rights activist and leader of Burma's National League for Democracy, who was detained in 1989 by SLORC, the ruling military junta, and today remains under house arrest. In 1991, her courage and ideals were internationally recognized when she was awarded the Nobel Peace Prize.

Memories of a Catholic Girlhood Mary McCarthy

'Many a time in the course of doing these memoirs,' Mary McCarthy says, 'I have wished that I were writing fiction.' 'Superb . . . so heartbreaking that in comparison Jane Eyre seems to have got off lightly' – *Spectator*

A Short Walk from Harrods Dirk Bogarde

In this volume of memoirs, Dirk Bogarde pays tribute to the corner of Provence that was his home for over two decades, and to Forwood, his manager and friend of fifty years, whose long and wretched illness brought an end to a paradise. 'A brave and moving book' – *Daily Telegraph*

When Shrimps Learn to Whistle Denis Healey

The Time of My Life was widely acclaimed as a masterpiece. Taking up the most powerful political themes that emerge from it Denis Healey now gives us this stimulating companion volume. 'Forty-three years of ruminations . . . by the greatest foreign secretary we never had' – *New Statesman & Society*

Eating Children Jill Tweedie

Jill Tweedie's second memoir, *Frightening People*, incomplete due to her tragically early death in 1993, is published here for the first time. 'Magnificent . . . with wit, without a shred of self-pity, she tells the story of an unhappy middle-class suburban child with a monstrously cruel father, and a hopeless mother' – *Guardian*